ENERGY AND THE ENVIRONMENT

Energy intersects with the environment at all stages of its life cycle by affecting nature and public health and is subject to government measures concerning low-carbon growth, energy efficiency and conservation, renewable energy and ecologically safe supply of nuclear and other energy resources. This timely book provides a comprehensive analysis of the role of international economic law in regulating such an energy–environment nexus under the regimes of the WTO, the Energy Charter Treaty, regional trade agreements and investment treaties. The author discusses the international environmental and economic law foundations of this nexus and extensively examines the relevant rules, jurisprudence and practices regarding trade restrictions, subsidies, technical standards, investment protection and technology policies. This book highlights the existing gaps and 'greening' solutions within the framework of international economic law. Where relevant, it draws comparisons between trade law and investment law to show their similarities, differences and (potential) conflicts at the energy–environment interface.

SHERZOD SHADIKHODJAEV is a Professor at the KDI School of Public Policy and Management and the author of the books *Industrial Policy and the World Trade Organization: Between Legal Constraints and Flexibilities* (2018) and *Retaliation in the WTO Dispute Settlement System* (2009) and articles published in *American Journal of International Law*, *European Journal of International Law*, *Journal of International Economic Law*, *World Trade Review* and others. He is an editorial board member of *Asia Pacific Law Review*.

ENERGY AND THE ENVIRONMENT

Exploring the Nexus under International Economic Law

SHERZOD SHADIKHODJAEV

KDI School of Public Policy and Management

CAMBRIDGE
UNIVERSITY PRESS

CAMBRIDGE
UNIVERSITY PRESS

Shaftesbury Road, Cambridge CB2 8EA, United Kingdom

One Liberty Plaza, 20th Floor, New York, NY 10006, USA

477 Williamstown Road, Port Melbourne, VIC 3207, Australia

314–321, 3rd Floor, Plot 3, Splendor Forum, Jasola District Centre, New Delhi – 110025, India

103 Penang Road, #05–06/07, Visioncrest Commercial, Singapore 238467

Cambridge University Press is part of Cambridge University Press & Assessment, a department of the University of Cambridge.

We share the University's mission to contribute to society through the pursuit of education, learning and research at the highest international levels of excellence.

www.cambridge.org
Information on this title: www.cambridge.org/9781009045469

DOI: 10.1017/9781009042239

First published 2024
First paperback edition 2025

A catalogue record for this publication is available from the British Library

Library of Congress Cataloging-in-Publication data
Names: Shadikhodjaev, Sherzod, author.
Title: Energy and the environment : exploring the nexus under international economic law / Sherzod Shadikhodjaev, KDI School of Public Policy and Management.
Description: Cambridge, United Kingdom ; New York, NY : Cambridge University Press, 2024. | Includes bibliographical references and index.
Identifiers: LCCN 2023045649 (print) | LCCN 2023045650 (ebook) | ISBN 9781316517444 (hardback) | ISBN 9781009045469 (paperback) | ISBN 9781009042239 (epub)
Subjects: LCSH: International economic relations. | Foreign trade regulation. | Law and economic development. | Renewable energy sources–Law and legislation. | Environmental law, International. | Investments, Foreign (International law)
Classification: LCC K3820 .S53 2024 (print) | LCC K3820 (ebook) | DDC 343.09/2–dc23/eng/20231005
LC record available at https://lccn.loc.gov/2023045649
LC ebook record available at https://lccn.loc.gov/2023045650

ISBN 978-1-316-51744-4 Hardback
ISBN 978-1-009-04546-9 Paperback

To Dinara with many thanks for everything

CONTENTS

FIGURES

TABLES

TABLE OF CASES

World Trade Organization (WTO)

Short Title (WTO)	Full Title (WTO)
Australia – Automotive Leather II (Article 21.5 – US)	Panel Report, *Australia – Subsidies Provided to Producers and Exporters of Automotive Leather – Recourse to Article 21.5 of the DSU by the United States*, WT/DS126/RW and Corr.1, adopted 11 February 2000, DSR 2000:III, p. 1189
Australia – Salmon	Appellate Body Report, *Australia – Measures Affecting Importation of Salmon*, WT/DS18/AB/R, adopted 6 November 1998, DSR 1998:VIII, p. 3327
Australia – Tobacco Plain Packaging	Panel Reports, *Australia – Certain Measures concerning Trademarks, Geographical Indications and Other Plain Packaging Requirements Applicable to Tobacco Products and Packaging*, WT/DS435/R, Add.1 and Suppl.1 *(Honduras)* / WT/DS441/R, Add.1 and Suppl.1 *(Dominican Republic)* / WT/DS458/R, Add.1 and Suppl.1 *(Cuba)* / WT/DS467/R, Add.1 and Suppl.1 *(Indonesia)*, WT/DS458/R and WT/DS467/R adopted 27 August 2018, DSR 2018:VIII, p. 3925, and WT/DS435/R and WT/DS441/R adopted 29 June 2020, as upheld by Appellate Body Reports WT/DS435/AB/R / WT/DS441/AB/R, DSR 2018:VIII, p. 3925

(*cont.*)

Short Title (WTO)	Full Title (WTO)
Brazil – Retreaded Tyres	Appellate Body Report, *Brazil – Measures Affecting Imports of Retreaded Tyres*, WT/DS332/AB/R, adopted 17 December 2007, DSR 2007:IV, p. 1527
Brazil – Taxation	Appellate Body Reports, *Brazil – Certain Measures Concerning Taxation and Charges*, WT/DS472/AB/R and Add.1 / WT/DS497/AB/R and Add.1, adopted 11 January 2019, DSR 2019:I, p. 7
Brazil – Taxation	Panel Reports, *Brazil – Certain Measures Concerning Taxation and Charges*, WT/DS472/R, Add.1 and Corr.1 / WT/DS497/R, Add.1 and Corr.1, adopted 11 January 2019, as modified by Appellate Body Reports WT/DS472/AB/R / WT/DS497/AB/R, DSR 2019:II, p. 345
Canada – Aircraft	Appellate Body Report, *Canada – Measures Affecting the Export of Civilian Aircraft*, WT/DS70/AB/R, adopted 20 August 1999, DSR 1999:III, p. 1377
Canada – Renewable Energy / Canada – Feed-in Tariff Program	Appellate Body Reports, *Canada – Certain Measures Affecting the Renewable Energy Generation Sector / Canada – Measures Relating to the Feed-in Tariff Program*, WT/DS412/AB/R / WT/DS426/AB/R, adopted 24 May 2013, DSR 2013:I, p. 7
Canada – Renewable Energy / Canada – Feed-in Tariff Program	Panel Reports, *Canada – Certain Measures Affecting the Renewable Energy Generation Sector / Canada – Measures Relating to the Feed-in Tariff Program*, WT/DS412/R and Add.1 / WT/DS426/R and Add.1, adopted 24 May 2013, as modified by Appellate Body Reports WT/DS412/AB/R / WT/DS426/AB/R, DSR 2013:I, p. 237
Canada – Wheat Exports and Grain Imports	Appellate Body Report, *Canada – Measures Relating to Exports of Wheat and Treatment of Imported Grain*, WT/DS276/AB/R, adopted 27 September 2004, DSR 2004:VI, p. 2739

(*cont.*)

Short Title (WTO)	Full Title (WTO)
China – Electronic Payment Services	Panel Report, *China – Certain Measures Affecting Electronic Payment Services*, WT/DS413/R and Add.1, adopted 31 August 2012, DSR 2012:X, p. 5305
China – Publications and Audiovisual Products	Appellate Body Report, *China – Measures Affecting Trading Rights and Distribution Services for Certain Publications and Audiovisual Entertainment Products*, WT/DS363/AB/R, adopted 19 January 2010, DSR 2010:I, p. 3
China – Publications and Audiovisual Products	Panel Report, *China – Measures Affecting Trading Rights and Distribution Services for Certain Publications and Audiovisual Entertainment Products*, WT/DS363/R and Corr.1, adopted 19 January 2010, as modified by Appellate Body Report WT/DS363/AB/R, DSR 2010:II, p. 261
China – Rare Earths	Appellate Body Reports, *China – Measures Related to the Exportation of Rare Earths, Tungsten, and Molybdenum*, WT/DS431/AB/R / WT/DS432/AB/R / WT/DS433/AB/R, adopted 29 August 2014, DSR 2014:III, p. 805
China – Rare Earths	Panel Reports, *China – Measures Related to the Exportation of Rare Earths, Tungsten, and Molybdenum*, WT/DS431/R and Add.1 / WT/DS432/R and Add.1 / WT/DS433/R and Add.1, adopted 29 August 2014, upheld by Appellate Body Reports WT/DS431/AB/R / WT/DS432/AB/R / WT/DS433/AB/R, DSR 2014:IV, p. 1127
China – Raw Materials	Appellate Body Reports, *China – Measures Related to the Exportation of Various Raw Materials*, WT/DS394/AB/R / WT/DS395/AB/R / WT/DS398/AB/R, adopted 22 February 2012, DSR 2012:VII, p. 3295
China – Raw Materials	Panel Reports, *China – Measures Related to the Exportation of Various Raw Materials*, WT/DS394/R, Add.1 and Corr.1 / WT/DS395/R, Add.1 and Corr.1 / WT/DS398/

(*cont.*)

Short Title (WTO)	Full Title (WTO)
	R, Add.1 and Corr.1, adopted 22 February 2012, as modified by Appellate Body Reports WT/DS394/AB/R / WT/DS395/AB/R / WT/DS398/AB/R, DSR 2012:VII, p. 3501
Colombia – Textiles	Appellate Body Report, *Colombia – Measures Relating to the Importation of Textiles, Apparel and Footwear*, WT/DS461/AB/R and Add.1, adopted 22 June 2016, DSR 2016:III, p. 1131
Dominican Republic – Import and Sale of Cigarettes	Appellate Body Report, *Dominican Republic – Measures Affecting the Importation and Internal Sale of Cigarettes*, WT/DS302/AB/R, adopted 19 May 2005, DSR 2005:XV, p. 7367
EC – Approval and Marketing of Biotech Products	Panel Reports, *European Communities – Measures Affecting the Approval and Marketing of Biotech Products*, WT/DS291/R, Add.1 to Add.9 and Corr.1 / WT/DS292/R, Add.1 to Add.9 and Corr.1 / WT/DS293/R, Add.1 to Add.9 and Corr.1, adopted 21 November 2006, DSR 2006:III, p. 847
EC – Asbestos	Appellate Body Report, *European Communities – Measures Affecting Asbestos and Asbestos-Containing Products*, WT/DS135/AB/R, adopted 5 April 2001, DSR 2001:VII, p. 3243
EC – Bananas III	Appellate Body Report, *European Communities – Regime for the Importation, Sale and Distribution of Bananas*, WT/DS27/AB/R, adopted 25 September 1997, DSR 1997:II, p. 591
EC – Hormones	Appellate Body Report, *European Communities – Measures Concerning Meat and Meat Products (Hormones)*, WT/DS26/AB/R, WT/DS48/AB/R, adopted 13 February 1998, DSR 1998:I, p. 135

(*cont.*)

Short Title (WTO)	Full Title (WTO)
EC – Sardines	Appellate Body Report, *European Communities – Trade Description of Sardines*, WT/DS231/AB/R, adopted 23 October 2002, DSR 2002:VIII, p. 3359
EC – Seal Products	Appellate Body Reports, *European Communities – Measures Prohibiting the Importation and Marketing of Seal Products*, WT/DS400/AB/R / WT/DS401/AB/R, adopted 18 June 2014, DSR 2014:I, p. 7
EC – Seal Products	Panel Reports, *European Communities – Measures Prohibiting the Importation and Marketing of Seal Products*, WT/DS400/R and Add.1 / WT/DS401/R and Add.1, adopted 18 June 2014, as modified by Appellate Body Reports WT/DS400/AB/R / WT/DS401/AB/R, DSR 2014:II, p. 365
EC – Tariff Preferences	Appellate Body Report, *European Communities – Conditions for the Granting of Tariff Preferences to Developing Countries*, WT/DS246/AB/R, adopted 20 April 2004, DSR 2004:III, p. 925
EC and certain member States – Large Civil Aircraft	Panel Report, *European Communities and Certain Member States – Measures Affecting Trade in Large Civil Aircraft*, WT/DS316/R, adopted 1 June 2011, as modified by Appellate Body Report WT/DS316/AB/R, DSR 2011:II, p. 685
EU – Energy Package	Panel Report, *European Union and its member States – Certain Measures Relating to the Energy Sector*, WT/DS476/R and Add.1, circulated to WTO Members 10 August 2018 [appealed by the European Union 21 September 2018]
India – Export Related Measures	Panel Report, *India – Export Related Measures*, WT/DS541/R and Add.1, circulated to WTO Members 31 October 2019, appealed 19 November 2019

(*cont.*)

Short Title (WTO)	Full Title (WTO)
India – Solar Cells	Appellate Body Report, *India – Certain Measures Relating to Solar Cells and Solar Modules*, WT/DS456/AB/R and Add.1, adopted 14 October 2016, DSR 2016:IV, p. 1827
India – Solar Cells	Panel Report, *India – Certain Measures Relating to Solar Cells and Solar Modules*, WT/DS456/R and Add.1, adopted 14 October 2016, as modified by Appellate Body Report WT/DS456/AB/R, DSR 2016:IV, p. 1941
Indonesia – Autos	Panel Report, *Indonesia – Certain Measures Affecting the Automobile Industry*, WT/DS54/R, WT/DS55/R, WT/DS59/R, WT/DS64/R, Corr.1 and Corr.2, adopted 23 July 1998, and Corr.3 and Corr.4, DSR 1998:VI, p. 2201
Japan – Film	Panel Report, *Japan – Measures Affecting Consumer Photographic Film and Paper*, WT/DS44/R, adopted 22 April 1998, DSR 1998:IV, p. 1179
Korea – Commercial Vessels	Panel Report, *Korea – Measures Affecting Trade in Commercial Vessels*, WT/DS273/R, adopted 11 April 2005, DSR 2005:VII, p. 2749
Korea – Radionuclides	Appellate Body Report, *Korea – Import Bans, and Testing and Certification Requirements for Radionuclides*, WT/DS495/AB/R and Add.1, adopted 26 April 2019, DSR 2019:VII, p. 3653
Korea – Radionuclides	Panel Report, *Korea – Import Bans, and Testing and Certification Requirements for Radionuclides*, WT/DS495/R and Add.1, adopted 26 April 2019, as modified by Appellate Body Report WT/DS495/AB/R, DSR 2019:VII, p. 3823
Korea – Various Measures on Beef	Appellate Body Report, *Korea – Measures Affecting Imports of Fresh, Chilled and Frozen Beef*, WT/DS161/AB/R, WT/DS169/AB/R, adopted 10 January 2001, DSR 2001:I, p. 5

(*cont.*)

Short Title (WTO)	Full Title (WTO)
Mexico – Taxes on Soft Drinks	Panel Report, *Mexico – Tax Measures on Soft Drinks and Other Beverages*, WT/DS308/R, adopted 24 March 2006, as modified by Appellate Body Report WT/DS308/AB/R, DSR 2006:I, p. 43
Ukraine – Ammonium Nitrate	Appellate Body Report, *Ukraine – Anti-Dumping Measures on Ammonium Nitrate*, WT/DS493/AB/R and Add.1, adopted 30 September 2019, DSR 2019:X, p. 5227
Ukraine – Ammonium Nitrate	Panel Report, *Ukraine – Anti-Dumping Measures on Ammonium Nitrate*, WT/DS493/R, Add.1 and Corr.1, adopted 30 September 2019, as upheld by Appellate Body Report WT/DS493/AB/R, DSR 2019:X, p. 5339
US – Anti-Dumping and Countervailing Duties (China)	Appellate Body Report, *United States – Definitive Anti-Dumping and Countervailing Duties on Certain Products from China*, WT/DS379/AB/R, adopted 25 March 2011, DSR 2011:V, p. 2869
US – Clove Cigarettes	Appellate Body Report, *United States – Measures Affecting the Production and Sale of Clove Cigarettes*, WT/DS406/AB/R, adopted 24 April 2012, DSR 2012:XI, p. 5751
US – Clove Cigarettes	Panel Report, *United States – Measures Affecting the Production and Sale of Clove Cigarettes*, WT/DS406/R, adopted 24 April 2012, as modified by Appellate Body Report WT/DS406/AB/R, DSR 2012:XI, p. 5865
US – COOL	Panel Reports, *United States – Certain Country of Origin Labelling (COOL) Requirements*, WT/DS384/R / WT/DS386/R, adopted 23 July 2012, as modified by Appellate Body Reports WT/DS384/AB/R / WT/DS386/AB/R, DSR 2012:VI, p. 2745
US – Countervailing Measures (China)	Panel Report, *United States – Countervailing Duty Measures on Certain Products from China*, WT/DS437/R and Add.1, adopted

(cont.)

Short Title (WTO)	Full Title (WTO)
	16 January 2015, as modified by Appellate Body Report WT/DS437/AB/R, DSR 2015:I, p. 183
US – Countervailing Measures (China) (Article 21.5 – China)	Appellate Body Report, *United States – Countervailing Duty Measures on Certain Products from China – Recourse to Article 21.5 of the DSU by China*, WT/DS437/AB/RW and Add.1, adopted 15 August 2019, DSR 2019:IX, p. 4737
US – Export Restraints	Panel Report, *United States – Measures Treating Exports Restraints as Subsidies*, WT/DS194/R and Corr.2, adopted 23 August 2001, DSR 2001:XI, p. 5767
US – Gambling	Panel Report, *United States – Measures Affecting the Cross-Border Supply of Gambling and Betting Services*, WT/DS285/R, adopted 20 April 2005, as modified by Appellate Body Report WT/DS285/AB/R, DSR 2005:XII, p. 5797
US – Gasoline	Appellate Body Report, *United States – Standards for Reformulated and Conventional Gasoline*, WT/DS2/AB/R, adopted 20 May 1996, DSR 1996:I, p. 3
US – Gasoline	Panel Report, *United States – Standards for Reformulated and Conventional Gasoline*, WT/DS2/R, adopted 20 May 1996, as modified by Appellate Body Report WT/DS2/AB/R, DSR 1996:I, p. 29
US – Large Civil Aircraft (2nd complaint)	Appellate Body Report, *United States – Measures Affecting Trade in Large Civil Aircraft (Second Complaint)*, WT/DS353/AB/R, adopted 23 March 2012, DSR 2012:I, p. 7
US – Large Civil Aircraft (2nd complaint)	Panel Report, *United States – Measures Affecting Trade in Large Civil Aircraft (Second Complaint)*, WT/DS353/R, adopted 23 March 2012, as modified by Appellate Body Report WT/DS353/AB/R, DSR 2012:II, p. 649

(cont.)

Short Title (WTO)	Full Title (WTO)
US – Large Civil Aircraft (2nd complaint) (Article 21.5 – EU)	Panel Report, *United States – Measures Affecting Trade in Large Civil Aircraft (Second Complaint) – Recourse to Article 21.5 of the DSU by the European Union*, WT/DS353/RW and Add.1, adopted 11 April 2019, as modified by Appellate Body Report WT/DS353/AB/RW, DSR 2019:V, p. 2171
US – Renewable Energy	Panel Report, *United States – Certain Measures Relating to the Renewable Energy Sector*, WT/DS510/R and Add.1, circulated to WTO Members 27 June 2019, appealed 15 August 2019
US – Shrimp	Appellate Body Report, *United States – Import Prohibition of Certain Shrimp and Shrimp Products*, WT/DS58/AB/R, adopted 6 November 1998, DSR 1998:VII, p. 2755
US – Softwood Lumber VII	Panel Report, *United States – Countervailing Measures on Softwood Lumber from Canada*, WT/DS533/R and Add.1, circulated to WTO Members 24 August 2020, appealed 28 September 2020
US – Tariff Measures (China)	Panel Report, *United States – Tariff Measures on Certain Goods from China*, WT/DS543/R and Add.1, circulated to WTO Members 15 September 2020, appealed 26 October 2020
US – Tuna II (Mexico)	Appellate Body Report, *United States – Measures Concerning the Importation, Marketing and Sale of Tuna and Tuna Products*, WT/DS381/AB/R, adopted 13 June 2012, DSR 2012:IV, p. 1837
US – Tuna II (Mexico)	Panel Report, *United States – Measures Concerning the Importation, Marketing and Sale of Tuna and Tuna Products*, WT/DS381/R, adopted 13 June 2012, as modified by Appellate Body Report WT/DS381/AB/R, DSR 2012:IV, p. 2013

(cont.)

Short Title (WTO)	Full Title (WTO)
US – Tuna II (Mexico) (Article 21.5 – Mexico)	Panel Report, *United States – Measures Concerning the Importation, Marketing and Sale of Tuna and Tuna Products –* Recourse to Article 21.5 of the DSU by Mexico, WT/DS381/RW, Add.1 and Corr.1, adopted 3 December 2015, as modified by Appellate Body Report WT/DS381/AB/RW, DSR 2015:X, p. 5409 and DSR 2015:XI, p. 5653
US – Washing Machines	Appellate Body Report, *United States – Anti-Dumping and Countervailing Measures on Large Residential Washers from Korea*, WT/DS464/AB/R and Add.1, adopted 26 September 2016, DSR 2016:V, p. 2275

General Agreement on Tariffs and Trade (GATT)

Short Title (GATT)	Full Title (GATT)
Canada – FIRA	GATT Panel Report, *Canada – Administration of the Foreign Investment Review Act*, L/5504, adopted 7 February 1984, BISD 30S/140
Japan – Alcoholic Beverages I	GATT Panel Report, *Japan – Customs Duties, Taxes and Labelling Practices on Imported Wines and Alcoholic Beverages*, L/6216, adopted 10 November 1987, BISD 34S/83
US – Superfund	GATT Panel Report, *United States – Taxes on Petroleum and Certain Imported Substances*, L/6175, adopted 17 June 1987, BISD 34S/136
US – Tuna (Mexico)	GATT Panel Report, *United States – Restrictions on Imports of Tuna*, DS21/R, DS21/R, 3 September 1991, unadopted, BISD 39S/155

Investor–State Dispute Settlement (ISDS)

Short Title (ISDS)	Full Title (ISDS)
Antaris and Göde v. Czech Republic	*Antaris Solar GmbH and Dr. Michael Göde v. The Czech Republic*, PCA Case No. 2014-01, Award, dated 2 May 2018
Arif v. Moldova	*Franck Charles Arif v. Republic of Moldova*, ICSID Case No. ARB/11/23, Award, dated 8 April 2013
Aven and others v. Costa Rica	*David R. Aven, Samuel D. Aven, Giacomo A. Buscemi and others v. Republic of Costa Rica*, ICSID Case No. UNCT/15/3, Final Award, dated 18 September 2018
Azurix v. Argentina (I)	*Azurix Corp. v. The Argentine Republic (I)*, ICSID Case No. ARB/01/12, Award, dated 14 July 2006
Bear Creek Mining v. Peru	*Bear Creek Mining Corporation v. Republic of Peru*, ICSID Case No. ARB/14/21, Award, dated 30 November 2017
Blusun v. Italy	*Blusun S.A., Jean-Pierre Lecorcier and Michael Stein v. Italian Republic*, ICSID Case No. ARB/14/3, Award, dated 27 December 2016
Burlington v. Ecuador	*Burlington Resources, Inc. v. Republic of Ecuador*, ICSID Case No. ARB/08/5, Decision on Counterclaims, dated 7 February 2017
Charanne and Construction Investments v. Spain	*Charanne B.V. and Construction Investments S.a. r.l. v. Spain*, SCC Case No. 062/2012, Final Award (unofficial English translation by Mena Chambers at www.italaw.com/sites/default/files/case-documents/italaw7162.pdf), dated 21 January 2016
Clayton/Bilcon v. Canada	*Clayton and Bilcon of Delaware Inc. v. Government of Canada*, PCA Case No. 2009-04, Award on Jurisdiction and Liability, dated 17 March 2015
Continental Casualty v. Argentina	*Continental Casualty Company v. Argentine Republic*, ICSID Case No. ARB/03/9, Award, dated 5 September 2008

(*cont.*)

Short Title (ISDS)	Full Title (ISDS)
Cube Infrastructure and others v. Spain	*Cube Infrastructure Fund SICAV and others v. Kingdom of Spain*, ICSID Case No. ARB/15/20, Decision on Jurisdiction, Liability and Partial Decision on Quantum, dated 19 February 2019
Eco Oro v. Colombia	*Eco Oro Minerals Corp. v. Republic of Colombia*, ICSID Case No. ARB/16/41, Decision on Jurisdiction, Liability and Directions on Quantum, dated 9 September 2021
Eiser and Energía Solar v. Spain	*Eiser Infrastructure Limited and Energía Solar Luxembourg S.à r.l. v. Kingdom of Spain*, ICSID Case No. ARB/13/36, Award, dated 4 May 2017
Electrabel v. Hungary	*Electrabel S.A. v. The Republic of Hungary*, ICSID Case No. ARB/07/19, Award, dated 25 November 2015
Eskosol v. Italy	*Eskosol S.p.A. in liquidazione v. Italian Republic*, ICSID Case No. ARB/15/50, Award, dated 4 September 2020
ESPF and others v. Italy	*ESPF Beteiligungs GmbH, ESPF Nr. 2 Austria Beteiligungs GmbH, and InfraClass Energie 5 GmbH & Co. KG v. Italian Republic*, ICSID Case No. ARB/16/5, Award, dated 14 September 2020
Europa Nova v. Czechia	*WA Investments-Europa Nova Limited v. The Czech Republic*, PCA Case No. 2014-19, Award, dated 15 May 2019
Eurus Energy v. Spain	*Eurus Energy Holdings Corporation v. Kingdom of Spain*, ICSID Case No. ARB/16/4, Decision on Jurisdiction and Liability, dated 17 March 2021
Foresight and others v. Spain	*Foresight Luxembourg Solar 1 S.Á.R.L., Foresight Luxembourg Solar 2 S.Á.R.L., Greentech Energy System A/S, GWM Renewable Energy I S.P.A and GWM Renewable Energy II S.P.A v. Kingdom of Spain*, SCC Case No. 2015/150, Final Award, dated 14 November 2018
GAMI v. Mexico	*GAMI Investments, Inc. v. United Mexican States*, UNCITRAL, Final Award, dated 15 November 2004

(*cont.*)

Short Title (ISDS)	Full Title (ISDS)
Greentech and NovEnergia v. Italy	*Greentech Energy Systems A/S, NovEnergia II Energy & Environment (SCA) SICAR, and NovEnergia II Italian Portfolio SA v. Italian Republic*, SCC Case No. 2015/095, Final Award, dated 23 December 2018
Hydro Energy 1 and Hydroxana v. Spain	*Hydro Energy 1 S.à r.l. and Hydroxana Sweden AB v. Kingdom of Spain*, ICSID Case No. ARB/15/42, Decision on Jurisdiction, Liability and Directions on Quantum, dated 9 March 2020
Isolux v. Spain	*Isolux Infrastructure Netherlands B.V. v. Kingdom of Spain*, SCC Case No. 2013/153, Award (unofficial English translation at www.energychartertreaty.org/fileadmin/DocumentsMedia/Cases/49_Isolux/Isolux_v._Spain_-_award_dis._opinion_unofficial_translationEN.pdf), dated 12 July 2016
Maffezini v. Spain	*Emilio Agustín Maffezini v. The Kingdom of Spain*, ICSID Case No. ARB/97/7, Award, dated 13 November 2000
Manolium-Processing v. Belarus	*OOO Manolium-Processing v. The Republic of Belarus*, PCA Case No. 2018-06, UNCITRAL, Final Award, dated 22 June 2021
Masdar v. Spain	*Masdar Solar & Wind Cooperatief U.A. v. Kingdom of Spain*, ICSID Case No. ARB/14/1, Award, dated 16 May 2018
Mesa Power v. Canada	*Mesa Power Group LLC v. Government of Canada*, PCA Case No. 2012–17, Award, dated 24 March 2016
Metalclad v. Mexico	*Metalclad Corporation v. The United Mexican States*, ICSID Case No. ARB(AF)/97/1, Award, dated 30 August 2000
Micula v. Romania (I)	*Ioan Micula, Viorel Micula and others v. Romania (I)*, ICSID Case No. ARB/05/20, Award, dated 11 December 2013
Mobil and Murphy v. Canada (I)	*Mobil Investments Canada Inc. and Murphy Oil Corporation v. Government of Canada (I)*, ICSID Case No. ARB(AF)/07/4, Decision on Liability and Principles of Quantum, dated 22 May 2012

(*cont.*)

Short Title (ISDS)	Full Title (ISDS)
NextEra v. Spain	*NextEra Energy Global Holdings B.V. and NextEra Energy Spain Holdings B.V. v. Kingdom of Spain*, ICSID Case No. ARB/14/11, Decision on Jurisdiction, Liability and Quantum Principles, dated 12 March 2019
Novenergia v. Spain	*Novenergia II – Energy & Environment (SCA), SICAR v. Kingdom of Spain*, SCC Case No. 063/2015, Final Arbitral Award, dated 15 February 2018
Nykomb v. Latvia	*Nykomb Synergetics Technology Holding AB v. The Republic of Latvia*, Arbitral Award, dated 16 December 2003
Perenco v. Ecuador	*Perenco Ecuador Limited v. Republic of Ecuador (Petroecuador)*, ICSID Case No. ARB/08/6, Decision on Perenco's Application for Dismissal of Ecuador's Counterclaims, dated 18 August 2017
Perenco v. Ecuador	*Perenco Ecuador Limited v. Republic of Ecuador (Petroecuador)*, ICSID Case No. ARB/08/6, Award, dated 27 September 2019
Philip Morris v. Uruguay	*Philip Morris Brand Sàrl (Switzerland), Philip Morris Products S.A. (Switzerland) and Abal Hermanos S.A. (Uruguay) v. Oriental Republic of Uruguay*, ICSID Case No. ARB/10/7, Award, dated 8 July 2016
Pope & Talbot v. Canada	*Pope & Talbot v. Government of Canada*, UNCITRAL, Award on the Merits of Phase 2, dated 10 April 2001
RWE Innogy v. Spain	*RWE Innogy GmbH and RWE Innogy Aersa S.A.U. v. Kingdom of Spain*, ICSID Case No. ARB/14/34, Decision on Jurisdiction, Liability and Certain Issues of Quantum, dated 30 December 2019
Saluka v. Czech Republic	*Saluka Investments BV v. The Czech Republic*, Partial Award, dated 17 March 2006
Santa Elena v. Costa Rica	*Compañia del Desarrollo de Santa Elena S.A. v. Republic of Costa Rica*, ICSID Case No. ARB/96/1, Final Award, dated 17 February 2000
Stadtwerke München and others v. Spain	*Stadtwerke München GmbH and others v. Kingdom of Spain*, ICSID Case No. ARB/15/1, Award, dated 2 December 2019

(cont.)

Short Title (ISDS)	Full Title (ISDS)
SunReserve v. Italy	*SunReserve Luxco Holdings SRL v. Italy*, SCC Case No. 132/2016, Final Award, dated 25 March 2020
The PV Investors v. Spain	*The PV Investors v. Spain*, PCA Case No. 2012-14, Final Award, dated 28 February 2020
Urbaser and CABB v. Argentina	*Urbaser S.A. and Consorcio de Aguas Bilbao Biskaia, Bilbao Biskaia Ur Partzuergoa v. Argentine Republic*, ICSID Case No. ARB/07/26, Award, dated 8 December 2016
Vattenfall v. Germany (I)	*Vattenfall AB, Vattenfall Europe AG, Vattenfall Europe Generation AG v. Federal Republic of Germany (I)*, ICSID Case No. ARB/09/6, Award Embodying the Parties' Settlement Agreement, dated 11 March 2011
Vattenfall v. Germany (II)	*Vattenfall AB and others v. Federal Republic of Germany (II)*, ICSID Case No. ARB/12/12, Order of the Tribunal Taking Note of the Discontinuance of the Proceeding, dated 9 November 2021
Vivendi v. Argentina (I)	*Compañía de Aguas del Aconquija S.A. and Vivendi Universal S.A. (formerly Compañía de Aguas del Aconquija, S.A. and Compagnie Générale des Eaux) v. Argentine Republic (I)*, ICSID Case No. ARB/97/3, Award, dated 20 August 2007
Windstream Energy v. Canada (I)	*Windstream Energy LLC v. The Government of Canada (I)*, PCA Case No. 2013-22, Award, dated 27 September 2016

International Court of Justice (ICJ)

Short Title (ICJ)	Full Title (ICJ)
Pulp Mills	*Pulp Mills on the River Uruguay (Argentina v. Uruguay)*, Judgment of 20 April 2010, ICJ Reports 2010, p. 14

Court of Justice of the European Union (EU)

Short Title (EU)	Full Title (EU)
Achmea	*Slowakische Republik v. Achmea BV*, Case C-284/16, Judgment of the Court (Grand Chamber) of 6 March 2018
Air Transport Association of America and Others	*Air Transport Association of America and Others v. Secretary of State for Energy and Climate Change*, Case C-366/10, Judgment of the Court (Grand Chamber) of 21 December 2011
Arcelor v. Parliament and Council	*Arcelor SA v. European Parliament and Council of the European Union*, Case T-16/04, Judgment of the General Court (Third Chamber) of 2 March 2010
Asteris and Others v. Greece and EEC	*Asteris AE and others v. Hellenic Republic and European Economic Community*, Case C-106/87, Judgment of the Court (Fifth Chamber) of 27 September 1988
Commission v. European Food and Others	*European Commission v. European Food SA and Others*, Case C-638/19 P, Judgment of the Court (Grand Chamber) of 25 January 2022
Commission v. Germany	*European Commission v. Federal Republic of Germany*, Case C-142/16, Judgment of the Court (Second Chamber) of 26 April 2017
Commission v. Netherlands	*European Commission v. Kingdom of the Netherlands*, Case C-368/10, Judgment of the Court (Third Chamber) of 10 May 2012
European Food and Others v. Commission	*European Food SA and Others v. European Commission*, Cases T-624/15, T-694/15 and T-704/15, Judgment of the General Court (Second Chamber, Extended Composition) of 18 June 2019
PL Holdings	*Republiken Polen v. PL Holdings Sàrl*, Case C-109/20, Judgment of the Court (Grand Chamber) of 26 October 2021
République de Moldavie	*République de Moldavie v. Komstroy LLC*, Case C-741/19, Judgment of the Court (Grand Chamber) of 2 September 2021

Canada's Supreme Court

References re Greenhouse Gas Pollution Pricing Act, Supreme Court Judgment (Canada), dated 25 March 2021, https://scc-csc.lexum.com/scc-csc/scc-csc/en/item/18781/index.do.

TABLE OF TREATIES

Agreement in Principle on the Modernisation of the Energy Charter Treaty, 24 June 2022.

Agreement on Agriculture, included in Marrakesh Agreement Establishing the World Trade Organization, Annex 1A, 15 April 1994.

Agreement on Fisheries Subsidies, included in WTO, Ministerial Conference – Twelfth Session – Geneva, 12–15 June 2022 – Agreement on Fisheries Subsidies – Ministerial Decision of 17 June 2022, WT/MIN(22)/33, WT/L/1144 (22 June 2022).

Agreement on the International Dolphin Conservation Program, 21 May 1998.

Agreement on Trade Facilitation, included in WTO, General Council – Protocol Amending the Marrakesh Agreement Establishing the World Trade Organization – Decision of 27 November 2014, WT/L/940 (28 November 2014).

Agreement on Trade in Civil Aircraft, 12 April 1979, included in Marrakesh Agreement Establishing the World Trade Organization, Annex 4, 15 April 1994.

Anti-dumping Agreement: Agreement on Implementation of Article VI of the General Agreement on Tariffs and Trade 1994, included in Marrakesh Agreement Establishing the World Trade Organization, Annex 1A, 15 April 1994.

Argentina–Qatar BIT (2016): The Reciprocal Promotion and Protection of Investments between the Argentine Republic and the State of Qatar, 6 November 2016.

Argentina–UAE BIT (2018): Agreement for the Reciprocal Promotion and Protection of Investments between the Argentine Republic and the United Arab Emirates, 16 April 2018.

Armenia–Singapore Agreement on Trade in Services and Investment (2019): Agreement on Trade in Services and Investment between the Republic of Armenia and the Republic of Singapore, 1 October 2019.

Australia–Hong Kong BIT (2019): Investment Agreement between the Government of Australia and the Government of the Hong Kong Special Administrative Region of the People's Republic of China, 26 March 2019.

Australia–UK FTA (2021): Free Trade Agreement between the United Kingdom of Great Britain and Northern Ireland and Australia, 17 December 2021.

Belgium–Luxembourg Economic Union–Montenegro BIT (2010): Agreement between the Belgium–Luxembourg Economic Union, on the One Hand, and Montenegro, on the Other Hand, on the Reciprocal Promotion and Protection of Investments, 16 February 2010.

Brazil–Ethiopia BIT (2018): Agreement between the Federative Republic of Brazil and the Federal Democratic Republic of Ethiopia on Investment Cooperation and Facilitation, 11 April 2018.

Brazil–Guyana BIT (2018): Cooperation and Investment Facilitation Agreement between the Federative Republic of Brazil and the Co-operative Republic of Guyana, 13 December, 2018.

Brazil–India BIT (2020): Investment Cooperation and Facilitation Treaty between the Federative Republic of Brazil and the Republic of India, 25 January 2020.

Brazil–Malawi BIT (2015): Investment Cooperation and Facilitation Agreement between the Federative Republic of Brazil and the Republic of Malawi, 25 June 2015.

Brazil–Suriname BIT (2018): Cooperation and Facilitation Investment Agreement between the Federative Republic of Brazil and the Republic of Suriname, 2 May 2018.

Brazil–UAE BIT (2019): Cooperation and Facilitation Investment Agreement between the Federative Republic of Brazil and the United Arab Emirates, 15 March 2019.

Burkina Faso–Canada BIT (2015): Agreement between the Government of Canada and the Government of Burkina Faso for the Promotion and Protection of Investments, 20 April 2015.

Canada–Benin BIT (2013): Agreement between the Government of Canada and the Government of the Republic of Benin for the Promotion and Reciprocal Protection of Investments, 9 January 2013.

Canada–Colombia FTA (2008): Free Trade Agreement between Canada and the Republic of Colombia, 21 November 2008.

Canada–Guinea BIT (2015): Agreement for the Promotion and Reciprocal Protection of Investments between Canada and the Republic of Guinea, 27 May 2015.

China–Mauritius FTA (2019): Free Trade Agreement between the Government of the People's Republic of China and the Government of the Republic of Mauritius, 17 October 2019.

Colombia–Japan BIT (2011): Agreement between Japan and the Republic of Colombia for the Liberalization, Promotion and Protection of Investment, 12 September 2011.

Convention on Biological Diversity, 5 June 1992.

CPTPP (2018): Comprehensive and Progressive Agreement for Trans-Pacific Partnership, 8 March 2018.

ECT (1994): Energy Charter Treaty, 17 December 1994.

EU–Armenia Comprehensive and Enhanced Partnership Agreement (2017): Comprehensive and Enhanced Partnership Agreement between the European Union and the European Atomic Energy Community and Their Member States, of the One Part, and the Republic of Armenia, of the Other Part, 24 November 2017.

EU–Canada CETA (2016): Comprehensive Economic and Trade Agreement (CETA) between Canada, of the One Part, and the European Union and Its Member States, of the Other Part, 30 October 2016.

EU–Colombia–Peru Trade Agreement (2012): Trade Agreement between the European Union and Its Member States, of the One Part, and Colombia and Peru, of the Other Part, 26 June 2012.

EU–Japan Economic Partnership Agreement (2018): Agreement between the European Union and Japan for an Economic Partnership, 17 July 2018.

EU–Kazakhstan Enhanced Partnership and Cooperation Agreement (2015): Enhanced Partnership and Cooperation Agreement between the European Union and Its Member States, of the One Part, and the Republic of Kazakhstan, of the Other Part, 21 December 2015.

EU–New Zealand FTA (2023): Free Trade Agreement between the European Union and New Zealand, 9 July 2023.

EU–Singapore FTA (2018): Free Trade Agreement between the European Union and the Republic of Singapore, 19 October 2018.

EU–Singapore Investment Protection Agreement (2018): Investment Protection Agreement between the European Union and Its Member States, of the One Part, and the Republic of Singapore, of the Other Part, 19 October 2018.

EU–UK Trade and Cooperation Agreement (2020): Trade and Cooperation Agreement between the European Union and the European Atomic Energy Community, of the One Part, and the United Kingdom of Great Britain and Northern Ireland, of the Other Part, 30 December 2020.

EU–Ukraine Association Agreement (2014): Association Agreement between the European Union and Its Member States, of the One Part, and Ukraine, of the Other Part, 21 March 2014.

EU–Viet Nam FTA (2019): Free Trade Agreement between the European Union and the Socialist Republic of Viet Nam, 30 June 2019.

EU–Viet Nam Investment Protection Agreement (2019): Investment Protection Agreement between the European Union and Its Member States, of the One Part, and the Socialist Republic of Viet Nam, of the Other Part, 30 June 2019.

European Free Trade Association–Indonesia Comprehensive Economic Partnership Agreement (2018): Comprehensive Economic Partnership Agreement between the Republic of Indonesia and the EFTA States, 16 December 2018.

Expanded Information Technology Agreement: WTO, Ministerial Conference – Tenth Session – Nairobi, 15–18 December 2015 – Ministerial Declaration on the Expansion of Trade in Information Technology Products – Nairobi, WT/MIN (15)/25 (16 December 2015).

GATS: General Agreement on Trade in Services, included in Marrakesh Agreement Establishing the World Trade Organization, Annex 1B, 15 April 1994.

GATT: General Agreement on Tariffs and Trade 1947, 30 October 1947, incorporated into the General Agreement on Tariffs and Trade 1994, as included in Marrakesh Agreement Establishing the World Trade Organization, Annex 1A, 15 April 1994.

GPA 1994: Agreement on Government Procurement, included in Marrakesh Agreement Establishing the World Trade Organization, Annex 4, 15 April 1994.

GPA 2012: Agreement on Government Procurement, as amended by the Protocol Amending the Agreement on Government Procurement, Appendix 1 to the Decision on the Outcomes of the Negotiations Under Article XXIV:7 of the

Agreement on Government Procurement, adopted 30 March 2012, GPA/113 (2 April 2012).

Hong Kong–Mexico BIT (2020): Agreement between the Government of the Hong Kong Special Administrative Region of the People's Republic of China and the Government of the United Mexican States for the Promotion and Reciprocal Protection of Investments, 23 January 2020.

Hungary–Kyrgyz Republic BIT (2020): Agreement between the Government of Hungary and the Government of the Kyrgyz Republic for the Promotion and Reciprocal Protection of Investments, 29 September 2020.

Hungary–Oman BIT (2022): Agreement between the Government of the Sultanate of Oman and the Government of Hungary for the Promotion and Reciprocal Protection of Investments, 2 February 2022.

Hungary–UAE BIT (2021): Agreement between the Government of Hungary and the Government of the United Arab Emirates for the Promotion and Reciprocal Protection of Investments, 15 July 2021.

IAEA Statute (1956): Statute of the International Atomic Energy Agency, approved 23 October 1956.

Iceland–Liechtenstein–Norway–UK FTA (2021): Free Trade Agreement between Iceland, the Principality of Liechtenstein and the Kingdom of Norway and the United Kingdom of Great Britain and Northern Ireland, 8 July 2021.

India–Belarus BIT (2018): Treaty between the Republic of Belarus and the Republic of India on Investments, 24 September 2018.

India–Kyrgyz Republic BIT (2019): Bilateral Investment Treaty between the Government of the Kyrgyz Republic and the Government of the Republic of India, 14 June 2019.

India–UAE Comprehensive Economic Partnership Agreement (2022): Comprehensive Economic Partnership Agreement between the Government of the Republic of India and the Government of the UAE, 18 February 2022.

Information Technology Agreement: WTO, Ministerial Conference, Singapore – Ministerial Declaration on Trade in Information Technology Products – Singapore, WT/MIN(96)/16 (13 December 1996).

International Energy Charter, 20 May 2015.

Investment Agreement for the COMESA Common Investment Area, 23 May 2007.

Japan–Bahrain BIT (2022): Agreement between Japan and the Kingdom of Bahrain for the Reciprocal Promotion and Protection of Investment, 23 June 2022.

Japan–Brunei Economic Partnership Agreement (2007): Agreement between Japan and Brunei Darussalam for an Economic Partnership, 18 June 2007.

Japan–Peru BIT (2008): Agreement between Japan and the Republic of Peru for the Promotion, Protection and Liberalisation of Investment, 21 November 2008.

Japan–UK Comprehensive Economic Partnership Agreement (2020): Agreement between the United Kingdom of Great Britain and Northern Ireland and Japan for a Comprehensive Economic Partnership, 23 October 2020.

Jordan–Singapore BIT (2004): Bilateral Investment Treaty between the Government of the Hashemite Kingdom of Jordan and the Government of the Republic of Singapore, 16 May 2004.

Korea–Australia FTA (2014): Free Trade Agreement between the Government of Australia and the Government of the Republic of Korea, 8 April 2014.

Korea–China FTA (2015): Free Trade Agreement between the Government of the People's Republic of China and the Government of the Republic of Korea, 1 June 2015.

Korea–Colombia FTA (2013): Free Trade Agreement between the Republic of Korea and the Republic of Colombia, 21 February 2013.

Korea–EU FTA (2010): Free Trade Agreement between the European Union and Its Member States, of the One Part, and the Republic of Korea, of the Other Part, 6 October 2010.

Korea–United States FTA (2007): Free Trade Agreement between the Republic of Korea and the United States of America, 30 June 2007.

Korea–Viet Nam FTA (2015): Free Trade Agreement between the Government of the Socialist Republic of Viet Nam and the Government of Republic of Korea, 5 May 2015.

Kyoto Protocol: Kyoto Protocol to the United Nations Framework Convention on Climate Change, 11 December 1997.

Lithuania–Turkey BIT (2018): Agreement between the Government of the Republic of Lithuania and the Government of the Republic of Turkey on the Reciprocal Promotion and Protection of Investments, 28 August 2018.

Malaysia–Australia FTA (2012): Malaysia–Australia Free Trade Agreement, 22 May 2012.

Malaysia–Turkey FTA (2014): Free Trade Agreement between the Government of Malaysia and the Government of the Republic of Turkey, 17 April 2014.

Morocco–Nigeria BIT (2016): Reciprocal Investment Promotion and Protection Agreement between the Government of the Kingdom of Morocco and the Government of the Federal Republic of Nigeria, 3 December 2016.

Myanmar–Singapore BIT (2019): Agreement between the Government of the Republic of Singapore and the Government of the Republic of the Union of Myanmar on the Promotion and Protection of Investments, 24 September 2019.

NAFTA (1992): North American Free Trade Agreement, 17 December 1992.

New Zealand–Chinese Taipei Economic Cooperation Agreement (2013): Agreement between New Zealand and the Separate Customs Territory of Taiwan, Penghu, Kinmen, and Matsu on Economic Cooperation, 10 July 2013.

New Zealand–UK FTA (2022): Free Trade Agreement between the United Kingdom of Great Britain and Northern Ireland and New Zealand, 28 February 2022.

Paris Agreement, 12 December 2015.

Protocol (2019) to Amend the Singapore–New Zealand Closer Economic Partnership Agreement: Protocol to Amend the Agreement between Singapore and New Zealand on a Closer Economic Partnership, 17 May 2019.

RCEP Agreement (2020): Regional Comprehensive Economic Partnership Agreement, 15 November 2020.

SCM Agreement: Agreement on Subsidies and Countervailing Measures, included in Marrakesh Agreement Establishing the World Trade Organization, Annex 1A, 15 April 1994.

Southern African Customs Union and Mozambique–UK Economic Partnership Agreement (2019): Economic Partnership Agreement between the Southern African Customs Union Member States and Mozambique, of the One Part, and the United Kingdom of Great Britain and Northern Ireland, of the Other Part, 9 October 2019.

SPS Agreement: Agreement on the Application of Sanitary and Phytosanitary Measures, included in Marrakesh Agreement Establishing the World Trade Organization, Annex 1A, 15 April 1994.

Switzerland–Georgia BIT (2014): Agreement between the Swiss Confederation and Georgia on the Promotion and Reciprocal Protection of Investments, 3 June 2014.

Switzerland–Japan Agreement on Free Trade and Economic Partnership (2009): Agreement on Free Trade and Economic Partnership between Japan and the Swiss Confederation, 19 February 2009.

Switzerland–Uruguay BIT (1988): Agreement between the Swiss Confederation and the Oriental Republic of Uruguay on the Reciprocal Promotion and Protection of Investments, 7 October 1988.

TBT Agreement: Agreement on Technical Barriers to Trade, included in Marrakesh Agreement Establishing the World Trade Organization, Annex 1A, 15 April 1994.

Tokyo Round Subsidies Code: Agreement on Interpretation and Application of Articles VI, XVI and XXIII of the General Agreement on Tariffs and Trade, 12 April 1979.

Tokyo Round TBT Code: Agreement on Technical Barriers to Trade, 12 April 1979.

Treaty on the Functioning of the European Union, as renamed by the Treaty of Lisbon amending the Treaty on European Union and the Treaty Establishing the European Community, 13 December 2007.

TRIMs Agreement: Agreement on Trade-Related Investment Measures, included in Marrakesh Agreement Establishing the World Trade Organization, Annex 1A, 15 April 1994.

TRIPS Agreement: Agreement on Trade-Related Aspects of Intellectual Property Rights, included in Marrakesh Agreement Establishing the World Trade Organization, Annex 1C, 15 April 1994.

Turkey–Cambodia BIT (2018): Agreement between the Government of the Republic of Turkey and the Government of the Kingdom of Cambodia on the Reciprocal Promotion and Protection of Investments, 21 October 2018.

UNFCCC (1992): United Nations Framework Convention on Climate Change, 9 May 1992.

USMCA (2018): Agreement between the United States of America, the United Mexican States, and Canada, 30 November 2018.

VCLT: Vienna Convention on the Law of Treaties, 23 May 1969.

WTO Agreement: Marrakesh Agreement Establishing the World Trade Organization, 15 April 1994.

TABLE OF OTHER LEGAL TEXTS (AND DRAFTS)

2022 APEC Joint Ministerial Statement, Bangkok (Thailand) (18 November 2022), www.apec.org/meeting-papers/annual-ministerial-meetings/2022/2022-apec-ministerial-meeting.

Agenda 21, adopted at the UN Conference on Environment and Development, Rio de Janerio (3–14 June 1992).

APEC 2009 Leaders' Declaration, Singapore (14 November 2009), www.apec.org/Meeting-Papers/Leaders-Declarations/2009/2009_aelm.aspx.

APEC 2012 Leaders' Declaration, Vladivostok (Russia) (8–9 September 2012), www.apec.org/Meeting-Papers/Leaders-Declarations/2012/2012_aelm.

Canada's Special Import Measures Act, R.S.C., 1985, c. S-15 (last amended 1 July 2020), https://laws-lois.justice.gc.ca/eng/acts/S-15/FullText.html.

Communication from the Commission: Guidelines on State Aid for Environmental Protection and Energy 2014–2020 (2014/C 200/01), OJ C 200 (28 June 2014).

Decision on Trade and Environment (15 April 1994) (Uruguay Round).

Declaration of the United Nations Conference on the Human Environment, adopted at the UN Conference on the Human Environment, Stockholm (5–16 June 1972).

Declaration on the Establishment of a New International Economic Order, UN General Assembly Resolution A/RES/S-6/3201 (1 May 1974).

Directive (EU) 2018/2001 of the European Parliament and of the Council of 11 December 2018 on the promotion of the use of energy from renewable sources (recast), OJ L 328 (21 December 2018).

Directive 2004/18/EC of the European Parliament and of the Council of 31 March 2004 on the coordination of procedures for the award of public works contracts, public supply contracts and public service contracts (OJ 2004 L 134, and corrigendum OJ 2004 L 351), as amended by Commission Regulation (EC) No. 1422/2007 of 4 December 2007, OJ 2007 L 317.

Directive 2008/101/EC of the European Parliament and of the Council of 19 November 2008 amending Directive 2003/87/EC so as to include aviation activities in the scheme for greenhouse gas emission allowance trading within the Community, OJ L 8 (13 January 2009).

Enabling Clause: GATT, Differential and More Favourable Treatment Reciprocity and Fuller Participation of Developing Countries – Decision of 28 November 1979, L/4903 (3 December 1979).

Energy Charter Protocol on Energy Efficiency and Related Environmental Aspects (17 December 1994).

European Parliament Resolution of 24 November 2022 on the Outcome of the Modernisation of the Energy Charter Treaty (2022/2934(RSP)), www.europarl .europa.eu/doceo/document/TA-9-2022-0421_EN.html.

European Parliament Resolution of 6 April 2011 on the future European international investment policy (2010/2203(INI)), OJ C 296 E (2 October 2012).

G7 Leaders' Communiqué, Elmau (Germany) (28 June 2022), www.g7germany.de/ resource/blob/974430/2062292/9c213e6b4b36ed1bd687e82480040399/2022-07-14-leaders-communique-data.pdf?download = 1.

G7 Statement on Climate Club (28 June 2022), www.g7germany.de/resource/blob/974430/ 2057926/2a7cd9f10213a481924492942dd660a1/2022-06-28-g7-climate-club-data.pdf.

G7 Trade Ministers' Communiqué (28 May 2021), www.gov.uk/government/news/g7-trade-ministers-communique.

G7 Trade Ministers' Statement (15 September 2022), www.meti.go.jp/policy/trade_ policy/G7G8/pdf/220914G7TradeMinistersStatementEN.pdf.

G20 Bali Leaders' Declaration, Bali (Indonesia) (15–16 November 2022), www.g20.org/en/.

G20 Leaders Statement: The Pittsburgh Summit, Pittsburgh (24–25 September 2009), www .g20.utoronto.ca/2009/2009communique0925.html.

General Assembly Resolution 1803 (XVII) of 14 December 1962, 'Permanent Sovereignty over Natural Resources'.

India's 1975 Customs Tariff Act.

India's 1995 Customs Tariff (Identification, Assessment and Collection of Countervailing Duty on Subsidized Articles and for Determination of Injury) Rules (as updated on 1 August 2018 at Ministry of Commerce and Industry, www.dgtr.gov.in/sites/default/ files/Compendium_of_Law%26Regulations_for-mail%281%29.pdf).

Italy's Model BIT (August 2022), https://investmentpolicy.unctad.org/international-investment-agreements/treaty-files/6438/download.

The Netherlands' Model BIT (22 March 2019), https://investmentpolicy.unctad.org/ international-investment-agreements/treaty-files/5832/download.

OECD Guidelines for Multinational Enterprises (1976).

OECD Principles of Corporate Governance (1999).

OECD, 'Arrangement on Officially Supported Export Credits' (January 2022 version), https://one.oecd.org/document/TAD/PG(2022)1/en/pdf.

'Recommendation of the Council on Guiding Principles Concerning International Economic Aspects of Environmental Policies', OECD/LEGAL/0102 (adopted 26 May 1972), https://legalinstruments.oecd.org/en/instruments/OECD-LEGAL-0102.

'Recommendation of the Council on the Implementation of the Polluter-Pays Principle', OECD/LEGAL/0132 (adopted 14 November 1974), https:// legalinstruments.oecd.org/en/instruments/OECD-LEGAL-0132.

Proposal for a Regulation of the European Parliament and the Council Establishing a Carbon Border Adjustment Mechanism, 2021/0214 (COD), COM(2021) 564 final (14 July 2021).

Rio Declaration on Environment and Development, adopted at the UN Conference on Environment and Development, Rio de Janeiro (3–14 June 1992).

Sharm el-Sheikh Implementation Plan, Decision 1/CP.27, Conference of the Parties, FCCC/CP/2022/10/Add.1 (17 March 2023).

Transforming Our World: The 2030 Agenda for Sustainable Development, Resolution adopted by the UN General Assembly on 25 September 2015, A/RES/70/1 (21 October 2015).

Tripartite Declaration of Principles Concerning Multinational Enterprises and Social Policy, adopted by the Governing Body of the International Labour Office at its 204th Session (Geneva, November 1977).

UN Global Compact (2000).

UN Guiding Principles on Business and Human Rights (adopted 16 June 2011).

US Congress, 'S.4355 – Clean Competition Act', 117th Congress (2021–2022), www.congress.gov/bill/117th-congress/senate-bill/4355/text.

US Inflation Reduction Act of 2022, www.democrats.senate.gov/imo/media/doc/inflation_reduction_act_of_2022.pdf.

US Model BIT (2012), https://ustr.gov/sites/default/files/BIT%20text%20for%20ACIEP%20Meeting.pdf.

WTO, Accession of the People's Republic of China – Decision of 10 November 2001, WT/L/432 (23 November 2001).

Australia – Schedule of Specific Commitments, GATS/SC/6 (15 April 1994).

Brazil – Schedule of Specific Commitments, GATS/SC/13 (15 April 1994).

Canada – Schedule of Specific Commitments, GATS/SC/16 (15 April 1994).

Colombia – Schedule of Specific Commitments, GATS/SC/20 (15 April 1994).

Communication from Sierra Leone – General Agreement on Trade in Services – Schedule of Specific Commitments, GATS/SC/105 (30 August 1995).

Decision of the Committee on Government Procurement on a Work Programme on Sustainable Procurement, Annex E to Appendix 2 of the Decision on the Outcomes of the Negotiations Under Article XXIV:7 of the Agreement on Government Procurement, adopted on 30 March 2012, GPA/113 (2 April 2012).

Decision of the Committee on Principles for the Development of International Standards, Guides and Recommendations with Relation to Articles 2, 5 and Annex 3 of the Agreement, attached to G/TBT/9 (13 November 2000), Annex 4.

Decision on Trade in Services and the Environment, S/L/4 (4 April 1995).

Disciplines on Domestic Regulation in the Accountancy Sector – Adopted by the Council for Trade in Services on 14 December 1998, S/L/64 (17 December 1998).

Iceland – Schedule of Specific Commitments, GATS/SC/41 (15 April 1994).

India – Schedule of Specific Commitments, GATS/SC/42 (15 April 1994).

Japan – Schedule of Specific Commitments, GATS/SC/46 (15 April 1994).

Joint Initiative on Services Domestic Regulation – Reference Paper on Services Domestic Regulation, INF/SDR/2 (26 November 2021) annexed to WTO, Declaration on the Conclusion of Negotiations on Services Domestic Regulation, WT/L/1129 (2 December 2021).

Kuwait – Schedule of Specific Commitments, GATS/SC/49 (15 April 1994).

Mexico – Schedule of Specific Commitments, GATS/SC/56 (15 April 1994).

Ministerial Conference – Fourth Session – Doha, 9–14 November 2001 – Declaration on the TRIPS Agreement and Public Health – Adopted on 14 November 2001, WT/MIN(01)/DEC/2 (20 November 2001).

Ministerial Conference – Fourth Session – Doha, 9–14 November 2001 – Ministerial Declaration – Adopted on 14 November 2001, WT/MIN(01)/DEC/1 (20 November 2001).

Ministerial Conference – Sixth Session – Hong Kong, 13–18 December 2005 – Doha Work Programme – Ministerial Declaration – Adopted on 18 December 2005, WT/MIN(05)/DEC (22 December 2005).

Norway – Schedule of Specific Commitments, GATS/SC/66 (15 April 1994).

Qatar – Schedule of Specific Commitments, GATS/SC/120 (10 November 1995).

Republic of Korea – Schedule of Specific Commitments, GATS/SC/48 (15 April 1994).

Sri Lanka – Schedule of Specific Commitments, GATS/SC/79 (15 April 1994).

Thailand – Schedule of Specific Commitments, GATS/SC/85 (15 April 1994).

Trade in Services – European Union – Schedule of Specific Commitments, GATS/SC/157 (7 May 2019).

Trade in Services – Georgia – Schedule of Specific Commitments, GATS/SC/129 (20 December 2000).

Trade in Services – Montenegro – Schedule of Specific Commitments, GATS/SC/146 (5 June 2012).

Trade in Services – Philippines – Schedule of Specific Commitments – Supplement 3, GATS/SC/70/Suppl.3 (26 February 1998).

Trade in Services – Russian Federation – Schedule of Specific Commitments, GATS/SC/149 (5 November 2012).

Trade in Services – Samoa – Schedule of Specific Commitments, GATS/SC/147 (5 June 2012).

Trade in Services – Tajikistan – Schedule of Specific Commitments, GATS/SC/151 (22 April 2013).

Trade in Services – The Kingdom of Cambodia – Schedule of Specific Commitments, GATS/SC/140 (25 October 2005).

Trade in Services – The People's Republic of China – Schedule of Specific Commitments, GATS/SC/135 (14 February 2002).

Trade in Services – The Republic of Bulgaria – Schedule of Specific Commitments, GATS/SC/122 (21 May 1997).

Trade in Services – The Republic of Croatia – Schedule of Specific Commitments, GATS/SC/130 (22 December 2000).

Trade in Services – The Republic of Kazakhstan – Schedule of Specific Commitments, GATS/SC/154 (15 February 2016).

Trade in Services – Viet Nam – Schedule of Specific Commitments, GATS/SC/142 (19 March 2007).

Tunisia – Schedule of Specific Commitments, GATS/SC/87 (15 April 1994).

Understanding on the Interpretation of Article XVII of the GATT 1994, included as part of the GATT 1994 in Marrakesh Agreement Establishing the World Trade Organization (15 April 1994).

United States – Schedule of Specific Commitments, GATS/SC/90 (15 April 1994).

Working Party on the Accession of Armenia – Report of the Working Party on the Accession of the Republic of Armenia, WT/ACC/ARM/23 (26 November 2002).

Working Party on the Accession of Cambodia – Report of the Working Party on the Accession of Cambodia, WT/ACC/KHM/21 (15 August 2003).

Working Party on the Accession of China – Report of the Working Party on the Accession of China, WT/ACC/CHN/49 (1 October 2001).

Working Party on the Accession of Saudi Arabia – Report of the Working Party on the Accession of the Kingdom of Saudi Arabia to the WTO, WT/ACC/SAU/61 (1 November 2005).

Working Party on the Accession of the Republic of Kazakhstan – Report of the Working Party on the Accession of the Republic of Kazakhstan – Schedule CLXXII – Republic of Kazakhstan – Addendum, WT/ACC/KAZ/93/Add.1 (23 June 2015).

Working Party on the Accession of the Republic of Tajikistan – Report of the Working Party on the Accession of the Republic of Tajikistan, WT/ACC/TJK/30 (6 November 2012).

Working Party on the Accession of the Russian Federation – Report of the Working Party on the Accession of the Russian Federation to the World Trade Organization – Schedule CLXV – The Russian Federation – Part I – Schedule of Concessions and Commitments on Goods – Addendum, WT/ACC/RUS/70/Add.1, WT/MIN(11)/2/Add.1 (17 November 2011).

Working Party on the Accession of the Russian Federation – Report of the Working Party on the Accession of the Russian Federation to the WTO, WT/ACC/RUS/70, WT/MIN(11)/2 (17 November 2011).

Working Party on the Accession of Ukraine – Report of the Working Party on the Accession of Ukraine to the WTO, WT/ACC/UKR/152 (25 January 2008).

ABBREVIATIONS

ACCTS	Agreement on Climate Change, Trade and Sustainability
ALOP	appropriate level of SPS protection
APEC	Asia-Pacific Economic Cooperation
ASEAN	Association of Southeast Asian Nations
BCA	border carbon adjustment
BTA	border tax adjustment
BIT	bilateral investment treaty
CBAM	carbon border adjustment mechanism
CETA	Comprehensive and Economic Trade Agreement
CO_2	carbon dioxide
CPC	Central Product Classification
CPTPP	Comprehensive and Progressive Agreement for Trans-Pacific Partnership
CSR	corporate social responsibility
DDA	Doha Development Agenda
ECT	Energy Charter Treaty
EGA	Environmental Goods Agreement
EPA	Environmental Protection Agency (United States)
ETS	emission trading system
EU	European Union
FDI	foreign direct investment
FET	fair and equitable treatment
FFSR	Fossil Fuel Subsidy Reform
FIT	feed-in tariff
FTA	free trade agreement
G7	Group of Seven
G20	Group of Twenty
GATS	General Agreement on Trade in Services
GATT	General Agreement on Tariffs and Trade
GHG	greenhouse gas
GPA	Government Procurement Agreement
HS	Harmonized System

ICSID	International Centre for Settlement of Investment Disputes
IDP	Informal Dialogue on Plastics Pollution and Sustainable Plastics Trade
IAEA	International Atomic Energy Agency
IEA	International Energy Agency
IEC	International Electrotechnical Commission
IIA	international investment agreement
IMF	International Monetary Fund
IRENA	International Renewable Energy Agency
ISDS	investor–State dispute settlement
ISO	International Organization for Standardization
LCR	local content requirement
LDC	least-developed country
MFN	most-favoured nation
NAFTA	North American Free Trade Agreement
NPR-PPMs	non-product-related processes and production methods
OECD	Organization for Economic Co-operation and Development
PCA	Permanent Court of Arbitration
ppm	parts per million
PPMs	processes and production methods
PV	photovoltaic
R&D	research and development
RCEP	Regional Comprehensive Economic Partnership
REN21	Renewable Energy Policy Network for the Twenty-First Century
RTA	regional trade agreement
S&D	special and differential (treatment)
SCC	Stockholm Chamber of Commerce
SCM	subsidies and countervailing measures
SDG	Sustainable Development Goal
SPS	sanitary and phytosanitary (measures)
STC	specific trade concern
TBT	technical barriers to trade
TESSD	Trade and Environmental Sustainability Structured Discussions
TPRB	Trade Policy Review Body
TRIMs	trade-related investment measures
TRIPS	trade-related aspects of intellectual property rights
UAE	United Arab Emirates
UN	United Nations
UNCITRAL	United Nations Commission on International Trade Law
UNCTAD	United Nations Conference on Trade and Development
UNEP	United Nations Environment Programme
UNFCCC	United Nations Framework Convention on Climate Change

USDOC	United States Department of Commerce
USMCA	United States–Mexico–Canada Agreement
VCLT	Vienna Convention on the Law of Treaties
WP.29	World Forum for Harmonization of Vehicle Regulations
WTO	World Trade Organization

Introduction

> Where there is ruin, there is hope for a treasure.
>
> Rumi (1207–1273)

Energy is an important component of economic activities. It includes non-renewable (fossil and nuclear) energy and renewable (typically, hydro, solar, wind, geothermal and biomass) energy in both primary and secondary forms.[1] Energy intersects with the environment at every stage of its life cycle, namely exploration, extraction, production, conversion, storage, transportation, distribution, use and disposal.

The energy supply chain can negatively affect nature and public health by polluting air, land and water or generating harmful waste, among others. Fossil fuel mining and excessive land use for growing biofuel feedstocks can damage the surrounding ecosystem. Nuclear power plant accidents bring about dangerous consequences felt even in regions far from the accident site. Climate change is probably the 'most global' acute problem associated with energy. Nearly 75 per cent of the world's greenhouse gas (GHG) emissions come from energy use in industry, transport, buildings and elsewhere.[2] This is so because almost 80 per cent of the world's energy is produced by burning fossil fuels, such as oil,

[1] The concept of 'energy' lacks a uniform definition and can change over time. By way of illustration, the United Nations (UN) energy statistics distinguish the following categories of 'energy products': solid fossil fuels (hard coal, brown coal, peat, oil shale, etc.), liquid fossil fuels (conventional crude oil, natural gas liquids, oil products, motor gasoline, etc.), gaseous fossil fuels (natural gas, gas works gas, coke oven gas, blast furnace gas, etc.), biofuels and waste (animal/vegetable waste, biogasoline, biodiesels, biogases, etc.), electricity and heat (primary/secondary electricity generated from fossil, nuclear or renewable energy sources; heat produced by primary/secondary processes, etc.). See UN, '2020 United Nations Energy Statistics Yearbook', 2020, pp. ix–xv, https://unstats.un.org/unsd/energystats/pubs/yearbook/2020/04d.pdf.

[2] Hannah Ritchie, Max Roser and Pablo Rosado, 'CO_2 and Greenhouse Gas Emissions', OurWorldInData.org, 2020, https://ourworldindata.org/co2-and-greenhouse-gas-emissions.

coal and gas.[3] Under the Paris Agreement (2015), governments agreed to pursue efforts to limit global warming to well below 2°C, preferably to 1.5°C, compared to pre-industrial levels.[4] But the preferable 1.5°C target requires achieving net-zero carbon dioxide (CO_2) emissions globally by the early 2050s.[5]

In order to reduce our dependence on high-carbon energy, more needs to be done to increase renewable energy generation and improve energy efficiency. It is thus not a mere coincidence that these are the two climate mitigation options that have been indicated most frequently in countries' nationally determined contributions, or action plans, under the Paris Agreement.[6] In parallel, greater efforts to conserve and sustainably exploit exhaustible energy resources will help avoid environmental pollution as well. In this respect, scientists suggest that in order to stabilize Earth's climate, a third of the world's oil reserves, half of its gas reserves and over 80 per cent of its coal reserves should remain unused.[7] Furthermore, environmentally safe production and use of carbon-free nuclear energy is another example of how properly managed energy can prevent harm to the environment.

As energy is involved in trade and investment projects, it is covered by the trade and investment branches of international economic law and regulated in these fields mainly by the rules of the World Trade Organization (WTO), the Energy Charter Treaty (ECT), regional trade agreements (RTAs) and international investment agreements (IIAs).

I.1 Recent Developments Regarding the Energy–Environment Agenda

Today, energy-related policies of virtually all nations, regardless of their geographical location or economic status, have incorporated

[3] World Trade Organization (WTO), 'Climate Change and International Trade', World Trade Report 2022, 2022, p. 20.

[4] Article 2.1(a) of the Paris Agreement (2015).

[5] Intergovernmental Panel on Climate Change, 'The Evidence Is Clear: The Time for Action Is Now. We Can Halve Emissions by 2030', 4 April 2022, www.ipcc.ch/2022/04/04/ipcc-ar6-wgiii-pressrelease/.

[6] UN, 'Nationally Determined Contributions under the Paris Agreement: Synthesis Report by the Secretariat', Conference of the Parties Serving as the Meeting of the Parties to the Paris Agreement, FCCC/PA/CMA/2022/4 (26 October 2022), paras. 33, 182.

[7] Christophe McGlade and Paul Ekins, 'The Geographical Distribution of Fossil Fuels Unused When Limiting Global Warming to 2°C', 517 *Nature* 187 (2015), p. 187.

environmental aspects, albeit with differing aspirations. As of 1 September 2022, 136 countries and the European Union (EU) have adopted or proposed net-zero targets to be achieved mostly by mid-century covering around 83 per cent of global carbon emissions.[8] To give just two examples, the European Green Deal (2019) lays down the EU strategy for reaching the bloc's climate neutrality by 2050 and decoupling economic growth from resource use through decarbonizing the energy system, mobilizing industry for a clean and circular economy, improving the energy performance of buildings and so on.[9] China's Fourteenth Five-Year Plan (2021–2025) expects the country to reach its CO_2 emissions peak by 2030 and carbon neutrality by 2060 and seeks to 'promote the clean, low-carbon, safe and efficient use of energy and advance the low-carbon transformation of industry, construction and transportation in an in-depth manner'.[10]

On the global stage, the Group of Twenty (G20) leaders made a political commitment to 'rapidly scale up the deployment of zero and low emission power generation, including renewable energy resources, and measures to enhance energy efficiency, abatement technologies as well as removal technologies, taking into account national circumstances'.[11] This corresponds to 'the importance of enhancing a clean energy mix, including low-emission and renewable energy, at all levels as part of diversifying energy mixes and systems, in line with national circumstances', as stressed by the Paris Agreement parties.[12]

Varying 'national circumstances' influence the pace of energy transition not only domestically but also at a regional level, including among

[8] Organization for Economic Co-operation and Development (OECD), 'The Climate Action Monitor 2022: Helping Countries Advance towards Net Zero', OECD, 2022, pp. 17, 19.

[9] See European Commission, 'The European Green Deal', Communication to the European Parliament, the European Council, the Council, the European Economic and Social Committee and the Committee of the Regions, COM(2019) 640 final (11 December 2019).

[10] China, 'Outline of the People's Republic of China 14th Five-Year Plan for National Economic and Social Development and Long-Range Objectives for 2035', 12 March 2021, Article XXVIII (section 4) (English translation at Centre for Security and Emerging Technology, https://cset.georgetown.edu/publication/china-14th-five-year-plan/).

[11] Group of Twenty (G20) Bali Leaders' Declaration, Bali (Indonesia), 15–16 November 2022, para. 12, www.g20.org/en/.

[12] Sharm el-Sheikh Implementation Plan, Decision 1/CP.27, para. 13, Conference of the Parties, FCCC/CP/2022/10/Add.1 (17 March 2023) in UN, 'Report of the Conference of the Parties on Its Twenty-Seventh Session, Held in Sharm el-Sheikh from 6 to 20 November 2022'.

developing countries. For example, the present energy cooperation policy of the Association of Southeast Asian Nations (ASEAN) aims to optimize the role of clean coal technology in decarbonization efforts and sets region-wide targets for reducing energy intensity and increasing renewables' portion in the total energy mix.[13] By contrast, the African Union does not have pre-defined 'greening' targets for the entire continent yet. Its current highest priority is to increase universal energy access in Africa in the short to medium term while the enhancement of the uptake of renewable energy is considered as a goal for the long term.[14]

Although the international trade and investment regimes focus on respective *economic* activities, the extent to which they are capable of addressing energy-related *environmental* issues is of increasing significance today. Indeed, new developments in international economic practice accentuate the energy–environment interplay more than ever. To name a few, there are ongoing WTO initiatives on trade and environmental sustainability, sustainable plastics trade and reforming fossil fuel subsidies; pro-environmental modernization efforts directed to the ECT; greening elements frequently entering today's investment and trade treaty-making; the growing number of trade and investment disputes on renewable energy; and international discussions on creating 'climate clubs' in the near future.[15] In addition, New Zealand, Costa Rica, Fiji, Iceland, Norway and Switzerland are currently negotiating an Agreement on Climate Change, Trade and Sustainability (ACCTS) seeking to liberalize trade in environmental goods and environmental services, eliminate harmful fossil fuel subsidies and develop guidelines concerning voluntary eco-labelling programmes and mechanisms. Once concluded, this agreement will then be open to other interested WTO members.[16]

[13] Association of Southeast Asian Nations (ASEAN) Centre for Energy, 'ASEAN Plan of Action for Energy Cooperation (APAEC) 2016–2025, Phase II: 2021–2025', 2020, pp. 2–3, https://aseanenergy.org/asean-plan-of-action-for-energy-cooperation-apaec-phase-ii-2021-2025/.

[14] See African Union, 'Africa Speaks with Unified Voice as AU Executive Council Adopts African Common Position on Energy Access and Just Energy Transition', 22 July 2022, https://au.int/en/pressreleases/20220722/africa-speaks-unified-voice-au-executive-council-adopts-african-common. See also Kigali Communique, 'Ensuring a Just and Equitable Energy Transition in Africa: Seven Transformative Actions for SDG 7', 19 May 2022, www.mininfra.gov.rw/index.php?eID=dumpFile&t=f&f=44024&token=c9d8a3e4e9ad4d22aa3c3b883055c9426760c584.

[15] See Sections 1.2.1, 1.2.2, 1.2.3, 1.2.4, 2.1.3, 3.2.2 and 5.2.

[16] See New Zealand Foreign Affairs and Trade, 'Agreement on Climate Change, Trade and Sustainability (ACCTS) Negotiations', www.mfat.govt.nz/en/trade/free-trade-agree

Furthermore, trade and clean energy are among the negotiating pillars of the Indo-Pacific Economic Framework for Prosperity launched by thirteen countries in 2022.[17] Importantly, on 19 January 2023, the European Commission, the EU Member States and twenty-six partner countries – both developed and developing countries – established a Coalition of Trade Ministers on Climate to build partnerships between trade and climate communities and identify ways in which trade and trade policies can promote global climate actions and support the most vulnerable developing and least-developed countries (LDCs).[18]

As for domestic policies, most of the environment-related trade measures notified to the WTO over the last ten years have been aimed at energy conservation and efficiency as well as alternative and renewable energy.[19] The EU legislative plans to introduce border adjustments for internal decarbonization costs and the United States' 2022 law disabling government financial support for the local use of many imported electric vehicles are among current hot issues that have energy–environment implications.[20]

I.2 Situating This Book within the Existing Literature

Energy has been in intense spotlight of academic research in international economic law, especially since 2010, partly in reflection of remarkable activism in the energy-related international discourse and dispute settlement in the realms of trade and investment. The literature on sustainability issues concerning energy production and use keeps growing. Without undermining the importance and intellectual value

ments/trade-and-climate/agreement-on-climate-change-trade-and-sustainability-accts-negotiations/.

[17] US White House, 'Statement on Indo-Pacific Economic Framework for Prosperity', 23 May 2022, www.whitehouse.gov/briefing-room/statements-releases/2022/05/23/statement-on-indo-pacific-economic-framework-for-prosperity.

[18] See Coalition of Trade Ministers on Climate, www.tradeministersonclimate.org; European Commission, 'Trade and Climate: EU and Partner Countries Launch the "Coalition of Trade Ministers on Climate"', 19 January 2023, https://ec.europa.eu/commission/presscorner/detail/en/IP_23_248.

[19] In the period 2009–2021, 'energy conservation and efficiency' and 'alternative and renewable energy' taken together were most frequently cited (or if taken separately, No. 2 and No. 3 among twenty-five) environment-related objectives of trade measures notified to the WTO. See 'Types of Environment-Related Objectives' in WTO Environmental Database (as of 1 April 2023), https://edb.wto.org/charts.

[20] See Sections 2.1.1 and 2.2.1.1.

of each work and given the spatial constraints that do not allow a review of all scholarship, one can distinguish a number of books in the fields of international trade and investment law that are particularly relevant to our topic.

In the area of trade law, Vranes, and Epps and Green examine the role of WTO law in addressing, respectively, trade–environment and trade–climate linkages.[21] While not energy-specific, these publications are comprehensive in considering complex intersectional issues from a multilateral trade perspective. By contrast, Selivanova's edited volume specifically deals with energy, underscoring the distinct status of energy as a commodity and service, and examines how it is regulated under both general and specialized frameworks, such as the WTO, the North American Free Trade Agreement (NAFTA) and the ECT. Some environmental aspects (e.g., bioenergy development and environmental impacts of energy dual pricing) are included but do not constitute the focal point of this book.[22] Marhold carries out an up-to-date comprehensive review of multilateral and preferential trade agreements and the ECT with particular reference to key concepts, historical developments and legal issues of market decentralization, decarbonization and security in the energy sector. The part on energy decarbonization is confined to dual pricing and fossil fuel subsidies.[23] Some other works are dedicated to specific issues of energy trade law but do not elaborate on environmental protection: for example, Azaria and Pogoretskyy provide an in-depth analysis of transit of energy via pipelines, looking into the concept of freedom of transit under the trade regime, among others.[24] Further, Hufbauer and others and Cottier and Espa edited a separate collection of papers on regulation of trade in sustainable energy/electricity.[25]

[21] Erich Vranes, *Trade and the Environment: Fundamental Issues in International Law, WTO Law, and Legal Theory* (Oxford: Oxford University Press, 2009); Tracey Epps and Andrew Green, *Reconciling Trade and Climate: How the WTO Can Help Address Climate Change* (Cheltenham and Northampton: Edward Elgar, 2010).

[22] Yulia Selivanova (ed.), *Regulation of Energy in International Trade Law: WTO, NAFTA and Energy Charter* (Alphen aan den Rijn: Kluwer Law International, 2011).

[23] Anna-Alexandra Marhold, *Energy in International Trade Law: Concepts, Regulations and Changing Markets* (Cambridge: Cambridge University Press, 2021).

[24] Danae Azaria, *Treaties on Transit of Energy via Pipelines and Countermeasures* (Oxford: Oxford University Press, 2015); Vitaliy Pogoretskyy, *Freedom of Transit and Access to Gas Pipeline Networks under WTO Law* (Cambridge: Cambridge University Press, 2017).

[25] Gary C. Hufbauer, Ricardo Meléndez-Ortiz and Richard Samans (eds.), *The Law and Economics of a Sustainable Energy Trade Agreement* (Cambridge: Cambridge University Press, 2016); Thomas Cottier and Ilaria Espa (eds.), *International Trade in Sustainable*

In the area of investment law, Viñuales extensively analyses synergetic and conflicting aspects of the relationship between foreign investment law and environmental law and points to the possibility for greater integration of environmental reasoning into investment adjudicative mechanisms.[26] Other representative monographs on the investment–environment interplay concern implications of the historical evolution of investment law for environmental protection (Miles), the right to regulate (Titi) and investment case law's impact on environmental policy (Tienhaara).[27] These works are not specific to energy per se, but they provide a useful framework for contextualizing the energy–environment nexus under international investment law. By contrast, a commentary on the ECT (Hobér), an edited volume on international energy arbitration (Scherer) and a book on stability in the energy investment regime (Cameron) specifically focus on the protection of energy investments across a wide spectrum of matters while dedicating only some parts to certain environmental issues.[28]

In addition, one cannot ignore the scholarship that discusses a broader picture of how to mainstream environmental sustainability under the international economic system. In this category, Condon and Sinha, Bacchus, and Petersmann discuss the transformation of global economic governance in response to climate change challenges and sustainable development needs.[29] This strand of literature offers solid intellectual grounds for urging greening actions within the world trade and investment architecture as a whole, including the energy part thereunder.

Electricity: Regulatory Challenges in International Economic Law (Cambridge: Cambridge University Press, 2017).

[26] Jorge E. Viñuales, *Foreign Investment and the Environment in International Law* (Cambridge: Cambridge University Press, 2012), pp. 392–393.

[27] Kate Miles, *The Origins of International Investment Law: Empire, Environment and the Safeguarding of Capital* (Cambridge: Cambridge University Press, 2013); Aikaterini Titi, *The Right to Regulate in International Investment Law* (Baden-Baden: Nomos, 2014); Kyla Tienhaara, *The Expropriation of Environmental Governance: Protecting Foreign Investors at the Expense of Public Policy* (Cambridge: Cambridge University Press, 2009).

[28] Kaj Hobér, *The Energy Charter Treaty: A Commentary* (Oxford: Oxford University Press, 2020); Maxi Scherer (ed.), *International Arbitration in the Energy Sector* (Oxford: Oxford University Press, 2018); Peter D. Cameron, *International Energy Investment Law: The Pursuit of Stability* (Oxford: Oxford University Press, 2010).

[29] Bradly J. Condon and Tapen Sinha, *The Role of Climate Change in Global Economic Governance* (Oxford: Oxford University Press, 2013); James Bacchus, *The Willing World: Shaping and Sharing a Sustainable Global Prosperity* (Cambridge: Cambridge University Press, 2018); Ernst-Ulrich Petersmann, *Transforming World Trade and Investment Law for Sustainable Development* (Oxford: Oxford University Press, 2022).

Last but not least, some monographs address the environmental intersection under international economic law with respect to specific issues pertaining to a wide range of economic activities, not necessarily confined to the energy sector. They deal with, for instance, processes and production methods (PPMs), emissions trading and carbon-related border adjustments.[30]

Without prejudice to the contents and merits of each publication, the literature above can be divided roughly into three groups: (i) works with a comprehensive scope on either energy trade law or energy investment law, with some environmental issues covered under each, or otherwise on the environmental linkage within 'general' trade or investment law; (ii) works focusing on a particular energy-related issue with/without environmental elements; and (iii) 'umbrella' works on the role of the global economic governance in accommodating sustainable development. Because of its comprehensive scope, our book is situated within the first group and intends to fill the existing gap there by focusing specifically on *the energy–environment nexus* under trade law *and* investment law. Its comprehensiveness applies to the range of covered issues as well as the breadth of the legal landscape spanning from multilateral to regional/preferential and energy-specialized agreements. While the previous literature in the first group has discussed either trade law or investment law, the consideration of both in this book allows, where relevant, for comparisons between these two to show their similarities, differences or even (potential) conflicts at the energy–environment interface. Given the intensifying interaction and convergence between the trade and investment law regimes,[31] this interdisciplinary approach has both doctrinal and practical importance in helping to promote coherence across energy-related trade and investment policies concerned. As another added value to academic research, our work includes some data-based observations where applicable. Data are being increasingly used in international

[30] See, for example, Christiane R. Conrad, *Processes and Production Methods (PPMs) in WTO Law: Interfacing Trade and Social Goals* (Cambridge: Cambridge University Press, 2011); David Sifonios, *Environmental Process and Production Methods (PPMs) in WTO Law* (Cham: Springer, 2018); James Munro, *Emissions Trading Schemes under International Economic Law* (Oxford: Oxford University Press, 2018); Felicity Deane, *Emissions Trading and WTO Law: A Global Analysis* (Cheltenham and Northampton: Edward Elgar, 2015); Kateryna Holzer, *Carbon-Related Border Adjustment and WTO Law* (Cheltenham and Northampton: Edward Elgar, 2014).

[31] See, for example, Jürgen Kurtz, *The WTO and International Investment Law: Converging Systems* (Cambridge: Cambridge University Press, 2016).

economic law research,[32] and in line with this practice, we rely on available and processed statistics and data related to the energy–environment nexus to provide more informed insights into recognizable trends and patterns concerning the topic.

I.3 The Purpose and Scope of This Book

Under international economic law, energy and the environment intersect in both factual and legal contexts. With respect to the factual context, this happens when States take action under any of the following policy domains:

- decarbonization of energy's life cycle;
- renewable energy;
- energy efficiency;
- environmentally safe energy supply chain (regarding nuclear energy, for instance); and
- conservation of exhaustible energy resources.

In these policy domains, trade and investment measures can take the form of laws, regulations, requirements, fiscal charges, restrictions, permissions, standards, stimuli and others, and they often pertain to more than one domain.

With respect to the legal context, the energy–environment nexus is discernible especially where trade law and investment law deal with States' right to regulate for the sake of environmental protection or create greening obligations in any of the policy domains above.

The purpose of this book is to examine such legal context, focusing on how far international economic law accommodates environmental concerns or values in energy-related trade and investment and what improvements are required here to better regulate the energy–environment nexus. Our approach in discussing both the legal status quo and the areas of improvement is similar to what some other authors have done with respect to their topics in the previous literature.[33] As shown throughout this book, greening reforms are currently being considered by governments on both trade and investment fronts, which

[32] See Wolfgang Alschner, Joost Pauwelyn and Sergio Puig, 'The Data-Driven Future of International Economic Law', 20 *Journal of International Economic Law* 217 (2017).

[33] See, for example, Pogoretskyy, supra note 24, pp. 8–9; Tienhaara, supra note 27, pp. 3, 267, 283.

amplifies the relevance of the narrative on necessary improvements in today's realities.

This book consists of six chapters. Chapter 1 discusses the foundations of the energy–environment nexus derivable from both 'external' and 'internal' legal sources. Intertwined with international economic law, the key principles and concepts of international (environmental) law, such as permanent sovereignty over natural resources, sustainable development, the polluter-pays principle, common but differentiated responsibilities and some others, are at the very base of the intersection of energy and the environment. In addition, the internal foundations are provided by international trade and investment rules that preserve regulatory sovereignty of States over environmental issues through exception clauses or other legal flexibilities.

The next chapters will focus on five topics, such as trade control, subsidies, technical standards, investment protection and technology policies. This selection covers all pertinent areas of international economic regulation and corresponds to the comprehensive nature of our analysis. Each topic is commonly tied to any of the aforementioned energy–environment policy domains but shows different aspects of government interventions with trade- and/or investment-related elements. Despite these differences, the five topics are linked to the same theme: how to strengthen environmental sustainability across various types of State measures, such as restrictions (Chapters 2, 4 and 5), incentives (Chapters 3, 5 and 6) and liberalization (Chapter 6). This linking theme serves to signal that governments must be consistent throughout their environmental responses when they apply, say, anti-carbon restrictions and measures to facilitate green technology dissemination, on the one hand, and incentives for carbon-emitting energy, on the other.

Chapter 2 starts with carbon pricing adjustments at the border as this matter is entering the mainstream of climate policymaking following the EU's recent legislative actions in this direction. Other trade control measures included in this chapter are import restrictions associated with air pollution, localization of renewable energy production, and radioactive pollution as well as export restrictions that governments often connect to their environmental rhetoric.

Unlike Chapter 2 about basically 'protective' government interventions, Chapter 3 discusses 'promotive' measures, namely subsidies for fossil fuels and renewable energy that generally have negative and positive environmental impacts, respectively. Thus, the examination of the energy–environment nexus here deals with eliminating unnecessary fossil fuel subsidies and exploring policy flexibilities for renewable energy subsidies.

Chapter 4 is about standardization policies in green trade and procurement that affect the international movement of energy-related goods and services. This chapter shows some trends in raising and addressing trade concerns in the WTO over pro-environmental energy standards, discusses the status of private standards and explores regulatory convergence options as a way of cutting trade costs for energy and energy-related products.

Energy subsidies attract foreign investors, but if they are suddenly cut or cancelled by a host country, this gives grounds for complaints under investment law. Government actions related to investment subsidies may cause a tension between trade law and investment law. Chapter 5 covers this issue and additionally offers some insights from ECT case law on the retraction of renewable energy incentives. This chapter also looks into the right of States to restrict energy investments in the public interest and discusses environmental accountability of energy investors.

Finally, green technologies are the key to advance low-carbon and resource-efficient growth without compromising the quality of our energy-dependent life. Chapter 6 demonstrates that international economic law applies to virtually any stage of the technological supply chain from the development to the final use of energy–environment technologies. Here, we discuss research and development (R&D) measures as well as the facilitation of green technology dissemination through trade liberalization and technology transfers.

1

Foundations of the Energy–Environment Nexus and International Economic Law

The intersection between energy and the environment is regulated on the basis of legal foundations that international economic law has developed on its own or 'borrowed' from (or otherwise relied on) such outside regimes as general international law and international environmental law. The borrowed principles, like sovereignty over natural resources or sustainable development, can find their reflection, directly or indirectly, in trade and investment agreements and case law and will continuously affect new developments in this field. Section 1.1 will show that such foundations stemming from external sources define the basic contours of State rights and duties associated with the energy–environment nexus. Moreover, the international trading and investment systems provide self-created legal foundations for environmental policy space as will be discussed in Section 1.2. They define the extent to which energy-related restrictive measures driven by environmental considerations can be accepted. The case of the ECT presented at the end of this chapter is a striking example for demonstrating that the legal foundations are not static and may undergo important changes.

1.1 The Underlying Principles and Concepts

The principles and rules of international (environmental) law on resource sovereignty, sustainable development, polluters' liability, precautionary measures, common but differentiated responsibilities and environmental impact assessments cut across the energy–environment interplay. Where they are not directly written into a trade or investment text itself, the pertinent external sources may still be consulted for interpreting that text. Indeed, Article 31(3)(c) of the Vienna Convention on the Law of Treaties (VCLT) (1969) requires that 'any relevant rules of international law applicable in the relations between the parties' should be taken into account 'together with the context' of a treaty term being interpreted. WTO panellists, for instance, invoked

Article 31(3)(c) of the VCLT to consider 'the international law principles of sovereignty over natural resources and sustainable development' for construing Article XX(g) of the General Agreement on Tariffs and Trade (GATT) on the conservation of exhaustible natural resources.[1] Like the principles above, the concepts of energy security and safety also raise cross-cutting energy–environment issues.

1.1.1 *Sovereignty over Natural Resources*

The principle of sovereignty over natural resources in international law started to crystallize in the wake of decolonization and nationalization of foreign property in Latin America, Africa, Asia and Eastern Europe after World War II. The underlying idea was that newly independent States must be entitled to exploit natural resources they possess to their own benefit.[2] As declared in the United Nations (UN) General Assembly Resolution on Permanent Sovereignty over Natural Resources (1962),[3] '[t]he right of peoples and nations to permanent sovereignty over their natural wealth and resources must be exercised in the interest of their national development and of the well-being of the people of the State concerned' (paragraph 1). This resolution confirms resource-owning States' regulatory authority for the exploration, development and disposition of resources as well as the import of necessary foreign capital (paragraph 2). It further elucidates some details on foreign investment treatment. In particular, when authorization is granted, the imported capital and the earnings on it are governed by national legislation and international law, and the profits must be shared as agreed upon by investors and the host State and with due care for that State's resource sovereignty (paragraph 3). In case of nationalization or expropriation, 'appropriate compensation' must be paid in accordance with the host State's rules and international law, and dispute settlement over compensation accommodates both the exhaustion of local remedies and international adjudication (paragraph 4). Many subsequent investment

[1] *China – Rare Earths*, WTO Panel Reports, para. 7.262. See also *China – Raw Materials*, WTO Panel Reports, paras. 7.380–7.381.

[2] See Nico J. Schrijver, 'Natural Resources, Permanent Sovereignty Over', in Rüdiger Wolfrum (ed.), *The Max Planck Encyclopedia of Public International Law* (Oxford: Oxford University Press, 2008), Vol. VII, p. 535.

[3] General Assembly Resolution 1803 (XVII) of 14 December 1962, 'Permanent Sovereignty over Natural Resources'.

treaties have, however, downplayed the relevance of national laws by setting out their own rules on compensation and enabling international arbitral procedures with no need for exhausting local remedies.[4] But overall, the 1962 resolution is widely considered as embodying a proper balance between the interests of capital-importing and capital-exporting countries,[5] inspiring subsequent international instruments to reiterate sovereignty over natural resources.[6]

The principle of sovereignty over natural resources has already gained universal acceptance, with the legal doctrine ascribing it different legal statuses, such as customary international law or *jus cogens*.[7] But just as sovereignty in general, resource sovereignty is not absolute. Among other things, it is 'inherently' constrained by a State's obligation not to cause transboundary environmental damage, with this obligation ensuring respect for the sovereign realm of other States.[8] Two declarations, representing important milestones in the evolution of international environmental law, make this point explicit. Principle 21 of the Declaration of the UN Conference on the Human Environment (1972)[9] places sovereignty together with environmental responsibility:

> States have, in accordance with the Charter of the United Nations and the principles of international law, the sovereign right to exploit their own resources pursuant to their own environmental policies, and the responsibility to ensure that activities within their jurisdiction or control do not cause damage to the environment of other States or of areas beyond the limits of national jurisdiction.

4 Yogesh Tyagi, 'Permanent Sovereignty over Natural Resources', 4 *Cambridge Journal of International and Comparative Law* 588 (2015), p. 606.

5 Nicolaas Schrijver, 'Self-Determination of Peoples and Sovereignty over Natural Wealth and Resources', in UN Human Rights Office of the High Commissioner, *Realizing the Right to Development: Essays in Commemoration of 25 Years of the United Nations Declaration on the Right to Development* (New York and Geneva: UN, 2013), p. 98.

6 See, for example, Schrijver, supra note 2, pp. 538–542.

7 See Ricardo Pereira and Orla Gough, 'Permanent Sovereignty over Natural Resources in the 21st Century: Natural Resource Governance and the Right to Self-Determination of Indigenous Peoples under International Law', 14 *Melbourne Journal of International Law* 451 (2013), pp. 461–464.

8 Franz Xaver Perrez, 'The Relationship between "Permanent Sovereignty" and the Obligation Not to Cause Transboundary Environmental Damage', 26 *Environmental Law* 1187 (1996), p. 1212.

9 Declaration of the UN Conference on the Human Environment, adopted at the UN Conference on the Human Environment, Stockholm, 5–16 June 1972.

Principle 2 of the Rio Declaration on Environment and Development (1992)[10] (hereinafter the 'Rio Declaration') reiterates Principle 21 above but with slight changes to the wording regarding the 'sovereign right to exploit their own resources pursuant to their own environmental *and developmental* policies' (emphasis added). The addition of 'and developmental', a source of varying interpretations, together with its textual context, appears to emphasize the sovereign right to development, on the one hand, while subjecting national development policies to the duty not to pollute across borders, on the other.[11] In order for State liability to arise, the transboundary environmental harm must be significant or substantial enough.[12]

The duty to avoid international environmental damage represents one aspect of the energy–environment nexus that constrains resource sovereignty. Another aspect – which is rather a State's own self-constraint in exploiting its natural resources – is embedded in the notion of *sustainable* use of natural resources when sovereignty mixes with the concept of sustainable development discussed below. This combination is present, for example, under Article XX(g) of the GATT that deals with the conservation of exhaustible natural resources. In interpreting Article XX(g), the WTO panel in *China – Raw Materials* took into account sovereignty over natural resources as a 'principle of international law' and found that such sovereignty could (and should) be exercised in harmony with Article XX(g) as economic development and conservation were not necessarily mutually exclusive.[13] Along the same lines and within the same legal context,[14] the panel in *China – Rare Earths* added:

> In recognition of the permanent sovereignty that every Member exercises over its natural resources, WTO law recognizes the right of Members to adopt conservation measures should they wish to do so, in the light of their own objectives and policy goals, including economic and sustainable development. In other words, resource-endowed WTO Members are entitled to design conservation policies that meet their development needs, determine how much of a resource should be exploited today and how much should be preserved for the future, including for use by

[10] Rio Declaration on Environment and Development, adopted at the UN Conference on Environment and Development, Rio de Janeiro, 3–14 June 1992.

[11] Perrez, supra note 8, pp. 1203–1204.

[12] See Philippe Sands et al., *Principles of International Environmental Law* (Cambridge: Cambridge University Press, 2018), 4th edn, pp. 743–745.

[13] *China – Raw Materials*, WTO Panel Reports, paras. 7.380–7.381.

[14] *China – Rare Earths*, WTO Panel Reports, paras. 7.265–7.266.

> future generations, in a manner consistent with their sustainable development needs and their international obligations.[15]

The ECT (1994) provides another legal context for conceptualizing energy sovereignty and its environmental implications. Article 18 ('Sovereignty over Energy Resources'), paragraph 1 of the ECT recognizes 'state sovereignty and sovereign rights over energy resources' that 'must be exercised in accordance with and subject to the rules of international law'. The rest of Article 18 elaborates on the associated rights of States without weakening the ECT's overall policy of facilitating access to energy resources:

> (2) Without affecting the objectives of promoting access to energy resources, and exploration and development thereof on a commercial basis, the Treaty shall in no way prejudice the rules in Contracting Parties governing the system of property ownership of energy resources.
> (3) Each state continues to hold in particular the rights to decide the geographical areas within its Area to be made available for exploration and development of its energy resources, *the optimisation of their recovery and the rate at which they may be depleted or otherwise exploited, . . . and to regulate the environmental and safety aspects of such exploration, development and reclamation within its Area*, and to participate in such exploration and exploitation, inter alia, through direct participation by the government or through state enterprises [emphasis added].
> (4) The Contracting Parties undertake to facilitate access to energy resources, inter alia, by allocating in a non-discriminatory manner on the basis of published criteria authorisations, licences, concessions and contracts to prospect and explore for or to exploit or extract energy resources.

The emphasized (italicized) parts of Article 18(3) above point to the rights of States to utilize energy resources in a sustainable and environmentally safe way. Article 18 is not justiciable under the ECT's investor–State dispute settlement (ISDS) procedures,[16] but the sovereignty over energy resources is not without any limits.[17] For example, it was clarified that Article 18(2) did not allow any party to circumvent the

[15] Ibid., para. 7.267.
[16] Article 18 of ECT (1994) is located in Part IV of the ECT while the ISDS provisions under Article 26 of the ECT are applicable to Part III on investment promotion and protection.
[17] Kaj Hobér, *The Energy Charter Treaty: A Commentary* (Oxford: Oxford University Press, 2020), pp. 348–349.

other ECT provisions and invoke its internal law as justification for its failure to perform treaty obligations.[18]

1.1.2 Sustainable Development

The term 'sustainable development' means 'development that meets the needs of the present without compromising the ability of future generations to meet their own needs'.[19] This concept is broad and covers economic growth, social inclusion and environmental protection. The 2030 Agenda for Sustainable Development, adopted by the UN General Assembly in 2015, represents a global 'plan of action' to attain 17 Sustainable Development Goals (SDGs) and 169 associated targets.[20] While all SDGs and targets are 'integrated and indivisible',[21] the SDGs and targets in Box 1.1 appear most relevant to the energy–environment context.

The 1992 UN Conference on Environment and Development in Rio de Janeiro acknowledged a positive role of the GATT 1947-based multilateral trading system in supporting sustainable development.[22] The preamble of the GATT 1947 spells out its objective of 'developing the full use of the resources of the world'. The preamble of the later-in-time WTO Agreement made noticeable changes to that objective. Now it reads 'the optimal use of the world's resources in accordance with the objective of sustainable development', with members 'seeking both to protect and preserve the environment and to enhance the means for doing so in a manner consistent with their respective needs and concerns at different levels of economic development'. Reflecting the intentions of the Uruguay Round negotiating parties, this preambular language gives 'colour, texture and shading' to the rights and obligations of members under WTO law and thus informs the interpretation of the WTO's

18 See Final Act of the European Energy Charter Conference, Declaration V and Chairman's Statement at Adoption Session on 17 December 1994, with relevant parts reproduced in Energy Charter Secretariat, 'The International Energy Charter Consolidated Energy Charter Treaty with Related Documents', 2015, p. 66.

19 World Commission on Environment and Development, 'Our Common Future', Report, UN, 1987, chapter 2, para. 1.

20 UN, 'Transforming Our World: The 2030 Agenda for Sustainable Development', Resolution adopted by the General Assembly on 25 September 2015, A/RES/70/1 (21 October 2015), preamble.

21 Ibid., para. 55.

22 See chapter 2 of Agenda 21, UN Conference on Environment and Development, Rio de Janeiro, 3–14 June 1992.

BOX 1.1 SDGS AND TARGETS RELATED TO THE ENERGY–ENVIRONMENT NEXUS

Goal 3. Ensure healthy lives and promote well-being for all at all ages

3.9 By 2030, substantially reduce the number of deaths and illnesses from hazardous chemicals and air, water and soil pollution and contamination.

Goal 6. Ensure availability and sustainable management of water and sanitation for all

6.3 By 2030, improve water quality by reducing pollution, eliminating dumping and minimizing release of hazardous chemicals and materials, halving the proportion of untreated wastewater and substantially increasing recycling and safe reuse globally.

Goal 7. Ensure access to affordable, reliable, sustainable and modern energy for all

7.1 By 2030, ensure universal access to affordable, reliable and modern energy services.

7.2 By 2030, increase substantially the share of renewable energy in the global energy mix.

7.3 By 2030, double the global rate of improvement in energy efficiency.

7.a By 2030, enhance international cooperation to facilitate access to clean energy research and technology, including renewable energy, energy efficiency and advanced and cleaner fossil-fuel technology, and promote investment in energy infrastructure and clean energy technology.

7.b By 2030, expand infrastructure and upgrade technology for supplying modern and sustainable energy services for all in developing countries, in particular least developed countries, small island developing States and landlocked developing countries, in accordance with their respective programmes of support.

Goal 9. Build resilient infrastructure, promote inclusive and sustainable industrialization and foster innovation

9.4 By 2030, upgrade infrastructure and retrofit industries to make them sustainable, with increased resource-use efficiency and greater adoption of clean and environmentally sound technologies and industrial processes, with all countries taking action in accordance with their respective capabilities.

Goal 11. Make cities and human settlements inclusive, safe, resilient and sustainable

11.6 By 2030, reduce the adverse per capita environmental impact of cities, including by paying special attention to air quality and municipal and other waste management.

BOX 1.1 (*CONT.*)

11.b By 2020, substantially increase the number of cities and human settlements adopting and implementing integrated policies and plans towards inclusion, resource efficiency, mitigation and adaptation to climate change, resilience to disasters, and develop and implement, in line with the Sendai Framework for Disaster Risk Reduction 2015–2030, holistic disaster risk management at all levels.

Goal 12. Ensure sustainable consumption and production patterns

12.2 By 2030, achieve the sustainable management and efficient use of natural resources.

12.4 By 2020, achieve the environmentally sound management of chemicals and all wastes throughout their life cycle, in accordance with agreed international frameworks, and significantly reduce their release to air, water and soil in order to minimize their adverse impacts on human health and the environment.

12.5 By 2030, substantially reduce waste generation through prevention, reduction, recycling and reuse.

12.6 Encourage companies, especially large and transnational companies, to adopt sustainable practices and to integrate sustainability information into their reporting cycle.

12.7 Promote public procurement practices that are sustainable, in accordance with national policies and priorities.

12.a Support developing countries to strengthen their scientific and technological capacity to move towards more sustainable patterns of consumption and production.

12.c Rationalize inefficient fossil-fuel subsidies that encourage wasteful consumption by removing market distortions, in accordance with national circumstances, including by restructuring taxation and phasing out those harmful subsidies, where they exist, to reflect their environmental impacts, taking fully into account the specific needs and conditions of developing countries and minimizing the possible adverse impacts on their development in a manner that protects the poor and the affected communities.

Goal 13. Take urgent action to combat climate change and its impacts

13.2 Integrate climate change measures into national policies, strategies and planning.

13.a Implement the commitment undertaken by developed-country parties to the United Nations Framework Convention on Climate Change to a goal of mobilizing jointly $100 billion annually by 2020 from all sources to address the needs of developing countries in the context of meaningful mitigation actions and transparency on implementation and fully operationalize the Green Climate Fund through its capitalization as soon as possible.

BOX 1.1 (*CONT.*)

Goal 15. Protect, restore and promote sustainable use of terrestrial ecosystems, sustainably manage forests, combat desertification, and halt and reverse land degradation and halt biodiversity loss

15.2 By 2020, promote the implementation of sustainable management of all types of forests, halt deforestation, restore degraded forests and substantially increase afforestation and reforestation globally.

15.a Mobilize and significantly increase financial resources from all sources to conserve and sustainably use biodiversity and ecosystems.

15.b Mobilize significant resources from all sources and at all levels to finance sustainable forest management and provide adequate incentives to developing countries to advance such management, including for conservation and reforestation.

Goal 17. Strengthen the means of implementation and revitalize the Global Partnership for Sustainable Development

17.7 Promote the development, transfer, dissemination and diffusion of environmentally sound technologies to developing countries on favourable terms, including on concessional and preferential terms, as mutually agreed.

Source: Author's selection from UN, 'Transforming Our World: The 2030 Agenda for Sustainable Development', Resolution adopted by the General Assembly on 25 September 2015, A/RES/70/1 (21 October 2015)

environment-related provisions, like Article XX of the GATT.[23] Further, the WTO Ministerial Decision on Trade and Environment (1994), which created the WTO Committee on Trade and Environment, insists on avoiding 'any policy contradiction' between keeping the multilateral trading system and acting for 'the promotion of sustainable development'.

In RTAs, sustainable development is often referenced in the preamble and less frequently in the main text.[24] Among trading economies, the EU is probably most active in systematically including detailed provisions on sustainable development in its trade deals. Beginning from the Korea–EU Free Trade Agreement (FTA) (2010), all subsequent EU trade agreements include a dedicated chapter on trade and sustainable development

[23] *US – Shrimp*, WTO Appellate Body Report, paras. 129, 152–153, 155; *China – Rare Earths*, WTO Panel Reports, para. 7.259.

[24] See José-Antonio Monteiro, 'Typology of Environment-Related Provisions in Regional Trade Agreements', WTO Working Paper No. ERSD-2016-13, 2016, pp. 19–21.

encompassing, inter alia, environmental and climate change issues.[25] They typically set forth any of the three types of obligations: those based on existing international standards (e.g., the implementation of multilateral environmental agreements), obligations related to domestic legislation (e.g., the ban on lowering domestic environmental standards) or aspirations towards higher levels of protection (e.g., best endeavours to enhance environmental protection).[26]

As for the investment domain, modern investment treaties also tend to include sustainable development provisions. Most of them address environmental issues and in doing so, generally, prevent the race to the bottom in environmental protection, confirm or recognize the parties' national or international environmental obligations or create policy carve-outs for environmental measures.[27] Some model bilateral investment treaties (BITs) contain a separate section on sustainable development that elaborates on investors' social responsibility and the host country's authority in promoting sustainable development.[28]

1.1.3 Polluter-Pays Principle

The polluter-pays principle essentially says that the cost of pollution should be borne by the polluter itself. Legally binding under many national jurisdictions, this principle appears not to have yet reached the level of customary international law despite its broad international acknowledgement.[29]

The Organization for Economic Co-operation and Development (OECD) was the first to expressly refer to this principle at an

[25] Jana Titievskaia, 'Sustainability Provisions in EU Free Trade Agreements: Review of the European Commission Action Plan', European Parliamentary Research Service, Briefing, 2021, p. 1.

[26] See Marco Bronckers and Giovanni Gruni, 'Retooling the Sustainability Standards in EU Free Trade Agreements', 24 *Journal of International Economic Law* 25 (2021), pp. 26–33.

[27] Manjiao Chi, 'Sustainable Development Provisions in Investment Treaties', UN Economic and Social Commission for Asia and the Pacific, 2018, pp. 17–18, 22.

[28] See section 3 of Italy's Model Bilateral Investment Treaty (BIT) (August 2022), https://investmentpolicy.unctad.org/international-investment-agreements/treaty-files/6438/download; section 3 of the Netherlands' Model BIT (22 March 2019), https://investmentpolicy.unctad.org/international-investment-agreements/treaty-files/5832/download.

[29] See Sands et al., supra note 12, pp. 240–241; Dirk Heine, Michael G. Faure and Goran Dominioni, 'The Polluter-Pays Principle in Climate Change Law: An Economic Appraisal', 10 *Climate Law* 94 (2020), p. 99 citing Benoit Mayer, *The International Law on Climate Change* (Cambridge: Cambridge University Press, 2018), p. 74.

international level. According to the OECD Guiding Principles Concerning the International Economic Aspects of Environmental Policies (1972), the polluter-pays principle means that environmental costs should be internalized in the price-setting of polluting goods and services, without being accompanied by subsidies that would create 'significant distortions in international trade and investment'.[30]

The follow-up OECD Recommendation on the Implementation of the Polluter-Pays Principle (1974) specifically discusses the relationship between subsidies and the polluter-pays principle. In particular, subsidization of the costs of pollution control should be avoided as a general rule. But 'the rapid implementation of a compelling and especially stringent pollution control regime' may cause significant socio-economic problems which may necessitate governmental assistance 'if the environmental policy objectives of a Member country are to be realised within a prescribed and specific time'. Thus, the granting of pollution control assistance should be selective and limited to situations where severe difficulties would otherwise occur, subject to transitional periods and without causing significant trade and investment distortions.[31] At the same time, the following is not considered to be incompatible with the polluter-pays principle:[32]

- aid for the experimentation with new pollution-control technologies and development of new pollution-abatement equipment; and
- aid for promoting specific socio-economic objectives, such as the reduction of serious interregional imbalances, that causes the incidental effect of aiding pollution-control purposes.

These OECD guidelines are only recommendations and do not extend to non-adhering countries. Nevertheless, they were helpful in informing external regimes. In the GATT case in *US – Superfund*, the complainant cited the above 1972 OECD's polluter-pays principle to argue that the United States should have taxed only domestic products for causing domestic environmental pollution but not imported products that could

[30] OECD, 'Recommendation of the Council on Guiding Principles Concerning International Economic Aspects of Environmental Policies', OECD/LEGAL/0102 (adopted 26 May 1972), Annex (para. 4), https://legalinstruments.oecd.org/en/instruments/OECD-LEGAL-0102.

[31] OECD, 'Recommendation of the Council on the Implementation of the Polluter-Pays Principle', OECD/LEGAL/0132 (adopted 14 November 1974), https://legalinstruments.oecd.org/en/instruments/OECD-LEGAL-0132, sections II:2, III:1, III:2.

[32] Ibid., sections II:3, II:4.

already have paid a pollution tax in an exporting country. The panel held that the GATT did not require the contracting parties to follow the polluter-pays principle although they were free 'to tax the sale of certain domestic products (because their production pollutes the domestic environment) and to impose a lower tax or no tax at all on like imported products (because their consumption or use causes fewer or no environmental problems)'.[33]

Furthermore, Principle 16 of the Rio Declaration (1992) mirrors the main contours of the OECD's conception of the polluter-pays principle:

> National authorities should endeavour to promote the internalization of environmental costs and the use of economic instruments, taking into account the approach that the polluter should, in principle, bear the cost of pollution, with due regard to the public interest and without distorting international trade and investment.

Likewise, Article 19(1) of the ECT (1994) states that 'the polluter in the Areas of Contracting Parties, should, in principle, bear the cost of pollution, including transboundary pollution, with due regard to the public interest and without distorting Investment in the Energy Cycle or international trade'.

The polluter-pays principle underlies such measures as carbon taxes, emission permits, environmental standards and so on.[34] This principle can also be linked to the environmental accountability of investors[35] as well as to partial (instead of full) compensation for, inter alia, expropriation of investors' assets that is set so to reflect environmental damage that the investors have caused in host countries.[36]

1.1.4 Precautionary Principle

The precautionary principle entitles States to take urgent action to address serious environmental threats in spite of scientific uncertainty. It began to appear in international instruments in the mid-1980s.[37] The essence of this principle is articulated in oft-cited Principle 15 of the Rio Declaration (1992):

[33] *US – Superfund*, GATT Panel Report, paras. 3.2.7–3.2.8, 5.2.3, 5.2.5.

[34] See Chapters 2 and 4.

[35] See Section 5.1.3.

[36] See Tomoko Ishikawa, 'The Role of the Precautionary and Polluter Pays Principles in Assessing Compensation', RIETI Discussion Paper Series No. 15-E-107, 2015, pp. 17–21.

[37] Sands et al., supra note 12, p. 230.

> In order to protect the environment, the precautionary approach shall be widely applied by States according to their capabilities. Where there are threats of serious or irreversible damage, lack of full scientific certainty shall not be used as a reason for postponing cost-effective measures to prevent environmental degradation.

Some authors indicate the customary international law nature of this principle,[38] but this stance still lacks universal acceptance. For example, the Appellate Body in *EC – Hormones* (and later the panel in *EC – Approval and Marketing of Biotech Products*[39]) noted the diversity of opinions among academics and law practitioners on the international legal status of this principle and refrained from taking a position on this issue, saying that 'the precautionary principle, at least outside the field of international environmental law, still awaits authoritative formulation'. The Appellate Body found that while the precautionary principle was not written into the Agreement on the Application of Sanitary and Phytosanitary (SPS) Measures as a ground for justifying otherwise illegal SPS measures, it was still reflected in Article 5.7 of the SPS Agreement.[40] Article 5.7 allows WTO members to take provisional SPS measures based on 'available pertinent information' where 'relevant scientific evidence is insufficient', provided that they will seek 'additional information' for a more objective risk assessment and review the SPS measure within a 'reasonable period of time'.

Under the investment regime, the tribunal in *Eco Oro v. Colombia* gave weight to the precautionary principle in concluding that a prohibition against mining activities in the region that required environmental protection did not constitute indirect expropriation within the meaning of the Canada–Colombia FTA (2008). There, the Colombian authorities deprived an investor of its right to mine in its concession area because that area overlapped with a high-mountain ecosystem rich in biodiversity and water resources.[41] The tribunal held that the precautionary principle, enshrined in the 1992 Convention on Biological Diversity and Principle 15 of the Rio Declaration (1992), was relevant to assessing the effect and proportionality of Colombia's measure (eventually found not to be

[38] See, for example, Owen McIntyre and Thomas Mosedale, 'The Precautionary Principle as a Norm of Customary International Law', 9 *Journal of Environmental Law* 221 (1997).

[39] See *EC – Approval and Marketing of Biotech Products*, WTO Panel Reports, paras. 7.88–7.89.

[40] *EC – Hormones*, WTO Appellate Body Report, paras. 123–124.

[41] *Eco Oro v. Colombia*, International Centre for Settlement of Investment Disputes (ICSID), Decision on Jurisdiction, Liability and Directions on Quantum, para. 86.

unreasonable or disproportionate) as 'it is . . . clear that once damaged it is uncertain whether or not [the high-mountain ecosystem] can be restored and, if so, the length of time such restoration will take'.[42]

1.1.5 Common but Differentiated Responsibilities

The principle of common but differentiated responsibilities, embodied in a number of environmental instruments, essentially acknowledges the shared responsibilities of States for preserving and protecting the common environment while placing different compliance burdens on them depending on their circumstances and capabilities. According to Principle 7 of the Rio Declaration (1992), common but differentiated responsibilities are attributable to 'the different contributions [of States] to global environmental degradation', so that 'developed countries acknowledge the responsibility that they bear in the international pursuit of sustainable development in view of the pressures their societies place on the global environment and of the technologies and financial resources they command'.

While developed countries are responsible for the majority of historical carbon emissions, developing countries are responsible for the majority of current carbon emissions.[43] This creates a difficult dilemma. On the one hand, placing all the burden of decarbonization on developed countries alone will not solve the climate problem. On the other hand, reducing carbon intensity of developing countries' economies poses a risk of slowing down their economic growth unless they are better equipped with a low-carbon and clean energy infrastructure, which necessitates technical and financial assistance from developed countries. Under the UN Framework Convention on Climate Change (UNFCCC) (1992), climate change is considered as 'a common concern of humankind', and developed countries 'should take the lead in combating climate change and the adverse effects thereof'.[44] The Paris Agreement (2015)

[42] Ibid., paras. 654–656.

[43] See, for example, Centre for Global Development, 'Developed Countries Are Responsible for 79 Percent of Historical Carbon Emissions', 2015, www.cgdev.org/media/who-caused-climate-change-historically#:~:text=Developed%20Countries%20Are%20Responsible%20for,Global%20Development%20%7C%20Ideas%20to%20Action; Centre for Global Development, 'Developing Countries Are Responsible for 63 Percent of Current Carbon Emissions', 2015, www.cgdev.org/media/developing-countries-are-responsible-63-percent-current-carbon-emissions.

[44] Preamble and Article 3.1 of the UN Framework Convention on Climate Change (UNFCCC) (1992).

recognizes 'common but differentiated responsibilities and respective capabilities, in the light of different national circumstances'[45] and obliges developed countries to provide climate-related financial assistance and capacity-building support to developing countries.[46]

The principle of common but differentiated responsibilities as such is not referenced in WTO agreements although it is not undetectable. The preamble of the WTO Agreement recognizes that the protection and preservation of the environment in the trade context should be sought consistently with members' 'respective needs and concerns at different levels of economic development'. Further, under Article XX of the GATT, the Appellate Body in *US – Shrimp* held that it was unacceptable for a member to apply a trade restriction to force other countries to adopt essentially the same environmental policy as that member's, *without taking into account different conditions that may exist in those countries.*[47] There, at issue was a US ban on imports of shrimp from countries that had not used a US-prescribed method of catching shrimp that would avoid killing sea turtles. Moreover, WTO provisions on special and differential (S&D) treatment, like those on technical assistance,[48] as well as the WTO-led Aid for Trade initiative can be used to address differentiated environmental capabilities of developing countries. Most of the current Aid for Trade disbursements for climate change mitigation covers the energy sector.[49]

The principle of common but differentiated responsibilities seems to be rarely mentioned by name in RTAs and IIAs. The only example with explicit references we could find is the EU–Colombia–Peru Trade Agreement (2012). The parties to this agreement commit to 'address global environmental challenges, in accordance with the principle of common but differentiated responsibilities'. In addition, they are 'resolved to enhance their efforts regarding climate change, which are led by developed countries, ... in accordance with their common but differentiated responsibilities and respective capabilities ..., and taking particularly into account the needs, circumstances, and high vulnerability to the adverse effects of climate change of those Parties which are

[45] Preamble, Articles 2.2, 4.3 and 4.19 of the Paris Agreement (2015).
[46] Articles 9.1, 11.3 and 13.9 of the Paris Agreement (2015).
[47] *US – Shrimp*, WTO Appellate Body Report, paras. 161–164.
[48] See, for example, Section 4.2.3.
[49] See WTO, 'Climate Change and International Trade', World Trade Report 2022, 2022, pp. 15, 74.

developing countries'.[50] Other international economic agreements may still include provisions that reflect the essence of the principle in question without specifically referencing it.

1.1.6 Environmental Impact Assessment

Environmental impact assessments, first introduced domestically by the US National Environmental Policy Act (1969) and required internationally since the 1972 UN Conference on the Human Environment in Stockholm, represent a legal technique of incorporating environmental considerations into a decision-making (or approval) process.[51] As stated in Principle 17 of the Rio Declaration (1992), '[e]nvironmental impact assessment, as a national instrument, shall be undertaken for proposed activities that are likely to have a significant adverse impact on the environment and are subject to a decision of a competent national authority'. Agenda 21, adopted at the 1992 UN Conference on Environment and Development, makes many references to environmental impact assessments, including also for energy production, calling for governments to adopt necessary procedures.[52] In the 2010 judgement, the International Court of Justice observed that 'it may now be considered a requirement under general international law' to undertake an environmental impact assessment where a proposed industrial activity has the potential to cause significant transboundary harm.[53]

As far as international economic treaties are concerned, over thirty RTAs encourage domestic environmental laws and policies to use environmental impact assessments.[54] Besides that and with respect to the energy sector, Article 19(1) of the ECT (1994) obligates parties to 'promote the transparent assessment at an early stage and prior to decision, and subsequent monitoring, of Environmental Impacts of environmentally significant energy investment projects', although it leaves it to each party to decide how to run domestic procedures for environmental impact assessments.[55]

To the extent that domestic laws mandate environmental impact assessments for investment activities, a foreign investment's compliance

[50] Articles 267.4 and 275.2 of the EU–Colombia–Peru Trade Agreement (2012).

[51] Sands et al., supra note 12, p. 657.

[52] See, for example, Agenda 21 (1992), supra note 22, paras. 4.20, 6.34(c)(i), 6.41(i).

[53] *Pulp Mills*, International Court of Justice, Judgment, para. 204.

[54] Monteiro, supra note 24, pp. 22, 35.

[55] See the Understanding of the Contracting Parties on Article 19(1)(i) of the ECT; *Blusun v. Italy*, ICSID, Award, para. 275.

with such domestic laws is often a prerequisite for it to be covered by an applicable IIA.[56] However, an improper manner of applying such domestic laws itself can trigger an investor–State dispute.[57] In *Clayton/Bilcon v. Canada*, the federal and provincial regulatory framework for investing in Canada's Nova Scotia included environmental assessment requirements. But a government-adopted environmental assessment of a quarry and marine terminal project at issue was found to violate the NAFTA provisions on minimum standard of treatment and national treatment.[58] The majority of the tribunal decried the domestic environmental assessment for concluding that this project conflicted with 'community core values' – a concept that was not envisaged by the Canadian rules, and hence 'unprecedented and unexpected' – and for failing to explore any related 'mitigation measures' that might have been taken to avoid the significant environmental effects of the project.[59]

In addition to environmental impact assessments of business activities or projects, some domestic procedures (e.g., in the EU, the United States and Canada) require environmental or broader sustainability impact assessments of trade agreements.[60] Typically, they are about an *ex ante* assessment of a trade agreement being negotiated – notably its potential impact on domestic environmental regulations and the state of the environment – with the purpose to give trade negotiators more insight into how environmental considerations could be reflected in trade treaty-making. For example, in response to the results of sustainability impact assessments of certain trade agreements, the European Commission announced that in ongoing negotiations it would, inter alia, work on:

[56] See, for example, Article 14 ('Impact Assessment') of the Morocco–Nigeria Bilateral Investment Treaty (BIT) (2016). As another example, the tribunal in *Maffezini v. Spain* found that the host country's domestic law required environmental impact assessments for investments in the chemical industry, and the applicable BIT called for the promotion of investment *in compliance with* domestic law. See *Maffezini v. Spain*, ICSID, Award, paras. 66, 69, 71.

[57] Graham Mayeda, 'Integrating Environmental Impact Assessments into International Investment Agreements: Global Administrative Law and Transnational Cooperation', 18 *Journal of World Investment & Trade* 131 (2017), p. 138.

[58] *Clayton/Bilcon v. Canada*, Permanent Court of Arbitration (PCA), Award on Jurisdiction and Liability, paras. 604, 731–732.

[59] Ibid., paras. 452, 503–505, 600–603.

[60] See, for example, WTO, Committee on Trade and Environment – Environmental (Sustainability) Assessments of Trade Liberalization Agreements at the National Level – Item 2 of the Work Programme – Note by the Secretariat, WT/CTE/W/171 (20 October 2000).

- the inclusion of a robust chapter on trade and sustainable development with dedicated provisions on climate change, sustainable forest management and conservation of forest cover;[61]
- fast-track trade liberalization for environmental goods and services and the promotion of bilateral cooperation on clean energy, air pollution and environmental monitoring;[62]
- the inclusion of a monitoring mechanism for an *ex post* environmental and social impact of the trade agreement;[63] and
- the reduction or removal of tariff/non-tariff barriers in the energy sector.[64]

An environmental impact assessment can also pertain to an already concluded trade agreement. More than twenty RTAs deal with such *ex post* (or post-negotiation) assessments of the agreement. They provide for a joint committee's consideration of the RTA's environmental review prepared by each party, the parties' commitment to conduct domestic environmental/sustainability assessments of the RTA being implemented, cooperation via the exchange of information or experience on RTA-related environmental/sustainability assessments and so on.[65]

Notwithstanding methodological challenges,[66] environmental or sustainability evaluations of trade agreements provide an important tool for coordinating trade and environmental policies and greening trade.

61 European Commission, 'European Commission Services' Position Paper on the Sustainability Impact Assessment in Support of Negotiations on a Trade Agreement between the European Union and Indonesia', 26 June 2020, p. 10, https://policy.trade.ec.europa.eu/analysis-and-assessment/sustainability-impact-assessments_en.

62 European Commission, 'Commission Services Position Paper on the Trade Sustainability Impact Assessment for the FTA between the EU and the Republic of India', March 2010, p. 11, https://policy.trade.ec.europa.eu/analysis-and-assessment/sustainability-impact-assessments_en.

63 European Commission, 'European Commission Services' Position Paper on the Trade Sustainability Impact Assessment in Support of Negotiations of a Deep and Comprehensive Free Trade Agreement between the European Union and Morocco', April 2015, p. 8, https://policy.trade.ec.europa.eu/analysis-and-assessment/sustainability-impact-assessments_en.

64 European Commission, 'European Commission Services' Position Paper on the Trade Sustainability Impact Assessment in Support of Negotiations of a Deep and Comprehensive Free Trade Area between the European Union and Jordan', December 2016, p. 17, https://policy.trade.ec.europa.eu/analysis-and-assessment/sustainability-impact-assessments_en.

65 See Monteiro, supra note 24, pp. 84–85.

66 See in general Evdokia Moïsé and Stela Rubínová, 'Sustainability Impact Assessments of Free Trade Agreements: A Critical Review', OECD Trade Policy Paper No. 255, 2021.

Unsurprisingly, the WTO Doha Declaration (2001), taking note of 'the efforts by Members to conduct national environmental assessments of trade policies on a voluntary basis', has encouraged the sharing of 'expertise and experience . . . with Members wishing to perform environmental reviews at the national level'.[67] Yet, such environmental assessments continue to be conducted by a handful of jurisdictions, mainly developed countries, with many others still lacking capacity. In the light of climate change and global environmental degradation, technical assistance to developing countries, including under RTAs, should necessarily embrace the sharing of know-how in this field.

Finally, since environmental impact assessments are mainly domestic procedures, time is ripe for introducing international-level impact assessments of trade and investment agreements at least with respect to their effects on climate change as a pressing global problem. For example, WTO negotiations and treaty-making could be accompanied by *ex ante* and/or *ex post* environmental assessments by international experts to help reach more environmentally sound outcomes. Such international impact assessments would focus on the effects on the shared environment and respond to the lack of capabilities of those negotiating/signatory countries that are unable to conduct such environmental impact assessments on their own.

1.1.7 Energy Security and Safety

In addition to serious humanitarian and geopolitical consequences, the outbreak of the war in Ukraine in 2022 has caused widespread energy supply disruptions, re-emphasizing the strategic importance of energy security.[68] The International Energy Agency (IEA) defines 'energy security' as 'the uninterrupted availability of energy sources at an affordable price' and distinguishes between 'long-term energy security' (necessitating timely energy investments in line with economic developments and environmental needs) and 'short-term energy security' (i.e., the energy

[67] WTO, Ministerial Conference – Fourth Session – Doha, 9–14 November 2001 – Ministerial Declaration – Adopted on 14 November 2001, WT/MIN(01)/DEC/1 (20 November 2001), paras. 6, 33.

[68] See, for example, Tim G. Benton, Antony Froggatt and Laura Wellesley, 'The Ukraine War and Threats to Food and Energy Security: Cascading Risks from Rising Prices and Supply Disruptions', Research Paper, Royal Institute of International Affairs, 2022.

system's responsiveness to sudden changes in supply and demand).[69] According to the WTO panel's interpretation in *EU – Energy Package*, 'security of energy supply is a fundamental interest of society' whose protection may serve to maintain 'public order'.[70] The role of trade and investment in enhancing energy security is internationally recognized.[71]

Availability of fossil fuel energy has traditionally been seen as a key to achieving energy security. Energy conservation and energy efficiency measures are required to preserve the longevity of such availability.[72] In addition, energy security can also be fostered through the diversification of energy sources[73] via a greater utilization of renewables. But the intermittency, or variability, of some renewables, like solar or wind power, necessitates technological solutions enabling effective power storage and real-time adaptations to minimize supply disruptions associated with the integration of such renewables into the energy mix.

While a country's self-sufficiency in energy production promotes its energy security, energy product supplies from different international sources can also be supportive. In *India – Solar Cells*, India's renewable electricity programme under its Jawaharlal Nehru National Solar Mission required the use of locally produced solar cells and solar modules. India hoped that this requirement would help develop the domestic capacity for manufacturing these solar power generating technologies and hence reduce the risks (i.e., supply-side vulnerabilities and fluctuations) arising from the country's import dependence on these products. In India's view, such local solar technologies, if readily available, could serve the objectives of 'energy security' and 'ecologically sustainable growth'.[74] Citing Article XX(j) of the GATT, which allows trade restrictions 'essential to

[69] International Energy Agency (IEA), 'Energy Security: Ensuring the Uninterrupted Availability of Energy Sources at an Affordable Price', www.iea.org/areas-of-work/ensuring-energy-security.

[70] *EU – Energy Package*, WTO Panel Report, para. 7.1156.

[71] See, for example, the preamble of the International Energy Charter (2015); Article 16.17.1 of the Korea–Australia Free Trade Agreement (FTA) (2014).

[72] For example, the preamble of the Energy Charter Protocol on Energy Efficiency and Related Environmental Aspects (1994) takes note of 'the improvements in supply security ... which result from the implementation of cost-effective energy efficiency measures'.

[73] For example, 'stimulating the diversification of energy sources and routes' is considered part of 'the enhancement of energy security' under Article 42.2(b) of the EU–Armenia Comprehensive and Enhanced Partnership Agreement (2017).

[74] *India – Solar Cells*, WTO Appellate Body Report, paras. 5.46, 5.84. See also Sherzod Shadikhodjaev, 'India – Certain Measures Relating to Solar Cells and Solar Modules', 111 *American Journal of International Law* 139 (2017).

the acquisition or distribution of products in general or local short supply', India claimed that its low manufacturing capacity pointed to the existence of a 'general or local short supply' of the solar products at issue in the internal market.[75] The Appellate Body admitted that the measure's policy rationales, such as energy security or sustainable development, could inform the nature and extent of supply and demand on the market. But it rejected India's claim due to a lack of evidence regarding the inadequacy of *both* domestic *and* international sources to meet India's domestic demand for solar cells and modules and evidence regarding actual disruptions in solar imports that would create supply-related risks.[76]

Energy security is to be distinguished from energy safety, which, in this book, is about safeguarding people and the environment from the dangers of energy production, supply or use. Take nuclear safety as an example. It was at the centre of some international tensions in the past. Following the nuclear accident at Chernobyl in the Soviet Union, the European Economic Community in May 1986 suspended food imports from certain East European countries. In a GATT meeting, Hungary argued that the selection of countries within a 1,000-kilometre radius from the place of the accident was unjustified and arbitrary, contrary to Article XX of the GATT. It contended that the radiation level had risen across most of Europe since the accident, and some countries outside that radius had even a greater radiation level than some (like Hungary) within it. But the European Economic Community countered that the measure was temporary to allow for more time to obtain and verify scientific information so that it could calm public anxiety and reassure its population.[77]

Twenty-five years later, another tragic occurrence gave rise to similar nuclear safety concerns. The accident at Japan's Fukushima Dai-ichi Nuclear Power Plant on 11 March 2011 prompted many countries to ban seafood products from this area out of fear of radioactive contamination, which led to a trade dispute in the WTO.[78] The Fukushima accident's repercussions went beyond the trade domain, triggering policy

[75] *India – Solar Cells*, WTO Appellate Body Report, paras. 5.51–5.52.

[76] Ibid., paras. 5.73–5.79.

[77] See GATT, Council – Minutes of Meeting – Held in the Centre William Rappard on 22 May 1986, GATT Doc., C/M/198 (12 June 1986), pp. 28–31.

[78] See Section 2.2.1.3.

amendments on nuclear power production in some countries and irritating affected foreign investors as a result.[79]

The use of nuclear energy is good for zero-carbon emissions into the atmosphere, but safety must be adequately ensured. Nuclear safety generally deals with the protection of people and the environment from radiation risks as well as with the safety of facilities and activities carrying radiation risks. This notion embraces the safety of nuclear installations, radiation safety, the safety of radioactive waste management and safety in the transport of radioactive material.[80] Nuclear safety is distinct from nuclear security, which is concerned with criminal or intentional unauthorized acts involving nuclear or other radioactive material and associated facilities/activities that could cause or threaten health or environmental harm.[81] The main nuclear safety treaties, adopted under the auspices of the International Atomic Energy Agency, deal with the safety of nuclear installations (i.e., land-based civil nuclear power plants), the safety of spent fuel management and radioactive waste management, early notification of a nuclear accident as well as assistance in the case of a nuclear accident or radiological emergency.[82]

While nuclear safety per se has been regulated mainly under the nuclear law framework, the EU–Armenia Comprehensive and Enhanced Partnership Agreement (2017), which covers trade matters, is remarkable for articulating the parties' commitment to ensuring high levels of nuclear safety and nuclear security and to cooperating in the fight against 'radiological and nuclear terrorism'.[83] Their energy cooperation regarding safety and security in the civil nuclear sector focuses on the exchange of technologies, best practices and training aimed at 'the safe operation of nuclear power plants' as well as on the closure and safe decommissioning of Armenia's Medzamor nuclear power plant.[84]

[79] See Section 5.1.1.

[80] International Atomic Energy Agency (IAEA), 'IAEA Nuclear Safety and Security Glossary', 2022 (Interim) Edition, 2022, pp. 139–140, 188.

[81] Ibid., p. 140.

[82] See IAEA, 'Nuclear Safety Conventions', www.iaea.org/topics/nuclear-safety-conventions.

[83] The preamble and Article 19.1(g) of the EU–Armenia Comprehensive and Enhanced Partnership Agreement (2017).

[84] Article 42.2(g) of the EU–Armenia Comprehensive and Enhanced Partnership Agreement (2017).

1.2 International Economic Framework for Environmental Policy Space

Originally developed outside, but intertwined with, international economic law, the principles and concepts discussed in the preceding analysis are the energy–environment foundations of 'external' origin. The following sections will focus on the 'internal' foundations, namely multilateral and regional trade and investment rules that preserve regulatory sovereignty of States over environmental issues through exception clauses or other legal flexibilities.

1.2.1 WTO

Established in 1995 as a successor to the GATT, the WTO has governed international trade by providing a global forum for lowering trade barriers, setting and administering rules, discussing and monitoring pertinent policies and settling inter-government disputes. While not being tailored to energy per se, the WTO-led multilateral trading system is inclusive enough to regulate energy trade.

Despite its great achievements, the WTO is currently in need of reform. To name some important bottlenecks, the first, and so far the only officially launched, WTO round of multilateral trade negotiations, including on trade and environment issues, has failed to conclude. Consensus-building difficulties have significantly hampered the WTO's rule-making activities, preventing timely legislative trade responses at the global level to climate change and other emerging challenges. Because of the persistent dysfunctionality of the Appellate Body for the last few years, many panel reports have been appealed into the void.[85] The troubling lack of required notifications of trade measures undermines the credibility of the WTO's transparency procedures.

Yet, amid this hardship, the WTO has recently progressed on the environmental front. The Twelfth Ministerial Conference in 2022 adopted a first WTO environmental treaty – the Agreement on Fisheries Subsidies, which is designed to preserve ocean sustainability in line with the UN SDG 14.6 mandate for curbing harmful subsidies that contribute to the depletion of global fish stocks. In 2020 and 2021, the WTO launched new initiatives on trade and environmental sustainability, plastics pollution and fossil fuel subsidies (see Table 1.1) to complement the

[85] See Sherzod Shadikhodjaev, 'United States – Safeguard Measure on Imports of Crystalline Silicon Photovoltaic Products', 116 *American Journal of International Law* 842 (2022), pp. 849–850.

Table 1.1 *Recent WTO environmental initiatives*

	Trade and Environmental Sustainability Structured Discussions (TESSD)	Informal Dialogue on Plastics Pollution and Sustainable Plastics Trade (IDP)	Fossil Fuel Subsidy Reform (FFSR)
Date of Launch	November 2020	November 2020	December 2021
Co-sponsors (participants)	74 members	75 members	48 members
Mission	• To organize structured discussions for interested WTO members and a dialogue with external stakeholders (including business community, civil society, international organizations and academic institutions) regarding the intersection of trade and environmental sustainability; • To identify concrete actions and work on deliverables to increase the supportiveness of trade and environment.	• To identify opportunities for enhanced trade cooperation within the WTO rules and mechanisms to support domestic, regional and global efforts to reduce plastics pollution and transition to a more circular and environmentally sustainable global plastics economy; • To be part of broader WTO deliberations to advance shared trade and environmental sustainability objectives.	• To rationalize and phase out inefficient fossil fuel subsidies that encourage wasteful consumption, taking fully into account developing countries' needs and conditions; • To share information and experiences to advance discussion in the WTO aimed at achieving ambitious and effective disciplines on these subsidies, including through enhanced WTO transparency and reporting.

Table 1.1 (*cont.*)

	Trade and Environmental Sustainability Structured Discussions (TESSD)	Informal Dialogue on Plastics Pollution and Sustainable Plastics Trade (IDP)	Fossil Fuel Subsidy Reform (FFSR)
Key Discussion Topics	• Trade-related climate measures; • Environmental goods and services; • Circular economy – circularity; • Subsidies.	• Cross-cutting issues (technical assistance, transparency, international cooperation, etc.); • Promoting trade to tackle plastics pollution; • Circularity and reduction to tackle plastics pollution.	• International efforts related to FFSR; • Development and social aspects of FFSR; • Members' actions on transparency and reforms.
Energy–Environment Aspects	Environmental sustainability of energy trade	Fossil fuels as a primary feedstock for plastic production; carbon emission throughout plastics' life cycle[a]	Wasteful fossil energy consumption

Source: Author's compilation from WTO documents as of 1 April 2023.

[a] See Centre for International Environmental Law, 'Plastic & Climate: The Hidden Costs of a Plastic Planet', 2019.

existing work of the Committee on Trade and Environment and other relevant WTO bodies. At the time of writing, these open-ended initiatives did not engage all WTO members yet, but thematic discussions were going on smoothly, leaving hope for concrete actions to be eventually agreed.

The WTO regime does not foreclose the use of trade restrictions for achieving legitimate policy objectives, like the protection of public health or the environment. But policy space here is not unfettered as members have committed to trade liberalization. Thus, the possibility of a tension between trade and non-trade concerns is well recognized.[86] The next sections discuss how such tension can be addressed under the WTO's general exceptions and other legal contexts.

1.2.1.1 General Exceptions

Scattered across several WTO agreements, the general exceptions can be invoked to justify otherwise WTO-incompatible measures on the pertinent legitimate policy grounds. As a most representative example, Article XX of the GATT lists general exceptions in paragraphs (a) to (j) for ten types of socially desirable trade restrictions. These paragraphs use different wording, characterizing such measures as, inter alia, 'necessary', 'essential' or 'relating to . . .' to express different degrees of 'connection or relationship' between the measure concerned and the covered policy interest.[87] To succeed, the party invoking Article XX must prove in two consecutive steps that its GATT-inconsistent measure (i) seats under any of the exceptions in the related paragraph and (ii) meets the requirements of the opening clause (or '*chapeau*') of Article XX.[88] The first step appraises the 'general design' of a challenged measure under the applicable paragraph while the second step checks the 'manner' in which that measure is applied to ensure that the invoking member is not abusing or misusing the covered exceptions.[89] Paragraphs (b) and (g) of Article XX are of particular relevance to the energy–environment nexus:

> Subject to the requirement that such measures are not applied in a manner which would constitute a means of arbitrary or unjustifiable discrimination between countries where the same conditions prevail, or

[86] See *Brazil – Retreaded Tyres*, WTO Appellate Body Report, para. 210.

[87] *US – Gasoline*, WTO Appellate Body Report, p. 17.

[88] Ibid., p. 22; *US – Shrimp*, WTO Appellate Body Report, paras. 119–120.

[89] *US – Gasoline*, WTO Appellate Body Report, p. 22; *US – Shrimp*, WTO Appellate Body Report, paras. 116, 156.

> a disguised restriction on international trade, nothing in this Agreement shall be construed to prevent the adoption or enforcement by any contracting party of measures:
>
> ...
>
> (b) necessary to protect human, animal or plant life or health;
>
> ...
>
> (g) relating to the conservation of exhaustible natural resources if such measures are made effective in conjunction with restrictions on domestic production or consumption;

The past energy–environment cases under paragraphs (b) and/or (g) of Article XX concerned trade measures aimed at reducing air pollution from gasoline use (*US – Gasoline* and *Brazil – Taxation*), lowering health and environmental risks associated with mining activities (*China – Raw Materials* and *China – Rare Earths*), conserving certain mineral resources (*China – Raw Materials* and *China – Rare Earths*) and improving fuel efficiency of motor vehicles (*Brazil – Taxation*).[90]

Under the analytical framework for Article XX(b), a measure at issue must be (i) 'designed' to protect human, animal or plant life or health and (ii) 'necessary' to achieve that objective, with the imposing member having discretion in determining its own level of protection.[91] The first element examines the design and structure of the measure to check whether its objective is indeed the life and health protection.[92] The second element consists in 'weighing and balancing' of the importance of the protected interests and values at stake, the measure's contribution to the achievement of the policy objective, and its trade restrictiveness, followed by a comparison of the measure with less-trade-restrictive alternatives that are reasonably available to the imposing member.[93]

As for Article XX(g), an analysis here basically looks into the challenged measures' design and structure in connection with the features of the relevant market, such as the exhaustible natural resource at issue, the market structure, the product and geographical scope of the market as

[90] See Section 2.2.

[91] *China – Raw Materials*, WTO Panel Reports, paras. 7.479–7.480 (and the accompanying footnotes referring to previous jurisprudence).

[92] Ibid., para. 7.479.

[93] *Brazil – Retreaded Tyres*, WTO Appellate Body Report, paras. 178, 182; *Colombia – Textiles*, WTO Appellate Body Report, para. 5.70.

well as the role of foreign and local market participants.[94] The term 'exhaustible natural resources' in Article XX(g) is not static but evolutionary, so it has been interpreted broadly to cover not only mineral or non-living resources but also living animals and plants susceptible of extinction as well as clean air, which can deplete because of the atmospheric pollution.[95] While 'conservation' means 'the preservation of the environment, especially of natural resources',[96] the Appellate Body said that the precise interpretation would depend on the natural resource involved:

> It seems to us that, for the purposes of Article XX(g), the precise contours of the word 'conservation' can only be fully understood in the context of the exhaustible natural resource at issue in a given dispute. For example, 'conservation' in the context of an exhaustible mineral resource may entail preservation through a reduction in the pace of its extraction, or by stopping its extraction altogether. In respect of the 'conservation' of a living natural resource, such as a species facing the threat of extinction, the word may encompass not only limiting or halting the activities creating the danger of extinction, but also facilitating the replenishment of that endangered species.[97]

The inquiry as to whether the measure is 'relating to' the conservation necessitates 'a close and genuine relationship of ends and means', namely between the claimed conservation and that measure.[98] Article XX(g) additionally imposes 'a requirement of even-handedness' by demanding the applying member to limit domestic production or consumption of the natural resource to be conserved. The domestic production/consumption must be subject to real restrictions rather than possible limitations sometime in the future.[99]

In addition, a measure qualifying for Article XX defence must also be cleared under the *chapeau* as a measure that is not applied to constitute 'a means of arbitrary or unjustifiable discrimination' or 'a disguised restriction on international trade'. The concept of 'arbitrary or unjustifiable discrimination' is not the same as discrimination envisaged by other

[94] *China – Rare Earths*, WTO Appellate Body Reports, paras. 5.96–5.97.

[95] *US – Shrimp*, WTO Appellate Body Report, paras. 128–131; *US – Gasoline*, WTO Panel Report, para. 6.37.

[96] *China – Rare Earths*, WTO Appellate Body Reports, para. 5.89 (citing *China – Raw Materials*, WTO Appellate Body Reports, para. 355).

[97] *China – Rare Earths*, WTO Appellate Body Reports, para. 5.89 (footnote omitted).

[98] *US – Shrimp*, WTO Appellate Body Report, para. 136; *China – Raw Materials*, WTO Appellate Body Reports, para. 355.

[99] *China – Rare Earths*, WTO Appellate Body Reports, paras. 5.92–5.93.

GATT provisions.[100] Rather, the discrimination is 'arbitrary or unjustifiable', referring to the case where the cause or rationale of discrimination bears no relationship to the achievement of the Article XX-covered policy objective or goes against that objective.[101] Such discrimination can occur between different exporting members or between exporting members and the importing member concerned.[102] The concepts of 'arbitrary or unjustifiable discrimination' and 'disguised restriction on international trade' are related terms that impart meaning to one another.[103]

Like Article XX of the GATT, Article XIV of the General Agreement on Trade in Services (GATS) sets out general exceptions and requires a two-tier analysis under a relevant paragraph and the *chapeau*.[104] But the GATS envisages an environmental exception for measures 'necessary to protect human, animal or plant life or health' (Article XIV(b)), while omitting the GATT-like conservation exception. In the Uruguay Round, it was concluded that the exception for the conservation of exhaustible natural resources appeared unnecessary for the GATS because it would not provide an additional cover beyond that already contained in Article XX(g) of the GATT.[105] If so, it appears to be a mystery how this rationale would make the GATS-omitted conservation exception any different from the GATS-included life/health-related exception that has the GATT counterpart too. The WTO Ministerial Decision on Trade in Services and the Environment (1995) notes that 'since measures necessary to protect the environment typically have as their objective the protection of human, animal or plant life or health, it is not clear that there is a need to provide for more than is contained in paragraph (b) of Article XIV'. However, WTO members decided to request the Committee on Trade and Environment to examine and report on the

[100] *US – Gasoline*, WTO Appellate Body Report, p. 23; *US – Shrimp*, WTO Appellate Body Report, para. 150.

[101] *Brazil – Retreaded Tyres*, WTO Appellate Body Report, para. 246.

[102] *US – Shrimp*, WTO Appellate Body Report, para. 150.

[103] *US – Gasoline*, WTO Appellate Body Report, p. 25.

[104] *US – Gambling*, WTO Appellate Body Report, paras. 291–292.

[105] WTO, Committee on Trade and Environment – Environment and Services, WT/CTE/W/9 (8 June 1995), para. 9. The underlying idea might be that trade-restrictive conservation measures, even if associated with services, would take place in merchandise trade, not services trade per se (see, e.g., WT/CTE/W/9, paras. 21, 32; WTO, Report (1996) of the Committee on Trade and Environment, WT/CTE/1 (12 November 1996), para. 154; WTO, Committee on Trade and Environment – Report of the Meeting Held on 24–25 November 1997 – Note by the Secretariat, WT/CTE/M/16 (19 December 1997), para. 10.).

relationship between services trade and the environment in order to determine whether any modification of Article XIV of the GATS is required.[106] But the work in this direction has not changed the status quo.

1.2.1.2 Other Policy Flexibilities

Not all WTO agreements contain general exceptions. Yet, the right to regulate in the public interest may still be deduced from a relevant context where applicable. For example, the Agreement on Technical Barriers to Trade (TBT) does not have a general exceptions clause, but its preamble sets a trade-liberalization objective and recognizes that 'no country should be prevented from taking measures necessary … for the protection of human, animal or plant life or health, of the environment … at the levels it considers appropriate', subject to the *chapeau*-like conditions. The Appellate Body found this to be akin to a legal balance under the GATT:

> The balance set out in the preamble of the *TBT Agreement* between, on the one hand, the desire to avoid creating unnecessary obstacles to international trade and, on the other hand, the recognition of Members' right to regulate, is not, in principle, different from the balance set out in the GATT 1994, where obligations such as national treatment in Article III are qualified by the general exceptions provision of Article XX.[107]

Members can also seek policy flexibilities under exceptions to or derogations from specific WTO provisions that are applicable to energy–environment issues, among others. For example, government procurement of clean energy goods falling within Article III:8(a) of the GATT is insulated from the GATT national treatment obligations. Where appropriate, preferential (but discriminatory) trade in green goods and services could be excused by the WTO exceptions for RTAs or preferential schemes for developing countries.

Further, Article IX (paragraphs 3 and 4) of the WTO Agreement empowers the Ministerial Conference to temporarily waive a requesting member from its WTO obligations in 'exceptional circumstances', subject to the attached 'terms and conditions'. Waivers exceeding one year are to be reviewed until full termination. None of the existing WTO waiver decisions has concerned the energy–environment nexus

[106] WTO, Decision on Trade in Services and the Environment, S/L/4 (4 April 1995), para. 1.
[107] *US – Clove Cigarettes*, WTO Appellate Body Report, para. 96 (emphasis in original).

per se.[108] James Bacchus, a former Chairman of the Appellate Body, is a strong advocate for adopting a 'WTO climate waiver', namely 'a [collective] waiver from WTO obligations for all trade-restrictive climate response measures that are based on the amount of carbon used or emitted in making a product, and that are taken in furtherance of and in compliance with the Paris Agreement and the UNFCCC'.[109] Collective waivers are indeed not unknown in WTO practice, but all of the adopted collective waivers specified concrete WTO obligations waived,[110] which is in line with 'the exceptional nature of waivers' that must be interpreted 'with great care'.[111] As many WTO members would likely oppose a *catch-all* climate waiver, the focus should rather be on narrowly defined measures (e.g., border adjustments of carbon payments[112]) and specific provisions (on, e.g., non-discrimination) to be waived. To garner greater support among members, such waiver should also be supplemented with concrete actions regarding climate-related technical and financial assistance for developing countries that are particularly susceptible to external environmental restrictions, such as carbon emission or energy efficiency regulations, which may hinder their economic growth.

In the case of nuclear energy, members tend to ensure the maximum of the right to regulate, even without specifying underlying environmental concerns. For example, Colombia's services schedule under the GATS does not allow foreign direct investments (FDIs) in 'the processing and disposal of toxic, hazardous or radioactive waste not produced in Colombia'.[113] Bulgaria remains 'unbound', or free to restrict, in relation to providing market access for foreign 'Services Relating to the Use of Nuclear Energy for Peaceful Purposes' in all four modes of service

[108] See WTO, General Council – Waivers – 2021 – Note by the Secretariat, WT/GC/W/840 (17 December 2021); WTO, General Council – Waivers – 1995–2020 – Note by the Secretariat – Revision, WT/GC/W/718/Rev.1 (25 January 2021).

[109] James Bacchus, 'The Case for a WTO Climate Waiver', Centre for International Governance Innovation, Special Report, 2017, p. 20.

[110] See Isabel Feichtner, *The Law and Politics of WTO Waivers: Stability and Flexibility in Public International Law* (New York: Cambridge University Press, 2011), pp. 124–157. For the waiver decision on COVID-19 vaccines regarding trade-related aspects of intellectual property rights (TRIPS), see WTO, Ministerial Conference – Twelfth Session – Geneva, 12–15 June 2022 – Ministerial Decision on the TRIPS Agreement – Adopted on 17 June 2022, WT/MIN(22)/30, WT/L/1141 (22 June 2022).

[111] *EC – Bananas III*, WTO Appellate Body Report, para. 185.

[112] See Section 2.1.2.

[113] WTO, Colombia – Schedule of Specific Commitments, GATS/SC/20 (15 April 1994).

supply.[114] Furthermore, the WTO security exceptions are applicable to members' actions 'relating to fissionable materials or the materials from which they are derived'.[115] Fissionable materials contain nuclides that are 'capable of supporting a self-sustaining nuclear chain reaction with neutrons of any speed'[116] and also extend to 'special fissionable materials', like plutonium-239 and uranium-233.[117] This security exception was included out of concern that fissionable materials could be used in the production of nuclear weapons.[118] But whether fissionable materials used for peaceful purposes, such as electric power generation, are relevant to WTO-protectable security interests is far from clear.[119]

Finally, the WTO entitles developing country members to S&D treatment so that they can have flexibility in undertaking commitments or using policy instruments, use transitional periods and rely on technical assistance, among other things.[120] Ideally, S&D flexibilities, including for addressing energy–environment issues, should help developing countries better their trading capabilities and increase their readiness to accept further trade commitments.[121] However, many S&D provisions lack implementation guidelines or contain vague formulations and soft law

[114] WTO, Trade in Services – The Republic of Bulgaria – Schedule of Specific Commitments, GATS/SC/122 (21 May 1997).

[115] Article XX1(b)(i) of the General Agreement on Tariffs and Trade (GATT). Article XIV *bis* of the General Agreement on Trade in Services (GATS), paragraph 1(b)(ii), speaks of 'fissionable and fusionable materials . . .'.

[116] IAEA, supra note 80, p. 88.

[117] Article XX:1 of the IAEA Statute (1956).

[118] Rüdiger Wolfrum, Peter-Tobias Stoll and Holger P. Hestermeyer (eds.), *WTO – Trade in Goods* (Leiden, Boston: Martinus Nijhoff Publishers, 2011), p. 586.

[119] For example, an Australian representative in 1947 negotiations on the International Trade Organization Charter worried that the 'fissionable materials' exception 'would have an unfortunate effect in the event that atomic energy became an important or major source of industrial energy'. UN Doc., E/PC/T/A/SR/30 (16 July 1947), p. 3. For the security exceptions on services, see also WTO, Council for Trade in Services – Energy Services – Background Note by the Secretariat, S/C/W/52 (9 September 1998), para. 28 (noting: 'It is unclear whether "essential" security interests could be at stake in the international trade of nuclear energy services for pacific purposes, also considering the potential spillovers in the military field.').

[120] See WTO, Committee on Trade and Development – Special and Differential Treatment Provisions in WTO Agreements and Decisions – Note by the Secretariat, WT/COMTD/W/271 (16 March 2023), p. 4, para. 1.5.

[121] See Vineet Hegde and Jan Wouters, 'Special and Differential Treatment under the World Trade Organization: A Legal Typology', 24 *Journal of International Economic Law* 551 (2021), p. 569.

obligations, and virtually all transitional periods have already expired.[122] The overall performance of the S&D regime has not met developing countries' expectations, and the S&D reforming attempts prescribed by the Doha Round mandate[123] have not improved the troubling situation. The WTO Agreement on Trade Facilitation, being in force since 2017, introduced a new S&D model for bridging the gap between members' implementation capacity and their obligation to implement: namely, developing countries can self-designate the status of envisaged commitments and link the implementation of some commitments to receipt of technical assistance and capacity building support from donor countries. Future S&D components could follow this innovative approach. If the WTO's long-standing practice of treating self-declared developing countries as a homogeneous group eligible for the same S&D treatment eventually changes towards greater heterogeneity among S&D recipients,[124] the level of vulnerability to climate change (or other environmental problems) should arguably be considered in allocating pertinent S&D benefits among developing countries. The rough idea here, which itself requires a further in-depth analysis, is to create a category of most climate (or environmentally) vulnerable developing countries and entitle them to greater-than-usual S&D assistance and policy space for coping with climate change, pollution and decarbonization challenges. In a sense, this would correspond to several members' calls for customizing S&D to 'the specific development needs of Members' and 'the particular situations faced by developing Members in different areas of economic activity'.[125]

1.2.2 RTAs

Regional trade agreements – FTAs and customs unions – have accommodated environmental concerns within preferential trade. Roughly

[122] See Sonia E. Rolland, *Development at the World Trade Organization* (Oxford: Oxford University Press, 2012), pp. 109–138.

[123] WT/MIN(01)/DEC/1, supra note 67, para. 44.

[124] See WTO, General Council – 9–11 December 2019 – Draft General Council Decision – Procedures to Strengthen the Negotiating Function of the WTO – Decision of X Date – Revision, WT/GC/W/764/Rev.1 (25 November 2019); WTO, General Council – An Undifferentiated WTO: Self-Declared Development Status Risks Institutional Irrelevance – Communication from the United States, WT/GC/W/757 (16 January 2019).

[125] WTO, General Council – 7 May 2019 – Pursuing the Development Dimension in WTO Rule-Making Efforts – Communication from Norway; Canada; Hong Kong, China; Iceland; Mexico; New Zealand; Singapore and Switzerland – Revision, WT/GC/W/770/Rev.3 (8 May 2019), para. 2.4.

97 per cent of RTAs notified to the WTO include at least one provision mentioning the environment, with RTAs concluded in 1992–2005 containing mainly environment-related exceptions or preambular language, and post-2005 RTAs also incorporating other, more elaborate environmental provisions.[126] The environmental exceptions, usually located in the part of the treaty text that details general and security exceptions, are mainly modelled after GATT Article XX or GATS Article XIV, but some use the amended WTO language or clarify the parties' understanding regarding the contents.[127]

More than 110 RTAs recognize the right to regulate environmental issues in environment chapters, side agreements or chapters on TBT measures, SPS measures, investment and government procurement.[128] To give a recent example, the environment chapter of the New Zealand–United Kingdom (UK) FTA (2022) recognizes 'the sovereign right of each Party to establish its own environmental priorities and levels of environmental protection relating to the environment, including mitigation of and adaptation to climate change, and those which a Party establishes pursuant to the multilateral environmental agreements to which it is a party, and to establish, maintain, or modify its relevant law and policies accordingly'.[129]

At least sixty-nine RTAs contain environment-related provisions on energy and mineral resources. These provisions often deal with cooperation (on renewable energy, energy conservation and efficiency, nuclear safety and so on) and less frequently with the promotion of environmental goods and services, import/export restrictions and internal measures (sometimes in connection with environment-related general exceptions), environmental management and others.[130]

1.2.3 IIAs

Close to 3,300 IIAs – BITs and treaties with investment provisions – concluded to date[131] constitute a divergent legal basis for regulating

[126] Monteiro, supra note 24, pp. 6–7.
[127] See ibid., pp. 36, 38–40.
[128] Ibid., p. 23.
[129] Article 22.4.1 of the New Zealand–United Kingdom (UK) FTA (2022).
[130] Monteiro, supra note 24, pp. 64–66.
[131] See UN Conference on Trade and Development (UNCTAD), 'International Investment Agreements Navigator', https://investmentpolicy.unctad.org/international-investment-agreements.

multinational business activities. Because of this large number of agreements, the international investment regime is highly fragmented and inconsistent throughout. Energy investments fall within the subject matter jurisdiction of IIAs unless provided otherwise.

International investment agreements have focused on promoting investment flows and protecting foreign investors and their assets from unwarranted restrictive measures of host countries. Thus, IIAs are typically imbalanced in creating obligations for States but virtually none for investors. Although IIAs are complementary to trade agreements in encouraging cross-border economic activities, they differ from them in several ways. As pointed out by two authors, while the trade regime is 'about overall welfare, efficiency, liberalization, state-to-state exchanges of market access, and trade opportunities – not individual rights', the investment regime traditionally concerns 'fairness grounded in customary rules on treatment of aliens, not efficiency' and is 'about protection, not liberalization, and about individual rights, not state-to-state exchanges of market opportunities'.[132]

As of September 2022, all known ISDS cases over State measures dealing with environmental protection or renewable energy were brought on the basis of so-called old-generation IIAs.[133] Old-generation IIAs – those concluded in the period 1959–2009 and constituting over 85 per cent of all IIAs ever signed – often lack explicit provisions preserving governments' regulatory space for environmental issues.[134] As a result, tribunals with 'neo-liberal biases' have interpreted States' obligations to foreign investors rather expansively while showing little deference to the regulatory space.[135] Therefore, the right to regulate for protecting public

[132] Nicholas DiMascio and Joost Pauwelyn, 'Nondiscrimination in Trade and Investment Treaties: Worlds Apart or Two Sides of the Same Coin?', 102 *American Journal of International Law* 48 (2008), pp. 54, 56 (footnote omitted).

[133] UNCTAD, 'Treaty-Based Investor–State Dispute Settlement Cases and Climate Action', IIA Issues Note: International Investment Agreements, Issue No. 4, 2022, p. 3, Annexes 1 and 3.

[134] UNCTAD, 'The International Investment Treaty Regime and Climate Action', IIA Issues Note: International Investment Agreements, Issue No. 3, 2022, p. 3. See also Kathryn Gordon and Joachim Pohl, 'Environmental Concerns in International Investment Agreements: A Survey', OECD Working Papers on International Investment No. 2011/01, 2011, p. 8 (finding that only 8.2 per cent of IIAs signed between 1959 and 2010 contain environmental language).

[135] Suzanne A. Spears, 'The Quest for Policy Space in a New Generation of International Investment Agreements', 13 *Journal of International Economic Law* 1037 (2010), pp. 1045–1047.

health and the environment is being given greater attention under 'new-generation' IIAs as discussed below.

1.2.3.1 General Exceptions

One study reveals that 51 (mostly BITs) out of 113 IIAs signed between 2010 and 2015 contained WTO-style general exceptions for the environment and concludes that 'general exceptions are mainstreaming into IIAs'.[136] Indeed, this trend sustains with the proliferation of new-generation IIAs.[137]

General exceptions typically apply to investment measures 'necessary to protect human, animal or plant life or health', subject to the GATT-like *chapeau* requirement where envisaged,[138] and may also cover environment-preserving measures, like 'the conservation of living or non-living exhaustible natural resources'.[139] Depending on the text, the exceptions apply across the board or vis-à-vis selective provisions only. The WTO judicial interpretations could be helpful in construing the meaning of words used in the WTO-like IIA general exceptions.[140] But ISDS tribunals (except few[141]) have actually been reluctant to 'borrow' from WTO jurisprudence[142] in support of the legal autonomy of the investment regime.

However, unlike in the WTO, there is considerable uncertainty regarding the legal status of IIA general exceptions partly because they are a relatively new trend with limited case law. Some authors expect little benefit (if any) or even warn that these exceptions may undermine,

[136] Amelia Keene, 'The Incorporation and Interpretation of WTO-Style Environmental Exceptions in International Investment Agreements', 18 *Journal of World Investment & Trade* 62 (2017), pp. 65, 69, 72, 91, Annex I.

[137] See UNCTAD, 'International Investment Agreements Reform Accelerator', 2020, pp. 26–27.

[138] See, for example, Article 18.1 of the Japan–Bahrain BIT (2022).

[139] See, for example, Article 22.7 of the Hungary–United Arab Emirates (UAE) BIT (2021).

[140] See Giorgio Sacerdoti, 'The Application of BITs in Time of Economic Crisis: Limits to Their Coverage, Necessity and the Relevance of WTO Law', in Giorgio Sacerdoti et al. (eds.), *General Interests of Host States in International Investment Law* (Cambridge: Cambridge University Press, 2014), pp. 19–23.

[141] One tribunal found it 'more appropriate' to refer to GATT/WTO case law for Article XX of the GATT, rather than customary international law, in interpreting the concept of necessity under a BIT exception for measures 'necessary' for maintaining public order and protecting essential security interests of the State. See *Continental Casualty v. Argentina*, ICSID, Award, paras. 192–195.

[142] See Keene, supra note 136, pp. 81–82.

rather than improve, the policy balance in the investment regime.[143] Others paint an optimistic prospect, citing, inter alia, the binding nature of the general exceptions as compared to the doctrinal reasoning for pro-environmental, and yet discretionary, interpretations of IIAs.[144]

The existing ISDS jurisprudence, albeit still scarce, tends to side with the pessimists. For example, the tribunal in *Bear Creek Mining v. Peru* indicated that the existence of the general exceptions for investment obligations could foreclose 'other exceptions from general international law or otherwise', like the police power exception.[145] The tribunal in *Eco Oro v. Colombia* concluded that the GATT-modelled general exception for the life and health protection, applicable to the investment chapter of the Canada–Colombia FTA (2008), did not negate the State's obligation to pay compensation for the breach of investment provisions. The tribunal observed that the interpretation to the contrary would create a conflict between the FTA general exception in question and the FTA provision on indirect expropriation under which certain environmental measures not covered by the envisaged carve-out would constitute indirect expropriation. Specifically, the investor would cite the latter provision to claim compensation while the State would invoke the general exception to deny compensation. The general exception in question, the tribunal said, was 'permissive' and merely ensured that the State was not forbidden from taking environmental measures, without explicitly waiving the State from its liability for compensation. Colombia as the responding State in this dispute could not explain why non-compensation was necessary for environmental protection.[146]

143 See Barton Legum and Ioana Petculescu, 'GATT Article XX and International Investment Law', in Roberto Echandi and Pierre Sauvé (eds.), *Prospects in International Investment Law and Policy* (Cambridge: Cambridge University Press, 2013), p. 362; Céline Lévesque, 'The Inclusion of GATT Article XX Exceptions in IIAs: A Potentially Risky Policy', in Echandi and Sauvé (eds.), *Prospects in International Investment Law and Policy*, pp. 364, 370.

144 See Keene, supra note 136, pp. 89, 91.

145 *Bear Creek Mining v. Peru*, ICSID, Award, paras. 473–474.

146 *Eco Oro v. Colombia*, ICSID, Decision on Jurisdiction, Liability and Directions on Quantum, paras. 829, 831–832, 837. For similar findings, see also *Bear Creek Mining v. Peru*, ICSID, Award, paras. 471–478. With respect to the carve-out from indirect expropriation, Annex 811(2)(b) of the Canada–Colombia FTA (2008) reads:

> Except in rare circumstances, such as when a measure or series of measures is so severe in the light of its purpose that it cannot be reasonably viewed as having been adopted in good faith, non-discriminatory measures by a Party that are designed and applied to protect legitimate public

While general exceptions in investment law are inspired by trade law counterparts, the ISDS developments so far indicate rather limited practical benefits of general exceptions for IIA environmental policy space. In the WTO, general exceptions justify relevant illegal measures and hence *preclude* counteracting remedies as long as the prescribed conditions are met. In contrast, the justification under investment treaties turns out to not necessarily free a violating State from the duty to compensate. This appears rather absurd as it is unlikely that treaty drafters – already being aware of the legal implications from the WTO general exceptions – have included general exceptions just for symbolic reasons, agreeing to mandatory compensation in any case. Thus, for greater meaningfulness, general exceptions in the investment law domain should be accompanied with unequivocal compensation waivers, except where this would bring about a conflict within the same IIA as indicated in *Eco Oro v. Colombia* above. Probably it is to avoid an internal conflict of this kind that the proposed text of the modernized ECT does not extend general exceptions – otherwise applicable to most investment provisions of the modernized agreement – to the provisions on expropriation under which measures not falling within the scope of the defined carve-out could constitute indirect expropriation.[147]

1.2.3.2 Other Policy Flexibilities

Apart from general exceptions, the environmental policy space under IIAs can also be explored in various other ways.[148] To start with, preambular clauses of IIAs can acknowledge the importance of environmental considerations in investment promotion or protection. For example, the preamble of the ECT (1994) stresses the necessity for the highest efficiency in energy exploration, production, conversion, storage, transport, distribution and use; recognizes 'the increasingly urgent need for measures to protect the environment, including the decommissioning of energy installations and waste disposal'; and recalls 'international environmental agreements with energy-related aspects' like the

welfare objectives, for example health, safety and the protection of the environment, do not constitute indirect expropriation.

[147] See Section 1.2.4.

[148] See, for example, Shunta Yamaguchi, 'Greening Regional Trade Agreements on Investment', OECD Trade and Environment Working Paper No. 2020/03, 2020, pp. 11–42.

UNFCCC. Preambles constitute a context for treaty interpretation[149] and may thus inform the meaning of other provisions in the course of defining the scope of the right to regulate.

Recently, several IIAs have explicitly reaffirmed the right to regulate for attaining public policy objectives including the protection of public health and the environment.[150] This new trend codifies what customary international law or the legal doctrine would otherwise ascribe to State sovereignty[151] and police powers[152]. Such text-based reconfirmation provides a context for interpreting other provisions and may at least serve to emphasize that a signatory State has not relinquished its right to regulate for the sake of the public welfare even if it committed itself to protecting foreign investment.

Perhaps more importantly, new-generation IIAs tend to set forth environmental carve-outs, or exemptions, from legal obligations. Such carve-outs make a particular provision (on, e.g., expropriation) inapplicable to a specified measure, and this contrasts with general exceptions that defend a measure that is otherwise inconsistent with an *applicable* provision. One crystallizing pattern of environmental carve-outs provides that non-discriminatory regulatory actions protecting public health, the environment and other legitimate welfare objectives do not constitute indirect expropriation, 'except in rare circumstances' (if mentioned so in the text).[153]

Furthermore, the most-favoured-nation (MFN) treatment and national treatment provisions of some agreements clarify that an assessment of treatment of foreign investors/investments in 'like circumstances' would consider a totality of circumstances, including whether distinctions in treatment are based on legitimate public policy objectives.[154] This codifies early ISDS jurisprudence under which a 'like

[149] Article 31.2 of the Vienna Convention on the Law of Treaties (VCLT) (1969).

[150] See, for example, Article 8.9.1 of the EU–Canada Comprehensive Economic and Trade Agreement (CETA) (2016); the preambles of the Myanmar–Singapore BIT (2019), the India–UAE Comprehensive Economic Partnership Agreement (2022), the Australia–UK FTA (2021) and the China–Mauritius FTA (2019).

[151] *Manolium-Processing v. Belarus*, PCA, Final Award, para. 424.

[152] See Section 5.1.2.

[153] See, for example, Annex 10(B), para. 4, of the Regional Comprehensive Economic Partnership (RCEP) Agreement (2020); Annex 9-B, para. 3(b), of the Comprehensive and Progressive Agreement for Trans-Pacific Partnership (CPTPP) (2018). See also Section 5.1.2.

[154] See, for example, Articles 14.4.4 and 14.5.4 of the United States–Mexico–Canada Agreement (USMCA) (2018); Article 9.4, footnote 14, of the CPTPP (2018).

circumstances' determination was not confined to only whether relevant investments/investors were competing in the same business or economic sectors but also extended to other pertinent factors, such as whether the difference in treatment stemmed from rational public policies not motivated by nationality preference for investments/investors.[155] As a result and subject to case-specific facts, different treatment driven solely by nationality-neutral environmental considerations would not necessarily violate IIA anti-discrimination clauses. In this context, one agreement clarifies that its general exceptions in the investment chapter do not diminish a government's right to treat investors differently based on legitimate regulatory distinctions.[156] This exemplifies a way of preventing the general exceptions from foreclosing the use of other built-in policy flexibilities.

RTAs with investment chapters tend to list each party's existing or future non-conforming measures and exempt them from specified investment-related provisions. Some lists of this kind envisage reservations for the right to regulate nuclear energy, electricity, renewable energy or mining activities, taking into account public interest considerations among others.[157]

Last but not least, IIAs may discourage race to the bottom in domestic investment policies. To this end, they recognize the achievability of IIA objectives without relaxing health and environmental standards[158] or the inappropriateness of such relaxation in attracting investment.[159] Some

[155] See, for example, *Pope & Talbot v. Canada*, UN Commission on International Trade Law (UNCITRAL), Award on the Merits of Phase 2, paras. 77–79; *GAMI v. Mexico*, UNCITRAL, Final Award, paras. 111–115. See also CPTTP (2018), 'Drafters' Note on Interpretation of "In Like Circumstances" under Article 9.4 (National Treatment) and Article 9.5 (Most-Favoured-Nation Treatment)', www.mfat.govt.nz/assets/Trade-agreements/CPTPP/Interpretation-of-In-Like-Circumstances.pdf.

[156] See footnote 24 to Article 3.26 ('General Exceptions') of the Armenia–Singapore Agreement on Trade in Services and Investment (2019) (stating that 'the application of the general exception to these provisions shall not be interpreted so as to diminish the ability of governments to take measures where investors are not in like circumstances due to the existence of legitimate regulatory objectives'.).

[157] See, for example, Annexes I and II (Korea's schedules) of the Korea–United States FTA (2007); Annex IX, Appendix 2 (Switzerland's list of reservations) of the Switzerland–Japan Agreement on Free Trade and Economic Partnership (2009); Annex III (Malaysia's reservations and non-conforming measures) of the RCEP Agreement (2020).

[158] See, for example, the preambles of the Japan–Bahrain BIT (2022) and the Turkey–Cambodia BIT (2018).

[159] See, for example, Article 5.2 of the Belgium–Luxembourg Economic Union–Montenegro BIT (2010).

IIAs also envisage a State-to-State procedure, like consultations, for handing revealed cases of such environmental regime weakening.[160] These anti-relaxation provisions are notable for restraining a host country's own desire to voluntarily diminish its right to regulate.

1.2.4 ECT

The ECT (1994) is an international agreement on energy cooperation among fifty-plus parties (including the EU and Euratom), covering both trade and investment elements. It focuses on energy trade and transit, investment promotion and protection, trade and investment dispute settlement and energy efficiency.

The ECT's trade-related provisions are largely based on, and overlap with, the relevant GATT/WTO rules.[161] Article 4 of the ECT explicitly states: 'Nothing in this Treaty shall derogate, as between particular Contracting Parties which are members of the WTO, from the provisions of the WTO Agreement as they are applied between those Contracting Parties'. By incorporating pertinent WTO norms, the trade part of the ECT is especially of importance to regulating energy trade with non-WTO contracting parties – currently, Azerbaijan, Belarus, Bosnia and Herzegovina, Turkmenistan and Uzbekistan – to which the WTO rules do not apply yet.

The investment part of the ECT sets forth legal standards of protecting foreign investors and their investments. It is remarkable that renewable energy cases account for the lion's share, or 60 per cent, of all 150 known investment arbitration cases brought under the ECT.[162]

With respect to environmental and energy efficiency issues, two ECT elements are worth noting. First, Article 19 ('Environmental Aspects') of the ECT requires parties to 'strive to minimise in an economically efficient manner harmful Environmental Impacts' occurring from all operations along the entire energy chain. Article 19 further lists essentially political commitments of parties to promote, inter alia:

[160] See, for example, Article 2.7 of the Hungary–Kyrgyz Republic BIT (2020).

[161] See Anna-Alexandra Marhold, *Energy in International Trade Law: Concepts, Regulations and Changing Markets* (Cambridge: Cambridge University Press, 2021), pp. 110–141.

[162] Energy Charter Secretariat, 'Statistics of ECT Cases (as of 01/06/2022)', www.energychartertreaty.org/fileadmin/user_upload/All_statistics_-_1_June_2022.pdf.

- market-oriented price formation and a fuller reflection of environmental costs and benefits;
- international cooperation;
- information sharing on environmentally sound and economically efficient energy policies;
- environmental impact assessment activities and public awareness of environmental impacts of energy systems;
- R&D and application of energy efficient and environmentally sound technologies; and
- technology transfer.

Second, the Energy Charter Protocol on Energy Efficiency and Related Environmental Aspects (1994) builds on the ECT and pursues the objectives to promote energy efficiency policies 'consistent with sustainable development', create framework conditions for inducing producers and consumers towards energy efficiency and foster cooperation in this field.[163] In Parts II and III, the protocol defines policy principles (on cooperation and assistance regarding energy efficiency, promotion of market mechanisms and so on), requires parties to formulate policy aims and strategies for energy efficiency, encourages them to incentivize energy efficiency and related investments and promote energy efficient technologies, mandates the implementation and regular updating of domestic programmes on energy efficiency and indicates possible areas of international cooperation. Article 13(1) of the protocol states that in case of its inconsistency with the ECT, the latter prevails.

Overall, the energy efficiency provisions lack substantive details as to concrete legally binding actions. Therefore, unlike other activities in the Energy Charter process, the work on energy efficiency focuses not on legal obligations but policy discussions. Within their participation in the protocol above, parties share good practices, experiences and policy advice on energy efficiency issues, paying particular attention to such aspects of national energy efficiency strategies as taxation, energy pricing, environment-related subsidies and other financing mechanisms.[164]

[163] Article 1(2) of the Energy Charter Protocol on Energy Efficiency and Related Environmental Aspects (1994).

[164] Energy Charter Secretariat, 'The Protocol on Energy Efficiency and Related Environmental Aspects (PEEREA)', www.energycharter.org/process/energy-charter-treaty-1994/energy-efficiency-protocol/; 'Energy Efficiency Group', 14 December 2016, www.energycharter.org/who-we-are/subsidiary-bodies/energy-efficiency-group/.

In June 2022, the ECT parties concluded negotiations on modernizing the ECT by reaching an agreement in principle on the modernized treaty text. Remarkably, many textual revisions are closely relevant to the greening of the energy sector, and some correspond to the aforementioned patterns of new-generation IIAs.[165]

First, the scope of ECT-covered economic activities is extended to include the capture, utilization and storage of CO_2 in order to decarbonize energy systems. The updated list of subject energy materials and products comprises new items, such as hydrogen, biomass, biogas, synthetic fuels and others.

Second, the modernized ECT's 'flexibility mechanism' allows parties to exclude investment protection for fossil fuels in their territories. The EU and the UK have already opted for such exclusions in relation to existing fossil fuel investments after ten years from the entry into force of the relevant provisions as well as in relation to new investments made after 15 August 2023. The underlying rationale is to discourage investment activities related to 'dirty' energy.

Third, a new provision is added to the ECT's investment part to reaffirm the right to regulate for the sake of environmental, climate change, public health, safety or public morals objectives.

Fourth, the modernized ECT provides that non-discriminatory environmental (including climate), public health or safety measures generally do not constitute indirect expropriation.

Fifth, revised Article 19 (renamed from 'Environmental Aspects' to 'Sustainable Development') of the ECT disallows weakening domestic environmental and labour laws as a means of encouraging energy trade or investment and reconfirms parties' rights and obligations under multilateral environmental and labour agreements, such as the UNFCCC (1992), the Paris Agreement (2015) and the International Labour Organization's fundamental conventions. A provision, added to original Article 19, requires parties to encourage investors to adopt principles of responsible business conduct. Any dispute between contracting parties regarding the ECT's sustainable development provisions

[165] The following explanation of the modernized ECT is based on: the text of the modernized ECT attached to the Agreement in Principle on the Modernisation of the Energy Charter Treaty (ad hoc meeting of the Energy Charter Conference, 24 June 2022), www.bilaterals.org/IMG/pdf/reformed_ect_text.pdf; Energy Charter Secretariat, 'Finalisation of the Negotiations on the Modernisation of the Energy Charter Treaty', Public Communication Approved by the Energy Charter Conference on 24 June 2022, www.energycharter.org/fileadmin/DocumentsMedia/CCDECS/2022/CCDEC202210.pdf.

will be handled under a new specialized dispute settlement mechanism, including conciliation procedures.

Sixth, a new article ('Climate Change and Clean Energy Transition') reaffirms parties' commitments to: effectively implement the UNFCCC and the Paris Agreement; enhance the mutual supportiveness of investment and climate policies; promote climate-related trade and investment by removing obstacles to low-carbon energy technologies and services; and cooperate on investment-related aspects of climate policies.

Finally, Article 24 (renamed from 'Exceptions' to 'General Exceptions') in the modernized text contains two environmental exceptions: one already existing exception for the protection of human, animal or plant life or health and one newly introduced exception for the conservation of exhaustible natural resources. Under the current ECT's Article 24(2), the exception for life/health protection does not apply to the ECT's investment-related provisions. In contrast, the revised text makes both general exceptions in question applicable to the ECT's investment part too, except the provisions on compensation for losses (in case of wars or other emergencies) and the provisions on expropriation.

The formal adoption of the modernized ECT was postponed from November 2022 to a later date due to the lack of consensus within the EU as a number of the EU members, including Spain, the Netherlands, France, Germany and others, recently declared their intention to withdraw from the ECT altogether. These countries fear that the ECT regime, even if modernized, would undercut their climate efforts aimed at coal plant closures, oil and gas production reductions and so on.[166] Along the same lines, in November 2022, the European Parliament disapproved of the modernized ECT text (including, inter alia, the ten-year guaranteed protection for the existing investments in fossil fuels) as being not aligned with the Paris Agreement and the EU climate law and urged a coordinated exit of the EU and its members from the ECT.[167] In February 2023, the European Commission announced that a joint EU exit from the ECT appeared to be 'unavoidable'.[168] However, under the current ECT (1994),

[166] For fossil fuel investment complaints, see Section 5.1.1.

[167] European Parliament Resolution of 24 November 2022 on the Outcome of the Modernisation of the Energy Charter Treaty (2022/2934(RSP)), paras. 5, 7, 18–20, www.europarl.europa.eu/doceo/document/TA-9-2022-0421_EN.html.

[168] See European Commission, 'Non-paper from the European Commission: Next Steps as Regards the EU, Euratom and Member States' Membership in the Energy Charter Treaty', 2023, www.euractiv.com/wp-content/uploads/sites/2/2023/02/Non-paper_ECT_nextsteps.pdf; Euractive, 'LEAK: Exit from Energy Charter Treaty "unavoidable",

its provisions will continue to apply to existing investments for twenty years after a party's withdrawal (Article 47(3)). The irony is that most ISDS cases under the ECT have actually been brought by renewable energy investors against the scaling-back of support schemes,[169] so massive ECT withdrawals could turn out to be a blow to green investments too if no alternative protections are provided instead.

1.3 Concluding Remarks

The legal foundations for the energy–environment nexus seek to accommodate the public interest of internal and/or external communities. States are sovereign in conducting their energy and environmental policies, which entitles them to utilize their energy resources in accordance with their needs, preserve energy security, take action against polluters and apply precautionary measures where warranted. But this sovereignty is subject to the sustainability needs of States as well as their duties to avoid transboundary environmental damage, ensure safety of the energy cycle and adopt environmental impact assessment procedures. In addition, the principle of common but differentiated responsibilities allows for different degrees of legal rigidity and lenience among States.

In trade law, the right to regulate has been recognized on a textual basis from the very beginning of the multilateral trading system, so it is the legal texts that have been the main source for determining the scope of environmental policy space. General exceptions for qualified measures exempt governments from adverse legal consequences that would otherwise arise in the case of trade violations. By contrast, in investment law with the prevalence of the old-generation IIAs, policy space has traditionally been sought through non-textual avenues. Here, general exceptions are a new trend, and even if modelled after the WTO provisions, they do not necessarily preclude adverse consequences for violating States. Nevertheless, the text-based solidification of the public interest is increasingly evolving under new-generation IIAs, so it remains to be seen how exactly this would contribute to the rebalancing of the investment regime.

EU Commission Says', 9 February 2023, www.euractiv.com/section/energy/news/exit-from-energy-charter-treaty-unavoidable-eu-commission-says/.

169 See Section 5.2.

2

Energy Trade Control and Environmental Protection

As noted in the Introduction, fossil fuel energy is a major source of carbon emissions. Governments may decide to impose a carbon emission charge to address environmental externalities. If implemented, this will drive up the cost of energy-intensive production. In order to level the playing field, domestic carbon pricing can be extended to carbon-embedding imports. The recent legislative movements in the EU and elsewhere show that the issue of adjusting carbon prices at the border is entering the mainstream of climate policymaking. At the same time, carbon is not the only target of energy-affecting trade control measures. Other typical examples of such measures include air quality regulations with import-restrictive impacts and the localization of clean energy production, which some States may portray as environmentally necessary. Products with health-threatening content associated with unsafe energy use can face market access barriers as well. When energy production causes ecological or public health problems at home or depletes natural resources, export restrictions are usually among candidate measures that governments consider to employ for mitigating such adverse effects. Therefore, it is imperative to examine the existing trade rules and case law to check the legality of these energy–environment measures.

2.1 Carbon Pricing and Border Adjustments

GHG (or carbon) pricing links the external cost of GHG emissions, borne by society, to emission sources by imposing a price usually based on CO_2 emitted.[1] Through such internalization of negative externalities, a carbon price signals emitters to either alter their activities and emit less or continue emitting but pay for emissions accordingly.[2] So far, carbon

1 World Bank, 'What Is Carbon Pricing?', https://carbonpricingdashboard.worldbank.org/what-carbon-pricing.

2 Ibid.

pricing has been a domestic policy choice, but some recent developments in trade treaty-making mark the gradual switch towards making this an internationally binding practice. In particular, the EU–UK FTA (2020) requires the parties to operate 'an effective system of carbon pricing as of 1 January 2021' to cover GHG emissions from electricity generation, heat generation, industry and aviation. The parties must cooperate on carbon pricing and give 'serious consideration to linking their respective carbon pricing systems'.[3] As another example, the New Zealand–UK FTA (2022) obligates the parties to 'promote carbon pricing as an effective policy tool for reducing greenhouse gas emissions efficiently, and promote environmental integrity in the development of international carbon markets'.[4]

Most common forms of direct, or explicit, carbon pricing – that is, pricing directly proportional to emissions – include carbon tax and emission trading system (ETS).[5] Carbon taxes put a price on GHG emissions, without capping emissions. There are two types of ETS that enable emitters to trade emission units to meet their emission targets. A 'cap-and-trade' ETS places an upper limit (or 'cap') on total GHG emissions in designated sectors and auctions or distributes emission permits (or 'allowances') to emitters covered by the cap, allowing them to buy additional or sell surplus allowances. A 'baseline-and-credit' ETS has no fixed limit on total emissions per sector but defines baseline emission levels for regulated individual emitters and issues credits to covered emitters that have reduced their emissions below their baseline level, which they can then sell to other emitters in need.

2.1.1 Carbon Leakage and Countermeasures

In 2022, around seventy carbon pricing instruments (carbon taxes and ETSs) were operating in more than forty-five national jurisdictions, covering approximately 23 per cent of total global GHG emissions.[6] Because of such limited geographical scope, carbon pricing imposing extra costs on domestic firms make them less competitive than firms from countries that do not operate similar mechanisms. This, in turn, may cause 'carbon leakage' – generally speaking, an increase in GHG emissions in one

[3] Article 392 of the EU–UK Trade and Cooperation Agreement (2020).

[4] Article 22.6.2(c) of the New Zealand–UK FTA (2022).

[5] The following descriptions of carbon taxes and ETS are based on World Bank, 'State and Trends of Carbon Pricing 2022', 2022, p. 13.

[6] World Bank, 'State and Trends of Carbon Pricing 2022', p. 15.

country provoked by emission reduction measures by another country[7] – where, for example, affected firms move their carbon-intensive production to countries with weaker climate policies, or 'pollution havens'.

At least one of two approaches can help prevent or minimize carbon leakage. First, governments may initially relieve polluters from the payment obligation by, for example, allocating ETS allowances for free in the initial years. This gives subject polluters more time to adapt to a carbon pricing environment, avoiding the need to relocate to pollution havens. Second, governments may use so-called border carbon adjustments (BCAs) by putting a domestic carbon price on carbon-embedding imports. Such BCAs will level the playing field between domestic products that bear carbon cost and competing foreign products that otherwise do not, and this measure can also exert political pressure on other nations to adopt comparable climate action.[8]

With respect to the first approach above, if the relaxation of the carbon pricing regime is uneven across covered polluters, more generous relaxation for select polluters may be found to constitute a countervailable subsidy. This is what the investigative records of the US Department of Commerce (USDOC) suggest. In its final countervailing duty determinations (2020) on fluid end blocks from Italy and Germany, the USDOC concluded that the EU's ETS had subsidized polluting installations placed on a 'carbon leakage list' by granting them *additional* free allowances as compared to the remaining installations that were given only a 'standard amount' of free allowances. In essence, the USDOC reasoned that when the government did not charge *all* covered installations for the *same* amount of emissions, there was no government revenue that was *otherwise* due. But when the government additionally did not charge a *narrower* group of installations for *extra* emissions as opposed to the rest of installations, the USDOC qualified this as the foregoing of government revenue. In particular, the relevant part of the USDOC's findings reads:[9]

7 See Andrei Marcu et al., 'Carbon Leakage: An Overview', Centre for European Policy Studies, CEPS Special Report No. 79 (2013), pp. 1–3; Meredith Fowlie and Mar Reguant, 'Challenges in the Measurement of Leakage Risk', 108 *AEA Papers and Proceedings* 124 (2018), p. 124.

8 See Michael A. Mehling et al., 'Designing Border Carbon Adjustments for Enhanced Climate Action', 113 *American Journal of International Law* 433 (2019), pp. 440–441; Joost Pauwelyn and David Kleimann, 'Trade Related Aspects of a Carbon Border Adjustment Mechanism: A Legal Assessment', Briefing, European Parliament, 2020, p. 7.

9 US Department of Commerce (USDOC), Issues and Decision Memorandum for the Final Affirmative Determination of the Countervailing Duty Investigation of Forged Steel Fluid

> [U]nder the ETS program, installations are allocated emissions allowances to cover 44.2 percent of the emissions of the most efficient installations in that sector. However, certain installations, deemed to be at significant risk of carbon leakage, are provided additional free allowances to meet 100 percent of the allowances needed by the benchmark (i.e. the most efficient) installations during the POI.
>
> On this basis, we find that the ETS program has established a system in which all installations (regardless of whether the installation is on the carbon leakage list) are allocated a certain amount of allowances based on the standards of that industry. In other words, we find that there is a standard amount of allowances that are provided throughout the country on a consistent, equal basis. Therefore, we find that the allowances that cover 44.2 percent of the emissions of the most efficient installations, regardless of whether they are provided to a company on the carbon leakage list, are not countervailable, as there is no revenue forgone that is otherwise due.
>
> However, the ETS program also provides for additional emissions allowances to specific company installations as a result of those installations being placed on the carbon leakage list. We find that these additional allowances are countervailable. Companies on the carbon leakage list that receive these additional allowances are relieved of the obligation to purchase additional allowances – beyond the standard allocation of free allowances – from the government or other parties .... [T]he regulatory system specifically establishes a distinct set of rules for the companies on the carbon leakage list that is unique from the set of rules for other companies under this program. In other words, the ETS system specifically designates certain companies that do not have to incur the full costs incurred by other companies ....
>
> Further, we find it significant that the ETS program, which the EU characterizes as an environmental protection program, provides additional free allowances to pollute to essentially the worst polluters, while installations that are not on the carbon leakage list are not entitled to these additional allowances. By allowing these listed installations to not have to purchase additional emissions from the government, the government has given up its entitlement to collect revenue.

As for the second anti-leakage approach above, BCAs have been widely discussed for the last two decades, but the real practice of

End Blocks from the Federal Republic of Germany [C-428-848], 7 December 2020, pp. 48–49 (footnotes omitted); USDOC, Issues and Decision Memorandum for the Final Determination in the Countervailing Duty Investigation of Forged Steel Fluid End Blocks from Italy [C-475-841], 7 December 2020, p. 14.

domestic implementation is rather very scarce.[10] Representing a rare example of actually applied BCAs, California's cap-and-trade system, launched in 2013, requires emission allowances for imports of electricity. California is part of the Western Interconnection – a power grid passing through Canada, the United States and Mexico – and consumes over 30 per cent of electricity from out-of-state imports.[11] California's case confirms practical feasibility of BCAs but also reveals some implementation difficulties in ensuring their environmental effectiveness. In particular, local policymakers have been wrestling with preventing market players from undermining the BCA's climate efforts through 'resource shuffling'. The latter typically refers to the practice of switching from 'dirty' to 'cleaner' electricity imports so as to lessen the financial burden of paying for emission allowances, with dirty electricity going to pollution haven jurisdictions instead, which eventually causes nearly a zero effect on overall emissions.[12]

Apart from California's case, BCAs in other pertinent jurisdictions have so far remained mostly in the planning stage, with the EU recently advancing a detailed legislative draft. On 14 July 2021, the European Commission proposed a carbon border adjustment mechanism (CBAM) that will obligate importers of certain goods to report and pay for the emissions embedded in those goods. The reporting obligation will apply in the transitional period (2023–2025) and thereafter, and the payment obligation will ensue from 2026 onwards.[13] According to the proposed regulation, the CBAM aims 'to prevent the risk of carbon leakage' and 'will progressively become an alternative to' the free allocation of EU ETS emission allowances that pursues the same anti-leakage purpose.[14] Until such free allowances are completely phased out by 2035, the CBAM will

[10] Andrew Prag, 'The Climate Challenge and Trade: Would Border Carbon Adjustments Accelerate or Hinder Climate Action?', OECD, 2020, p. 14. See also Mehling et al., supra note 8, pp. 448–456.

[11] Stefan U. Pauer, 'Including Electricity Imports in California's Cap-and-Trade Program: A Case Study of a Border Carbon Adjustment in Practice', 31 *The Electricity Journal* 39 (2018), pp. 39–40.

[12] Ibid., pp. 41–45.

[13] The description of the carbon border adjustment mechanism (CBAM) below is based on EU, 'Proposal for a Regulation of the European Parliament and the Council Establishing a Carbon Border Adjustment Mechanism', 2021/0214 (COD), COM(2021) 564 final, 14 July 2021 (hereinafter the 'CBAM Draft Regulation'); European Commission, 'Carbon Border Adjustment Mechanism: Questions and Answers', 14 July 2021, https://ec.europa.eu/commission/presscorner/detail/en/qanda_21_3661.

[14] Articles 1.1 and 1.3 of the CBAM Draft Regulation, supra note 13.

apply only to the proportion of emissions that is not covered by the EU free allowances. The CBAM is comparable to, but not the same as, the ETS in various aspects, including, among others, in the following:[15]

> The EU ETS and the CBAM have a common objective of pricing GHG emissions embedded in the same sectors and goods through the use of specific allowances or certificates. Both systems have a regulatory nature and are justified by the need to curb GHG emissions, in line with the environmental objective set out in Union.
>
> However, while the EU ETS sets an absolute cap on the GHG emissions from the activities under its scope and allows tradability of allowances . . ., the CBAM should not establish quantitative limits to import, so as to ensure that trade flows are not restricted. Moreover, while the EU ETS applies to installations based in the Union, the CBAM should be applied to certain goods imported into the customs territory of the Union.

Initially, the CBAM will cover selected goods exposed to a high risk of carbon leakage (e.g., iron and steel, cement, fertilizers, aluminium and electricity), with the possibility of expanding the scope of goods later on. EU importers will have to annually declare the quantity of those goods and the amount of embedded emissions in the total goods imported in the preceding year and to surrender the corresponding amount of 'CBAM certificates' they have purchased in advance from national authorities. The excess of the purchased CBAM certificates cannot be traded among importers but can be resold to the national authorities up to one third of the total certificates purchased, with the remaining unused certificates to be cancelled. Embedded emissions of imported goods will be calculated based on verified actual emissions or else certain default values typically linked to exporting country data on the average emission intensity of the subject good. By contrast, emission levels for imported electricity will be determined by reference to default values unless the declarant chooses to use actual emission values. The CBAM will apply to direct carbon emissions in a good's production process, but the EU may later decide whether to also extend it to indirect emissions from the production of electricity used to produce the subject goods. Each CBAM certificate corresponds to one tonne of embedded emissions in goods. The price of certificates will be based on the weekly average auction price of EU ETS allowances. The idea is to peg the CBAM price to the carbon price that would have been paid, had the subject goods been produced

[15] Recitals 18 and 19 of the CBAM Draft Regulation, supra note 13.

under the EU carbon pricing regime. However, if it is shown that a carbon price has already been paid in a third country, that price will be deducted from the CBAM payment for related EU imports. Countries participating in, or connected to, the EU ETS – currently, Iceland, Liechtenstein, Norway and Switzerland – are excluded from the CBAM. On 13 December 2022, the European Parliament and the Council of the EU reached a political agreement on the implementation of the CBAM, which builds on the European Commission's 2021 proposal.[16] The proposed CBAM may undergo changes before taking effect.

As for non-EU jurisdictions, the US President's 2021 Trade Policy Agenda, for example, envisages international cooperation for developing 'market and regulatory approaches' to address GHG emissions in the world trading system. In particular, '[a]s appropriate, and consistent with domestic approaches to reduce U.S. greenhouse gas emissions, this includes consideration of carbon border adjustments'.[17] In June 2022, US Senator Sheldon Whitehouse introduced the Clean Competition Act in Congress proposing the imposition of a US 'carbon intensity charge' on domestic and imported goods beginning after 2023.[18] The government of Canada has recently explored the potential of BCAs and discussed with its partners on how BCAs could meet climate targets and secure a fair business environment.[19] In early 2023, the UK was considering introducing a carbon border tax on steel imports.[20]

BCAs have received mixed comments as to climate effectiveness and trade implications.[21] With respect to climate effectiveness, *ex ante* studies

[16] European Commission, 'European Green Deal: Agreement Reached on the Carbon Border Adjustment Mechanism (CBAM)', 13 December 2022, https://ec.europa.eu/commission/presscorner/detail/en/ip_22_7719.

[17] US Trade Representative, '2021 Trade Policy Agenda and 2020 Annual Report of the President of the United States on the Trade Agreements Program', 2021, p. 3.

[18] See US Congress, 'S.4355 – Clean Competition Act', 117th Congress (2021–2022), www.congress.gov/bill/117th-congress/senate-bill/4355/text; Shuting Pomerleau, 'What's in the Carbon Border Adjustment Bill Introduced by Senator Whitehouse?', 8 June 2022, Niskanen Center, www.niskanencenter.org/whats-in-the-carbon-border-adjustment-bill-introduced-by-senator-whitehouse.

[19] Government of Canada, 'Consultation on Border Carbon Adjustments', 1 February 2022, www.canada.ca/en/department-finance/programs/consultations/2021/border-carbon-adjustments.html.

[20] Sylvia Pfeifer and Jim Pickard, 'UK to Propose Carbon Border Tax as Part of Steel Industry Aid Package', *Financial Times*, 24 January 2023, www.ft.com/content/94eab3e5-87dd-424f-9c5a-be0d79d7cb5c.

[21] See, for example, Pascal Lamy, Geneviève Pons and Pierre Leturcq, 'Greening EU Trade 3: A European Border Carbon Adjustment Proposal', Policy Paper, Europe Jacques

generally assume that BCAs would be at least partially effective in reducing carbon leakage in energy-intensive trade-exposed sectors, but the lack of BCA practice does not allow for sufficient *ex post* assessments on the real impact.[22] Furthermore, by exerting leverage on other countries to adopt rigorous climate measures, BCAs would serve global decarbonization purposes but, depending on the design, could also conflict with the principle of common but *differentiated* responsibilities and the concept of countries' *self-defined* nationally determined contributions under the Paris Agreement.[23] As for trade effects, there is some alarm about a potential misuse of BCAs as disguised protectionism[24] as well as about trade distortions that may occur when BCAs target specific carbon-intensive inputs (e.g., steel) but omit other parts of the value chain (e.g., nails), leading to the replacement of BCA-affected input imports with unaffected downstream imports.[25] In WTO meetings, several members have expressed their concerns about the proposed CBAM's potential trade restrictiveness and discrimination against third countries and thus insisted on ensuring compliance with the WTO rules.[26] Therefore, the climate and trade-law validity of BCAs will largely hinge upon how exactly they are designed and applied.

2.1.2 BCAs and WTO Law

Under the WTO system, BCAs for carbon pricing, such as carbon tax and ETS, can raise the issue of border adjustment of taxes or regulations as considered in the following sub-sections. The focus will be on the multilateral trade provisions on tariff bindings, national treatment and

Delors, 2020; Georg Zachmann and Ben McWilliams, 'A European Carbon Border Tax: Much Pain, Little Gain', Policy Contribution No. 5, Bruegel, 2020; Henrik Horn and Petros C. Mavroidis, 'To B(TA) or Not to B(TA)? On the Legality and Desirability of Border Tax Adjustments from a Trade Perspective', 34 *The World Economy* 1911 (2011).

22 OECD, 'Climate Policy Leadership in an Interconnected World: What Role for Border Carbon Adjustments?', 2020, p. 13.

23 Ibid., pp. 28–29.

24 Henrik Horn and André Sapir, 'Can Border Carbon Taxes Fit into the Global Trade Regime?', Policy Brief No. 2013/06, Bruegel, 2013, p. 6.

25 Zachmann and McWilliams, supra note 21, pp. 9–10.

26 See, for example, WTO, Council for Trade in Goods – Minutes of the Meeting of the Council for Trade in Goods – 7 and 8 July 2022, G/C/M/143 (6 October 2022), paras. 16.1–16.48, 41.1–41.70. See also James Bacchus, 'Legal Issues with the European Carbon Border Adjustment Mechanism', CATO Briefing Paper No. 125, CATO, 2021.

subsidies. As the actual BCA practice is scarce and evolving, this is a preliminary legal analysis on BCAs.

2.1.2.1 Tax-Related BCAs

The WTO consistency of imposing domestic carbon taxes on imports is closely tied to the issue of border tax adjustment (BTA). As carbon taxes apply to domestic (and, where applicable, imported) carbon-intensive products, they qualify as an internal 'tax' rather than a customs duty, which by definition applies to imported products only.[27] A BTA is the practice of subjecting imports to, and exempting exports from, internal taxes and charges. In particular, the OECD's definition of BTAs used by the 1970 Report of the GATT Working Party on BTAs refers to:

> any fiscal measures which put into effect, in whole or in part, the destination principle (i.e. which enable exported products to be relieved of some or all of the tax charged in the exporting country in respect of similar domestic products sold to consumers on the home market and which enable imported products sold to consumers to be charged with some or all of the tax charged in the importing country in respect of similar domestic products).[28]

The destination principle mentioned in the OECD definition prescribes the collection of taxes at the final point of consumption. This contrasts with the origin principle of taxing in the country of production that obviates any need for BTAs. As domestic taxation systems remain largely disharmonized, BTAs aim to level the playing field between taxed domestic and untaxed foreign products and to prevent double taxation on a product crossing the borders from one jurisdiction to another.

With respect to the BTA-related provisions, the 1970 Working Party report above identified, inter alia, Articles II (schedules of concessions) and III (national treatment) of the GATT on the import side and Article XVI (subsidies) of the GATT on the export side.[29] Following the principle of destination, the WTO rules allow BTAs for indirect taxes imposed on products and connected to internal consumption rather than direct taxes that are imposed on producers and hence in the country of

27 WTO, Committee on Trade and Environment – Taxes and Charges for Environmental Purposes – Border Tax Adjustment – Note by the Secretariat, WT/CTE/W/47 (2 May 1997), para. 55.

28 GATT, 'Report by the Working Party on Border Tax Adjustments', L/3464 (20 November 1970), para. 4.

29 Ibid., para. 7.

production.[30] As defined in footnote 58 to Annex I(e) of the Subsidies and Countervailing Measures (SCM) Agreement, direct taxes are 'taxes on wages, profits, interests, rents, royalties, and all other forms of income, and taxes on the ownership of real property'; indirect taxes are 'sales, excise, turnover, value added, franchise, stamp, transfer, inventory and equipment taxes, border taxes and *all taxes other than direct taxes and import charges*' (emphasis added). Given that the SCM Agreement details Article XVI of the GATT, this list of taxes may well be stretched to the GATT provisions too. In the light of the italicized words above, carbon taxes seem to qualify as indirect taxes as they are not listed among direct taxes and do not fall within 'import charges' that footnote 58 of the SCM Agreement distinguishes from domestic *taxes*.[31]

On the import-side BTAs, *Ad* Article III of the GATT envisages the possibility of collecting internal taxes or charges on imported products at the border. In addition, Article II of the GATT reads in relevant part:

> 2. Nothing in this Article shall prevent any contracting party from imposing at any time on the importation of any product:
>
> (a) a charge equivalent to an internal tax imposed consistently with the provisions of paragraph 2 of Article III* in respect of the like domestic product or *in respect of an article from which the imported product has been manufactured or produced in whole or in part* [emphasis added];

The italicized part in this passage suggests border adjustability of relevant taxes targeting a product's content. The GATT's drafters explained the term 'equivalent' in Article II:2(a) as meaning that, for example, 'if a [charge] is imposed on perfume because it contains alcohol, the [charge] to be imposed must take into consideration the value of the alcohol and not the value of the perfume, that is to say the value of the content and not the value of the whole'.[32] Article III:2 of the GATT – cross-referred in Article II:2(a) – outlaws discriminatory internal taxes or charges applied, 'directly or indirectly', to products. The drafters introduced the word 'indirectly' to Article III:2 to embrace 'even a tax not on a

[30] WT/CTE/W/47, supra note 27, paras. 31–36. See also L/3464, supra note 28, para. 21.

[31] See also Christine Kaufmann and Rolf H. Weber, 'Carbon-Related Border Tax Adjustment: Mitigating Climate Change or Restricting International Trade?', 10 *World Trade Review* 497 (2011), p. 520.

[32] WTO, *Guide to GATT Law and Practice* (Geneva: WTO, 1995), Analytical Index, Vol. 1, p. 86 (citing EPCT/TAC/PV/26, p. 21).

product as such but on the *processing* of the product'.[33] Later, this point was confirmed in the GATT panel's finding in *Japan – Alcoholic Beverages I* that 'indirect' taxation under Article III:2 includes 'taxing the raw materials used in the product during the various stages of its production'.[34] Similarly, a soft drink tax – subjected to Article III:2 – in the WTO case in *Mexico – Taxes on Soft Drinks* was found to apply 'indirectly' to non-cane sugar sweeteners used for the production of taxed soft drinks and syrups.[35]

Therefore, the drafting history of the GATT and case law indicate the applicability of Articles II:2(a) and III:2 even to taxes on what a product contains. But there still remains some legal uncertainty as to the availability of BTAs to taxes targeting inputs (e.g., embedded carbon content) that are not physically present in the imported product. As a relevant case, *US – Superfund* centred on the legality of a US tax on imported substances produced from certain chemicals that were subject to US tax. The amount of tax on imported substances, in principle, equaled the amount of the US tax that would have been levied on the used chemicals if those chemicals had been sold in the United States for the use in producing substances.[36] It was alleged that the US tax was not eligible for the BTA as it was designed to tax polluting activities within the United States, and the polluter-pays principle would require the US authorities to tax only domestic products as the sole cause of pollution in the United States.[37] But the panel found that environmental purposes of taxation were not relevant to the tax's eligibility for BTA and that the BTA at issue was lawfully available to imported products derived from the chemicals that constituted a taxable base.[38] However, the panel's decision left it unclear whether those chemicals were physically present in the final product or whether they had been exhausted in the production process, making no distinction to that effect.[39]

As for export-side BTAs, footnote 1 to Article 1.1(a)(1)(ii) of the SCM Agreement does not consider as a 'subsidy' certain qualified tax exemptions or remissions on exports 'in amounts not in excess of those which have accrued'. Depending on the design and application of carbon taxes, paragraph (g) or (h) of Annex I of the SCM Agreement, connected to

[33] Ibid., p. 141 (citing EPCT/A/PV/9, p. 19; EPCT/W/181, p. 3) (emphasis added).
[34] *Japan – Alcoholic Beverages I*, GATT Panel Report, para. 5.8.
[35] *Mexico – Taxes on Soft Drinks*, WTO Panel Report, paras. 8.44–8.45, 8.59.
[36] *US – Superfund*, GATT Panel Report, paras. 2.4–2.5.
[37] Ibid., para. 5.2.3.
[38] Ibid., paras. 5.2.4, 5.2.7–5.2.8.
[39] WT/CTE/W/47, supra note 27, para. 70.

footnote 1, may apply to export-related carbon tax refunds. Specifically, Annex I(g) of the SCM Agreement allows non-excessive BTAs on indirect taxes (and carbon taxes seem to be indirect taxes as noted before) 'in respect of the production and distribution of exported products', possibly covering production/distribution-related emissions.[40] Furthermore, BTAs for 'prior-stage cumulative indirect taxes' under Annex I(h) are applicable to 'inputs that are consumed in the production of the exported product'. Carbon taxes are generally not 'cumulative', but it may be possible to make them so.[41] The definition of 'inputs' in footnote 61 of the SCM Agreement is relevant to Annex I(h)[42] and means 'inputs physically incorporated, energy, fuels and oil used in the production process and catalysts which are consumed in the course of their use to obtain the exported product'. By permitting such BTAs on exports that were produced with the use of physically unembedded 'energy, fuels and oil', the SCM Agreement here remarkably contrasts with the Tokyo Round Subsidies Code that confined export-side BTAs only to inputs 'physically incorporated' in the exported product.[43] Yet, it is not completely clear whether carbon content of products is a qualified 'input' for export BTAs under the SCM Agreement. In *India – Export Related Measures*, the panel interpreted footnote 61 above as setting forth an 'exhaustive' definition of 'inputs consumed in the production process' to the exclusion of unlisted items.[44] There, India submitted that capital goods, like machinery and equipment, used for export production contributed to the cost of exported products and were thus inputs eligible for duty drawback – an export-side BTA-like scheme for import duties. But the panel disagreed and held that an input's contribution to a product's cost was not the same as being an input 'consumed' in the production

[40] See Joost Pauwelyn, 'U.S. Federal Climate Policy and Competitiveness Concerns: The Limits and Options of International Trade Law', Working Paper No. NI WP 07-02, Nicholas Institute for Environmental Policy Solutions at Duke University, 2007, p. 20.

[41] Gary Clyde Hufbauer, Steve Charnovitz and Jisun Kim, *Global Warming and the World Trading System* (Washington, DC: Peterson Institute for International Economics, 2009), p. 45.

[42] Annex I(h) of the Subsidies and Countervailing Measures (SCM) Agreement states that it 'shall be interpreted in accordance with the guidelines on consumption of inputs in the production process contained in Annex II', and footnote 61 is included in Annex II of the SCM Agreement.

[43] See paragraphs (h) and (i) of the Annex of the Agreement on Interpretation and Application of Articles VI, XVI and XXIII of the GATT (Tokyo Round). See also WT/CTE/W/47, supra note 27, para. 74.

[44] *India – Export Related Measures*, WTO Panel Report, paras. 7.199–7.200, 7.211.

process.[45] If such exhaustiveness of the inputs list is interpreted narrowly to mean its strict limitation to the exact wording of the inputs, Annex I (h) BTA is not available to *carbon* embedded in exports. However, a broader way of interpretation may still accommodate carbon as being *part* of 'energy, fuels and oil' consumed in the production of exported products.

The WTO provisions on export-related BTAs may serve as a legal context for interpreting the reference in Article II:2(a) to 'an article from which the imported product has been manufactured or produced in whole or in part'. It is argued in the literature that such 'article', read together with the definition of 'inputs' under the SCM Agreement above, includes not only physically incorporated inputs but also inputs (like energy) that are *necessary* to the manufacturing of imported products.[46] Therefore, the existing textual acceptance, under the WTO subsidy rules, of export-side BTAs for qualified physically untraceable components (namely, energy, fuels and oil as well as possibly carbon if considered as part thereof) of a processed product could arguably open the door for supporting permissibility of such BTAs on the import side as well.

2.1.2.2 Regulation-Related BCAs

If ETS emission permits, or allowances, and CBAM certificates mirroring the ETS price qualify as a tax, the obligation to purchase them on the import side would be linked to BTAs discussed in the preceding part. Referring to the OECD's tax definition, some authors consider emission allowances as a tax because they serve community interests, and the subject entities as taxpayers do not receive anything identifiable in return.[47] The opposite view, however, is that the entities actually do obtain an identifiable benefit in the form of the permission to emit to the level that is directly proportional to the amount paid.[48]

45 Ibid., paras. 7.206–7.207.

46 Robert Howse and Antonia L. Eliason, 'Domestic and International Strategies to Address Climate Change: An Overview of the WTO Legal Issues', in Thomas Cottier, Olga Nartova and Sadeq Z. Bigdeli (eds.), *International Trade Regulation and the Mitigation of Climate Change* (New York: Cambridge University Press, 2009), p. 66.

47 See R. Ismer and K. Neuhoff, 'Border Tax Adjustments: A Feasible Way to Address Nonparticipation in Emission Trading', CMI Working Paper No. 36, 2004, p. 11; Javier de Cendra, 'Can Emissions Trading Schemes Be Coupled with Border Tax Adjustments? An Analysis vis-à-vis WTO Law', 15 *RECIEL* 131 (2006), pp. 135–136; Pauwelyn, supra note 40, p. 21.

48 Tracey Epps and Andrew Green, *Reconciling Trade and Climate: How the WTO Can Help Address Climate Change* (Cheltenham and Northampton: Edward Elgar, 2010), p. 138.

In *Air Transport Association of America and Others*, the Court of Justice of the EU examined the EU requirement for airline companies to hold allowances for CO_2 emitted during all their operated flights entering and leaving EU airspace. The number of allowances for aircraft operators was based on their fuel consumption for the covered flights in the preceding year and an emission factor.[49] The Court of Justice of the EU found that this scheme did not constitute 'a duty, tax, fee or charge' on fuel consumption on the following grounds: there was no direct link between the quantity of fuel consumed by an aircraft and the actual cost of obtaining allowances; the scheme did not intend to generate public revenues; and the price of allowances was set by the market rather than pre-determined by the government.[50]

The 'non-tax' view is also deducible from the 2021 decision of the Supreme Court of Canada on constitutionality of the country's 2018 Greenhouse Gas Pollution Pricing Act. The Supreme Court concluded that excess emission charges – paid by covered facilities for emitting above the fixed caps under an 'output-based pricing system' – were *not* a 'tax' but a 'regulatory charge'. The charges at issue were not qualified as a tax because they served to change individual behaviour towards reducing GHG emissions and were set at a specific level necessary for that purpose rather than for generating revenue to recover the cost of the related emission reduction scheme.[51]

Should the reasoning of the Court of Justice of the EU and Canada's Supreme Court be used for identifying taxes covered by WTO law, one may argue that emission permits and CBAM certificates are not internal taxes under Article III:2 of the GATT[52] and thus not eligible for BTAs under Article II:2(a) of the GATT. If not a tax, they can still fall within

[49] See Directive 2008/101/EC of the European Parliament and of the Council of 19 November 2008 amending Directive 2003/87/EC so as to include aviation activities in the scheme for greenhouse gas emission allowance trading within the Community, OJ L 8, 13 January 2009, pp. 3–21.

[50] *Air Transport Association of America and Others*, Judgment of the Court (EU), paras. 142–143.

[51] *References re Greenhouse Gas Pollution Pricing Act*, Supreme Court Judgment (Canada), 25 March 2021, paras. 212–219.

[52] See Lorand Bartels, 'The WTO Legality of the Application of the EU's Emission Trading System to Aviation', 23 *European Journal of International Law* 429 (2012), pp. 439–440. For the opposing view, see Joshua Meltzer, 'Climate Change and Trade – The EU Aviation Directive and the WTO', 15 *Journal of International Economic Law* 111 (2012), pp. 130–131.

'laws, regulations and requirements affecting . . . internal sale, offering for sale, purchase, transportation, distribution or use' of products within the meaning of Article III:4 of the GATT. The proposed CBAM regulation states explicitly that both the EU ETS and the CBAM 'have a *regulatory* nature'.[53] According to the Appellate Body in *Korea – Various Measures on Beef*, Article III:4 is deemed to be violated when all three following factors exist: (i) imported and domestic products are 'like products'; (ii) the measure at issue is a 'law, regulation, or requirement'; and (iii) the imported products are accorded 'less favourable' treatment.[54] The first and third factors are especially controversial.

In particular, the first factor above will check whether carbon intensity can make, say, high-carbon foreign cement and low-carbon domestic cement 'unlike' so as to justify the requirement for the former to obtain the bigger number of allowances or CBAM certificates. In the WTO, panellists have largely avoided directly addressing the relevance of so-called non-product-related processes and production methods (NPR-PPMs) – that is, PPMs not leaving any physical traces on the product – such as genetic modification,[55] fishing methods[56] or hunting methods[57] to the likeness test. By contrast, the unadopted GATT panel report in *US – Tuna (Mexico)* was straightforward in stating that a difference in NPR-PPMs was irrelevant to the likeness determination as 'Article III covers only measures affecting products as such'.[58] This rationale is yet questionable in the light of WTO jurisprudence. Indeed, in *Brazil – Taxation*, the Appellate Body disagreed with Brazil that contended that

[53] Recital 18 of the CBAM Draft Regulation (emphasis added), supra note 13.

[54] *Korea – Various Measures on Beef*, WTO Appellate Body Report, para. 133.

[55] See *EC – Approval and Marketing of Biotech Products*, WTO Panel Reports, para. 7.3422 (see also paras. 7.3418, 7.3420) on judicial economy for the consistency of safeguard measures with Article III:4 of the GATT as applied to subject biotech agricultural products versus domestic non-biotech products.

[56] See *US – Tuna II (Mexico) (Article 21.5 – Mexico)*, WTO Panel Report, paras. 7.71, 7.496 where the panel accepted the parties' agreement that tuna products at issue were 'like', without considering whether the difference in fishing methods affected the likeness of those products. In the context of Article 2.1 (non-discrimination) of the Technical Barriers to Trade (TBT) Agreement in the original dispute, the panel focused on 'a comparison between Mexican tuna products and tuna products of US origin and tuna products originating in any other country, not between dolphin-safe and not dolphin-safe tuna' (*US – Tuna II (Mexico)*, WTO Panel Report, para. 7.250).

[57] See *EC – Seal Products*, WTO Panel Reports, paras. 7.138–7.140, 7.607 relying on the absence of the parities' doubt about the likeness of seal products, regardless of seal hunting.

[58] *US – Tuna (Mexico)*, GATT Panel Report, paras. 5.11, 5.15.

Article III was 'applicable only to measures which affect a *product* once it has been produced and enters the marketplace' and 'not to production (pre-market)' measures that do not concern a product as such but rather impose 'process and production-step requirements'.[59] The Appellate Body countered that neither Article III:2 on tax discrimination nor Article III:4 on regulatory discrimination excludes, from its respective scope, measures 'directed at producers' that modify the conditions of competition between imported and domestic products.[60] Therefore, a likeness determination under Article III:4 – which is 'fundamentally, a determination about the nature and extent of a competitive relationship between and among products'[61] – may consider carbon-related PPMs in principle, although the outcome would vary depending on facts in each case. In particular, if consumers' preferences in the importing country are affected by the climate (un)friendliness of PPMs, carbon intensity would matter in the context of at least consumers' tastes and habits. The latter is one of the four commonly used 'like product' criteria, along with the products' properties, end-uses and tariff classification. In *EC – Asbestos*, the Appellate Body admitted that health risks (such as carcinogenicity or toxicity) posed by products could be evaluated under the likeness criteria of physical properties and of consumers' tastes and habits.[62] But the Appellate Body there also emphasized that the 'like product' standard requires a *cumulative* analysis of *all* relevant criteria, without tilting to a single criterion alone:[63]

> It is our view that, having adopted an approach based on the four [likeness] criteria . . ., the Panel should have examined the evidence relating to *each* of those four criteria and, then, weighed *all* of that evidence, along with any other relevant evidence, in making an *overall* determination of whether the products at issue could be characterized as 'like'. . .. [A] determination on the 'likeness' of products cannot be made on the basis of a partial analysis of the evidence, after examination of just one of the criteria the Panel said it would examine.
>
> . . .
>
> In many cases, the evidence will give conflicting indications, possibly within each of the four criteria. For instance, there may be some evidence of similar physical properties and some evidence of differing physical

[59] *Brazil – Taxation*, WTO Appellate Body Reports, paras. 5.8, 5.14 (emphasis in original).
[60] Ibid., paras. 5.15–5.16. See also *Brazil – Taxation*, WTO Panel Reports, paras. 7.63–7.70.
[61] *EC – Asbestos*, WTO Appellate Body Report, para. 99.
[62] Ibid., paras. 113–114, 122.
[63] Ibid., paras. 109 (emphasis in original), 120.

properties. Or the physical properties may differ completely, yet there may be strong evidence of similar end-uses and a high degree of substitutability of the products from the perspective of the consumer.

Thus, even if environmentally conscious consumers distinguish otherwise identical products by their carbon footprint (based on, for example, a carbon label), such consumers' tastes and habits alone do not suffice to make high-carbon and low-carbon products unlike.[64] Rather, it must be a holistic determination showing that these products are unlike.

As for the third element of the Article III:4 test, treatment of imported products is 'less favourable' when a governmental measure worsens the conditions of competition for them relative to domestic counterparts.[65] This may happen where, for instance, the granting of free allowances to domestic products can give them a competitive advantage over imported like products that are subject to BCAs. As another example, the now-unrealized Lieberman–Warner Bill (2007) on introducing a cap-and-trade system in the United States envisaged that the number of allowances to be purchased by domestic firms was proportional to their *own* emissions in relation to a *particular good*, but that for importers was based on the *average* of emissions by the exporting country's all firms producing *multiple goods within a particular category*.[66] If designed so or in a similar way, ETS schemes with such uneven-handed features could be found to treat imported goods less favourably in violation of Article III:4. In the case of the EU CBAM proposal, it allows the use of *actual* emissions of imported goods in calculations as a principle. For electricity, it prefers the use of default values due to 'the impossibility to follow the actual flow of electrons', but it gives declarants the opportunity to claim

64 See, for example, Erich Vranes, *Trade and the Environment: Fundamental Issues in International Law, WTO Law, and Legal Theory* (Oxford: Oxford University Press, 2009), p. 324; Reinhard Quick and Christian Lau, 'Environmentally Motivated Tax Distinctions and WTO Law: The European Commission's Green Paper on Integrated Product Policy in Light of the "Like Product-" and "PPM-" Debates', 6 *Journal of International Economic Law* 419 (2003), p. 432. On the other hand, some commentators defend source-neutral PPMs as being consistent with Article III. See Robert Howse and Donald Regan, 'The Product/Process Distinction – An Illusory Basis for Disciplining "Unilateralism" in Trade Policy', 11 *European Journal of International Law* 249 (2000); Steve Charnovitz, 'The Law of Environmental "PPMs" in the WTO: Debunking the Myth of Illegality', 27 *Yale Journal of International Law* 59 (2002).

65 *Dominican Republic – Import and Sale of Cigarettes*, WTO Appellate Body Report, para. 93.

66 Paul-Erik Veel, 'Carbon Tariffs and the WTO: An Evaluation of Feasible Policies', 12 *Journal of International Economic Law* 749 (2009), p. 769.

CBAM calculations based on actual emissions (instead of default values) subject to certain criteria.[67] In addition, the exclusion from the CBAM of emissions benefiting from EU ETS free allowances would prevent imports from paying for the carbon cost for which EU producers do not, which appears to avoid less favourable treatment vis-à-vis imports.[68]

Should BCAs – whether tax-based or regulation-based – be found to be illegal under WTO law, they may still rely on the WTO exceptions where applicable. For example, the Appellate Body has already confirmed the invocability of the GATT general exceptions for GATT-inconsistent NPR-PPM policies affecting the transboundary environment.[69]

2.1.2.3 Some External Implications of BCAs

Unlike the case of BTAs that are applicable to both imports and exports in general, many commentators suggest BCAs on imports, not on exports, because otherwise export-side BCAs may undermine climate policy efforts by incentivizing domestic carbon-intensive production to work for export, with carbon cost refunded.[70] Along the same lines, the complainants in *US – Superfund* argued that it was 'inappropriate' for the United States to exempt exports of certain chemicals from a tax as this would essentially free those chemicals from bearing the cost of environmental pollution caused by their production in the United States.[71] Besides environmental considerations, export-related refunds of (or exemptions from) some carbon payments for, say, ETS allowances, if considered as a regulatory measure rather than a border-adjustable tax/charge, may not qualify as proper BTAs under the SCM Agreement.[72] On the other hand, without export-side BCAs, carbon-paying products

[67] Recital 45, Article 7 and Annex III of the CBAM Draft Regulation, supra note 13.

[68] The European Commission explains that 'until [free allowances] are completely phased out in 2035, the CBAM will apply only to the proportion of emissions that does not benefit from free allowances under the EU ETS, thus ensuring that importers are treated in an even-handed way compared to EU producers'. See European Commission, supra note 13.

[69] See, for example, *US – Shrimp*, WTO Appellate Body Report, para. 121.

[70] See, for example, OECD, supra note 22, p. 21; Mehling et al., supra note 8, pp. 473–474; Aaron Cosbey, Michael Bernstein and Seton Stiebert, 'Enabling Climate Ambition: Border Carbon Adjustment in Canada and Abroad', International Institute for Sustainable Development and Clean Prosperity, 2021, p. 12.

[71] *US – Superfund*, GATT Panel Report, para. 3.2.7. At issue was, however, the import-side border tax adjustment (BTA), and the panel declined to examine the environmental aspect of the US measure (paras. 5.2.4–5.2.6).

[72] See Kateryna Holzer, *Carbon-Related Border Adjustment and WTO Law* (Cheltenham and Northampton: Edward Elgar, 2014), pp. 201–205.

may lose their competitiveness in overseas markets. At a minimum, BCA jurisdictions should agree, with respect to products traded across their borders, to mutually recognize carbon payments already made in one jurisdiction and prevent double remedies for embedded emissions.[73] However, in order for this to be effective, the number of BCA jurisdictions should increase so that the expanded geography of carbon-taxed trade would lessen the probability for these products to move to non-BCA jurisdictions and face carbon-related competitive disadvantages there. The 'climate clubs' discussed in the following section could likely contribute to the proliferation of BCAs.

Furthermore, BCAs should reflect the interests of vulnerable countries many of which have historically not emitted much but desire industrialization for economic development. In this respect, a recent study (2021) of the UN Conference on Trade and Development (UNCTAD) using a general equilibrium model estimates that the EU CBAM will reduce exports of developing countries, but not developed countries, in targeted sectors and will create a similar gap between the two in terms of welfare.[74] While BCAs do not put an outright import prohibition as it was in *US – Shrimp*, the Appellate Body's comment made in that dispute in the context of the *chapeau* of Article XX is quite telling:

> [I]t is not acceptable, in international trade relations, for one WTO Member to use an economic embargo to *require* other Members to adopt essentially the same comprehensive regulatory program, to achieve a certain policy goal, as that in force within that Member's territory, *without* taking into consideration different conditions which may occur in the territories of those other Members.[75]

Therefore, in order to avoid 'arbitrary or unjustifiable discrimination' (as proscribed by the *chapeau* of Article XX) and to be in line with the environmental principle of common but differentiated responsibilities,

[73] A source of inspiration could come from, for example, linking arrangements entered into by some emission trading system (ETS) jurisdictions to accept each other's allowance units for compliance under their respective ETS. See James Munro, *Emissions Trading Schemes under International Economic Law* (Oxford: Oxford University Press, 2018), pp. 129–132.

[74] UNCTAD, 'A European Union Carbon Border Adjustment Mechanism: Implications for Developing Countries', 2021, pp. 3, 23–24. See also Zachmann and McWilliams, supra note 21, p. 11; Christoph Böhringer, Jared C. Carbone and Thomas F. Rutherford, 'Embodied Carbon Tariffs', 120 *Scandinavian Journal of Economics* 183 (2018), pp. 183, 207–208.

[75] *US – Shrimp*, WTO Appellate Body Report, para. 164 (emphasis in original).

the BCA-imposing jurisdictions should take account of special conditions of LDCs and other vulnerable developing countries. One conceivable approach would be, for instance, to exempt them from BCAs, relying on, inter alia, the 1979 Decision on Differential and More Favourable Treatment, Reciprocity and Fuller Participation of Developing Countries (also known as the 'Enabling Clause') as a possible legal context for justification.[76] When non-horizontal, or selective, BCA exclusions within the developing country group are adopted, these should be subject to *objective* eligibility criteria like the level of development, climate change effects, climate mitigation efforts and so on, as one can infer from WTO jurisprudence on the Enabling Clause.[77] WTO waivers could also be sought. However, such country-specific exemptions, even if legally defendable, may spur carbon leakage to the exempted countries concerned. Instead, an environmentally better alternative would be to increase decarbonization financing/technical assistance and green technology transfers to LDCs and other developing countries in need.[78] The existing S&D and Aid for Trade regimes could provide necessary legal avenues for this. Revenues from BCAs could be used here as a source of financing.[79] Such assistance approach would help beneficiary countries continue their development path without compromising the climate.

2.1.3 Climate Clubs

Carbon pricing policies can be synchronized through 'climate clubs' – a coalition of countries with harmonized emission reductions that gives

[76] See Kateryna Holzer, 'Proposals on Carbon-Related Border Adjustments: Prospects for WTO Compliance', 1 *Carbon & Climate Law Review* 51 (2010), p. 59; OECD, supra note 22, pp. 16, 20–21.

[77] See *EC – Tariff Preferences*, WTO Appellate Body Report, paras. 178–188.

[78] See, for example, Recital 55 of the CBAM Draft Regulation, supra note 13; European Commission, 'Impact Assessment Report Accompanying the Document: Proposal for a Regulation of the European Parliament and of the Council Establishing a Carbon Border Adjustment Mechanism', Commission Staff Working Document, SWD(2021) 643 final (14 July 2021), p. 30.

[79] For example, 25 per cent of revenues raised under the US Clean Competition Act proposal (2022) was planned for spending to help developing countries decarbonize. See Shuting Pomerleau, 'What's in the Carbon Border Adjustment Bill Introduced by Senator Whitehouse?', 8 June 2022, Niskanen Center, www.niskanencenter.org/whats-in-the-carbon-border-adjustment-bill-introduced-by-senator-whitehouse. See also Tatiana Falcão, 'Toward Carbon Tax Internationalism: The EU Border Carbon Adjustment Proposal', 98 *Tax Notes International* 1047 (2020), p. 1052.

benefits to members and penalties to non-members.[80] Climate clubs are meant to curb free riding by non-members in relation to carbon emission reductions by members. Recently, two initiatives have been proposed to put this concept into practice.

First, in June 2022, the Group of Seven (G7) nations agreed to establish a 'Climate Club'. Under the adopted terms of reference, this club 'will provide a high-ambition intergovernmental forum for discussion and serve as an enabling framework for increased cooperation, improved coordination and potential collective action'. In particular, the club will advance ambitious and transparent climate mitigation policies, facilitate sectoral industry decarbonization and boost international climate cooperation and partnerships. Its agenda includes, inter alia, the countering of carbon leakage and cooperation in the funding of industry decarbonization in emerging and developing countries. Specific activities of the club can engage all or a subset of members. Planned for a full launch in 2023, the Climate Club is open to 'climate-ambitious countries' that are committed to the full and effective implementation of the Paris Agreement, a zero-emission transition by mid-century, accelerated industrial decarbonization and the collective promotion of the club's objectives.[81]

Second, in October 2021, the EU and the United States agreed to negotiate a global steel and aluminium arrangement (also known as a 'Global Arrangement on Sustainable Steel and Aluminium') to 'restore market-oriented conditions and address carbon intensity'. This industry-specific initiative would essentially restrict market access for non-participants that fall short of market economy conditions and contribute to non-market overcapacity and that do not meet low-carbon intensity standards.[82] The idea is to create a global club of like-minded market-oriented economies for low-carbon metals trade that would erect trade

[80] See William Nordhaus, 'Climate Clubs: Overcoming Free-Riding in International Climate Policy', 105 *American Economic Review* 1339 (2015).

[81] See Group of Seven (G7), 'G7 Statement on Climate Club', 28 June 2022, www.g7germany.de/resource/blob/974430/2057926/2a7cd9f10213a481924492942dd660a1/2022-06-28-g7-climate-club-data.pdf; G7, 'Terms of Reference for the Climate Club', 12 December 2022, www.g7germany.de/resource/blob/974430/2153140/a04dde2adecf0ddd38cb9829a99c322d/2022-12-12-g7-erklaerung-data.pdf?download=1.

[82] See USDOC, 'Steel and Aluminum U.S.–EU Joint Statement', 31 October 2021, www.commerce.gov/news/fact-sheets/2021/10/steel-and-aluminum-us-eu-joint-statement. For steel overcapacity, see Sherzod Shadikhodjaev, 'Steel Overcapacity and the Global Trading System', 16 *Asian Journal of WTO & International Health Law and Policy* 179 (2021).

barriers for non-participants. A US concept paper, presented to the EU in December 2022, reportedly proposes imposing a carbon intensity tariff on intra-club trade, which would be higher for non-member countries.[83] However, the embedded approach to combine both market economy and decarbonization issues within the same legal framework appears to be environmentally questionable and counterproductive. Indeed, it is not ruled out that countries with non-market practices in steel and aluminium can produce in an environmentally friendly way and pollute less than club members. If so, their exclusion from the club may lower the decarbonization ambition of this initiative. But if these countries are heavy polluters and refuse to abandon their non-market practices, they will not have any motivation to green their metal industries. As non-members, they will have to pay higher tariffs anyway just because of their non-market policies, which they do not want to relinquish. In short, greening efforts should be delinked from the market economy conditions in order to effectively promote environmentally sustainable behaviour.

The two initiatives above are evolving, so precise trade-law implications are yet to be seen. But the potential for discriminating against non-participating countries is worrisome. The availability of WTO environmental exceptions for possible discriminatory treatment largely hinges upon how climate clubs would eventually operate. Moreover, climate clubs could be made part of RTAs to be justified by the WTO provisions on preferential trade, subject to the strict requirements laid down by those provisions for valid RTAs, inter alia, to cover 'substantially all the trade' and not to raise barriers to trade with third countries.[84] Another alternative would be to negotiate a WTO open-ended climate club agreement, and the ongoing TESSD could serve as a forum for exploring this possibility.

Climate clubs look promising in harmonizing domestic decarbonization policies, which can be enabled through the establishment of common rules and the sharing of information, expertise and best

[83] See David Lawder, 'U.S. Floats New Steel, Aluminum Tariffs Based on Carbon Emissions', Reuters, 8 December 2022, www.reuters.com/business/sustainable-business/us-floats-new-steel-aluminum-tariffs-based-carbon-emissions-2022-12-08/; Ana Swanson, 'U.S. Proposes Green Steel Club That Would Levy Tariffs on Outliers', *The New York Times*, 7 December 2022, www.nytimes.com/2022/12/07/business/economy/steel-tariffs-climate-change.html.

[84] For the WTO rules on RTAs, see Sherzod Shadikhodjaev, 'Checking RTA Compatibility with Global Trade Rules: WTO Litigation Practice and Implications from the Transparency Mechanism for RTAs', 45 *Journal of World Trade* 529 (2011), pp. 530–536.

practices among members. But to become truly meaningful, such clubs should not leave out major emitters and developing countries. Using penalties against outsiders can divert their trade from climate clubs towards non-club members. More green assistance is needed to developing countries to make them prepared for accepting the club-anticipated level of climate ambition. It is true that at the UNFCCC's Conference of Parties in 2009, developed countries already committed to a goal of mobilizing jointly $100 billion per year by 2020 for climate action in developing countries. But this goal was never reached, so it was extended to 2025.[85] Perhaps even more funding would be needed to accelerate global decarbonization.

2.2 Energy-Related Trade Restrictions

Border adjustments linked to carbon pricing policies can help reduce the fossil-energy intensity of trade. In addition to these decarbonization measures, governments may also employ other types of trade restrictions against energy, energy-using or energy-affected products in the name of the environment. As the following sections will show, these measures connected to internal environmental factors or external risks are not always successful in passing trade-law scrutiny.

2.2.1 Import Restrictions and Environmental Policy Space

Because the scope of import restrictions and associated legal issues is broad, this part of the book will focus on WTO jurisprudence regarding import-related measures on vehicle fuels, solar energy products and radioactively contaminated fishery products. Specifically, *US – Gasoline* and *Brazil – Taxation* explore whether discrimination by anti-pollution policies is justifiable under the GATT environmental exceptions. The *India – Solar Cells* case offers some insights into whether a member's compliance with its international environmental obligations can justify its WTO violations. Unlike these three cases, *Korea – Radionuclides (Japan)* about food safety measures adopted in response to external 'energy–environment' risks deals with a more specialized WTO regime, accommodating environmental considerations, than GATT Article XX.

[85] OECD, 'Climate Finance and the USD 100 Billion Goal', www.oecd.org/climate-change/finance-usd-100-billion-goal/.

2.2.1.1 Improvement of Air Quality

More than 92 per cent of the world's population lives in areas that do not meet the World Health Organization's guideline for healthy air.[86] Unsurprisingly, an increasing number of countries have been adopting policy actions – typically, incentives, requirements and standards – to improve air quality in manufacturing, transportation, waste management, agriculture and elsewhere.[87]

Remarkably, the very first adjudication case in the WTO was about an anti-pollution measure. In particular, in *US – Gasoline*, US clean air rules aimed at reducing vehicle emissions permitted only gasoline of certain cleanliness to be sold on the domestic market. These rules violated national treatment under Article III of the GATT as importers had to comply with an *average* (or 'statutory') baseline for cleanliness that was not connected to the specific gasoline imported while, at the same time, refiners of domestic gasoline had only to meet *individual* baselines linked to their *own* product.[88] The US measure fell within the scope of Article XX(g) of the GATT on the conservation of exhaustible natural resources given that 'a policy to reduce the depletion of clean air was a policy to conserve a natural resource'.[89] But even so, it was inconsistent with the *chapeau* of Article XX as the United States could actually have avoided 'unjustifiable discrimination' and a 'disguised restriction on international trade' by imposing a statutory baseline without differentiation between domestic and imported gasoline or by making individual baselines available to not only domestic but also foreign refiners.[90]

In *Brazil – Taxation*, an INOVAR-Auto programme maintained discriminatory tax preferences and accreditation requirements in the automotive sector contrary to Article III of the GATT. Brazil invoked Article XX(b) of the GATT on life or health protection and contended that this programme actually sought to improve vehicle safety and reduce CO_2 emissions through better energy efficiency.[91] It also argued that

[86] UN Environment Programme (UNEP), 'Actions on Air Quality: A Global Summary of Policies and Programmes to Reduce Air Pollution', 2021, p. 13.

[87] See ibid., pp. 5–47.

[88] *US – Gasoline*, WTO Panel Report, paras. 6.10, 6.14–6.16.

[89] Ibid., para. 6.37.

[90] *US – Gasoline*, WTO Appellate Body Report, pp. 25, 27–29.

[91] *Brazil – Taxation*, WTO Panel Reports, para. 7.864. Brazil submitted that 78 per cent of total national carbon emissions in transportation derived from the use of individual vehicles, so that anti-pollution measures in this field had a direct impact on improving air quality and reducing the risks of respiratory problems (para. 7.878).

less-trade-restrictive alternatives (such as the extension of fiscal benefits to all vehicles meeting safety and energy efficiency standards, regardless of the origin) would actually undermine another objective of the INOVAR-AUTO programme, namely the technological development of the Brazilian automotive industry.[92] The panel did recognize that the reduction of CO_2 emissions was indeed a policy objective covered by Article XX(b).[93] However, reasonably available alternatives, the panel said, could not be rejected simply because they did not contribute to a different objective that was not protected under Article XX.[94] As for Article XX(g) also invoked by Brazil, the panel agreed that petroleum – which could be conserved through increased vehicle fuel efficiency – was a finite exhaustible natural resource.[95] But it concluded that Brazil had not demonstrated that there was 'a close and genuine relationship of ends and means' between the discriminatory features of the INOVAR-AUTO programme and the objective of increasing energy efficiency.[96] Interestingly enough, the panel admitted that 'under certain circumstances', the discriminatory aspects of the programme in question could potentially contribute in the long term to the environmental objectives claimed under Articles XX(b) and XX(g):[97]

> In the view of the Panel, it is conceivable that the protection afforded to domestic producers by the discriminatory aspects of the measure could enable such domestic producers to develop their industry. The development of the industry could enable an otherwise uncompetitive domestic industry to become competitive, resulting in technological development within the industry, and ultimately enabling the domestic industry to produce more energy-efficient and safer motor vehicles. Ultimately, by elevating the domestic industry from a position of technological and competitive inferiority to a position in which the domestic industry could compete with foreign motor vehicles, the INOVAR-AUTO programme could conceivably contribute in the long-run to overall vehicle safety as well as overall reductions in CO_2 emissions.[98]

However, Brazil failed to present evidence demonstrating how this possibility was likely to materialize. In fact, the counterargument was that

[92] Ibid., para. 7.936.
[93] Ibid., paras.7.880–7.881.
[94] Ibid., paras. 7.941–7.942, 7.947, 7.952, 7.956.
[95] Ibid., para. 7.986 (referring to *US – Shrimp*, WTO Appellate Body Report, para. 128).
[96] Ibid., para. 7.996.
[97] Ibid., paras. 7.903, 7.905, 7.994–7.995.
[98] Ibid., para. 7.904.

the discriminatory treatment excluding many imported fuel-efficient vehicles from the market could actually weaken domestic industry's competitiveness and technological capabilities.[99]

Both *US – Gasoline* and *Brazil – Taxation* cases address the same question: why is discrimination necessary for improving air quality? Unjustified burden on foreign products or preferences solely for domestic products could generally indicate the protectionist nature of measures camouflaged with environmental rationales. The *Brazil – Taxation* panel did agree that hypothetically, protectionism (or, in the panel's words, 'the protection afforded to domestic producers by the discriminatory aspects of the measure') has the potential to develop local green industries and thereby contribute to the decarbonization goals, but how exactly this would work in practice remains unclear. The overall message, deducible from these cases, is that protectionist measures are unlikely to pass the Article XX standards for environmental exceptions if the imposing government can realistically accomplish the underlying environmental objectives without discriminating. This has important implications for many pertinent policies. For example, the US Inflation Reduction Act of 2022, aimed to 'build a new clean energy economy',[100] offers tax credits of up to $7,500 to purchasers of qualified electric vehicles, or 'clean vehicles', that underwent final assembly in North America. To be eligible for the maximum tax credit, a certain amount of the vehicle battery's critical minerals must be extracted or processed in the United States or the US FTA signatory country or recycled in North America, and a specified value of the battery's components must be produced or assembled in North America.[101] These requirements clearly discriminate against many electric cars produced in other parts of the world, and the environmental relevance of these requirements is questionable. The Inflation Reduction Act could actually achieve greater and faster

[99] Ibid., paras. 7.919–7.921, 7.995.

[100] US White House, 'Biden-Harris Administration Releases Inflation Reduction Act Guidebook for Clean Energy and Climate Programs', 15 December 2022, www.whitehouse.gov/briefing-room/statements-releases/2022/12/15/biden-harris-administration-releases-inflation-reduction-act-guidebook-for-clean-energy-and-climate-programs/.

[101] See Molly F. Sherlock, 'Clean Vehicle Tax Credits in the Inflation Reduction Act of 2022', US Congressional Research Service, 2022, https://crsreports.congress.gov/product/pdf/IN/IN11996. The original text of the US Inflation Reduction Act of 2022 is available at www.democrats.senate.gov/imo/media/doc/inflation_reduction_act_of_2022.pdf.

decarbonization if those discriminatory elements were removed to promote the domestic consumption of green cars from everywhere. Non-discriminatory incentives here could also prevent or minimize subsidy-related trade frictions as no country would likely complain against foreign consumption subsidies that benefit its products.

2.2.1.2 Localization of Clean Energy Production

Local content requirements (LCRs) in solar and wind energy industries have been on the rise globally especially since 2009, with twenty-four developed and developing countries having active solar and wind LCRs as of 2021.[102] In the anticipation of greater industrial development and increased employment, governments apply LCRs typically in the form of the requirement for solar or wind electricity generators to use a minimum amount of locally produced goods (solar cells, wind blades, etc.) or services as a precondition for granting financial or fiscal support, public procurement awards or preferential electricity tariffs.[103] While politically attractive, renewable energy LCRs may turn out to be costly and economically inefficient.[104] If a domestic product or service is competitive and good enough, producers would make use of it without LCRs. But if their choice is limited by LCRs, this would encourage import substitution, consequently discouraging competition for local content suppliers, which, in turn, would drive up the costs of renewable energy

[102] Megan Hogan, 'Local Content Requirements Threaten Renewable Energy Uptake: Featuring a List of Local Content Requirements in Wind and Solar Industries', Peterson Institute for International Economics, 6 December 2021, www.piie.com/blogs/trade-and-investment-policy-watch/local-content-requirements-threaten-renewable-energy-uptake.

[103] See Jan-Christoph Kuntze and Tom Moerenhout, 'Local Content Requirements and the Renewable Energy Industry – A Good Match?', International Centre for Trade and Sustainable Development, 2013, p. 5. See also Sherzod Shadikhodjaev, 'Industrial Policy in Asia-Pacific Integration: Localization Measures and Subsidies in ASEAN Countries, 31 *Asia Pacific Law Review* 618 (2023).

[104] See Morgan Bazilian, Victoria Cuming and Thomas Kenyon, 'Local-Content Rules for Renewables Projects Do Not Always Work', 32 *Energy Strategy Reviews* (2020) 100569; Benedict Probst et al., 'The Short-Term Costs of Local Content Requirements in the Indian Solar Auctions', 5 *Nature Energy* 842 (2020). For local content requirements (LCRs) in general, see, for example, Gary Clyde Hufbauer et al., *Local Content Requirements: A Global Problem* (Washington, DC: Peterson Institute for International Economics, 2013); Sherzod Shadikhodjaev, *Industrial Policy and the World Trade Organization: Between Legal Constraints and Flexibilities* (Cambridge: Cambridge University Press, 2018), pp. 147–193.

production to the detriment of environmental policy efforts.[105] Instead of LCRs, governments could actually opt for providing incentives directly to the production of local content, in which case local content prices would fall, making downstream producers more willing to buy local content.[106]

Since 2010, LCRs concerning renewable energy have been challenged in the WTO often in connection with the subsidy rules as shown in Chapter 3.[107] Most recently, the EU in *UK – CfD Local Content (EU)* asked for consultations with the UK over the latter's LCR in low-carbon (mainly offshore wind) energy generation. The EU alleges that the UK is violating Article III (national treatment) of the GATT by making the use of local content an eligibility criterion for a governmental support scheme, which is 'covering the difference between the cost of low carbon electricity generation and the regular market price for electricity through the payment of a subsidy'.[108] In previous WTO cases, LCRs under renewable energy programmes were found to be inconsistent with the WTO trade-in-goods provisions on national treatment.[109] Where a government purchased renewable electricity produced under LCR-conditioned incentives, such purchases were not considered to be WTO-perceived government procurement that would otherwise exempt LCRs from the national treatment provisions. Because the government was procuring renewable electricity rather than LCR-subjected electricity-generating inputs, discrimination by LCRs against foreign electricity-generating inputs was found to be not covered by the government procurement's derogation from the WTO national treatment principle.[110]

In *India – Solar Cells*, India obligated solar power developers to use locally produced solar cells and solar modules in exchange for long-term government-guaranteed purchases of renewable electricity. As mentioned in Chapter 1, India considered the LCR as a means of developing the

[105] For economic effects of LCRs, see, for example, OECD, 'Overcoming Barriers to International Investment in Clean Energy', OECD, 2015, pp. 59–64.

[106] From a legal perspective, this could, of course, raise allegations about actionable subsidies, but these subsidies are anyway not prohibited in the WTO as local content subsidies are.

[107] See Sections 3.2.2 and 3.2.3.

[108] WTO, *United Kingdom – Measures Relating to the Allocation of Contracts for Difference in Low Carbon Energy Generation* – Request for Consultations by the EU, WT/DS612/1, G/L/1428 (30 March 2022).

[109] See *US – Renewable Energy*, WTO Panel Report, paras. 7.339–7.340, 8.4–8.6; *India – Solar Cells*, WTO Panel Report, paras. 8.2–8.3; *Canada – Renewable Energy / Canada – Feed-in Tariff Program*, WTO Panel Reports, paras. 8.2, 8.6.

[110] See, for example, *India – Solar Cells*, WTO Appellate Body Report, paras. 5.25–5.44.

domestic solar energy capacity to reduce the risks of supply disruption and hence preserve the country's energy security. To justify its national treatment violation, India also invoked Article XX(d) of the GATT and claimed that the LCR met that provision's wording as a measure 'necessary to secure compliance with laws or regulations which are not inconsistent with the provisions of [the GATT]'. India stated that such 'laws or regulations' included certain international environmental instruments, namely the preamble of the WTO Agreement, the UNFCCC, the Rio Declaration and the UN General Assembly Resolution A/RES/66/288 (2012) (Rio + 20 Document: 'The Future We Want'). India contended that these instruments embodied its obligation 'to ensure ecologically sustainable growth while addressing India's energy security challenge, and ensuring compliance with its obligations relating to climate change'.[111]

Although India's defence under Article XX(d) failed,[112] the Appellate Body's interpretation here have important implications for the energy–environment nexus. The Appellate Body acknowledged that international (environmental) instruments could qualify as 'laws or regulations' in the sense of Article XX(d) under two conditions. First, these instruments must become part of the member's domestic legal system through any of the three means: incorporation via legislative or executive implementation, direct effect without such implementation or 'other ways' available under the domestic system.[113] Second, these instruments must operate with 'a sufficient degree of normativity and specificity under the domestic legal system of a Member so as to set out a rule of conduct or course of action'.[114] As clarified, normativity may be proved not only by legal enforceability but also by other possible characteristics derivable from the respective national regime and the instrument itself.[115] In particular, the Appellate Body held:

> We do not consider that the scope of 'laws or regulations' is limited to instruments that are legally enforceable (including, e.g. before a court of law), or that are accompanied by penalties and sanctions to be applied in situations of non-compliance. Instead, as we see it, the concept is broader and may, in appropriate cases, include rules in respect of which a Member

[111] Ibid., para. 5.94, n. 275 to para. 5.92, para. 5.96.

[112] For details, see Sherzod Shadikhodjaev, 'India – Certain Measures Relating to Solar Cells and Solar Modules', 111 *American Journal of International Law* 139 (2017), pp. 142–143, 145–146.

[113] *India – Solar Cells*, WTO Appellate Body Report, para. 5.140.

[114] Ibid., para. 5.141, footnote omitted.

[115] Ibid., para. 5.121.

> seeks to 'secure compliance', even when compliance is not coerced, for example, through the imposition of penalties or sanctions.[116]

The appellate ruling in this case is remarkable for accepting 'other ways' of making international law part of the domestic legal order (subject to the respective national system) in addition to the incorporation and direct effect methods as is commonly contemplated as well as for broader interpretation of normativity. This opens the door wider (than one could otherwise expect) for qualifying, say, GATT-consistent international energy–environment rules – even soft law with sufficient normativity – as part of municipal law, compliance with which could justify associated trade-restrictive environmental measures under Article XX(d) of the GATT.

2.2.1.3 Restrictions against Radioactive Contamination of Foods

On 11 March 2011, the Great East Japan Earthquake, measuring 9.0 on the Richter scale, triggered a tsunami that reached the Fukushima Daiichi Nuclear Power Plant, causing a nuclear emergency and a release of radioactive material into the environment. Immediately following this accident, many countries banned food imports from this area.[117] Korea, for example, imposed import bans and additional testing requirements for fishery and non-fishery products from Japan to protect human health from the risks arising from contaminants, notably certain radionuclides, contained in those products. Radionuclides, such as caesium, strontium, plutonium and radioactive iodine, are a source of ionizing radiation, exposure to which can cause cancer and various bone diseases.[118]

In *Korea – Radionuclides*, Japan challenged Korea's import measures under the SPS Agreement.[119] According to Article 5.6 of the SPS Agreement, WTO members must ensure that SPS measures are 'not more trade-restrictive than required to achieve their appropriate level of sanitary or phytosanitary protection, taking into account technical and economic feasibility'. SPS measures are deemed to be so unless there is another 'reasonably available' measure that achieves such appropriate

[116] Ibid., para. 5.109.
[117] Yong-Shik Lee, 'Regulatory Autonomy under the WTO Agreement on Sanitary and Phytosanitary Measures: Implications of *Korea–Import Bans, and Testing and Certification Requirements for Radionuclides*', 20 *World Trade Review* 321 (2021), p. 324.
[118] See *Korea – Radionuclides*, WTO Panel Report, paras. 2.1, 2.12–2.18.
[119] Ibid., paras. 2.12–2.13, 2.112–2.116, 7.26.

level and is 'significantly less restrictive to trade' (footnote 3 to Article 5.6). The panel accepted Korea's own definition of the appropriate level of SPS protection (hereinafter 'ALOP') as consisting of both qualitative and quantitative aspects regarding radioactivity levels in food consumed in Korea, namely: (i) the levels existing in the ordinary environment (i.e., in the absence of radiation from a major nuclear accident), (ii) the levels of radioactive contamination in food being 'as low as reasonably achievable' and (iii) a quantitative dose exposure of 1 millisievert per year as the upper limit of tolerable risk.[120] While accepting the multi-faceted nature of Korea's ALOP, the panel focused on the quantitative (third) element and concluded that Korea violated Article 5.6 as it could have used an alternative measure proposed by Japan to achieve ALOP in a less trade-restrictive manner.[121] However, the Appellate Body reversed this finding because of the panel's failure to additionally consider the qualitative elements of ALOP so as to examine whether the suggested alternative measure satisfied *all* of the elements of ALOP identified by Korea and accepted by the panel.[122] In addition, the Appellate Body reversed the panel's finding under Article 2.3 of the SPS Agreement that reads:

> Members shall ensure that their sanitary and phytosanitary measures do not arbitrarily or unjustifiably discriminate between Members where identical or similar conditions prevail, including between their own territory and that of other Members. Sanitary and phytosanitary measures shall not be applied in a manner which would constitute a disguised restriction on international trade.

In this context, the panel's analysis centred on actual contamination (radionuclide concentration) levels in food products in determining whether 'similar conditions' prevailed between Japan and other members. On appeal, Korea criticized the panel for ignoring other relevant factors too, in particular 'the environmental and ecological conditions in Japan and the status of the [Fukushima Dai-ichi Nuclear Power Plant]' as well as post-accident continuous releases of radionuclides which make conditions in Japan different.[123] Agreeing with Korea, the Appellate Body concluded that the panel should have examined both actual contamination levels *and* the potential for

[120] Ibid., paras. 7.162–7.163, 7.172, 7.247.

[121] Ibid., paras. 7.251–7.256, as summarized in *Korea – Radionuclides*, WTO Appellate Body Report, paras. 5.25–5.28.

[122] *Korea – Radionuclides*, WTO Appellate Body Report, paras. 5.36–5.39.

[123] Ibid., para. 5.54.

contamination. It faulted the panel for limiting the scope of relevant 'conditions' to the risk *present* in products, without accounting for different degrees of *potential* contamination or territorial conditions in Japan and the rest of the world. The panel omitted these factors despite its own recognition that there could be 'greater potential for contamination near the source' and that 'specific release events could result in a localized and incremental increase in the potential for contamination of food'.[124]

The *Korea – Radionuclides* case provides some lessons for defining acceptable boundaries of policy space on energy–environment issues under the SPS Agreement. As an important part of members' regulatory autonomy, setting ALOP is both the prerogative and implicit obligation of members under the SPS Agreement.[125] The Appellate Body in this dispute once again confirmed that ALOP does not need to be expressed in quantitative terms and may thus include qualitative elements. While Korea's self-determined ALOP had both quantitative and qualitative components, quantification may not necessarily be possible in other circumstances affected by environmental disasters. If so, ALOP based solely on qualitative considerations (e.g., seriousness of environmental or public health conditions) would be accepted under the SPS Agreement, provided that the definition of ALOP is sufficiently precise to allow the relevant provisions of the SPS Agreement including Article 5.6 to apply.[126] In addition, the Article 2.3 findings seem to approve of SPS measures vis-à-vis a particular foreign territory when *potential* (i.e., not-yet-manifested) risks from that territory differ from comparable potential risks from other territories. This arguably gives more room under members' regulatory autonomy to customize their preemptive SPS actions depending on severity of environmental risks abroad.

2.2.2 Export Restrictions and Environmental Policy Space

Broadly speaking, export restrictions comprise governmental measures that limit the quantity of exports, necessitate export permits or levy special charges (duties, taxes or fees) on exports.[127] These measures have also been imposed on energy products (Table 2.1).

[124] Ibid., paras. 5.89–5.93.
[125] *Australia – Salmon*, WTO Appellate Body Report, paras. 199, 206.
[126] See ibid., para. 206.
[127] See *US – Export Restraints*, WTO Panel Report, para. 8.17.

Table 2.1 *Selected export measures on energy products*

Measure	Targeted products	Applying member
Export duty	Mineral fuels, oil, waxes	China (2018)
	Electricity, mineral oils, solid hydrocarbons	Congo (2017)
	Coal	Kyrgyz Republic (2014)
	Natural gas	Russia (2016); Ukraine (2016)
	Coal, (crude) petroleum oil, oils obtained from bituminous minerals	Viet Nam (2021)
Export prohibition	Petroleum, petroleum products except those produced from natural gas	Bangladesh (2019)
	Kerosene components, jet fuel, diesel oil, biodiesel	Bolivia (2018)
	Liquefied petroleum gas	El Salvador (2016)
	Light fuels oils, petroleum products	Kyrgyz Republic (2014)
	Petrol, diesel, kerosene oil, liquefied petroleum gas, air fuel	Nepal (2019)
Export quota	Coal, crude oil, refined oil	China (2018)
Export permit/ licensing	Nuclear materials	Australia (2020); Kyrgyz Republic (2014)
	Automotive gas oil (diesel), gasoline (premium and regular), kerosene	Brunei Darussalam (2015)
	Liquid hydrocarbons from oil fields, refined petroleum etc.	Bolivia (2018)
	Natural gas	El Salvador (2016)
	Coal, coal-based products	Indonesia (2021)
	Radioactive materials	Philippines (2018); Tanzania (2019)
	Petroleum products	Senegal (2018); Malawi (2016); Nigeria (2017)
	Coal, petroleum products	Tunisia (2016)
	Natural gas, electric power	United States (2019)
	Nuclear and radioactive substances	Georgia (2016)
	Oil, gas	Indonesia (2021)

Table 2.1 (*cont.*)

Measure	Targeted products	Applying member
	Mineral fuels, mineral oils and products of their distillation, bitumen substances, mineral wax, engine oil	Kuwait (2012)
	Coal, coke	Malaysia (2018)
	Electricity, nuclear substances, radioactive minerals/sources	Mongolia (2021)
	Radioactive and nuclear waste	Norway (2019)
	Radioactive materials, filled gas cylinders	Saudi Arabia (2021)
Minimum export price	Coal	Colombia (2018)
Export recommendation	Electricity, petroleum, natural gas	Myanmar (2021)

Source: Author's compilation from information in the WTO Secretariat's trade policy review reports (WT/TPR/S/*).
Note: The year in parentheses next to the applying member is the year of issue of the respective trade policy review report.

Export restrictions on resource products are quite often linked to health and environmental concerns.[128] For example, during the WTO accession, Cambodia explained that it 'levied export taxes on certain unprocessed raw materials and products to encourage local processing, encourage exports of finished products and *to protect human health*'.[129] A number of WTO trade policy review reports mention such export control rationales as protection of the environment or health, conservation of natural resources and non-proliferation of nuclear materials.[130]

128 Jeonghoi Kim, 'Recent Trends in Export Restrictions on Raw Materials', in OECD, *The Economic Impact of Export Restrictions on Raw Materials* (OECD Trade Policy Studies, 2010), p. 18.

129 WTO, Working Party on the Accession of Cambodia – Report of the Working Party on the Accession of Cambodia, WT/ACC/KHM/21 (15 August 2003), para. 109 (emphasis added).

130 See, for example, WTO, Trade Policy Review Body (TPRB) – Trade Policy Review – Report by the Secretariat – China – Revision, WT/TPR/S/375/Rev.1 (14 September 2018), p. 62, para. 3.76; WTO, TPRB – Trade Policy Review – Report by the Secretariat – Australia – Revision, WT/TPR/S/396/Rev.1 (29 July 2020), p. 60,

2.2.2.1 Legal Constraints

While export restrictions are subject to several WTO provisions,[131] Articles XI and XX of the GATT are especially relevant to our topic. Article XI:1 of the GATT outlaws any 'prohibitions or restrictions other than duties, taxes or other charges, whether made effective through quotas, import or export licences or other measures' applied to 'the exportation or sale for export of any product'. In other words, this provision bans quantitative export restrictions but allows export duties ('duties, taxes or other charges' on exports).

The WTO prohibition against quantitative export restrictions, in principle, applies to all members alike, but the permission of export duties does not. When considered together with accession commitments, the WTO regime regarding export duties creates 'unequal rights and obligations'.[132] Indeed, unlike the overwhelming majority of members that are free to use export duties allowed by Article XI:1, less than twenty members have committed to restrict the use of export duties by minimizing their use, eliminating, reducing, binding such duties or foreclosing any future use.[133] Some members' export duty commitments concern hydrocarbon energy products.[134]

para. 3.60; WTO, TPRB – Trade Policy Review – Report by the Secretariat – Bangladesh – Revision, WT/TPR/S/385/Rev.1 (21 May 2019), p. 52, para. 3.46; WTO, TPRB – Trade Policy Review – Report by the Secretariat – Georgia – Revision, WT/TPR/S/328/Rev.1 (18 March 2016), p. 53, para. 3.80; WTO, TPRB – Trade Policy Review – Report by the Secretariat – Indonesia – Revision, WT/TPR/S/401/Rev.1 (5 February 2021), Table 3.8, p. 97; WTO, TPRB – Trade Policy Review – Report by the Secretariat – The State of Kuwait – Revision, WT/TPR/S/258/Rev.1 (28 February 2012), Table III.8, p. 40.

131 See, for example, WTO, Working Party on the Accession of Armenia – Report of the Working Party on the Accession of the Republic of Armenia, WT/ACC/ARM/23 (26 November 2002), para. 112; WTO, Working Party on the Accession of Ukraine – Report of the Working Party on the Accession of Ukraine to the WTO, WT/ACC/UKR/152 (25 January 2008), para. 255.

132 Julia Ya Qin, 'Reforming WTO Discipline on Export Duties: Sovereignty over Natural Resources, Economic Development and Environmental Protection', 46 *Journal of World Trade* 1147 (2012), p. 1162.

133 Ibid., pp. 1161–1162; Chiedu Osakwe, Dayong Yu and Petra Beslać, 'Export Duty Commitments: The Treaty Dialogue and the Pattern of Commitments', in Uri Dadush and Chiedu Osakwe (eds.), *WTO Accessions and Trade Multilateralism: Case Studies and Lessons from the WTO at Twenty* (Cambridge: Cambridge University Press, 2015), p. 743.

134 See, for example, Part V of the Schedule of Concessions and Commitments on Goods (Schedule CLXV – The Russian Federation), reproduced in WTO, Working Party on the Accession of the Russian Federation – Report of the Working Party on the Accession of

As the literature suggests, the attempts of acceding members to textually link, in accession instruments, their export duty commitments to the GATT Article XX exceptions were generally opposed by working party members on the grounds that such linkage could undermine those commitments.[135] This might partly explain why only few acceded members secured policy space specifically for export duty commitments. In particular, Ukraine assured the working party that in implementing its binding schedule, it 'would not increase export duties, nor apply other measures having an equivalent effect, *unless justified under the exceptions of the GATT 1994*'.[136] Further, while not mentioning Article XX per se, Russia and Kazakhstan undertook not to exceed their bound levels for the scheduled export duties on energy and other listed products, 'except in accordance with' the provisions of the GATT 1994.[137] By contrast, the Appellate Body in *China – Raw Materials* agreed with the panel that because of the absence of any textual reference to Article XX in paragraph 11.3 of China's Accession Protocol regarding the accession commitment on export duties, China was not allowed to invoke Article XX for justifying export duty violations.[138] As acknowledged by the panel, China's situation here differs from that of many other WTO members:

> The Panel is mindful that excluding the applicability of Article XX justifications from the obligations contained in Paragraph 11.3 means

the Russian Federation to the World Trade Organization – Schedule CLXV – The Russian Federation – Part I – Schedule of Concessions and Commitments on Goods – Addendum, WT/ACC/RUS/70/Add.1, WT/MIN(11)/2/Add.1 (17 November 2011); WTO, Part V of the Schedule of Concessions and Commitments on Goods (Schedule CLXXII – Republic of Kazakhstan), reproduced in WTO, Working Party on the Accession of the Republic of Kazakhstan – Report of the Working Party on the Accession of the Republic of Kazakhstan – Schedule CLXXII – Republic of Kazakhstan – Addendum, WT/ACC/KAZ/93/Add.1 (23 June 2015).

135 Osakwe et al., supra note 133, pp. 744–745.

136 WT/ACC/UKR/152, supra note 131, para. 240 (emphasis added).

137 See Part V of the Schedule of Concessions and Commitments on Goods (Schedule CLXV – The Russian Federation) in WT/ACC/RUS/70/Add.1, WT/MIN(11)/2/Add.1, supra note 134; Part V of the Schedule of Concessions and Commitments on Goods (Schedule CLXXII – Republic of Kazakhstan) in WT/ACC/KAZ/93/Add.1, supra note 134.

138 *China – Raw Materials*, WTO Appellate Body Reports, paras. 306–307. Paragraph 11.3 of China's Accession Protocol states that China 'shall eliminate all taxes and charges applied to exports unless specifically provided for in Annex 6 of this Protocol or applied in conformity with the provisions of Article VIII of the GATT 1994'. See WTO, Accession of the People's Republic of China – Decision of 10 November 2001, WT/L/432 (23 November 2001).

> that China is in a position unlike that of most other WTO Members who are not prohibited from using export duties, either via the terms of their respective accession protocols or their membership to the WTO at the time of its inception. However, based on the text before us, the Panel can only assume that this was the intention of China and the WTO Members when negotiating China's Accession Protocol. The situation created by this provision taken in isolation may be perceived as imbalanced, but the Panel can find no legal basis in the Protocol or otherwise to interpret Paragraph 11.3 of China's Accession Protocol as permitting resort to Article XX of the GATT 1994.[139]

Unlike the above case with export duties being deprived of the defence of Article XX, quantitative export restrictions prohibited by GATT Article XI may still be justified by the exceptions under Article XX. The fragmented, or unequal, availability of the general exceptions across the WTO legal system is difficult to accept given the systemic importance of Article XX-based policy space to all members alike, so WTO legislative reforms are required to rectify this puzzling situation.[140]

2.2.2.2 Pro-environmental Considerations

One study observes that export duties could be used to avoid BCAs in export markets. The idea is that exporting countries could tax embedded emissions upon exportation of related products (and hence keep the fiscal revenue at home) into carbon-pricing countries that provide credits (carbon price deductions/exemptions) for imports that have already paid a carbon price abroad.[141] However, because such carbon export duties must comply with the MFN principle,[142] their application to products destined for countries *not* using BCAs would lead to unnecessary price increases for those products there. If export duties are nevertheless imposed only on products going to BCA-using jurisdictions to obtain carbon credits, the genuineness of the exporting country's climate actions is doubted as the primary objective of the export duties would be to avoid carbon pricing in the importing country rather than to tax embedded carbon.

139 *China – Raw Materials*, WTO Panel Reports, para. 7.160 (footnote omitted).

140 See Shadikhodjaev, supra note 104, pp. 224–227.

141 See Baris Karapinar and Kateryna Holzer, 'Legal Implications of the Use of Export Taxes in Addressing Carbon Leakage: Competing Border Adjustment Measures', 10 *New Zealand Journal of Public and International Law* 15 (2012).

142 Ibid., p. 34.

2.2.2.2.1 General Exceptions In *China – Raw Materials* and *China – Rare Earths*, Article XX was invoked for quantitative export restrictions and export duties. For export duties, the panels ruled out the applicability of Article XX to China's accession commitment as mentioned before but nevertheless decided to proceed to the merits of defence on the *arguendo* assumption that Article XX was applicable to these measures.[143]

To recall, Article XX(b) of the GATT deals with trade measures 'necessary to protect human, animal or plant life or health'. In *China – Raw Materials*, China linked this clause to its export duties and export quotas on 'energy-intensive, highly polluting, resource-based products', such as coke, magnesium metal, manganese metal and silicon carbide.[144] China argued that these measures would protect its population's health by reducing demand abroad and consequently domestic production and environmental pollution.[145] But the panel said that in general, export restrictions did not address environmental externalities as pollution costs derived from domestic production rather than exports or consumption abroad.[146]

In *China – Rare Earths*, the panel again turned down China's defence based on Article XX(b) in relation to export duties on rare earths, tungsten and molybdenum that China said were part of its 'comprehensive policy to protect the environment'. China contended that the mining and production of these products had caused soil, water and air pollution and hence 'grave harm' to the environment and consequently to the life and health of humans, animals and plants in China.[147] While accepting this fact, the panel found that the export duties did not make a 'material contribution' to the purported societal protection. These measures, albeit triggering possible price hikes abroad, could actually cause a fall in prices of the targeted materials at home and, as a result, an increase in domestic consumption for making value-added downstream products, eventually leading to greater mining/production and environmental pollution.[148] Furthermore, China failed to convince why making some other already-existing Chinese measures (i.e., volume restrictions and pollution

[143] *China – Raw Materials*, WTO Panel Reports, paras. 7.229–7.230; *China – Rare Earths*, WTO Panel Reports, para. 7.140.
[144] *China – Raw Materials*, WTO Panel Reports, para. 7.470.
[145] Ibid., paras. 7.471, 7.494.
[146] Ibid., para. 7.586.
[147] *China – Rare Earths*, WTO Panel Reports, paras. 7.149–7.155.
[148] Ibid., paras. 7.156–7.185.

controls on mining/production, resource and pollution taxes) *stricter* could not be an alternative to address ecological damage.[149]

Under Article XX(g) of the GATT on conservation measures, China contended that refractory-grade bauxite and fluorspar, used in steel and aluminium production, were scarce and not easily substitutable natural resources being 'essential for its sustainable development' and in need of protection.[150] However, the panel found that a policy of restricting extraction would better serve to achieve conservation than export restrictions, which could have 'long-term negative effects on conservation due to the increased demand from the downstream sector'.[151]

To conclude, unlawful export restrictions on energy resources driven by environmental considerations are not likely to pass the Article XX test when imposing members have failed to take alternative or additional internal restrictions to tackle the problem at the source through sustainable mining, production or consumption. Some developing countries are said to have 'better institutional capacity to control trade than to control domestic production and consumption', so that 'administering export restrictions could be a more, if not the only, feasible policy option to target environmental externalities'.[152] If so, these countries should still try to employ legally 'safer' options than prohibited quantitative export restrictions. For example, most WTO members are free to use MFN-compliant export duties, without any need to rely on Article XX. Being generally permitted, export duties have the potential to help conserve energy resources to some extent if an increase in domestic consumption of these resources caused by export duties does not completely offset a reduction in their overseas consumption.[153]

2.2.2.2.2 Carve-Out for Some Quantitative Export Restrictions Article XI:2(a) of the GATT states that the provisions of Article XI:1 banning quantitative trade restrictions 'shall not extend to … [e]xport prohibitions or restrictions temporarily applied to prevent or relieve critical shortages of foodstuffs or other products essential to the exporting contracting party'. According to the appellate interpretation,

149 Ibid., para. 7.186.

150 *China – Raw Materials*, WTO Panel Reports, paras. 7.356, 7.411.

151 Ibid., paras. 7.428, 7.430.

152 Baris Karapinar, 'Export Restrictions and the WTO Law: How to Reform the "Regulatory Deficiency"', 45 *Journal of World Trade* 1139 (2011), p. 1152.

153 Qin, supra note 132, p. 1171.

Article XI:2(a) covers 'a measure applied for a limited time, a measure taken to bridge a "passing need"' that addresses 'crucial' deficiencies in quantity of 'foodstuffs or otherwise absolutely indispensable or necessary products'.[154] The products here may include, for example, foodstuffs used in bioenergy production and energy products essential to the exporting member.

In *China – Raw Materials*, China argued that its export quota on refractory-grade bauxite – being in operation for about a decade – was needed to address the critical shortage of this material that, according to China's estimation, could be depleted in sixteen years or so.[155] While agreeing that refractory-grade bauxite was 'essential' to China because of its usage in the production of such important products as steel, the panel eventually rejected this defence (and the Appellate Body upheld this conclusion) as China had failed to show a 'critical shortage' of this material and that the quota at issue was 'temporarily applied' within the meaning of Article XI:2(a).[156] The panel noted that the textual differences of Article XX(g), in particular its *chapeau* requirements not existent in Article XI:2(a), lent support to its interpretation that the measure covered by Article XI:2(a) must be of a limited duration and not indefinite. To interpret otherwise, the panel said, would allow members to 'resort indistinguishably to either Article XI:2(a) or XX(g) to address the problem of an exhaustible natural resource'.[157] The Appellate Body, however, had reservations about the panel's concern over indistinguishable resort to Article XI:2(a) or XX(g):[158]

> Members can resort to Article XX of the GATT 1994 as an exception to justify measures that would otherwise be inconsistent with their GATT obligations. By contrast, Article XI:2 provides that the general elimination of quantitative restrictions *shall not extend to* the items listed under subparagraphs (a) to (c) of that provision. This language seems to indicate that the scope of the obligation not to impose quantitative restrictions itself is limited by Article XI:2(a). Accordingly, where the requirements of Article XI:2(a) are met, there would be no scope for the application of Article XX, because no obligation exists.[159]

[154] *China – Raw Materials*, WTO Appellate Body Reports, paras. 323, 324, 326.

[155] *China – Raw Materials*, WTO Panel Reports, paras. 7.239–7.242, 7.322, 7.348–7.350.

[156] Ibid., paras. 7.340, 7.346, 7.351, 7.355; *China – Raw Materials*, WTO Appellate Body Reports, para. 344.

[157] *China – Raw Materials*, WTO Panel Reports, paras. 7.257–7.258.

[158] *China – Raw Materials*, WTO Appellate Body Reports, para. 333.

[159] Ibid., para. 334 (emphasis in original).

Thus, when a quantitative restriction on exports of exhaustible energy resources falls within the scope of Article XI:2(a), it is considered to be a measure excluded from (and thus not violating) the prohibition of Article XI:1. Article XX(g) would not apply here as there is no violation of Article XI:1 to be justified. At the same time, the Appellate Body did not rule out the co-existence of quantitative restrictions and conservation measures on the same exhaustible resource:

> We do not exclude that a measure falling within the ambit of Article XI:2(a) could relate to the same product as a measure relating to the conservation of an exhaustible natural resource. It would seem that Article XI:2(a) measures could be imposed, for example, if a natural disaster caused a 'critical shortage' of an exhaustible natural resource, which, at the same time, constituted a foodstuff or other essential product. Moreover, because the reach of Article XI:2(a) is different from that of Article XX(g), an Article XI:2(a) measure might operate simultaneously with a conservation measure complying with the requirements of Article XX(g).[160]

The reach of Article XI:2(a) is not the same as that of Article XX(g) because, inter alia, the former relates to Article XI:1 only while the latter to GATT obligations more broadly.[161] This fact would allow for Article XX defence vis-à-vis a measure that falls within Article XI:2(a) – hence, derogating from Article XI:1 – but violates other GATT provisions, say, Article I on MFN to which Article XX is applicable.

2.3 Concluding Remarks

Carbon pricing mechanisms compel many producers into low-carbon production. However, the market concerned may be distorted when carbon-intensive like products are not equally exposed to the carbon payment. With the introduction of the EU CBAM, BCAs are gaining promise as a practical measure to maintain fair carbon competition within the EU market. This may set an example for other jurisdictions to follow. If properly designed and applied without unwarranted discrimination among targets, BCAs will likely pass the WTO legal scrutiny. At the same time, the interests of LDCs and other vulnerable developing countries should be preserved, and part of BCA revenues could be used for decarbonizing those countries. Furthermore, the idea of climate clubs

[160] Ibid., para. 337.

[161] *China – Raw Materials*, WTO Panel Reports, para. 7.300 as approved of by the Appellate Body in *China – Raw Materials*, WTO Appellate Body Reports, para. 337.

needs a careful thought to ensure maximum inclusivity and prevent the widening gap with pollution havens.

If protectionism underlies carbon measures and other 'environmental' trade measures, this is neither helpful nor effective in addressing environmental externalities. Restricting market access for imports of environmentally efficient goods, with the aim of shielding domestic goods from fair competition, can undermine the national green agenda. Likewise, export restrictions on energy resources may not accomplish the conservation or anti-pollution purposes when the root of the problem is actually in the production or domestic consumption that is not adequately curtailed or greened.

3

Energy Subsidies and the Environment

Import and export restrictions discussed in Chapter 2 are not the only trade measures connected to public interest at the intersection of energy and the environment. Besides them, such industry-aiding government interventions as energy subsidies also have environmental implications. The IEA defines 'energy subsidy' as 'any government action that concerns primarily the energy sector that lowers the cost of energy production, raises the price received by energy producers or lowers the price paid by energy consumers'.[1] Such subsidies are granted to promote energy security, employment and economic growth, foster innovation and achieve social and/or environmental goals.[2] Energy subsidies are subject to WTO disciplines. Removing fossil fuel subsidies will help reduce fossil CO_2 emissions to the levels necessary to contain global warming[3] and improve public health by cutting premature global air pollution deaths by more than half.[4] By contrast, providing subsidies for renewable energy can advance a climate-friendly policy of diversifying and decarbonizing national energy systems. Thus, the energy–environment nexus here centres on the issues of eliminating harmful fossil fuel subsidies, on the one hand, and exploring policy flexibilities for renewable energy subsidies, on the other.

[1] IEA, 'Carrots and Sticks: Taxing and Subsidising Energy', Note on Energy Subsidies and Taxes, 17 January 2006, www.iea.org/publications/freepublications/publication/oil_subsidies.pdf.

[2] Ilaria Espa and Sonia E. Rolland, 'Subsidies, Clean Energy, and Climate Change', International Centre for Trade and Sustainable Development and World Economic Forum, 2015, p. 1.

[3] Ian Parry, Simon Black and Nate Vernon, 'Still Not Getting Energy Prices Right: A Global and Country Update of Fossil Fuel Subsidies', IMF Working Paper No. WP/21/236, 2021, p. 5.

[4] David Coady et al., 'How Large Are Global Energy Subsidies?', IMF Working Paper No. WP/15/105, 2015, pp. 25–26.

3.1 Fossil Fuel Subsidies

The UN SDG 12 on ensuring sustainable consumption and production calls for the rationalization of inefficient fossil fuel subsidies that encourage wasteful consumption 'by removing market distortions . . . including by restructuring taxation and phasing out those harmful subsidies . . . to reflect their environmental impacts', taking fully into account development issues.[5] But the current multilateral treaties on climate change and trade are not sufficiently powerful in pushing countries into reforming fossil fuel subsidies.

3.1.1 The Scope of Subsidies and Policy Agenda

Fossil fuel subsidies are given to producers and/or consumers. The IEA, the OECD and the International Monetary Fund (IMF) operate related databases covering different methodologies, target countries and fuels (with or without electricity and heat).[6] The estimated amounts of fossil fuel subsidies vary significantly ranging from $440 billion in 2021 (IEA)[7] to $697.2 billion in 2021 (OECD and IEA)[8] and $5.9 trillion in 2020 (IMF).[9]

Under the IEA's price-gap approach, a fossil fuel subsidy is what constitutes the difference between a fuel's market price (usually an adjusted international reference price) and its actual (lower) price charged to domestic consumers. The IEA database captures consumption subsidies in forty-plus countries.[10]

By contrast, the OECD applies an inventory approach, which lists government measures (currently, around 1,500 individual policy measures in fifty-one economies), such as budgetary transfers and tax

5 UN, 'Transforming Our World: The 2030 Agenda for Sustainable Development', https://sustainabledevelopment.un.org/post2015/transformingourworld. See also Section 1.1.2.

6 See Masami Kojima and Doug Koplow, 'Fossil Fuel Subsidies: Approaches and Valuation', Policy Research Working Paper No. WPS7220, World Bank, 2015.

7 IEA, 'Energy Subsidies: Tracking the Impact of Fossil-Fuel Subsidies', www.iea.org/topics/energy-subsidies.

8 OECD, 'Support for Fossil Fuels Almost Doubled in 2021, Slowing Progress toward International Climate Goals, according to New Analysis from OECD and IEA', 29 August 2022, www.oecd.org/newsroom/support-for-fossil-fuels-almost-doubled-in-2021-slowing-progress-toward-international-climate-goals-according-to-new-analysis-from-oecd-and-iea.htm.

9 Parry et al., supra note 3, p. 1.

10 See IEA, supra note 7.

expenditures that provide a benefit or preference to fossil fuel producers or consumers.[11] The inventory approach is useful in understanding the overall scale and forms of energy-related public support.[12]

The IMF's database covering more than 170 countries distinguishes between 'pre-tax' and 'post-tax' fossil fuel subsidies. Pre-tax subsidies follow the IEA's price-gap concept. Post-tax subsidies include the cost of negative externalities, such as air pollution and climate change, not reflected in fuel prices through a corrective 'Pigouvian' tax. Post-tax subsidies are several times larger in size than pre-tax subsidies primarily because of the high environmental cost.[13] The IMF methodology helps us grasp the magnitude of fossil fuel under-pricing and environmental externalities.

Fossil fuel subsidies are problematic because they crowd out social spending, undermine energy efficiency, disproportionately benefit high-income households and encourage energy smuggling.[14] But subsidies are continuously provided due to the strategic importance of energy, misconceptions about their effectiveness in supporting economic and development objectives, the strong lobbying power of beneficiaries or governments' inability to adopt efficient alternative policies.[15]

The issue of fossil fuel subsidy reforms has frequently appeared on international agenda. In 2009, the G20 leaders recognized the negative role of fossil fuel subsidies in impeding clean energy investment and undermining climate change actions and therefore committed to '[r]ationalize and phase out over the medium term inefficient fossil fuel subsidies that encourage wasteful consumption' while providing targeted support to those in need.[16] Reconfirming this commitment,[17] the Asia-Pacific Economic Cooperation (APEC) now encourages 'those member economies that are

[11] See OECD, 'OECD Work on Support for Fossil Fuels', www.oecd.org/fossil-fuels/. For the OECD methodology, see www.oecd.org/fossil-fuels/methodology/.

[12] Kojima and Koplow, supra note 6, pp. 23–24.

[13] See Coady et al., supra note 4.

[14] Filip Savatic, 'Fossil Fuel Subsidy Reform: Lessons from the Indonesian Case', Studies No. 06/16, IDDRI, 2016, pp. 16–20.

[15] Shelagh Whitley and Laurie van der Burg, 'Fossil Fuel Subsidy Reform: From Rhetoric to Reality', Working Paper, New Climate Economy, 2015, pp. 26–28; Elizabeth Bast et al., 'Empty Promises: G20 Subsidies to Oil, Gas and Coal Production', Overseas Development Institute and Oil Change International, 2015, p. 67.

[16] G20 Information Centre, 'G20 Leaders Statement: The Pittsburgh Summit', Pittsburgh, 24–25 September 2009, para. 29, www.g20.utoronto.ca/2009/2009communique0925.html.

[17] APEC, '2009 Leaders' Declaration', Singapore, 14 November 2009, www.apec.org/Meeting-Papers/Leaders-Declarations/2009/2009_aelm.aspx.

in a position to do so, to implement a voluntary standstill on inefficient fossil fuel subsidies'.[18] The G7 pledged to eliminate inefficient fossil fuel subsidies by 2025 and 'end new direct public support for the international unabated fossil fuel energy sector by the end of 2022, except in limited circumstances clearly defined by each country consistent with a 1.5°C warming limit and the goals of the Paris Agreement'.[19]

Since 2010, an informal forum called 'Friends of Fossil Fuel Subsidy Reform' – consisting of non-G20 countries such as Costa Rica, Denmark, Ethiopia, Finland, the Netherlands, New Zealand, Norway, Sweden, Switzerland and Uruguay – has worked to raise international awareness of the fossil fuel subsidy problem and campaign for reform in this field.[20]

As for international monitoring procedures, the G20 facilitates voluntary peer reviews of inefficient fossil fuel subsidies among its member countries. This transparency mechanism promotes G20-wide information and knowledge sharing, capacity building in tracking and assessing fossil fuel policies, as well as inter-agency coordination within the countries under review.[21] Similar peer reviews also take place under the auspices of the APEC.[22] However, international peer reviews have inherent limitations as they are voluntary and lack compliance mechanisms.[23]

In the WTO, fossil fuel subsidies have been discussed in the Committee on Trade and Environment, the Trade Policy Review Body and the SCM Committee.[24] The newly established environmental initiatives – the FFSR and the TESSD – opened the door for more focused

[18] The 2022 APEC Joint Ministerial Statement, Bangkok (Thailand), 18 November 2022, para. 29, www.apec.org/meeting-papers/annual-ministerial-meetings/2022/2022-apec-ministerial-meeting.

[19] G7 Leaders' Communiqué, Elmau (Germany), 28 June 2022, www.g7germany.de/resource/blob/974430/2062292/9c213e6b4b36ed1bd687e82480040399/2022-07-14-leaders-communique-data.pdf?download=1.

[20] See Friends of Fossil Fuel Subsidy Reform, http://fffsr.org/.

[21] OECD and IEA, 'Update on Recent Progress in Reform of Inefficient Fossil-Fuel Subsidies That Encourage Wasteful Consumption', 2019, pp. 7–9; Henok Birhanu Asmelash, 'Phasing Out Fossil Fuel Subsidies in the G20: Progress, Challenges, and Ways Forward', International Centre for Trade and Sustainable Development, 2017, pp. 7–9.

[22] OECD and IEA, supra note 21, p. 17.

[23] Ivetta Gerasimchuk et al., 'A Guidebook to Reviews of Fossil Fuel Subsidies: From Self-Reports to Peer Learning', International Institute for Sustainable Development, 2017, p. vii.

[24] See Henok Asmelash, 'The Regulation of Environmentally Harmful Fossil Fuel Subsidies: From Obscurity to Prominence in the Multilateral Trading System', 33 *European Journal of International Law* 993 (2022), pp. 1004–1009.

discussions on this issue, taking into account development aspects as well.[25] The FFSR seeks 'the rationalization and phase out of inefficient fossil fuel subsidies that encourage wasteful consumption along a clear timeline' and, for this purpose, facilitates information and experience sharing to advance WTO discussion aimed at 'achieving ambitious and effective disciplines' on these subsidies.[26] The FFSR participants intend to 'elaborate concrete options' ahead of the Thirteenth Ministerial Conference in 2024.[27] In parallel, fossil fuel subsidies are also considered in the TESSD's Working Group on Subsidies, but some have voiced concern about duplication with the FFSR.[28]

Thanks to the international agenda and campaign, participants of the OECD Arrangement on Officially Supported Export Credits agreed in 2021 to ban official export credits or tied aid for:[29]

- the export of new coal-fired power plants without operational carbon capture, utilization and storage facilities; and
- the export supply of equipment to existing coal-fired power plants unless the purpose of the equipment supplied is pollution or CO_2 abatement and such equipment does not extend the useful lifetime or capacity of the plant, or unless it is for retrofitting to install carbon capture, utilization and storage.

Since export credits conforming to the OECD arrangement in question are not considered export subsidies prohibited by the SCM Agreement, it appears that the newly introduced ban in the OECD arrangement will no longer provide such a 'safe haven' for export credits for unabated coal-fired power plants mentioned above.[30] This is a welcome development,

[25] See Section 1.2.1.

[26] WTO, General Council – Ministerial Statement on Fossil Fuel Subsidies – Revision, WT/MIN(21)/9/Rev.2 (10 June 2022), para. 8.

[27] Ibid.

[28] WTO, Trade and Environmental Sustainability Structured Discussions – Meeting Held on 19 and 20 July 2022 – Informal Summary by the Coordinators, INF/TE/SSD/R/12 (20 September 2022), para. 5.4. See also WTO, 'Trade and Environmental Sustainability Structured Discussion: An Overview in Three Pages', p. 3, www.wto.org/english/tratop_e/tessd_e/tessd_overview_in_three_pages.pdf.

[29] OECD, 'Agreement Reached at OECD to End Export Credit Support for Unabated Coal-Fired Power Plants', 22 October 2021, www.oecd.org/newsroom/agreement-reached-at-oecd-to-end-export-credit-support-for-unabated-coal-fired-power-plants.htm; Article 6 of the Arrangement on Officially Supported Export Credits (January 2022 version), https://one.oecd.org/document/TAD/PG(2022)1/en/pdf.

[30] See Annex I(k) of the SCM Agreement which speaks of 'an international undertaking on official export credits' or 'a successor undertaking'.

but more needs to be done given the existing limitedness of the climate and trade regimes in curbing harmful fossil fuel subsidies.

3.1.2 Limited Responsiveness of the Global Climate and Trade Regimes

Fossil fuel subsidies do not bypass international legal radars altogether. In fact, they are already covered by the global climate and trade regimes to a certain extent. But these regimes are not without limitations. Multilateral agreements on climate change are toothless in curtailing fossil fuel subsidies as they may affect countries' sovereignty over natural resources and economic development.[31] Indeed, neither the UNFCCC (1992) nor the Paris Agreement (2015) makes any specific references to reforming fossil fuel subsidies other than calling for broader mitigation measures by the contracting parties.[32] An exception is Article 2.1(a)(v) of the 1997 Kyoto Protocol to the UNFCCC that required that the parties with mandatory emission reduction commitments '[i]mplement and/or further elaborate policies and measures' on 'progressive reduction or phasing out of market imperfections, fiscal incentives, tax and duty exemptions and subsidies in all greenhouse gas emitting sectors that run counter to the objective of the Convention and application of market instruments'. But this provision applied to a few countries whose latest commitment period ended in December 2020 anyway.

Admittedly, the Sharm el-Sheikh Implementation Plan (2022) of the Conference of the Parties to the Paris Agreement calls upon parties to 'accelerat[e] efforts towards the phasedown of unabated coal power and phase-out of inefficient fossil fuel subsidies, while providing targeted support to the poorest and most vulnerable'.[33] But it falls short of giving any substantive details. Further, the current global climate system provides for voluntary reporting of subsidies/reforms or inclusion of subsidy reforms in nationally appropriate mitigation actions and nationally

[31] Harro van Asselt and Kati Kulovesi, 'Seizing the Opportunity: Tackling Fossil Fuel Subsidies under the UNFCCC', 17 *International Environmental Agreements: Politics, Law and Economics* 357 (2017), pp. 360–361.

[32] For example, Article 2.1(c) of the Paris Agreement (2015) sets a goal to make 'finance flows consistent with a pathway towards low greenhouse gas emissions and climate-resilient development'.

[33] Sharm el-Sheikh Implementation Plan, para. 16 in UN, 'Report of the Conference of the Parties on Its Twenty-Seventh Session, Held in Sharm el-Sheikh from 6 to 20 November 2022', Decision 1/CP.27, FCCC/CP/2022/10/Add.1 (17 March 2023).

determined contributions.[34] However, contracting parties have considerable discretion in using these options[35] and can thus easily ignore them.

On the trade front, international rule-making on fossil fuel subsidy reforms is embryonic at this point and has so far achieved limited progress under few RTAs. At least four agreements are relevant. The EU–Singapore FTA (2018) recognizes 'the need to ensure that, when developing public support systems for fossil fuels, proper account is taken of the need to reduce greenhouse gas emissions and of the need to limit distortions of trade as much as possible'. Its parties 'share the goal of progressively reducing subsidies for fossil fuels' and state that such reductions 'may' necessitate 'measures to alleviate the social consequences associated with the transition to low carbon fuels'.[36] Under the Iceland–Liechtenstein–Norway–UK FTA (2021), the parties agreed to cooperate on 'the global phase-out of inefficient fossil fuel subsidies'.[37] Two other agreements were signed by New Zealand, which has been a coordinator of the WTO's FFSR, thus playing a leading role in advancing the international trade agenda on fossil fuel subsidies. In particular, the EU–New Zealand FTA (2023) confirms the parties' common goal of reforming fossil fuel subsidies and their commitment to cooperate in this field.[38] Like the EU–Singapore FTA, this agreement addresses the issue in question through soft law provisions. In contrast, the New Zealand–UK FTA (2022) sets out more concrete obligations of the parties to:[39]

- eliminate 'harmful fossil fuel subsidies', except those in support of 'legitimate public policy objectives';
- end 'unabated coal-fired electricity generation in their territories';
- publish subsidy information; and
- end new direct fossil fuel financing in third countries and international aid funding for fossil fuel energy, subject to certain (environmental/climate) exceptions.[40]

[34] Asselt and Kulovesi, supra note 31, pp. 364–366.

[35] Ibid.

[36] Article 12.11.3 of the EU–Singapore FTA (2018).

[37] Article 13.22.3(h) of the Iceland–Liechtenstein–Norway–UK FTA (2021).

[38] Article 19.7 ('Trade and Fossil Fuel Subsidy Reform') of the EU–New Zealand FTA (2023).

[39] Article 22.8 ('Fossil Fuel Subsidy Reform and Transition to Clean Energy') of the New Zealand–UK FTA (2022).

[40] These exceptions include: 'new direct financial support, such as officially supported export credits, for fossil fuel energy in non-parties … where it meets a legitimate policy

The ongoing negotiations on the ACCTS – launched in 2019 and currently involving New Zealand, Costa Rica, Fiji, Iceland, Norway and Switzerland – are likely to introduce disciplines to eliminate harmful fossil fuel subsidies.[41]

As for WTO law, the SCM Agreement is applicable to fossil fuel subsidies in principle, but it is not effective enough in capturing them specifically. In addition, governments may get around the WTO rules when they implement dual pricing schemes or operate State-owned enterprises (SOEs). The next sections will discuss these issues in detail.

3.1.3 Limitations of the SCM Agreement

Article 1 of the SCM Agreement defines 'subsidy' as a 'financial contribution' – transfers of funds, fiscal favours and other listed measures – by a government or public body (or alternatively 'any form of income or price support') that confers a 'benefit'.[42] A benefit is considered to be

goal, such as improved safety or environmental standards; or supports a clean energy transition aligned with the goals of the Paris Agreement' (Article 22.8.2(e) of the New Zealand–UK FTA (2022)); and 'international aid funding for fossil fuel energy . . . where it is not feasible to provide access to energy solely from renewable sources and the aid: is essential as part of a humanitarian response; is to meet a legitimate policy goal such as improved safety or environmental standards; or supports a clean energy transition aligned with the goals of the Paris Agreement' (Article 22.8.2(f) of the New Zealand–UK FTA (2022)).

41 See New Zealand Foreign Affairs and Trade, 'New Zealand with Costa Rica, Fiji, Iceland, Norway and Switzerland Have Launched a New Initiative – the Agreement on Climate Change, Trade and Sustainability (ACCTS)', www.mfat.govt.nz/en/trade/free-trade-agreements/trade-and-climate/agreement-on-climate-change-trade-and-sustainability-accts-negotiations/.

42 Article 1 of the SCM Agreement states in relevant part:

1.1 For the purpose of this Agreement, a subsidy shall be deemed to exist if:

(a)(1) there is a financial contribution by a government or any public body within the territory of a Member (referred to in this Agreement as "government"), i.e. where:

(i) a government practice involves a direct transfer of funds (e.g. grants, loans, and equity infusion), potential direct transfers of funds or liabilities (e.g. loan guarantees);

(ii) government revenue that is otherwise due is foregone or not collected (e.g. fiscal incentives such as tax credits); [footnote 1 omitted]

(iii) a government provides goods or services other than general infrastructure, or purchases goods;

conferred if the recipient is made better off in the market,[43] which necessitates comparisons with relevant commercial transactions.[44] Subsidies contingent upon export performance (i.e., export subsidies) or upon the use of domestic over imported goods (i.e., local content or import substitution subsidies) are 'prohibited' by the SCM Agreement and deemed to be 'specific' as such.[45] All other subsidies that are specific to particular enterprises, industries or regions and causing 'adverse effects' to the interests of other members are 'actionable'.[46] Prohibited and actionable subsidies can be challenged through the WTO dispute settlement procedures (the multilateral track) or countered through countervailing duty procedures (the national track).

In practice, the SCM Agreement has almost never been used to directly challenge fossil fuel subsidies.[47] The low push from interest groups[48] and the reluctance of governments to take legal actions can be attributed to a number of supply- and demand-side factors, as follows.

On the supply side, production subsidies (e.g., R&D support, tax incentives, grants, concessional loans, insurance and other pertinent favours) linked to any of the stages of fossil fuel production[49] can be considered as 'specific' to the energy sector and hence 'actionable' at least. However, these subsidies are 'complex and often opaque',[50] which makes them difficult to track. Moreover, they are concentrated in countries that are principal producers of oil, gas and coal,[51] and the relatively small

(iv) a government makes payments to a funding mechanism, or entrusts or directs a private body to carry out one or more of the type of functions illustrated in (i) to (iii) above which would normally be vested in the government and the practice, in no real sense, differs from practices normally followed by governments;

43 *Canada – Aircraft*, WTO Appellate Body Report, paras. 154, 157–158.

44 See Article 14 of the SCM Agreement.

45 Articles 2.3 and 3 of the SCM Agreement.

46 Part III of the SCM Agreement.

47 See Henok Birhanu Asmelash, 'Energy Subsidies and WTO Dispute Settlement: Why Only Renewable Energy Subsidies are Challenged', 18 *Journal of International Economic Law* 261 (2015), p. 268.

48 Ibid., pp. 283–284.

49 Such production stages include gaining access to resource sites, exploration and appraisal; development; extraction and preparation; transport to refineries and power stations; construction and operation of plants; distribution to consumers; and decommissioning and other post-operations. Bast et al., supra note 15, pp. 33–35.

50 Laura Merrill et al., 'Tackling Fossil Fuel Subsidies and Climate Change: Levelling the Energy Playing Field', Nordic Council of Ministers, 2015, pp. 18–19.

51 UNEP, 'Measuring Fossil Fuel Subsidies in the Context of the Sustainable Development Goals', 2019, p. 6.

number of such countries allows them to have extensive market access both at home and abroad and avoid trade frictions among themselves. Besides, countries dependent on fossil fuel imports are not likely to take issue with foreign production subsidies that have price-lowering effects on these imports. Unsurprisingly, one study could find only two (minor) instances of direct attacks against fossil fuel production subsidies under the GATT/WTO system, neither of which had resulted in formal cases.[52]

As for the demand side, consumption subsidies are more prevalent and widespread. In particular, roughly 80 per cent of the government support in the OECD inventory goes to consumers (rather than producers) of fossil fuels (especially petroleum).[53] As consumption subsidies can boost global demand for fossil fuels, the probability of WTO dispute initiations by fossil-fuel-producing members against those subsidies is close to zero.[54] Although energy-importing countries could actually challenge foreign consumption subsidies for artificially increasing global demand and consequently international prices of fossil fuels, this line of thinking has never been advanced in the WTO.[55] Moreover, WTO-based actions against consumption subsidies may face some high legal hurdles. First, because these subsidies are often available to energy-consuming industries across the board, they do not tend to be 'specific'.[56] Second, for challenging a production subsidy at the consumption level (e.g., tax exemptions for extracting natural gas that is used by manufacturing industries after extraction), one must meet the onerous standard of

[52] Under the GATT system in the early 1990s, Australia took issue with coal production subsidies of the European Communities but did not proceed to a formal challenge after reaching a bilateral agreement with the European Communities on a standstill in subsidized coal production. The other instance involves a failed attempt of an American oil company to initiate US anti-dumping and countervailing duty investigations on imports of crude petroleum oil products in 2000. See Ronald Steenblik, Jehan Sauvage and Christina Timiliotis, 'Fossil Fuel Subsidies and the Global Trade Regime', in Jakob Skovgaard and Harro van Asselt (eds.), *The Politics of Fossil Fuel Subsidies and Their Reform* (Cambridge: Cambridge University Press, 2018), p. 127.

[53] OECD and IEA, supra note 21, pp. 9, 34; OECD, 'OECD Inventory of Support Measures for Fossil Fuels: Database Brochure', 2019, pp. 4–5, www.oecd.org/fossil-fuels/data/OECD-Fossil-Fuels-Support-database-brochure-2019.pdf.

[54] Steenblik et al., supra note 52, p. 128.

[55] Ibid.

[56] However, such subsidies may turn out to be 'specific' under Article 2.1(c) of the SCM Agreement in the light of such factors as 'use of a subsidy programme by a limited number of certain enterprises, predominant use by certain enterprises, the granting of disproportionately large amounts of subsidy to certain enterprises, and the manner in which discretion has been exercised by the granting authority in the decision to grant a subsidy'.

proving that this subsidy has been passed through from the production to the consumption level, and that it is specific at both levels.[57] Third, bringing a WTO complaint against a fossil-fuel-producing member with an undiversified economy may turn out to be useless. For example, if such a member loses a case over its export restrictions on crude oil (which has a price-lowering impact on domestic *consumers*), it may nevertheless wish to continue those restrictions without fear of any strong retaliation. The complainant will not likely retaliate against that member by restricting oil imports it relies upon, while (cross-)retaliation in non-oil sectors will be impracticable or ineffective given the respondent's undiversified economic structure.[58]

Finally, the undervaluation of externalities associated with fossil fuels – classified as fossil fuel subsidies under the IMF methodology – is also difficult to challenge under the SCM Agreement. The idea that a government's failure to internalize environmental externalities, like pollution costs, into firms' price-setting is tantamount to an indirect way of subsidizing local industries does not appear to have enough legal underpinnings under the existing subsidy rules. The prevailing view in the literature is that the WTO's definition of 'subsidy' does not cover 'implicit' or 'regulatory' subsidies that lower production costs by downgrading environmental or social standards.[59] Perhaps this is the reason why the United States proposed in 2020, albeit unsuccessfully, that the WTO Ministerial Conference officially declare that poor environmental policies constitute actionable subsidies under the SCM Agreement.[60]

[57] See Sherzod Shadikhodjaev, 'How to Pass a Pass-through Test: The Case of Input Subsidies', 15 *Journal of International Economic Law* 621 (2012), pp. 636–642.

[58] Timothy Meyer, 'Explaining Energy Disputes at the World Trade Organization', 17 *International Environmental Agreements: Politics, Law and Economics* 391 (2017), pp. 401–403.

[59] See, for example, Asmelash, supra note 47, pp. 270–271; Dominic Coppens, *WTO Disciplines on Subsidies and Countervailing Measures: Balancing Policy Space and Legal Constraints* (Cambridge: Cambridge University Press, 2014), pp. 448–449.

[60] WTO, General Council – Advancing Sustainability Goals through Trade Rules to Level the Playing Field – Draft Ministerial Decision, WT/GC/W/814 (17 December 2020). The draft ministerial decision, proposed by the United States, reads:

1. The failure of a government to adopt, maintain, implement and effectively enforce laws and regulations that ensure environmental protections at or above a threshold of fundamental standards shall constitute an actionable subsidy under the ASCM.
2. If an industry disproportionately benefits from pollution controls or other environmental measures set below a threshold of fundamental standards, a Member may

As subsidization patterns involving both the supply and demand sides vary significantly, we will now proceed to examine only dual pricing and SOEs – the two controversial issues that are common to many economies and highly relevant to fossil fuel subsidies.

3.1.4 *Dual Pricing*

Dual pricing occurs when a country sets a lower price for its product sold domestically compared to the price it charges for that product's export.[61] Major targets of dual pricing are coal, natural gas, petroleum and other raw materials.[62] Resulting mainly from direct price controls or indirect measures, like export restrictions, dual pricing distorts trade by making domestic energy-reliant downstream industries more competitive than their foreign rivals. Dual pricing has been discussed in the GATT/WTO system since the oil crises in the 1970s, but all attempts to introduce specific multilateral rules have failed mainly because of the resistance of countries using dual pricing as a means of exploiting their comparative trade advantages.[63]

WTO law limits dual pricing mainly in two contexts. First, Article XI of the GATT explicitly bans quantitative export restrictions other than temporary 'export prohibitions or restrictions' on certain 'essential' products being in 'critical shortages' or other than export restraints 'necessary to the application of standards or regulations for the classification, grading or marketing of commodities in international trade'. To recall from Chapter 2, export restrictions can generate a decline in the domestic price of the subject product but an increase in its export/international price.[64] An export quota on coke, or coal-based fuel, together with other export restrictions were found to be inconsistent with Article XI in *China – Raw Materials*.[65] Second, some members' accession instruments contain relevant WTO-plus restrictions.

impose a countervailing duty equal to the benefit received by the industry when the goods from such an industry enter the Member's customs territory.

[61] WTO, 'Trade in Natural Resources', World Trade Report 2010, 2010, p. 173.

[62] Anna Marhold, 'Fossil Fuel Subsidy Reform in the WTO: Options for Constraining Dual Pricing in the Multilateral Trading System', International Centre for Trade and Sustainable Development, 2017, p. 1.

[63] Ibid., pp. 6–7.

[64] See also, for example, K. C. Fung and Jane Korinek, 'Economics of Export Restrictions as Applied to Industrial Raw Materials', OECD Trade Policy Paper No. 155, 2013, pp. 32–33.

[65] *China – Raw Materials*, WTO Panel Reports, paras. 7.222, 7.224. See Section 2.2.2.2.2.

In particular, China committed to 'eliminate dual pricing practices as well as differences in treatment accorded to goods produced for sale in China in comparison to those produced for export'.[66] Saudi Arabia, Russia and Tajikistan committed to maintaining the normal commercial conditions for pricing the energy supplies concerned.[67] Several members assumed accession obligations to limit the use of export duties with the varying scope of goods (including energy products), commitments and exceptions.[68]

However, in many other legal contexts, WTO law is weak in constraining dual pricing. As one of the most relevant provisions, Article III:9 of the GATT reads that 'internal maximum price control measures' can have 'prejudicial' effect on the interests of other members supplying imported products and that members applying such measures 'shall take account of the interests of exporting [members] with a view to avoiding to the fullest practicable extent such prejudicial effects'. When a State under-prices its energy products in the domestic market, it can be seen as creating an (implicit) upper limit on the energy price in the sense of Article III:9. But the overall language of Article III:9 seems to imply rather the soft law nature of the importing country's obligation under that provision.[69]

Further, Article XVII of the GATT can be linked to dual pricing if the price-setting occurs through State trading enterprises that have 'exclusive or special rights or privileges, including statutory or constitutional powers, in the exercise of which they influence through their purchases

[66] WTO, Working Party on the Accession of China – Report of the Working Party on the Accession of China, WT/ACC/CHN/49 (1 October 2001), para. 18.

[67] See, for example, WTO, Working Party on the Accession of Saudi Arabia – Report of the Working Party on the Accession of the Kingdom of Saudi Arabia to the WTO, WT/ACC/SAU/61 (1 November 2005), para. 33; WTO, Working Party on the Accession of the Russian Federation – Report of the Working Party on the Accession of the Russian Federation to the WTO, WT/ACC/RUS/70, WT/MIN(11)/2 (17 November 2011), para. 132; WTO, Working Party on the Accession of the Republic of Tajikistan – Report of the Working Party on the Accession of the Republic of Tajikistan, WT/ACC/TJK/30 (6 November 2012), para. 59.

[68] See Julia Ya Qin, 'Reforming WTO Discipline on Export Duties: Sovereignty over Natural Resources, Economic Development and Environmental Protection', 46 *Journal of World Trade* 1147 (2012), pp. 1161–1162.

[69] See Julia Selivanova, 'World Trade Organization Rules and Energy Pricing: Russia's Case', 38 *Journal of World Trade* 559 (2004), p. 594; Vitaliy Pogoretskyy, 'Energy Dual Pricing in International Trade: Subsidies and Anti-Dumping Perspectives', in Yulia Selivanova (ed.), *Regulation of Energy in International Trade Law: WTO, NAFTA and Energy Charter* (Alphen aan den Rijn: Kluwer Law International, 2011), pp. 190–191.

or sales the level or direction of imports or exports'.[70] Subparagraph (a) of Article XVII:1 states that the subject enterprise must, in its purchases or sales involving imports or exports, comply with 'the general principles of non-discriminatory treatment prescribed . . . for governmental measures affecting imports or exports by private traders'. Subparagraph (b) of Article XVII:1 adds that subparagraph (a) 'shall be understood to require' such enterprise to purchase or sell 'solely in accordance with commercial considerations'. According to the Appellate Body's interpretation, subparagraph (b) is 'dependent upon the content of subparagraph (a)' and 'operates to clarify the scope of the requirement not to discriminate in subparagraph (a)'.[71] Because the anti-discrimination requirement of Article XVII:1 appears to entail MFN treatment,[72] the literature suggests that the provision in question does not apply to dual pricing by State trading enterprises as this practice discriminates between domestic and export markets without affecting MFN.[73] Therefore, it is questionable whether Article XVII can effectively address dual pricing.

Likewise, the WTO subsidy and anti-dumping rules are not effective either. Under the SCM Agreement, dual pricing may qualify as a 'subsidy' in the form of, for instance, the government provision of a good (natural gas, oil, electricity, etc.) to downstream industries at a less-than-adequate remuneration. However, the underselling of energy in this case would often benefit virtually any energy-using industry, which would make such scheme a non-specific subsidy out of the SCM Agreement's reach. Neither would it be a genuine prohibited subsidy.[74]

Furthermore, the SCM Agreement does not seem to effectively limit dual pricing caused by export restrictions. In *US – Export Restraints*, the panel rejected 'the US approach that, because, or to the extent that, an export restraint causes an increased domestic supply of the restrained good, it is the same as if a government had expressly entrusted or directed a private body to provide the good domestically' as captured by the notion of 'financial contribution' in the SCM Agreement. The panel concluded that export restraints did not involve an 'explicit and affirmative action of delegation or command' as implied by the concepts

[70] WTO, Understanding on the Interpretation of Article XVII of the GATT 1994.

[71] *Canada – Wheat Exports and Grain Imports*, WTO Appellate Body Report, para. 89.

[72] John H. Jackson, *World Trade and the Law of GATT* (Indianapolis: Bobbs-Merrill Company, 1969), pp. 345–347.

[73] Pogoretskyy, supra note 69, pp. 198–199.

[74] See Selivanova, supra note 69, pp. 569–584; Sergey Ripinsky, 'The System of Gas Dual Pricing in Russia: Compatibility with WTO Rules', 3 *World Trade Review* 463 (2004).

of entrustment or direction and that the mere effect of export restraints on the market did not differ from the effect of many other governmental (non-subsidy) measures impacting on the marketplace.[75] The panel in *US – Countervailing Measures (China)* was also sceptical about the characterization of export restraints as entrustment or direction within the meaning of the SCM Agreement.[76]

As for the anti-dumping mechanism, WTO jurisprudence outlawed a methodology of input cost adjustment being applied by an importing government in response to, inter alia, dual pricing effects. Anti-dumping duties can be imposed when a product's export price is less than its domestic price (or 'normal value') in an exporting country. When domestic sales in the exporting country do not permit proper price comparisons, Article 2.2 of the WTO Anti-Dumping Agreement allows an investigating authority to construct the normal value from 'the cost of production in the country of origin plus a reasonable amount for administrative, selling and general costs and for profits'. In doing so, some investigating authorities replace distorted production costs, reported by a producer or exporter, with market-based surrogate costs considered to be more reliable. This leads to 'artificial' inflations of dumping margins and corresponding anti-dumping duty rates to the detriment of exporters' interests.[77] For instance, in *Ukraine – Ammonium Nitrate*, the Ukrainian investigating authority determined that ammonium nitrate from Russia was produced with the use of the natural gas that was under-priced because of the following factors:[78]

> a. the gas price in the domestic Russian market was not a market price, as the state controlled the price for gas;
> b. due to the existence of state control, *the price of gas for the investigated Russian producers was much lower than the selling price of gas exported from Russia* and the prices for producers in other countries, as well as the market price in certain countries such as the United States, Canada, Japan, or the European Union;

[75] *US – Export Restraints*, WTO Panel Report, paras. 8.75, 8.28–8.44.

[76] See *US – Countervailing Measures (China)*, WTO Panel Report, paras 7.362, 7.392, 7.399–7.406.

[77] For a detailed analysis of this issue, see Sherzod Shadikhodjaev, 'Input Cost Adjustments and WTO Anti-Dumping Law: A Closer Look at the EU Practice', 18 *World Trade Review* 81 (2019); Sherzod Shadikhodjaev, 'Non-Market Economies, Significant Market Distortions, and the 2017 EU Anti-Dumping Amendment', 21 *Journal of International Economic Law* 885 (2018).

[78] *Ukraine – Ammonium Nitrate*, WTO Panel Report, para. 7.73 (footnotes omitted, emphasis added).

c. calculations that showed that JSC Gazprom (Gazprom), a Russian supplier of gas, was selling below its cost of production and that the profitability of this supplier was due to export sales.

On these grounds, the Ukrainian authority substituted the reported gas cost for the adjusted (higher) price of gas exported from Russia to the German border.[79] But the Appellate Body found that such cost adjustment methodology was in violation of Article 2.2 of the Anti-Dumping Agreement under which the constructed normal value must include, inter alia, the production cost in the *country of origin* (i.e., Russia in the given case).[80] In addition, it confirmed the breach of Article 2.2.1.1 of the Anti-Dumping Agreement, which states that the costs must normally be calculated on the basis of the investigated *exporter or producer's records*, provided that the records (i) comply with 'the generally accepted accounting principles' and (ii) 'reasonably reflect' the relevant costs.[81] Importantly, the Appellate Body interpreted the words 'reasonably reflect' in the second condition as requiring that the cost *records* be reasonable (in other words, accurate enough) and not the cost per se be reasonable. Thus, 'there is no standard of reasonableness under that condition that governs the meaning of "costs" itself, which would allow investigating authorities to disregard domestic input prices when such prices are lower than other prices internationally'.[82]

3.1.5 SOEs

Through SOEs, governments control roughly 70 per cent of global oil and gas production and about 60 per cent of coal production and coal-fired power plants worldwide.[83] Governments distort 'competitive neutrality' in markets by granting advantages to SOEs over private enterprises.[84] In general, SOEs are often entitled to preferential financing,

[79] Ibid., paras. 7.64, 7.94. The EU has also applied a similar approach towards Russian energy-intensive products. See Sherzod Shadikhodjaev, 'Russia and Energy Issues under the WTO System', 50 *Journal of World Trade* 705 (2016), pp. 716–719.

[80] *Ukraine – Ammonium Nitrate*, WTO Appellate Body Report, para. 7.8.

[81] Ibid., paras. 7.5–7.6.

[82] Ibid., para. 7.5.

[83] David Nelson et al., 'Moving to a Low-Carbon Economy: The Impact of Policy Pathways on Fossil Fuel Asset Values', Climate Policy Initiative, 2014, pp. 9–10.

[84] See Antonio Capobianco and Hans Christiansen, 'Competitive Neutrality and State-Owned Enterprises: Challenges and Policy Options', OECD Corporate Governance Working Papers No. 1, 2011; Sherzod Shadikhodjaev, 'Steel Overcapacity and the

privileged access to information, implicit or explicit State guarantees, grants, tax concessions, in-kind subsidies, regulatory exemptions, preferences in public procurement, commercial diplomacy support and other forms of government support.[85]

Apart from receiving these governmental favours, SOEs may also grant advantages to others. When State-owned banks provide financing to fossil fuel producers/consumers at below the market rates or when SOEs supply under-priced fossil fuels to downstream industries, they may qualify as a subsidizing 'public body' within the meaning of Article 1.1(a)(1) of the SCM Agreement. The Appellate Body in *US – Anti-Dumping and Countervailing Duties (China)* reversed the proposition – shared by a panel in a previous case[86] – that the term 'public body' under the SCM Agreement means any entity controlled by a government. Instead, the Appellate Body found that a public body 'must be an entity that possesses, exercises or is vested with governmental authority'.[87] The mere existence of a government's control, ownership or majority shareholding in an entity does not necessarily show that that entity has been bestowed with governmental authority so as to qualify as a 'public body'.[88] Rather, one needs to holistically assess all relevant characteristics of an entity to check if it is vested with authority to carry out a governmental function.[89] However, this narrow interpretation poses practical difficulties of countering many favours by SOEs.

Interestingly enough, one Appellate Body member, in a separate (dissenting) opinion in *US – Countervailing Measures (China) (Article 21.5 – China)*, disagreed with the previous WTO judicial practice of adhering to the possession/exercise of governmental authority as '*the* essential criterion in every case' for verifying a public body and suggested that '[a]n entity may be found to be a public body when the government has the ability to control that entity and/or its conduct to convey financial value'.[90]

Global Trading System', 16 *Asian Journal of WTO & International Health Law and Policy* 179 (2021), p. 205.

85 OECD, 'State-Owned Enterprises as Global Competitors: A Challenge or an Opportunity?', 2016, pp. 28–30.

86 *Korea – Commercial Vessels*, WTO Panel Report, para. 7.50.

87 *US – Anti-Dumping and Countervailing Duties (China)*, WTO Appellate Body Report, para. 317.

88 Ibid., para. 318.

89 Ibid., paras. 318–319.

90 *US – Countervailing Measures (China) (Article 21.5 – China)*, WTO Appellate Body Report, paras. 5.245–5.248 (emphasis in original).

3.1.6 The Way Forward

In order to successfully reform fossil fuel subsidies at home, the package of State actions should include a comprehensive reform plan, communication campaigns for gaining sufficient domestic support, prudent energy price increases, energy SOE reforms, targeted assistance to negatively affected groups and depoliticized mechanisms for setting energy prices.[91] The WTO system should put a higher international pressure on its members for them to take necessary steps in this direction.

3.1.6.1 Horizontal Improvements

As seen from the previous chapters, fossil fuels are already included in WTO law even where agreements do not mention them explicitly. Therefore, any improvement of 'product-neutral' (or 'horizontal') rules in this system will automatically apply to fossil fuel subsidies where relevant.

Like for any industrial subsidy, transparency in government policies is important for identifying and assessing fossil fuel subsidies. Article 25 of the SCM Agreement requires WTO members to notify specific subsidies. For fossil fuels, this is applicable to many production subsidies as well as qualified consumption subsidies that are specific because of disproportionately benefiting targeted industries using a fossil fuel.[92] However, the notification requirement is largely diminished by the notoriously 'chronic low compliance' of members,[93] with the portion of members not making any subsidy notification increasing from 25 per cent in 1995 to 58 per cent in 2021.[94] Since 2018, a group of WTO members have proposed new

[91] David Coady, Valentina Flamini and Louis Sears, 'The Unequal Benefits of Fuel Subsidies Revisited: Evidence for Developing Countries', IMF Working Paper No. WP/15/250, 2015, p. 14. See also Kathryn Chelminski, 'Fossil Fuel Subsidy Reform in Indonesia: The Struggle for Successful Reform', in Skovgaard and Asselt (eds.), supra note 52, pp. 193–211; Abhishek Jain, Shalu Agrawal and Karthik Ganesan, 'Lessons from the World's Largest Subsidy Benefit Transfer Scheme: The Case of Liquefied Petroleum Gas Subsidy Reform in India', in Skovgaard and Asselt (eds.), supra note 52, pp. 212–228; Djavad Salehi-Isfahani, Bryce Wilson Stucki and Joshua Deutschmann, 'The Reform of Energy Subsidies in Iran: The Role of Cash Transfers', 51 *Emerging Markets Finance and Trade* 1144 (2015).

[92] See supra note 56.

[93] WTO, 'Subsidies Committee Members Again Cite Concerns on Lack of Transparency', 30 April 2019, www.wto.org/english/news_e/news19_e/scm_30apr19_e.htm.

[94] WTO, Committee on SCM – Notification Provisions under the Agreement on Subsidies and Countervailing Measures – Background Note by the Secretariat – Revision, G/SCM/W/546/Rev.13 (31 March 2022), p. 4, para. 9.

procedures for enhancing transparency and improving compliance with the WTO notification requirements. Their initial proposal envisaged both carrots and sticks, such as the WTO Secretariat's expanded assistance and capacity building support, on the one hand, and some punitive 'administrative measures' for persistent non-notification, on the other.[95] Due to the fierce opposition by many developing country members, a more recent version of that proposal omits the punitive elements and instead focuses on targeted technical assistance and capacity building.[96] The proposal also suggests that 'all trade policy reviews include a specific, standardized focus on the Member's compliance with its notification obligations'.[97] The proposal has continuously been discussed in the General Council's meetings.[98] Because of the horizontal reach, the proposed procedures, if eventually approved, are expected to improve transparency of national practices in subsidizing fossil fuels.

As for SOEs, some WTO members have recently called for revisiting the related WTO rules – as part of the overall WTO reform package – to better capture enterprises associated with governments.[99] In this regard, the Comprehensive and Progressive Agreement for Trans-Pacific Partnership (CPTPP) (2018) representing 'a crucial step in SOE rulemaking'[100] may

[95] WTO, General Council – Council for Trade in Goods – Procedures to Enhance Transparency and Strengthen Notification Requirements under WTO Agreements – Communication from Argentina, Costa Rica, the EU, Japan, and the United States, JOB/GC/204, JOB/CTG/14 (1 November 2018).

[96] WTO, General Council – Council for Trade in Goods – Procedures to Enhance Transparency and Improve Compliance with Notification Requirements under WTO Agreements – Communication from Albania; Argentina; Australia; Brazil; Canada; Chile; Colombia; Costa Rica; the EU; [. . .]; and Uruguay – Revision, JOB/GC/204/Rev.12, JOB/CTG/14/Rev.12 (2 November 2022).

[97] Ibid.

[98] See, for example, WTO, General Council – Minutes of the Meeting – Held in the Centre William Rappard and in Virtual Format on 25–26 July 2022, WT/GC/M/200 (21 October 2022), paras. 8.1–8.92.

[99] See, for example, the EU's Concept Paper on WTO Modernization, 18 September 2018, http://trade.ec.europa.eu/doclib/docs/2018/september/tradoc_157331.pdf; WTO, General Council – Strengthening and Modernizing the WTO: Discussion Paper – Communication from Canada, JOB/GC/201 (24 September 2018). See also G7 Trade Ministers' Communiqué, 28 May 2021, para. 5 in 'Market-Distorting Policies and Practices', www.gov.uk/government/news/g7-trade-ministers-communique; G7 Trade Ministers' Statement, 15 September 2022, p. 4 on 'Levelling the Playing Field and Addressing Economic Coercion', www.meti.go.jp/policy/trade_policy/G7G8/pdf/220914G7TradeMinistersStatementEN.pdf.

[100] Julien Sylvestre Fleury and Jean-Michel Marcoux, 'The US Shaping of State-Owned Enterprise Disciplines in the Trans-Pacific Partnership', 19 *Journal of International Economic Law* 445 (2016), p. 451.

provide some readily available templates for improving the WTO disciplines. Chapter 17 of the CPTPP contains WTO-plus provisions on SOEs in two respects. First, each contracting party must ensure that its SOE 'acts in accordance with commercial considerations in its purchase or sale of a good or service',[101] that is, as the agreement explains, on such conditions and terms that privately owned enterprises in the relevant business or industry would normally take into account in their commercial decisions.[102] Unlike Article XVII:1 of the GATT, Chapter 17 of the CPTPP *defines* and imposes the 'commercial considerations' requirement upon SOEs *in addition to* (rather than as part of) a non-discrimination requirement. Second, the CPTPP regulates 'non-commercial assistance' provided *by* State enterprises or SOEs (in addition to assistance by governments) *to* SOEs as the only/major recipient.[103] Unlike the SCM Agreement, the CPTPP does *not* require SOEs to be a public body and disciplines non-commercial assistance given *specifically* to SOEs. The latter aspect introduces a new concept of SOE-specificity of covered subsidies[104] with a view to countering SOE-oriented advantages and securing 'competitive neutrality' mentioned above.

Finally, WTO members could agree on a text restricting dual pricing outright. As observed above, this has already been reflected in some accession texts. Inspiration may also been drawn from recent non-WTO arrangements.[105] For example, Article 270(1) of the EU–Ukraine

[101] Article 17.4.1(a) of the CPTPP (2018).

[102] Article 17.1 of the CPTPP (2018).

[103] The scope of 'non-commercial assistance' as defined by Article 17.1 of the CPTPP (2018) ('direct transfers of funds or potential direct transfers of funds or liabilities' as well as 'goods or services other than general infrastructure' made available at commercially favourable terms) includes the situation where 'the Party or any of the Party's state enterprises or state-owned enterprises:

(i) explicitly limits access to the assistance to the Party's state-owned enterprises;
(ii) provides assistance which is predominately used by the Party's state-owned enterprises;
(iii) provides a disproportionately large amount of the assistance to the Party's state-owned enterprises; or
(iv) otherwise favours the Party's state-owned enterprises through the use of its discretion in the provision of assistance;'

[104] Although China's WTO Accession Protocol envisages a similar notion of SOE-specificity of subsidies, this is confined to Chinese subsidies only. See section 10.2 of the Accession Protocol in WTO, Accession of the People's Republic of China – Decision of 10 November 2001, WT/L/432 (23 November 2001).

[105] See Marhold, supra note 62, pp. 16–18.

Association Agreement (2014) stipulates that 'neither Party or a regulatory authority thereof, shall adopt or maintain a measure resulting in a higher price for exports of energy goods to the other Party than the price charged for such goods when intended for domestic consumption'.[106] Under such wording, dual pricing can be removed not only by equalizing domestic and export prices but also either (i) by charging higher prices on domestically sold fossil fuels or (ii) by lowering their export prices. From an environmental perspective, option one is preferable because it would encourage improving energy efficiency and potentially switching to green energy in dual-pricing countries. But depending on the circumstances, option two may also inflate domestic prices as the exporting country cannot rely on high export prices any longer to 'cross-subsidize' the under-pricing of fossil fuels at home.[107] Although previous attempts to directly prohibit dual pricing in multilateral rules under the GATT/WTO system have failed, the urgency of climate change today could exert increased global pressure to reconsider this issue.

3.1.6.2 Sectoral Improvements

In 2013, former Director-General of the WTO Pascal Lamy lamented that 'the ongoing political debate on reforming fossil fuel subsidies has largely bypassed the WTO' and that 'the absence of this topic from the WTO radar screen can be considered as a missed opportunity'.[108] But the ongoing FFSR and TESSD discussions gave new impetus to revisiting this issue in the WTO system, leaving the door open for some possible statutory improvements specifically tied to fossil fuel subsidies. Furthermore, fuel subsidies could potentially be included in future WTO disciplines on fisheries subsidies that contribute to overcapacity or overfishing. These subsidies were included in the draft Agreement on Fisheries Subsidies but eventually removed from the adopted final text to make way for further discussions in the follow-up negotiations.[109] Last

[106] According to Article 268(1) of the EU–Ukraine Association Agreement (2014), the term 'energy goods' includes natural gas, electrical energy and crude oil.

[107] It is possible that a government intentionally sets high export prices of energy goods to compensate their low domestic prices, thereby causing dual pricing. See Selivanova, supra note 69, pp. 562, 597.

[108] WTO, 'Lamy Calls for Dialogue on Trade and Energy in the WTO', 29 April 2013, www.wto.org/english/news_e/sppl_e/sppl279_e.htm.

[109] See WTO, Ministerial Conference – Twelfth Session – Geneva, 12–15 June 2022 – Agreement on Fisheries Subsidies – Ministerial Decision of 17 June 2022, WT/MIN(22)/33, WT/L/1144 (22 June 2022), para. 4 (on future negotiations on outstanding

but not least, some progress (to be) reached on the non-WTO trade front above may also contribute to the possibility of creating fossil fuel subsidy rules in the WTO.

To enhance transparency of fossil fuel subsidies specifically, the WTO could reorganize its surveillance procedures. The practice shows that members' comments and information on fossil fuel subsidies provided in the WTO, and in particular the Trade Policy Review Body and the SCM Committee, tend to be rather scarce, sporadic and unfocused.[110] Therefore, the WTO body/bodies concerned should hold dedicated meetings or sessions on a regular basis for more thorough discussions on fossil fuel subsidies as connected to each member, region and/or the entire world. The purpose here is to allow for more focused deliberations and information sharing among members to improve their understanding of the state of play on fossil fuel subsidies and best practices in phasing them out. This issue could be included in the ongoing WTO reform talks on revitalizing the WTO's monitoring and deliberative function.[111]

In parallel with the transparency track, new WTO rules could be negotiated to restrict fossil fuel subsidies per se.[112] For this purpose, members could use the operative negotiating mandate for clarifying and improving the SCM Agreement[113] or use the FFSR and TESSD channels. In line with the global agenda, the WTO efforts should be aimed, first of

issues, including overcapacity and overfishing subsidies). See Articles 5.1(c) and 8.2 of the 2022 draft text of the Agreement on Fisheries Subsidies (WTO, Ministerial Conference – Twelfth Session – Geneva, 12–15 June 2022 – Agreement on Fisheries Subsidies – Draft Text, WT/MIN(22)/W/20 (10 June 2022)).

[110] See Liesbeth Casier et al., 'Shining a Light on Fossil Fuel Subsidies at the WTO: How NGOs Can Contribute to WTO Notification and Surveillance', 13 *World Trade Review* 603 (2014), pp. 613–619.

[111] See WTO, General Council – Reinforcing the Deliberative Function of the WTO to Respond to Global Trade Policy Challenges – Communication from the EU, WT/GC/W/864 (22 February 2023); WTO, General Council – WTO Reform: Incremental Changes to Improve the Functioning of the Various WTO Bodies – Communication from India, WT/GC/W/874 (1 May 2023); WTO, General Council – Improving the Operation of WTO Bodies to Revitalise the WTO's Monitoring and Deliberative Function – Communication from Australia; Brunei Darussalam; Canada; Chile; Costa Rica; Guatemala; Iceland; Israel; Japan; Republic of Korea; New Zealand; [. . .]; and the UK, WT/GC/W/877 (4 May 2023).

[112] See Gary Horlick and Peggy A. Clarke, 'Rethinking Subsidy Disciplines for the Future: Policy Options for Reform', 20 *Journal of International Economic Law* 673 (2017), p. 684.

[113] WTO, Ministerial Conference – Fourth Session – Doha, 9–14 November 2001 – Ministerial Declaration – Adopted on 14 November 2001, WT/MIN(01)/DEC/1 (20 November 2001), para. 28; WTO, Negotiating Group on Rules – Report by the

all, at prohibiting 'inefficient fossil fuel subsidies that encourage wasteful consumption'. While the term 'subsidy' is already defined in the SCM Agreement, the rest of this expression needs further clarification.[114] Despite the confusing reference to 'wasteful consumption', it is considered that 'inefficient subsidies' cover both producer and consumer subsidies leading to wasteful consumption as it follows from the G20 countries' inclusion of both in their national implementation strategies.[115]

For the clarification purpose, at least two approaches are conceivable. A 'top-down' approach could give a blanket definition of the inefficient subsidies concerned, list some particular subsidy forms or provide a combination of both. This would correspond to the SCM Agreement's way of laying down across-the-board subsidy definition and parameters. Alternatively, a more flexible 'bottom-up' approach could let members decide for themselves what subsidies to include into this category, subject to periodic updates. To this end, individual members could inquire into whether their subsidy is efficient (adequate) enough to reach the underlying objectives, like protection of the poor, which would necessitate a cost–benefit analysis; and whether the subsidy avoids encouraging wasteful (excessive) energy consumption in satisfying basic needs as compared with the subsidy-free situation, which would require considering social and equity aspects.[116] Either approach could be supplemented by member-specific schedules on phasing out 'prohibited' inefficient subsidies and binding the amounts of other 'actionable' fossil fuel subsidies.

Like many other WTO texts, including the SCM Agreement, the new rules on fossil fuel subsidies should give more leeway to developing country members. This would also correspond to SDG 12, target 12.C that calls for 'taking fully into account the specific needs and conditions of developing countries' in fossil fuel subsidy reforms. Besides

Chairman, H. E. Mr Wayne McCook to the Trade Negotiations Committee, TN/RL/28 (29 November 2017), paras. 1, 6.

114 So far, there has not been any official definition of 'inefficient fossil fuel subsidies that encourage wasteful consumption' as noted by Vernon Rive, 'Anatomy of an International Norm Entrepreneur: The Friends of Fossil Fuel Subsidy Reform', in Skovgaard and Asselt (eds.), supra note 52, p. 165.

115 Asmelash, supra note 21, p. 4.

116 See IEA, Organization of the Petroleum Exporting Countries, OECD and World Bank, 'Analysis of the Scope of Energy Subsidies and Suggestions for the G-20 Initiative', Joint Report (prepared for submission to the G-20 Summit Meeting in Toronto (Canada), 26–27 June 2010), 2010, pp. 33–34.

transitional periods for implementation and other possible flexibilities, the S&D regime here could also link such reforms in developing countries to donors' assistance and technical support for identifying subsidies to be phased out, optimizing the consumption of fossil fuels and other relevant purposes.

3.2 Renewable Energy Subsidies

Fossil fuel subsidy reforms will have long-term positive impacts on emission reductions if they are supplemented with other decarbonization policies[117] aimed at clean energy, among other things.[118] Despite the global climate change concerns, it is ironic that clean energy has garnered much lower subsidies than dirty energy. Specifically, fossil fuel consumption subsidies provided worldwide are approximately more than twice global renewable energy subsidies.[119] This gap may widen further if production subsidies in fossil fuels are additionally considered.

It is true that renewables are getting cheaper,[120] and the speed of growth in installed capacity of renewable energy has outpaced many predictions since 2000.[121] This can be attributed to, inter alia, renewable energy support policies that are currently present in virtually every jurisdiction at the national and/or regional levels.[122] But these efforts are still insufficient to reach international climate goals.[123] According to some estimates, in order to keep the average global temperature rise below 2°C, the global share of renewable energy must increase from around 15 per cent of the total primary energy supply in 2015 to around 66 per cent by 2050 while the current and planned policies would likely

[117] Harro van Asselt, Laura Merrill and Kati Kulovesi, 'Fossil Fuel Subsidies and the Global Climate Regime', in Skovgaard and Asselt (eds.), supra note 52, p. 143.

[118] See Laura Merrill et al., 'Making the Switch: From Fossil Fuel Subsidies to Sustainable Energy', Nordic Council of Ministers, 2017, pp. 30, 39–64.

[119] Wataru Matsumura and Zakia Adam, 'Commentary: Fossil Fuel Consumption Subsidies Bounced Back Strongly in 2018', 13 June 2019, www.iea.org/newsroom/news/2019/june/fossil-fuel-consumption-subsidies-bounced-back-strongly-in-2018.html.

[120] See International Renewable Energy Agency (IRENA), 'Renewable Power Generation Costs in 2018', 2019.

[121] Carbon Tracker Initiative, 'Carbon Supply Cost Curves: Evaluating Financial Risk to Coal Capital Expenditures', 2014, p. 11, www.carbontracker.org/wp-content/uploads/2014/09/CTI-Coal-report-Sept-2014-WEB1.pdf.

[122] See Renewable Energy Policy Network for the Twenty-First Century (REN21), 'Renewables 2019: Global Status Report', 2019.

[123] Ibid., pp. 20, 49.

lead to only 27 per cent share by then.[124] Thus, more is needed to reach SDG 7.2 target to 'increase substantially the share of renewable energy in the global energy mix'.

3.2.1 Renewable Energy Support Policies

A joint study of three international energy bodies finds that a genuine energy transition can be achieved only with a combination of the following comprehensive policies aimed at the transformation of both the energy sector itself and the socio-economic structure upon which it is built.[125] First, 'direct policies' encourage the development and deployment of renewable energy through mandatory actions (e.g., obligatory quotas for renewable electricity use, biofuel use requirements and so on), pricing or regulatory incentives (e.g., feed-in policies, tradeable certificates and so on) and fiscal or financial stimuli.[126] Second, 'integrating policies' seek to incorporate renewables into a larger energy and economic ecosystem and consumers' daily life by ensuring the presence of a required infrastructure (e.g., charging stations for electric cars), enhancing operational flexibility (e.g., R&D support for renewable electricity storage), encouraging behavioural change (e.g., raising awareness programmes) and so on.[127] Third, 'enabling policies' secure smooth operation of the renewable energy system by levelling the playing field across the energy segments, managing land use for, inter alia, renewable energy installations or biofuel crops, adopting tailor-made technical requirements, educational and labour programmes and others.[128]

Roughly 32 per cent of environment-related subsidies notified to the WTO in 2009–2021 concern alternative and renewable energy.[129] The existing support policies for renewables worldwide are especially ambitious for power generation but relatively modest in the heating/cooling and transport sectors.[130] The policies in each sector can be summarized as follows.

[124] IRENA, 'Global Energy Transformation: A Roadmap to 2050', 2018, pp. 8–9, 23.
[125] IRENA, IEA and REN21, 'Renewable Energy Policies in a Time of Transition', 2018, pp. 102–103.
[126] Ibid.
[127] Ibid.
[128] Ibid.
[129] WTO Environmental Database, 'Subsidies and Countervailing Measures' (see 'Types of Environment-related Objectives'), https://edb.wto.org/notifications/14305.
[130] REN21, supra note 122, p. 20.

In the power sector, feed-in pricing is a prevalent support scheme where governments pay for renewable electricity a feed-in tariff (FIT) – a long-term guaranteed fixed price – or otherwise a feed-in premium – a fixed or floating premium on top of the market price for renewable electricity, subject to possible upper and lower limits.[131] By contrast, quota obligations – generally known as 'renewable portfolio standards', 'renewable purchase obligations' or 'renewables obligations' – commonly require a specified portion of renewable electricity within the energy-mix but vary by type of quota, technology, timing, target entities and compliance rules.[132] Such quota obligations often operate together with tradeable renewable energy certificates or credits issued for the units of power produced from renewable sources. As another scheme, competitive tendering/bidding procedures or auctions, which invite potential project developers to compete and submit bids, can help discover real prices and cost-efficient support levels that can serve as a reference point for setting feed-in prices or capacity payments per installed kilowatt.[133] As for net metering and net billing systems, households and entities having solar photovoltaic (PV) or wind installations can feed the surplus of produced renewable electricity into the grid and take electricity from the grid in times of shortage, paying only for the difference between the taken and injected electricity and hence the 'net' energy use.[134]

With respect to heating and cooling, government support for using renewables (mainly, bioenergy, solar thermal, geothermal and renewable electricity) in buildings and industries is often implemented together with energy efficiency policies.[135] For example, building codes can indirectly incentivize renewable heating or cooling by prescribing relevant energy performance standards.[136] Besides various financial and fiscal

[131] See Council of European Energy Regulators, 'Key Support Elements of RES in Europe: Moving Towards Market Integration', C15-SDE-49-03, 2016, pp. 29–40; Energypedia, 'Feed-in Tariffs (FIT)', https://energypedia.info/wiki/Feed-in_Tariffs_(FIT); Energypedia, 'Feed-in Premiums (FIP)', https://energypedia.info/wiki/Feed-in_Premiums_(FIP).

[132] IRENA, IEA and REN21, supra note 125, p. 61; See also Sadie Cox and Sean Esterly, 'Renewable Electricity Standards: Good Practices and Design Considerations', Technical Report No. NREL/TP-6A20-65507, National Renewable Energy Laboratory, 2016.

[133] See Council of European Energy Regulators, supra note 131, pp. 15–23.

[134] Rodolfo Dufo-López and José L. Bernal-Agustín, 'A Comparative Assessment of Net Metering and Net Billing Policies. Study Cases for Spain', 84 *Energy* 684 (2015), pp. 684–685.

[135] REN21, supra note 122, p. 51.

[136] See ibid., pp. 52–54.

incentives for developing and deploying necessary technologies, countries have also designed more specific schemes, such as FITs, quotas for renewable heat and mandates for installing particular heating and cooling technologies.[137]

In the transport sector, policy promotion of renewables concerns energy carriers and fuels, vehicles and energy infrastructure.[138] Green energy usable in this sector includes biofuels, bio-methane, renewable electricity, renewable-electricity-derived hydrogen, ammonia and synthetic fuels.[139] Government support here is mainly concentrated in road transport in the form of supply- and demand-stimulating incentives for fuel-efficient vehicles and non-fossil fuels/electricity used in powering vehicles.[140] Regulatory measures, like blending mandates for biofuels, may supplement a variety of fiscal incentives and public financing adopted in this field.

In economics, the measures above can be justified where the market cannot produce optimal and efficient outcomes on its own. Such 'market failures' typically occur in the case of externalities, coordination failures and asymmetric information.[141] Governments respond to positive externalities of renewable energy production by granting incentives to producers for creating societal benefits in the form of a cleaner environment. By subsidizing both renewable power generation and related technology deployment, governments can correct the market's failure to coordinate these two and thereby achieve the harmonious 'greening' of the energy system. In the presence of information asymmetry as to the real market price of renewables, competitive biddings or auctions help governments identify the optimal price to be paid for renewable energy on the basis of offers by producers that, unlike governments, often have more realistic information about costs and profits (i.e., price components). If some of the market failures are already addressed by other policies or measures

[137] See IRENA, IEA and REN21, supra note 125, pp. 26–37.

[138] See IEA–RETD, 'Driving Renewable Energy for Transport: Next Generation Policy Instruments for Renewable Transport (Res-T-Next)', 2015.

[139] IRENA, IEA and REN21, supra note 125, p. 41.

[140] See REN21, supra note 122, pp. 54–59.

[141] See Sherzod Shadikhodjaev, *Industrial Policy and the World Trade Organization: Between Legal Constraints and Flexibilities* (Cambridge: Cambridge University Press, 2018), pp. 14–18. The justifications in question are also recognized in official documents, such as European Commission, Communication from the Commission: Guidelines on State Aid for Environmental Protection and Energy 2014–2020 (2014/C 200/01), OJ C 200, 28 June 2014, paras. 34–35.

(e.g., anti-pollution taxes or regulations), government stimuli are still warranted in economics to the extent they correct residual market failures or otherwise supplement the existing measures to make them more effective in remedying the same market imperfection.[142]

3.2.2 Legal Actions against Renewable Energy Subsidies

Unlike fossil fuel subsidies, renewable energy subsidies have already been targeted by a number of WTO disputes. As Table 3.1 shows, ten WTO disputes citing the SCM Agreement in consultation requests challenged renewable energy support by the EU (and some of its Member States), Canada, China, India and the United States. In four disputes resulting in panel/appellate decisions, the adjudicators ruled against discriminatory local content elements of the contested policies. But under the SCM Agreement, they either exercised judicial economy or were unable to complete a legal analysis, or the complainant did not raise subsidy claims in the panel request despite doing so in its earlier consultation request.

In sharp contrast to fossil fuel subsidies, government support for renewable energy has been attacked so intensively through the multilateral track for several reasons. Renewable energy and related technologies are produced in a larger number of countries, which naturally results in higher competition and trade tensions.[143] Moreover, the surge of the WTO disputes corresponds to the trend in international practice of challenging *new* trade-distorting measures (here, renewable energy subsidies) more often than long-standing, and hence expected, ones (here, fossil fuel subsidies).[144] Last but not least, the green subsidies at issue in all WTO disputes above had discriminatory LCRs while this is generally not typical of fossil fuel subsidies.[145]

In addition, the national track has also been frequently used. Table 3.2 captures twenty-two countervailing measures on renewable energy imports imposed worldwide since 2009.

Because of sparse trade in electricity in many parts of the world today, government support of renewable *electricity* as such is currently less prone to multilateral or national-track challenges than public favours

[142] See European Commission, supra note 141, paras. 36–37.
[143] Steenblik et al., supra note 52, pp. 128–129.
[144] See Meyer, supra note 58, pp. 394, 403–405.
[145] Asmelash, supra note 47, p. 281.

Table 3.1 *WTO disputes on renewable energy subsidies (as of 1 April 2023)*

Dispute number	Dispute title	Consultation request	Current status	Subsidy allegations in consultation request	Key findings
DS600	*European Union and Certain Member States – Certain Measures Concerning Palm Oil and Oil Palm Crop-Based Biofuels* (Complainant: Malaysia)	15/01/2021	Panel composed	Prohibited (local content) subsidies and actionable subsidies	
DS593	*European Union – Certain Measures Concerning Palm Oil and Oil Palm Crop-Based Biofuels* (Complainant: Indonesia)	09/09/2019	Panel composed	Prohibited (local content) subsidies and actionable subsidies	
DS563	*United States – Certain Measures Related to Renewable Energy* (Complainant: China)	14/08/2018	In consultations	Prohibited (local content) subsidies	
DS510	*United States – Certain Measures Relating to the Renewable Energy Sector* (Complainant: India)	09/09/2016	Panel report under appeal	Prohibited (local content) subsidies and actionable subsidies	Violations of national treatment (GATT); Judicial economy on prohibited subsidies; Actionable subsidies were not before the panel.

Table 3.1 (*cont.*)

Dispute number	Dispute title	Consultation request	Current status	Subsidy allegations in consultation request	Key findings
DS459	*European Union – Certain Measures on the Importation and Marketing of Biodiesel and Measures Supporting the Biodiesel Industry* (Complainant: Argentina)	15/05/2013	In consultations	Prohibited (local content) subsidies and actionable subsidies	
DS456	*India – Certain Measures Relating to Solar Cells and Solar Modules* (Complainant: United States)	06/02/2013	Panel report and Appellate Body report adopted on 14/10/2016; Compliance proceedings ongoing; Authorization to retaliate requested	Prohibited (local content) subsidies and actionable subsidies (as mentioned in the first consultation request)	Violations of national treatment (GATT and Agreement on Trade-Related Investment Measures (TRIMs)); Subsidy issues were not before the panel.
DS452	*European Union and Certain Member States – Certain Measures Affecting the Renewable Energy Generation Sector* (Complainant: China)	05/11/2012	In consultations	Prohibited (local content) subsidies	

DS426	*Canada – Measures Relating to the Feed-in Tariff Program* (Complainant: EU)	11/08/2011	Panel report and Appellate Body report adopted on 24/05/2013; Implementation notified by respondent	Prohibited (local content) subsidies	Violations of national treatment (GATT and TRIMs Agreement); Unable to complete subsidy-related legal analysis
DS419	*China – Measures Concerning Wind Power Equipment* (Complainant: United States)	22/12/2010	In consultations	Prohibited (local content) subsidies	
DS412	*Canada – Certain Measures Affecting the Renewable Energy Generation Sector* (Complainant: Japan)	13/07/2010	Panel report and Appellate Body report adopted on 24/05/2013; Implementation notified by respondent	Prohibited (local content) subsidies	Violations of national treatment (GATT and TRIMs Agreement); Unable to complete subsidy-related legal analysis

Source: Author's compilation from data at WTO, www.wto.org, on dispute complaints (consultation requests) brought under the SCM Agreement.

Table 3.2 *WTO members' countervailing measures on renewable energy products*

Imposing member	Subject product	Exporting member	Measure in force from	Investigation number
United States	Utility scale wind towers	India	06/12/2021	C-533-898
United States	Utility scale wind towers	Malaysia	04/08/2021	C-557-822
UK	Biodiesel	United States	01/01/2021	2020/05 US
UK	Biodiesel	Argentina	01/01/2021	2020/26 AR
UK	Biodiesel	Indonesia	01/01/2021	2020/36 ID
United States	Utility scale wind towers	Canada	26/08/2020	C-122-868
United States	Utility scale wind towers	Viet Nam	26/08/2020	C-552-826
United States	Utility scale wind towers	Indonesia	26/08/2020	C-560-834
Colombia	Fuel alcohol (ethanol)	United States	07/05/2020	SB-249-01-01/ Alcohol carburante
EU	Biodiesel	Indonesia	09/12/2019	AS650 ID
EU	Biodiesel	Argentina	12/02/2019	AS644 AR
United States	Biodiesel	Argentina	04/01/2018	C-357-821
United States	Biodiesel	Indonesia	04/01/2018	C-560-831
Peru	Biodiesel	Argentina	28/01/2016	Exp. N° 009-2014-CFD-ARG
Canada	Certain photovoltaic modules and laminates	China	04/07/2015	CV/140/CN
United States	Crystalline silicon photovoltaic cells	China	18/02/2015	C-570-011
EU	Solar glass	China	14/05/2014	AS599 CN
China	Solar-grade polysilicon	United States	20/01/2014	12-0007
United States	Utility scale wind towers	China	15/02/2013	C-570-982

Table 3.2 (*cont.*)

Imposing member	Subject product	Exporting member	Measure in force from	Investigation number
United States	Crystalline silicon photovoltaic cells, whether or not assembled into modules	China	07/12/2012	C-570-980
Peru	Pure biodiesel (B100) and blends containing more than 50 per cent biodiesel (B50)	United States	22/08/2010	Exp.N°019-2009-CFD-USA
EU	Biodiesel	United States	10/07/2009	AS532 US

Source: Author's compilation from data, covering the period 1995–2022, at the WTO's Trade Remedies Data Portal, https://trade-remedies.wto.org/en (accessed 1 April 2023).
Note: At the time of writing, the WTO trade remedies database, used for retrieving data for Table 3.2, presented measures that were in force on or after 1 January 2020 while historical information on measures that were terminated before 31 December 2019 were being verified by the WTO Secretariat.

for renewable energy-generating equipment that is already extensively traded on a global scale.[146] But as EU case law may suggest,[147] subsidy-related frictions over green electricity trade can occur at least in regional or other international markets that have integrated electricity systems.

[146] Ilaria Espa and Gracia Marín Durán, 'Renewable Energy Subsidies and WTO Law: Time to Rethink the Case for Reform beyond *Canada – Renewable Energy / Fit Program*', 21 *Journal of International Economic Law* 621 (2018), pp. 626, 637–643.

[147] For EU case law involving renewable electricity subsidies, see Sherzod Shadikhodjaev, 'Promotion of "Green" Electricity and International Dispute Settlement: Trade and Investment Issues', 49 *International Lawyer* 343 (2016), pp. 352–361.

In addition to the EU,[148] ASEAN provides an example of expanding intra-regional trade in electricity, including from renewable energy sources, facilitated by the ASEAN Power Grid initiative.[149] In 2021, the African Union officially launched an 'African Single Electricity Market' covering 'the world's largest continent-wide energy trading program' and interconnected grid with the plan to incorporate renewable electricity in the future.[150] Furthermore, the literature envisions the possibility of creating a pan-continental 'global grid' powered by renewable sources from various locations worldwide.[151] Thus, it is realistic to expect that the intensification of cross-border movement of identifiable renewable electricity, benefiting from government support measures, can lead to a rise in anti-subsidy measures against this particular commodity.

3.2.3 *Key Messages from WTO Jurisprudence*

The WTO rulings in *Canada – Renewable Energy / Canada – Feed-in Tariff Program* are remarkable for providing important findings on the scope of policy space in the clean energy field.[152] In these cases, the EU and Japan complained about Canadian province Ontario's FIT programme that was launched in 2009 to offer guaranteed payments to solar and wind power generators under twenty- or forty-year contracts if they met the LCR, or the 'Minimum Required Domestic Content Level', for using the qualifying electricity generation equipment. The FIT programme at issue was the third in a series of renewable energy initiatives adopted by the local government since 2004 to diversify Ontario's electricity supply-mix and reduce coal-fired facilities.[153]

[148] See European Commission, 'Electricity Market Design', https://energy.ec.europa.eu/topics/markets-and-consumers/market-legislation/electricity-market-design_en.

[149] ASEAN Centre for Energy, 'ASEAN Plan of Action for Energy Cooperation (APAEC) 2016–2025, Phase II: 2021–2025', 2020, pp. 12–17, https://aseanenergy.org/asean-plan-of-action-for-energy-cooperation-apaec-phase-ii-2021–2025/.

[150] African Union, 'African Union Launches World's Largest Single Electricity Market (AFSEM)', 4 June 2021, https://au.int/en/pressreleases/20210604/african-union-launches-worlds-largest-single-electricity-market-afsem.

[151] See, for example, Spyros Chatzivasileiadis, Damien Ernst and Göran Andersson, 'The Global Grid', 57 *Renewable Energy* 372 (2013).

[152] See Sherzod Shadikhodjaev, 'First WTO Judicial Review of Climate Change Subsidy Issues', 107 *American Journal of International Law* 864 (2013).

[153] *Canada – Renewable Energy / Canada – Feed-in Tariff Program*, WTO Panel Reports, paras. 7.64–7.65.

While the LCR of this programme was found to discriminate against competing foreign equipment in violation of the WTO national treatment provisions under the GATT and the Agreement on Trade-Related Investment Measures (TRIMs),[154] this case could not confirm that the FIT *was* a 'subsidy' within the meaning of the SCM Agreement. The Appellate Body did find that FIT-covered electricity purchases by the Ontario Power Authority was a financial contribution in the form of the government purchase of goods as envisaged by Article 1.1(a)(1)(iii) of the SCM Agreement.[155] But at the stage of verifying the existence of a benefit, it could not uphold that FIT prices were more attractive for the generators than non-FIT electricity prices. Among other things, three important findings of the Appellate Body leading to this outcome have far-reaching repercussions for renewable energy support in potentially carving out some room for manoeuvre for policymakers.

First, the Appellate Body held that unlike government support of certain participants in an established market, a State intervention creating a *new* market did not 'in and of itself' provide a benefit, and hence a subsidy, because the market which did not exist yet could not be said to be distorted by the government.[156] In practice, this would imply that if the renewables market is in its infancy in the region of competence of the 'subsidizing' government, the latter can shy away from the WTO strictures by proving that the public support at issue was necessary for creating a renewables market. However, the appellate decision in question left it unanswered how to ascertain the maturity of a particular market so as to determine properly whether a government measure is a WTO-regulated 'subsidy'. In this dispute, even though the renewable energy policy was adopted by the government of Ontario five years before the inception of the contested FIT scheme, nothing in this ruling seems to indicate a particular development level of the renewable energy market there.[157]

Second, the Appellate Body held that when defining an appropriate market for comparing government-backed FIT prices with non-FIT prices, one must examine both demand- and supply-side factors to check whether renewable and conventional electricity are substitutable enough

[154] *Canada – Renewable Energy / Canada – Feed-in Tariff Program*, WTO Appellate Body Reports, para. 6.1. For LCRs, see also Section 2.2.1.2.

[155] *Canada – Renewable Energy / Canada – Feed-in Tariff Program*, ibid., para. 5.128.

[156] Ibid., para. 5.188.

[157] Shadikhodjaev, supra note 152, p. 877.

to be deemed to be in the same market of electricity. Unlike consumers (or the demand side), the generators (or the supply side) can distinguish conventional and renewable electricity due to 'important differences in cost structures and operating costs and characteristics among generating technologies'.[158] Such supply-side non-substitutability of both electricity types necessitates price comparisons within the renewable electricity market alone, rather than across the blended electricity market as a whole.[159] The policy implication is that as long as renewable energy remains 'unlike' to cheaper conventional energy under the subsidy rules, proving the existence of a benefit for renewables would generally be more difficult than if one would do so through cross-energy price comparisons.

Third, where subsidy determinations within a particular renewable energy segment, like solar power or wind power, involve price comparisons across different support programmes to establish the benefit under one of them, the comparison must be made 'between prices referring to the same period, the same type of generation technology, the same overall supply-mix, projects of the same or similar scale, and supply contracts of the same duration'.[160] In practice, however, these apparently strict criteria of ensuring accuracy may be hard to meet to successfully challenge a renewable energy scheme. Indeed, in reviewing proposed price comparisons under the FIT and competitive bidding procedures in *Canada – Renewable Energy / Canada – Feed-in Tariff Program*, the Appellate Body itself could not complete the benefit analysis due to the insufficient factual determinations on record. The price comparisons here concerned wind power only as no appropriate data existed for solar energy.[161]

The second implication regarding renewable and conventional energy comparisons above can find support in *US – Softwood Lumber VII* as well. There, at issue was the USDOC's countervailing duty determination that a Canadian State-owned utility company had purchased biomass electricity at a higher-than-usual price (hence subsidizing the electricity purchases) within a single market of electricity generated from all energy sources. But because it was Canada's specific regulatory regime on clean energy that required the utility company to purchase electricity generated

[158] *Canada – Renewable Energy / Canada – Feed-in Tariff Program*, WTO Appellate Body Reports, para. 5.178.
[159] Ibid., para. 5.178.
[160] Ibid., para. 5.235.
[161] Ibid., paras. 5.236, 5.245–5.246.

from biomass, the panel indicated that the relevant market for price comparisons should have been defined under that specific regime. Thus, in the context of *that* regime, biomass electricity was considered not to be substitutable with electricity generated from other sources. Moreover, the USDOC's approach was found to be flawed as it selected a benchmark that reflected prevailing market conditions for the sale of electricity at the retail level where the prevailing market conditions were not shaped by the same regulatory regime.[162]

Overall, the judicial findings above increase the burden of proof for contesting renewable energy projects under the WTO subsidy rules. This probably explains why the United States omitted the SCM Agreement in its panel request in *India – Solar Cells* although it did invoke that agreement in the consultation request when the appellate rulings in *Canada – Renewable Energy / Canada – Feed-in Tariff Program* were not issued yet.[163] However, if government support for renewables is conditioned upon compliance with LCRs, the latter can be found to be illegal under the WTO national treatment provisions even if the government support itself is not determined to be a subsidy.

3.2.4 Creating More Policy Space for Renewable Energy Subsidies

Strictly speaking, the judicial climate-friendly subsidy interpretations above are binding upon the disputing parties with respect to the examined measure, but the WTO adjudicators have generally followed previous case law on a de facto basis. However, given that the de facto 'precedent' practice has been one of the main reasons for the United States to continuously criticize and paralyse the Appellate Body,[164] it is not ruled out that the precedential value of previous jurisprudence may diminish over time. While WTO dispute settlement is a useful route for defining policy space on a case-by-case basis, the reforming of the SCM Agreement could be an alternative, albeit admittedly difficult, track for accommodating green policies in a securer and more predictable way.[165]

[162] See *US – Softwood Lumber VII*, WTO Panel Report, paras. 7.634, 7.639–7.642, 7.648–7.650; see also paras. 7.667–7.680.

[163] See *India – Solar Cells*, WTO Panel Report, n. 1 to para. 1.1.

[164] See US Trade Representative, 'Report on the Appellate Body of the World Trade Organization', 2020, pp. 55–64.

[165] For a detailed discussion of certain 'greening' options in the sections below, see Sherzod Shadikhodjaev, 'Renewable Energy and Government Support: Time to "Green" the SCM Agreement?', 14 *World Trade Review* 479 (2015), pp. 494–505.

The existing WTO mandate for improving the SCM Agreement could be used for this purpose.[166] In addition, the TESSD could be another available avenue to tackle this issue.[167]

Given that LCRs are environmentally counterproductive in general,[168] the SCM Agreement can be said to be already pro-environmental in prohibiting subsidies that are conditional on compliance with LCRs. But this is not sufficient, and further greening is needed. Indeed, actionable subsidies for renewable energy always remain prone to WTO challenges as some disputes in Table 3.1 suggest. Moreover, the proliferation of countervailing measures on renewable energy products constrains subsidizing members' environmental policy space, as well.[169] Finally and importantly, ongoing decarbonization actions worldwide and international rule-making efforts against harmful fossil fuel subsidies will necessitate more policy space for renewable energy subsidies to replace fossil fuels. Thus, it is not surprising to see that in order to foster support measures for the net-zero transition, the EU temporarily loosened its State aid rules in March 2023 to allow Member States to grant aid for: accelerating the rollout of renewable energy, energy storage and renewable heat; decarbonizing industrial production processes; and accelerating investments in key net-zero-enabling sectors (e.g., solar panels, wind turbines, heat-pumps, electrolysers and carbon capture, usage and storage).[170]

3.2.4.1 Due Restraint for Renewable Energy Subsidies

Initially, now-defunct Article 8 of the SCM Agreement treated certain environmental and R&D subsidies – both relevant to renewable energy support – as 'non-actionable', or permissible, subsidies. However, the overly strict eligibility criteria significantly narrowed the scope of non-actionable subsidies, rendering Article 8 virtually inoperative in

[166] See WT/MIN(01)/DEC/1, supra note 113, para. 28; TN/RL/28, supra note 113, paras. 1, 6.

[167] See INF/TE/SSD/R/12, supra note 28, para. 5.2; 'Trade and Environmental Sustainability Structured Discussion', supra note 28, p. 3.

[168] See Section 2.2.1.2.

[169] Espa and Durán, supra note 146, pp. 632, 647, 651.

[170] See European Commission, 'State Aid: Commission Adopts Temporary Crisis and Transition Framework to Further Support Transition towards Net-Zero Economy', 9 March 2023, https://ec.europa.eu/commission/presscorner/detail/en/ip_23_1563; European Commission, 'Temporary Crisis and Transition Framework' (applicable as of 9 March 2023), https://competition-policy.ec.europa.eu/state-aid/ukraine_en.

practice.[171] Therefore, the revival of Article 8 in its original version in the SCM Agreement appears rather unhelpful for shielding clean energy subsidies today although nothing prevents WTO members from unilaterally incorporating Article 8 into domestic countervailing duty rules and RTAs.[172]

Instead, we suggest that WTO members negotiate an interim *renewables-specific* 'due restraint' clause that would prevent SCM measures against actionable subsidies in this field.[173] In order to minimize trade distortions, such clause should cover products directly associated with renewable energy and benefit only deserving members depending on their green development level. This would require defining a list of renewable energy products and specifying competitiveness criteria (or thresholds) for including members' products in, and graduating them from, the due restraint protection. Like under the Agreement on Agriculture, the due restraint in question could apply to the bound/scheduled amounts of renewable energy subsidies to be reduced over time.

In addition, the due restraint could also apply to subsidies switching from fossil fuels to renewables. The idea here is to encourage subsidies' redirection from dirty to clean energy to achieve greater decarbonization. In this regard, one study estimated that the elimination of fossil fuel subsidies in selected twenty countries – including big subsidizers – could cut national GHG emissions by 11 per cent, but this number could climb to 18 per cent if only some share (30 per cent) of savings from such subsidy reform were reinvested into renewable energy and energy efficiency.[174] For the sake of the due restraint in this context, WTO members would need to work out a mechanism of tracking such subsidy shifts. For example, any well-documented shift of budgetary spending on fossil fuels to renewables could rely on the protection from anti-subsidy

171 See Rüdiger Wolfrum, Peter-Tobias Stoll and Michael Koebele (eds.), *WTO – Trade Remedies* (Leiden/Boston: Martinus Nijhoff Publishers, 2008), p. 552; Robert Howse, 'Climate Mitigation Subsidies and the WTO Legal Framework: A Policy Analysis', International Institute for Sustainable Development, 2010, p. 21.

172 See Section 6.1.2; José-Antonio Monteiro, 'Typology of Environment-Related Provisions in Regional Trade Agreements', WTO Working Paper No. ERSD-2016-13, 2016, p. 43.

173 For a list of some earlier works insisting on a renewed shelter for 'good' subsidies including renewable energy subsidies, see Luca Rubini, '*Ain't Wastin' Time No More*: Subsidies for Renewable Energy, the SCM Agreement, Policy Space, and Law Reform', 15 *Journal of International Economic Law* 525 (2012), p. 571 (n. 165).

174 Merrill et al., supra note 50, p. 11.

measures as long as the affected renewable energy product of the member concerned would remain internationally uncompetitive under the predefined criteria (or thresholds) mentioned before.

3.2.4.2 Technology Transfer Exemption

As will be considered in Chapter 6, the WTO Agreement on Trade-Related Aspects of Intellectual Property Rights (TRIPS) obligates developed country members to incentivize technology transfer to LDCs. But under the SCM Agreement, developed countries are still subject to the ban against export subsidies, which may partly explain relatively modest results on such technology transfers.

To be complementary to the TRIPS Agreement, the SCM Agreement could be revised to exempt developed countries from the export subsidy ban in the case of their incentives promoting technology transfer to LDCs (and other deserving developing countries). This exemption could be confined to the transfer of specified green technologies if reaching consensus for the revision here covering all types of technologies is otherwise not possible. At present, Article 27.2 of the SCM Agreement already exempts some developing countries listed in Annex VII from the ban on export subsidies. The existence of this precedent should encourage members to create a similar carve-out for the technology transfer in question that would be supportive of sustainable development in the beneficiary countries. This would also correspond to the calls of environmental treaties upon developed countries to promote and finance the transfer of green technologies to developing countries.[175]

3.2.4.3 Increasing Thresholds for Negligible Subsidies

WTO members could agree to green the current requirements for the termination of countervailing duty investigations vis-à-vis *de minimis* subsidies and negligible imports.[176] Under the SCM Agreement, the amount of a subsidy is *de minimis* if it is less than 1 per cent ad valorem (or 2 per cent for developing countries);[177] negligible volumes of subsidized imports are specified only for developing countries at the level of less than 4 per cent of total imports.[178] But members could agree to increase these thresholds for imports of renewable energy products.

[175] See Section 6.2.2.1.
[176] See Article 11.9 of the SCM Agreement.
[177] Articles 11.9 and 27.10(a) of the SCM Agreement.
[178] Article 27.10(b) of the SCM Agreement.

In the case of *de minimis*, all countervailable subsidy programmes benefiting an investigated producer would typically be counted towards the determination of such an increased *de minimis* level in line with the general methodology of calculating subsidization rates. In addition, members could also agree to establish a separate *de minimis* margin for each subsidy programme considered in an investigation on renewables. If so, any individual progamme below such margin would be treated as negligible and consequently excluded from the net subsidy rate calculations.[179]

3.2.4.4 Application of General Exceptions

It is controversial whether general (environmental) exceptions under Article XX of the GATT can justify green subsidies found to be inconsistent with the SCM Agreement.[180] Unlike the legal texts that explicitly accept the applicability of Article XX (e.g., the TRIMs Agreement) or exclude its applicability due to *lex specialis* on general exceptions (e.g., the GATS), the SCM Agreement, the Anti-Dumping Agreement and few others are silent on this issue. Even if one assumes that footnote 56 to Article 32.1 of the SCM Agreement does not rule out the Article XX application, this would work only for anti-subsidy measures rather than subsidization.[181]

179 For some jurisdictions' calculation practice concerning negligible subsidy programmes, see, for example, USDOC, Issues and Decision Memorandum for the Final Determination in the Countervailing Duty Investigation of Crystalline Silicon Photovoltaic Cells, Whether or Not Assembled Into Modules, from the People's Republic of China [C-570-980], 9 October 2012, pp. 20, 22; USDOC, Issues and Decision Memorandum for the Final Determination on Countervailing Duty (CVD) Investigation: Utility Scale Wind Towers (Wind Towers) from the People's Republic of China (the PRC) [C-570-982], 17 December 2012, p. 26; EU, Commission Decision of 20 December 2012 terminating the anti-subsidy proceeding concerning imports of bioethanol originating in the United States of America and terminating the registration of such imports imposed by Regulation (EU) No. 771/2012, OJ L 352, 21 December 2012, paras. 78, 143, 168, 188.

180 See, for example, Paolo D. Farah and Elena Cima, 'Energy Trade and the WTO: Implications for Renewable Energy and the OPEC Cartel', 16 *Journal of International Economic Law* 707 (2013), pp. 726–728.

181 Article 32.1 of the SCM Agreement reads:

> No specific action against a subsidy of another Member can be taken except in accordance with the provisions of GATT 1994, as interpreted by this Agreement.[56]
>
> 56 This paragraph is *not intended to preclude action under other relevant provisions of GATT 1994*, where appropriate [emphasis added].

WTO jurisprudence has accepted the invocability of Article XX only in the presence of a specific textual basis. For example, in *China – Publications and Audiovisual Products*, China invoked the public moral exception under Article XX(a) of the GATT vis-à-vis paragraph 5.1 of its Accession Protocol that imposes the obligation to 'progressively liberalize the availability and scope of the right to trade' – so that all enterprises in the country could freely import and export goods – '[w]ithout prejudice to China's right to regulate trade in a manner consistent with the WTO Agreement'. Because the 'WTO Agreement' covers the GATT and the consistency with the WTO Agreement can be achieved, inter alia, through justification by GATT Article XX, the Appellate Body confirmed China's right to rely on Article XX(a) defence in the legal context in question.[182] By contrast, the availability of Article XX was rejected in *China – Raw Materials* vis-à-vis paragraph 11.3 of China's Accession Protocol which lacks any textual link to Article XX.[183]

Therefore, renewable energy subsidies found to be illegal under the SCM Agreement are not likely to be eligible for the GATT general exceptions. To change the status quo, WTO members could amend the SCM Agreement accordingly. Alternatively, they could take a more comprehensive step affecting *all* WTO obligations by adopting a ministerial decision, declaration or another instrument that would make it explicit that the provisions of GATT Article XX (and Article XXI on security exceptions) apply to all WTO texts without prejudice to the existing exceptions and flexibilities. This would fill a lacuna where the relevant text, like the current SCM Agreement, is silent on the applicability of the GATT exceptions.

3.3 Concluding Remarks

Both fossil fuel subsidies and renewable energy subsidies create cost (or price) advantages for beneficiary producers to the detriment of competitors. Thus, the SCM Agreement, being concerned with subsidy-related market distortions, applies to both dirty and clean energy alike. But the actual SCM practice presents negative environmental implications for State energy promotion. In particular, the limitations of the WTO subsidy regime in curtailing fossil fuel subsidies, on the one hand, and the

[182] *China – Publications and Audiovisual Products*, WTO Appellate Body Report, paras. 218–223, 233.

[183] See Section 2.2.2.1.

contrasting upward trend in attacking clean energy subsidies, on the other, are environmentally unwelcome facts.

Remaining on the international agenda for more than a decade, the issue of reforming fossil fuel subsidies is currently being discussed under the recently launched environmental initiatives in the WTO. This may create once-missed momentum in the WTO for taking action in this sphere. As discussed in this chapter, members should enhance the WTO's role in restricting and controlling harmful fossil fuel subsidies through horizontal and sectoral approaches. As for renewable energy subsidies, WTO jurisprudence offers some significant interpretations in favour of environmental policy space. But for greater legal security and predictability, the WTO subsidy regime should be improved to afford better treatment to green policies. In short, the WTO should readjust the existing subsidy rules to more effectively align with the environmental sustainability needs.

4

Pro-environmental Energy Standards and Trade

Standardization of products and services pursues certain public policy objectives and thus takes into account environmental needs and the concerns of society. This chapter examines trade rules and practices regarding technical standards on energy efficiency, carbon emissions and renewable energy. Such standards usually complement anti-pollution, decarbonization and subsidization measures discussed in the previous chapters, by establishing limits on pollutants, energy performance requirements, sustainability criteria for government-promoted energy products and so on. The way in which standard-related measures are adopted and applied affects the international movement of goods and services. The active use and trade implications of these measures in the energy–environment context have intensified the pace of raising related trade concerns in the WTO. Often tensions arise because of regulatory divergence that stems from differences in domestic situations, conditions and preferences as reflected in national standardization policies. But the notion that regulatory convergence is important in cutting trade costs is widely recognized, with many jurisdictions being increasingly involved in regulatory cooperation. Clean energy products can be supplied together with the associated services. Yet international trade rules on service standards are nearly under-developed and lack substantive details, which gives leeway to national regulators. Finally, apart from 'general' markets, green goods and services also find their use in the segment of government procurement where environmental aspects are made part of technical specifications.

4.1 Trade Concerns over Pro-environmental Energy Standards

Energy–environment standard-related measures concerning goods have been discussed in the WTO's TBT Committee. The latter regularly meets to consult on 'any matters relating to the operation of [the TBT] Agreement or the furthering of its objectives' and carries out the assigned 'responsibilities'.[1] Since its first meeting in 1995, the TBT Committee has discussed 'specific trade concerns' (STCs) – trade issues raised by members in relation to proposed or implemented TBT measures (technical regulations, standards or conformity assessment procedures) of other members.[2] The TBT Committee's work on STCs is very important in providing an 'informal' avenue for resolving non-tariff 'trade conflicts' often in a 'low-cost, expedient and effective way'.[3] This mechanism can prevent many formal disputes. Indeed, in 1995–2021, 728 STCs far outnumbered fifty-seven disputes under the TBT Agreement,[4] with only a small fraction (of about 2 per cent) of STCs being linked to WTO complaints.[5]

As for the procedures, a member wishing to include a particular STC in the TBT Committee's agenda notifies its intention to the WTO Secretariat and the targeted member before the committee meeting.[6] An STC can be withdrawn from the agenda if the concerned and targeted members engage in an informal bilateral dialogue prior to the meeting and settle the matter at that stage.[7] In the committee meeting, discussions on each new or previously raised STC typically start with comments of the concerned (and other interested) member followed by a response of the targeted member. In general, the STC process carries out three functions: to enable members to obtain more information about measures at issue, to influence regulations of other members and to address practical issues of meeting other members' regulatory requirements.[8]

Between 1 January 1995 and 31 December 2021, WTO members raised seventy-four STCs over energy–environment TBT measures

[1] Article 13.1 of the TBT Agreement.

[2] WTO, Committee on TBT – Decisions and Recommendations Adopted by the WTO Committee on Technical Barriers to Trade since 1 January 1995 – Note by the Secretariat – Revision, G/TBT/1/Rev.14 (24 September 2019), p. 55.

[3] Henrik Horn, Petros C. Mavroidis and Erik N. Wijkström, 'In the Shadow of the DSU: Addressing Specific Trade Concerns in the WTO SPS and TBT Committees', 47 *Journal of World Trade* 729 (2013), p. 730; Kateryna Holzer, 'Addressing Tensions and Avoiding Disputes: Specific Trade Concerns in the TBT Committee', WTO Staff Working Paper No. ERSD-2018-11, 31 October 2018, p. 10.

[4] See STCs at https://eping.wto.org/ and WTO disputes under the TBT Agreement at www.wto.org/english/tratop_e/dispu_e/dispu_agreements_index_e.htm.

[5] In 1995–2021, TBT disputes concerned measures previously addressed in seventeen STCs: fifteen STCs (1995–2017), identified in Holzer (supra note 3, p. 14), plus two more STCs (*IMS ID 553* and *IMS ID 664*) linked to disputes brought in 2018–2021.

[6] G/TBT/1/Rev.14, supra note 2, p. 56.

[7] Holzer, supra note 3, p. 4.

[8] Marianna B. Karttunen, *Transparency in the WTO SPS and TBT Agreements: The Real Jewel in the WTO's Crown* (Cambridge: Cambridge University Press, 2020), p. 297.

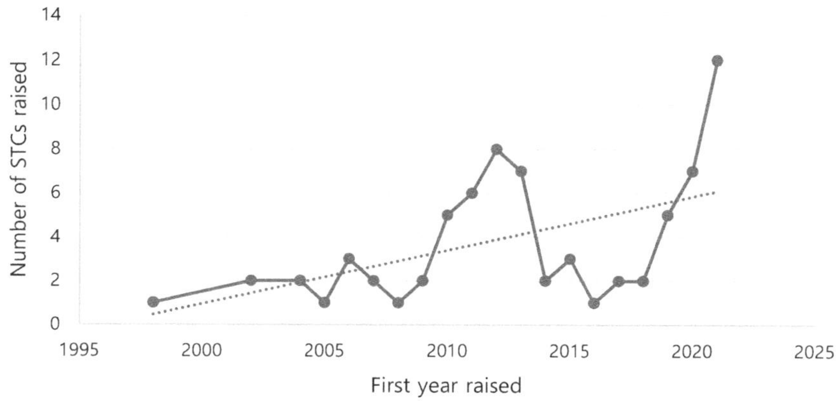

Figure 4.1 Trend in raising energy–environment STCs in TBT Committee (1995–2021).
Source: Author's compilation from data (as of 1 April 2023) at WTO, 'SPS & TBT Platform', https://eping.wto.org, as arranged in Appendix A.

concerning energy efficiency (73 per cent of those STCs), emission control (17 per cent) and renewable energy (10 per cent).[9] The number of such STCs has noticeably increased in recent years (Figure 4.1), with forty-nine STCs (or 65 per cent) being raised in 2012–2021. The nature of members' concerns varies (Figure 4.2). Roughly 80 per cent of the energy–environment STCs concerned notified measures. The most frequent STC targets were the EU and its Member States, the United States, Korea, China, Colombia and Saudi Arabia; and the most frequent STC raisers were China, Korea, the United States, the EU and Japan.[10]

The number of times of raising a particular STC may indicate the degree of importance attached to the STC and/or the level of progress reached in addressing it.[11] STCs appearing in three or more meetings are likely to address 'serious' issues that go beyond simple clarifications.[12] The following sections briefly discuss some of the most frequent STCs on energy–environment measures captured by the database presented in Appendix A.

[9] Based on Appendix A.
[10] Ibid.
[11] WTO, Committee on TBT – Twenty-Fifth Annual Review of the Implementation and Operation of the TBT Agreement – Note by the Secretariat, G/TBT/44 (19 February 2020), para. 4.15.
[12] Horn et al., supra note 3, p. 746.

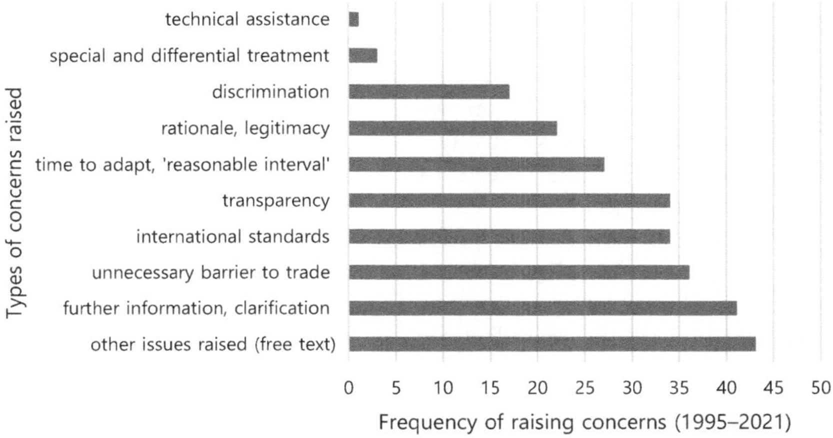

Figure 4.2 The nature of energy–environment STCs raised in TBT Committee (1995–2021).

Source: Author's compilation from data (as of 1 April 2023) at WTO, 'SPS & TBT Platform', https://eping.wto.org, as arranged in Appendix A.

Notes: There can be several types of concerns raised in one STC. 'Frequency of raising concerns' indicates the number of STCs for a particular type of concern.

4.1.1 *Energy Efficiency STCs*

A series of STCs (*ID 123*, *575* and *592*) discussed EU eco-design rules (a framework directive and regulations) affecting various household appliances and other energy-using devices. The measures at issue are about improving product design so as to ensure greater energy savings and lesser environmental damage during the product life cycle. In addition to energy efficiency, they lay down new 'circular economy' requirements for enhancing durability, reparability and reusability/recyclability of covered products. WTO members flagged concerns about the lack of transparency and consultation with stakeholders, adverse impacts on especially developing country exports, excessively strict energy standards, an unjustified ban on the use of some chemicals and so on.[13]

[13] See WTO, Committee on TBT – Minutes of the Meeting of 2 November 2005 – Note by the Secretariat, G/TBT/M/37 (22 December 2005), paras. 11–13; WTO, Committee on TBT – European Union – Draft Commission Regulation Laying Down Eco-Design Requirements for Electronic Displays Pursuant to Directive 2009/125/EC of the European Parliament and of the Council, Amending Commission Regulation (EC) No. 1275/2008 [. . .] – 6 and 7 March 2019, G/TBT/W/606 (22 March 2019); WTO,

In *ID 455* and *599*, Ecuador's energy efficiency standards for cloth dryers were criticized for being overly trade-restrictive in allowing the marketing of only 'A' and 'B' classes while international standards and practice accepted class 'C' as well.[14] In these and the above STCs, Ecuador and the EU, respectively, responded by justifying their measure concerned with the need to promote environment-friendly energy consumption.[15]

ID 527 dealt with China's proposed policy to increase the portion of new energy vehicles (plug-in electric or hydrogen fuel cell vehicles) in car production/importation to 8 per cent in 2018, 10 per cent in 2019 and 12 per cent in 2020. By manufacturing or purchasing such vehicles, companies could earn credits and use them for meeting compulsory limits on fleet-wide corporate average fuel consumption.[16] Some members pointed out timing constraints for adaptation and requested equal access for foreign producers to Chinese incentives (e.g., purchase subsidies) as well as flexibility for small-volume manufacturers' average fuel consumption targets. In response, China postponed the enforcement of the relevant rules from 2018 to 2019 and assured equal treatment between domestic and foreign producers. But members still insisted on revealing post-2020 plans and allowing for sufficient lead time for future regulatory developments in this field.[17]

Committee on TBT – Minutes of the Meeting of 20–21 June 2019 – Note by the Secretariat, G/TBT/M/78 (23 September 2019), paras. 3.110–3.113; WTO, Committee on TBT – European Union – Draft Commission Regulation Laying Down Eco-Design Requirements for Electronic Displays Pursuant to Directive 2009/125/EC of the European Parliament and of the Council, Amending Commission Regulation (EC) No. 1275/2008 [...] – 20 and 21 June 2019, G/TBT/W/672 (23 July 2019); WTO, Committee on TBT – Minutes of the Meeting of 12–15 November 2019 – Note by the Secretariat, G/TBT/M/79 (30 January 2020), paras. 2.113–2.116, 2.294–2.297.

14 See WTO, Committee on TBT – Minutes of the Meeting of 5–6 November 2014 – Note by the Secretariat – Revision, G/TBT/M/64/Rev.1 (6 March 2015), paras. 2.70–2.72; G/TBT/M/79, supra note 13, paras. 2.16–2.17.

15 WTO, Committee on TBT – Minutes of the Meeting of 18–19 March 2015 – Note by the Secretariat, G/TBT/M/65 (28 May 2015), para. 2.237; WTO, Committee on TBT – Minutes of the Meeting of 24–25 March 2010 – Note by the Secretariat, G/TBT/M/50 (28 May 2010), para. 180.

16 See Shikha Rokadiya and Zifei Yang, 'Overview of Global Zero-Emission Vehicle Mandate Programs', International Council on Clean Transportation, Briefing, 2019, pp. 6–7.

17 See WTO, Committee on TBT – Minutes of the Meeting of 29–30 March 2017 – Note by the Secretariat, G/TBT/M/71 (2 June 2017), paras. 2.23–2.32; WTO, Committee on TBT – Minutes of the Meeting of 8–9 November 2017 – Note by the Secretariat, G/TBT/M/73 (6 March 2018), paras. 2.179–2.183; WTO, Committee on TBT – Minutes of

4.1.2 Emission Control STCs

Since the notification in 2014, China's interim measures for quality management of commercial coal (*ID 477*) have been among most frequent STCs in the energy sector. Australia and Canada were disappointed with market access difficulties triggered by burdensome conformity assessment procedures, customs clearance delays and unrecognition of applicable international standards and testing practices. Despite being a member of the International Laboratory Accreditation Cooperation that supports the trade liberalization goal of 'accredited once, accepted everywhere',[18] China required retesting of foreign coal upon importation, which ended up with duplication of testing and inspection in the country of loading and China. Moreover, Australia argued that instead of using a relevant standard of the International Organization for Standardization (ISO), namely ISO 13909, China based its measure on the globalCOAL's Standard Coal Trading Agreement, which, according to Australia, 'was not recognized as a standard for testing coal quality'. However, China countered that it had introduced these measures to protect public health and the environment. China said that since 2012, it had continuously suffered severe air pollution and haze exacerbated by the growing domestic coal consumption. While China assured that the measures applied to domestic and imported coal alike, it fell short of a persuasive explanation about the need for duplicative inspection by the Chinese authority.[19]

In 2004 and 2006, Switzerland notified two draft ordinances that sought to impose a certain maximum limit on particle emissions for diesel engine cars. With these regulations, the authorities of this country intended to induce the equipping of diesel vehicles with special filters in order to significantly reduce the emission of carcinogenic

the Meeting of 21–22 March 2018 – Note by the Secretariat, G/TBT/M/74 (22 May 2018), paras. 2.202–2.206.

18 International Laboratory Accreditation Cooperation, 'ILAC MRA and Signatories', https://ilac.org/ilac-mra-and-signatories/.

19 See WTO, Committee on TBT – Minutes of the Meeting of 4–6 November 2015 – Note by the Secretariat, G/TBT/M/67 (3 February 2016), paras. 2.5–2.9; WTO, Committee on TBT – Minutes of the Meeting of 9–10 March 2016 – Note by the Secretariat, G/TBT/M/68 (12 May 2016), paras. 2.299–2.305; WTO, Committee on TBT – Minutes of the Meeting of 15–16 June 2016 – Note by the Secretariat, G/TBT/M/69 (22 September 2016), paras. 3.298–3.302; WTO, Committee on TBT – Minutes of the Meeting of 6–7 March 2019 – Note by the Secretariat, G/TBT/M/77 (15 May 2019), paras. 3.172–3.173.

particles.[20] However, the EU and the United States in *ID 110* questioned the reliability of the Swiss measurement methods and an unreasonable interval left between the measure's publication and entry into force. Taking into account these concerns, Switzerland eventually decided to withdraw the proposed regulations.[21]

ID 318 gives an example of national energy-related standards based on other members' standards. In order to reduce particulate emissions from diesel engines, Colombia introduced new rules that set a cap of 50 parts per million (ppm) on sulphur content in diesel fuel. Diesel trucks had to meet a certain EU emission standard, which Colombia viewed most appropriate for using the new 50 ppm sulphur diesel. The United States and Mexico asked Colombia to continuously allow into market diesel trucks meeting a relevant standard of the US Environmental Protection Agency (EPA) instead. Colombia stuck to its position but provided an adaptation period for producers to adjust to the new regulation.[22]

4.1.3 Renewable Energy STCs

STCs on renewable energy have regarded energy-generating equipment and biofuels. In *ID 271*, Korea's standard KS 61646 for thin-film solar panels was criticized for accepting only amorphous silicon type thin-film solar panels that were domestically produced while excluding two other types produced overseas. This deviated from the related international standard of the International Electrotechnical Commission (IEC), namely IEC 61646, that recognized all three types. Korea explained that this was a voluntary domestic standard that did not cover the two types

[20] WTO, Committee on TBT – Notification – Switzerland – Diesel Passenger Cars, G/TBT/N/CHE/39 (5 March 2004); WTO, Committee on TBT – Notification – Switzerland – Diesel Passenger Cars, G/TBT/N/CHE/67 (11 August 2006).

[21] See WTO, Committee on TBT – Minutes of the Meeting of 1 July 2004 – Chairperson: Mr. Sudhakar Dalela (India) – Note by the Secretariat, G/TBT/M/33 (31 August 2004), paras. 17–19; WTO, Committee on TBT – Minutes of the Meeting of 16–17 June 2005 – Note by the Secretariat, G/TBT/M/36 (4 August 2005), para. 18; WTO, Committee on TBT – Minutes of the Meeting of 9 November 2006 – Note by the Secretariat, G/TBT/M/40 (26 January 2007), paras. 4–5; WTO, Committee on TBT – Minutes of the Meeting of 5 July 2007 – Note by the Secretariat, G/TBT/M/42 (6 August 2007), paras. 104–106.

[22] WTO, Committee on TBT – Minutes of the Meeting of 6–7 March 2013 – Note by the Secretariat, G/TBT/M/59 (8 May 2013), paras. 2.198–2.202; WTO, Committee on TBT – Colombia – Proposed Modifications to Resolutions 910/2008 and 2604/2009 on Pollutant Emissions from Heavy Vehicles with Diesel Engines – (G/TBT/N/COL/185 and G/TBT/N/COL/186) – Statement by Mexico to the Committee on Technical Barriers to Trade – 6–7 March 2013, G/TBT/W/362 (21 March 2013).

because of their environmentally hazardous content, such as cadmium. But the counterargument was that Korea's measure in fact created a de facto market barrier to the excluded solar panels despite the acceptably low concentration levels of cadmium. After completing internal assessments, Korea decided to additionally certify one more solar panel type that met national environmental standards.[23]

As for biofuels, two STCs are noteworthy. In *ID 216*, some members took issue with Colombia's draft regulation that initially intended to require all gasoline-engine motor vehicles in the future to be capable of running on a fuel mixture including up to 85 per cent alcohol fuel. They worried that the proposed strict standard could prevent the development of alternative environment-friendly automotive technologies and sales of more fuel-efficient cars and that the schedule of implementing this regulation was too tight for carmakers to adapt to. Following a series of TBT Committee-level and bilateral discussions, Colombia revised the regulation to allow for flexibility in using ethanol blends and arranging timelines for compliance. It also assured that all future changes to the ethanol percentage in gasoline would be subject to technical and transparency procedures.[24]

A more recent STC (*ID 553*) concerns amendments to the EU Renewable Energy Directive under which biofuels produced from food or feed crops with a significant expansion of agricultural land into areas with high-carbon stock (such as forests, wetlands and peatlands) will not count towards EU renewable energy targets in the transport sector after 2030 any longer. The EU measure gradually reduces the portion of unsustainably produced biofuels in the calculation of the EU-prescribed share of renewable energy consumption. Some WTO members were alarmed that

[23] See WTO, Committee on TBT – Minutes of the Meeting of 23–24 June 2010 – Note by the Secretariat, G/TBT/M/51 (1 October 2010), paras. 33–35; WTO, Committee on TBT – Minutes of the Meeting of 24–25 March 2011 – Note by the Secretariat, G/TBT/M/53 (26 May 2011), paras. 273–275; G/TBT/M/59, supra note 22, paras. 2.193–2.196; WTO, Committee on TBT – Minutes of the Meeting of 17, 19 and 20 June 2013 – Note by the Secretariat, G/TBT/M/60 (23 September 2013), paras. 3.80–3.82; WTO, Committee on TBT – Minutes of the Meeting of 30–31 October 2013 – Chairperson: Mr. Jingo Kikukawa – Note by the Secretariat, G/TBT/M/61 (5 February 2014), paras. 2.62–2.63.

[24] See WTO, Committee on TBT – Minutes of the Meeting of 18–19 March 2009 – Note by the Secretariat, G/TBT/M/47 (5 June 2009), paras. 79–80; WTO, Committee on TBT – Minutes of the Meeting of 25–26 June 2009 – Note by the Secretariat, G/TBT/M/48 (29 September 2009), paras. 251–254; G/TBT/M/53, supra note 23, paras. 199–204; WTO, Committee on TBT – Minutes of the Meeting of 10–11 November 2011 – Note by the Secretariat, G/TBT/M/55 (9 February 2012), paras. 86–89.

this would phase out the use of palm oil-based biofuels under the EU renewable energy regime in contrast to biofuels derived from other feedstocks, causing discriminatory import restrictions against palm oil and palm oil-based biofuels. But the EU countered that palm oil biofuels would continuously be allowed on the EU market even if they would not qualify for meeting the renewable energy targets. Since the referral of this issue to the now-pending WTO dispute settlement procedures in *EU – Palm Oil (Indonesia)* and *EU and Certain Member States – Palm Oil (Malaysia)*,[25] the EU has refrained from addressing it in the TBT Committee.[26] This is actually the second time that the EU Renewable Energy Directive has been targeted by both an STC and WTO complaint. With respect to an earlier version of this directive, some members in *ID 307* took issue with certain sustainability criteria and emission reduction thresholds for biofuels as negatively impacting foreign soybean/palm oil biofuels. There, the EU argued that this issue was beyond the TBT Agreement and the TBT Committee's competence;[27] and the related WTO dispute remained at the consultation stage without moving to the formal adjudication.[28]

4.1.4 The Overall Picture

Ten per cent of all STCs raised between 1995 and 2021 were related to energy–environment issues, and only a few were referred to the dispute

[25] *European Union – Certain Measures Concerning Palm Oil and Oil Palm Crop-Based Biofuels* (DS593), complainant: Indonesia; *European Union and Certain Member States – Certain Measures Concerning Palm Oil and Oil Palm Crop-Based Biofuels* (DS600), complainant: Malaysia.

[26] See, for example, G/TBT/M/74, supra note 17, paras. 2.24–2.37; WTO, Committee on TBT – Minutes of the Meeting of 13–14 May 2020 – Written Procedure on Specific Trade Concerns – Note by the Secretariat, G/TBT/M/81 (26 June 2020), paras. 1.428–1.437; WTO, Committee on TBT – Minutes of the Meeting of 24–26 February 2021 – Note by the Secretariat, G/TBT/M/83 (21 April 2021), paras. 2.121–2.123; WTO, Committee on TBT – European Union – Amendments to the Directive 2009/28/EC, Renewable Energy Directive – Statement by the European Union to the Committee on Technical Barriers to Trade – 21 and 22 March 2018, G/TBT/W/474 (17 April 2018).

[27] See, for example, WTO, Committee on TBT – Minutes of the Meeting of 15–16 June 2011 – Note by the Secretariat, G/TBT/M/54 (20 September 2011), paras. 67–73; WTO, Committee on TBT – Minutes of the Meeting of 13–15 June 2012 – Note by the Secretariat, G/TBT/M/57 (18 September 2012), paras. 253–256; G/TBT/M/60, supra note 23, paras. 3.101–3.104.

[28] WTO, *European Union and Certain Member States – Certain Measures on the Importation and Marketing of Biodiesel and Measures Supporting the Biodiesel Industry* – Request for Consultations by Argentina, WT/DS459/1, G/L/1027, G/SCM/D97/1, G/TRIMS/D/36, G/TBT/D/44 (23 May 2013).

settlement procedures, indicating the effectiveness of the STC mechanism in minimizing the potential for energy–environment TBT disputes. Within those 10 per cent, the prevalence of energy efficiency STCs might suggest that most energy–environment TBT measures pertain to *energy-using* products, rather than energy or energy-generating products, as the scope of energy-using products is wider.

The above review of the selected STCs shows that targeted members generally were responsive to concerned members' comments. Some typical reactions consisted in the defensive narrative citing environmental or health rationales as well as assurances or acts to revise or cancel the measure concerned. By contrast, the persistent STC-raising in relation to the EU-amended renewable energy regime did not bring any significant change that could otherwise have prevented or stopped the now-ongoing WTO litigation. From an energy–environment perspective, the EU measure is remarkable for its 'double-greening' mission in expanding the share of bioenergy in the energy supply-mix and accepting only sustainably produced biofuels for this purpose. Whether the way of achieving this complies with the WTO rules is another issue currently being considered by WTO panellists.

4.2 Energy–Environment TBT Issues

The issues raised in the STC process are closely connected to the substantive and procedural requirements of the TBT Agreement. This agreement acknowledges members' right to regulate for protecting the environment, human/animal/plant life or health and other legitimate public interests and lays down certain disciplines (on non-discrimination, avoidance of unnecessary barriers to trade and others) against unwarranted TBT measures. The agreement covers mandatory 'technical regulations' and voluntary 'standards' as well as conformity assessment procedures. RTAs typically have TBT provisions confirming and/or adding to the existing WTO rules.[29] The following sections focus on some important energy–environment TBT issues.

4.2.1 Labelling and PPMs

Environmental labelling helps foster environmentally sound consumption by conveying information on, inter alia, energy efficiency, carbon

[29] See Ana Cristina Molina and Vira Khoroshavina, 'TBT Provisions in Regional Trade Agreements: To What Extent Do They Go beyond the WTO TBT Agreement?', WTO Staff Working Paper No. ERSD-2015-09, 2015.

footprint or source of energy. For example, a Eurobarometer survey (2019) revealed that 79 per cent of Europeans had been influenced by the EU energy label in their purchases of electric appliances, giving priority to more environment-friendly and/or more energy-efficient appliances.[30] Such demand-side preferences push the supply side towards greener production and products.

According to the OECD, there are more than 500 environmental labelling schemes worldwide, with the majority originating in Europe and North America.[31] The multiplication of such schemes is characterized by the deepening (or 'intensification') of traditional or prevalent labelling forms in such industries as food and agriculture or forestry as well as by a parallel process of broadening (or 'extensification') through new varieties of schemes bearing quantified carbon/environmental footprints or energy information.[32] Most of the schemes are voluntary in nature and owned/operated by non-governmental bodies. Mandatory schemes are rather exceptions and generally confined to energy efficiency labels, but some voluntary schemes' requirements become mandatory once an entity chooses to use the label.[33]

The ISO 14020 series of standards distinguishes three types of environmental labelling. Type I, also known as 'ecolabels' in the ISO system, consists of voluntary third-party-managed schemes that award labels (a mark or logo) upon a product's fulfilment of a set of criteria to indicate its environmental preferability based on life cycle, or from-production-to-disposal, considerations. The Global Ecolabelling Network – an association of Type I ecolabelling organizations[34] – captures close to sixty energy labels, used in individual or several countries, such as WindMade, GreenPower, China Energy Conservation Certification, ENERGY STAR,

[30] Special Eurobarometer 492, 'Europeans' Attitudes on EU Energy Policy: Summary', May 2019, p. 20, https://ec.europa.eu/commfrontoffice/publicopinion/index.cfm/survey/getsurveydetail/instruments/special/surveyky/2238.

[31] OECD, 'Environmental Labelling and Information Schemes', Policy Perspectives: Synthesis Report, 2016, p. 6.

[32] Andrew Prag, Thomas Lyon and Aimée Russillo, 'Multiplication of Environmental Labelling and Information Schemes (ELIS): Implications for Environment and Trade', OECD Environment Working Paper No. 106, ENV/WKP(2016)8, 2016, pp. 19–20; Guillaume Gruère, 'A Characterization of Environmental Labelling and Information Schemes', OECD Environment Working Paper No. 62, ENV/WKP(2013)9, 2013, pp. 32–33.

[33] OECD, supra note 31, pp. 2, 6.

[34] International Organization for Standardization (ISO), 'Environmental Labels and Declarations: How ISO Standards Help', 2012, p. 20.

Carbon Trust Standard and so on.[35] Type II environmental labels refer to self-declared environmental claims made by manufacturers, importers, distributers or any other interested entities, without third-party certification. Type III represents life cycle data declarations with quantified environmental performance information on, inter alia, energy used or emissions generated, allowing objective comparisons between products fulfilling the same function.[36]

Despite well-intended rationales, environmental labelling in energy may actually turn out to be counterproductive if inappropriately designed and implemented. From an environmental perspective, a label's effectiveness can be undermined by 'greenwashing' (i.e., labelling an environmentally poor product based on inaccurate self-reports or third-party certification) or 'greenbashing' (i.e., wrongly giving low environmental scores to products with genuinely good environmental performance).[37] From a trade perspective, environmental labels can be restrictive in extending only to a small portion of products in a tradeable product category, creating uneven compliance costs or effects for producers from different countries or using criteria favouring domestic over foreign producers.[38]

Labelling schemes provide environmental information either about (i) the product itself (e.g., biofuels) or (ii) the process by which the product was made (e.g., the level of sustainable electricity used or GHG emitted during a labelled product's energy consumption). The extent to which WTO law applies to the second item has been a controversial issue associated with environmental aspects of labelling programmes. Unlike the GATT-era TBT rules that limited the scope of 'technical regulation' and 'standard' solely to product characteristics,[39] the WTO's TBT Agreement additionally applies to PPMs. But it is not entirely clear

[35] Global Ecolabelling Network, 'All Ecolabels on Energy', www.ecolabelindex.com/ecolabels/?st=category,energy.

[36] See ISO, 'Environmental Labels', 2019; ISO, supra note 34; WTO, Committee on Trade and Environment – Internationally Agreed Definitions of Environmental Labelling within the International Organization for Standardization (ISO) and Related Work – Communication from the ISO, WT/CTE/W/114 (31 May 1999).

[37] Prag et al., supra note 32, pp. 23–24, 27; WTO, Committee on Trade and Environment – Report of the Meeting Held on 30 June 2014 – Note by the Secretariat, WT/CTE/M/57 (30 September 2014), para. 1.45.

[38] See OECD, 'Effects of Eco-Labelling Schemes: Compilation of Recent Studies', COM/ENV/TD(2004)34/FINAL, 2005, pp. 5, 20; Prag et al., supra note 32, pp. 11, 32–33; WT/CTE/M/57, supra note 37, para. 1.45.

[39] See Annex 1 of the Tokyo Round TBT Code.

whether the TBT Agreement is applicable to environmental labelling that causes trade discrimination merely on the grounds of NPR-PPMs, such as differences in energy consumption or emission levels in products' life cycle. At the outset, it should be noted that regardless of the TBT Agreement's applicability, NPR-PPM labelling schemes can still be scrutinized under the GATT provisions, including, for example, Articles III (national treatment), XI (ban on quantitative restrictions) or XX (general exceptions).[40]

Annex 1.1 of the TBT Agreement in two sentences defines 'technical regulation' as a binding document that lays down 'product characteristics or their related processes and production methods' (first sentence) and that 'may also include or deal exclusively with ... labelling requirements as they apply to a product, process or production method' (second sentence). Annex 1.2 defines 'standard' as an unbinding document that provides 'rules, guidelines or characteristics for products or related processes and production methods' (first sentence) and that 'may also include or deal exclusively with ... labelling requirements as they apply to a product, process or production method' (second sentence). The controversy around NPR-PPMs stems from the inclusion of 'their related'/'related' for PPMs in the first sentence as opposed to the omission of these words in the second sentence in both Annex 1.1 and Annex 1.2. When these definitions are considered in conjunction with the negotiating history, one may argue that only product-related PPMs are subject to the disciplines of the TBT Agreement.[41] Indeed, during the drafting of these provisions, the words 'their' and 'related' were inserted at the request of Mexico that wished to make it clear that the intent was to exclude NPR-PPMs from the coverage of the TBT Agreement.[42] At the same time, it follows from the WTO Secretariat's Note on the Uruguay

[40] Gabrielle Marceau and Joel P. Trachtman, 'The Technical Barriers to Trade Agreement, the Sanitary and Phytosanitary Measures Agreement, and the General Agreement on Tariffs and Trade: *A Map of the World Trade Organization Law of Domestic Regulation of Goods*', 36 *Journal of World Trade* 811 (2002), p. 862.

[41] See, for example, Seung Wha Chang, 'GATTing a Green Trade Barrier: Eco-Labelling and the WTO Agreement on Technical Barriers to Trade', 31 *Journal of World Trade* 137 (1997), pp. 142–147, 157.

[42] WTO, Committee on Trade and Environment – Committee on TBT – Negotiating History of the Coverage of the Agreement on Technical Barriers to Trade with Regard to Labelling Requirements, Voluntary Standards, and Processes and Production Methods Unrelated to Product Characteristics – Note by the Secretariat, WT/CTE/W/10, G/TBT/W/11 (29 August 1995), paras. 146–147.

Round negotiations on the TBT Agreement that the existing records could not confirm whether this intent was shared by all:[43]

> The negotiating history suggests that many participants were of the view that standards based inter alia on PPMs unrelated to a product's characteristics should not be considered eligible for being treated as being in conformity with the TBT Agreement.
>
> Towards the end of the negotiations, some delegations proposed changing the language contained in the 'definitions' in Annex 1 of the Agreement to make it unambiguous that only PPMs related to product characteristics were to be covered by the Agreement, but although no participant is on record as having opposed that objective, at that late stage of the negotiations it did not prove possible to find a consensus on the proposal.

Without referring to the negotiating history, the Appellate Body in *EC – Seal Products* made three important points. First, it acknowledged the exclusion of some PPMs from the TBT Agreement's purview by saying that 'the line between PPMs that fall, and those that do not fall, within the scope of the TBT Agreement raises important systemic issues'.[44] But it did not say expressly that PPMs uncovered by the agreement were NPR-PPMs. Second, it interpreted the phrase 'their related' PPMs in the first sentence of Annex 1.1 as encompassing only the PPMs that have a close bearing on the characteristics of a product (which appears to imply the exclusion of NPR-PPMs):

> A plain reading of Annex 1.1 thus suggests that a 'related' PPM is one that is 'connected' or 'has a relation' to the characteristics of a product. The word 'their,' which immediately precedes the words 'related processes and production methods,' refers back to 'product characteristics.' Thus, in the context of the first sentence of Annex 1.1, we understand the reference to 'or their related processes and production methods' to indicate that the subject matter of a technical regulation may consist of a process or production method that is *related* to product characteristics. In order to determine whether a measure lays down related PPMs, a panel thus will have to examine whether the processes and production methods prescribed by the measure have a sufficient nexus to the characteristics of a product in order to be considered related to those characteristics.[45]

Third, the Appellate Body held that the second sentence of Annex 1.1 defining 'technical regulation' includes elements that 'are additional to,

[43] Ibid., para. 3(c).
[44] *EC – Seal Products*, WTO Appellate Body Reports, para. 5.69.
[45] Ibid., para. 5.12 (emphasis in original).

and may be distinct from,' those in the first sentence.[46] To recall, the second sentence mentions 'labelling requirements as they apply to a product, process or production method', with the latter not preceded by the words 'their related' or 'related'. Therefore, unlike the first sentence that textually covers product-related PPMs, the second sentence seems to also embrace NPR-PPM labelling requirements as *additional or distinct* parts of technical regulations (and standards under Annex 1.2).[47]

Suppose member *A*'s technical regulation for biodiesel blends requires that an associated label show the percentage of biodiesel blended with mineral diesel and the level of sustainability of feedstock used in the biodiesel production (i.e., the impact of the feedstock on deforestation, biodiversity and/or land degradation). Following the Appellate Body's findings above, this technical regulation could be scrutinized under the first sentence of Annex 1.1 with respect to the blend ratio as biodiesel is physically detectable through chemical testing in the blended fuel; it could also be examined under the second sentence in relation to the feedstock's sustainability as an NPR-PPM.

Interestingly, the panel in *US – Tuna II (Mexico)* was pragmatic enough to bypass the tricky PPM coverage issue. In particular, the panel concluded that the US dolphin-safe labelling requirements fell within the scope of the second sentence of Annex 1.1 simply on the grounds that they 'apply to a product' (here, tuna) in accordance with the language of that sentence.[48] The underlying rationale here can be linked to an earlier opinion in the literature that all labels are actually 'attached to and an intrinsic part of the product itself, regardless of the criteria by which the label is awarded' or information it carries.[49] The panel's finding in question, albeit not appealed, shows how NPR-PPMs in energy – just like fishing methods here leaving no physical traces on tuna – can be examined without addressing the very issue of the TBT Agreement's scope for NPR-PPMs. Following this approach, the NPR-PPM concerning the sustainability characteristics of the used feedstock in our

[46] Ibid., para. 5.14.

[47] For a similar conclusion, see also Christiane R. Conrad, *Processes and Production Methods (PPMs) in WTO Law: Interfacing Trade and Social Goals* (Cambridge: Cambridge University Press, 2011), pp. 389–393; Jan McDonald, 'Domestic Regulation, International Standards, and Technical Barriers to Trade', 4 *World Trade Review* 249 (2005), p. 257; Marceau and Trachtman, supra note 40, p. 876.

[48] *US – Tuna II (Mexico)*, WTO Panel Report, para. 7.78.

[49] McDonald, supra note 47, p. 257 citing Erik P. Bartenhagen, 'The Intersection of Trade and the Environment: An Examination of the Impact of the TBT Agreement on Ecolabelling Programs', 17 *Virginia Environmental Law Journal* 51 (1997), p. 80.

hypothetical example above could be examined under the second sentence of Annex 1.1 just because that measure applies to the blended fuel as a product under consideration.

The WTO transparency procedures have addressed labelling requirements irrespective of the nature of associated PPMs. With respect to notifications, the TBT Committee agreed that members' obligation to notify 'all mandatory labelling requirements' (as specified under Article 2.9 of the TBT Agreement for technical regulations) was 'not dependent upon the kind of information which is provided on the label, whether it is in the nature of a technical specification or not'.[50] Further, 'without prejudice to the views of Members concerning the coverage and application of the Agreement', the TBT Committee clarified that 'the obligation to publish notices of draft standards containing voluntary labelling requirements' (as per paragraph L of Annex 3 for standards) was 'not dependent upon the kind of information provided on the label'.[51]

Remarkably, the TBT Committee addressed quite a number of STCs concerning energy-related labelling (see Appendix A), but none of them questioned the relevance of the NPR-PPM issue as such. In addition, the Committee on Trade and Environment was tasked to 'give particular attention to', and to check 'any need to clarify relevant WTO rules' on, 'labelling requirements for environmental purposes'.[52] Members have generally used this committee to share their national practices on environmental labelling on energy (and beyond) and raise concerns about possible negative impacts on trade, but they have never been united about the clarification of the existing rules.[53]

4.2.2 Private Standards

Private standards may restrict the cross-border movement or marketability of energy and energy-intensive products, but the role of the global trading system in regulating such standards is rather limited. In the TBT

[50] G/TBT/1/Rev.14, supra note 2, p. 29.

[51] Ibid., p. 36.

[52] WTO, Ministerial Conference – Fourth Session – Doha, 9–14 November 2001 – Ministerial Declaration – Adopted on 14 November 2001, WT/MIN(01)/DEC/1 (20 November 2001), para. 32.

[53] See Sherzod Shadikhodjaev, *Industrial Policy and the World Trade Organization: Between Legal Constraints and Flexibilities* (Cambridge: Cambridge University Press, 2018), pp. 219–220; Manuel A. J. Teehankee, *Trade and Environment Governance at the World Trade Organization Committee on Trade and Environment* (Alphen aan den Rijn: Kluwer Law International, 2020), pp. 142–155.

Committee and the Committee on Trade and Environment, several members raised concerns about proliferation of private (environmental) standards and their implications for trade and developing countries, but others doubted the relevance of such standards to the TBT Agreement.[54]

More intensive discussions have taken place in the WTO SPS Committee. In the 2005 meeting, Saint Vincent and the Grenadines raised an STC about private standards, complaining that EurepGAP (today, GLOBALG.A.P.) certification had been made a condition for selling bananas to UK supermarkets.[55] Since then, the SPS Committee has discussed the issue of private standards, albeit with no conclusive outcome.[56] WTO members could not agree to a nearly finalized definition of an 'SPS-related private standard' as 'a written requirement or condition, or a set of written requirements or conditions . . . that may be used in commercial transactions and that is applied by a non-governmental entity that is not exercising governmental authority'.[57] The EU and the United States opposed this definition for its reference to a 'non-governmental entity' that, if accepted, could impact on a future interpretation of the same term being currently used in the SPS Agreement and give the impression that private standards are already covered by the WTO.[58]

[54] See, for example, WTO, Committee on TBT – Fifth Triennial Review of the Operation and Implementation of the Agreement on Technical Barriers to Trade under Article 15.4, G/TBT/26 (13 November 2009), para. 26; WTO, Committee on TBT – Sixth Triennial Review of the Operation and Implementation of the Agreement on Technical Barriers to Trade under article 15.4, G/TBT/32 (29 November 2012), para. 7; WTO, Committee on Trade and Environment – Report of the Meeting Held on 29 September 2010 – Note by the Secretariat, WT/CTE/M/50 (2 November 2010), para. 50; WTO, Committee on Trade and Environment – Report of the Meeting Held on 14 November 2011 – Note by the Secretariat, WT/CTE/M/53 (27 January 2012), para. 41.

[55] WTO, Committee on Sanitary and Phytosanitary (SPS) Measures – Summary of the Meeting Held on 29–30 June 2005 – Note by the Secretariat – Revision, G/SPS/R/37/Rev.1 (18 August 2005), paras. 16–20; WTO, Committee on SPS Measures – Private Industry Standards – Communication from Saint Vincent and the Grenadines, G/SPS/GEN/766 (28 February 2007).

[56] See WTO, Committee on SPS Measures – Review of the Operation and Implementation of the SPS Agreement – Report adopted by the Committee on 14 July 2017, G/SPS/62 (25 July 2017), paras. 14.1–14.21.

[57] WTO, Committee on SPS Measures – Report of the Co-Stewards of the Private Standards E-Working Group to the March 2015 Meeting of the SPS Committee on Action 1 (G/SPS/55) – Submission by the Co-Stewards of the E-Working Group, G/SPS/W/283 (17 March 2015), paras. 2, 8–9, 21–22.

[58] Yoshiko Naiki, 'Meta-Regulation of Private Standards: The Role of Regional and International Organizations in Comparison with the WTO', 20 *World Trade Review* 1

As it follows from the aforementioned and some other definitions,[59] private standards are developed or applied by non-governmental/private entities that do not possess governmental authority. Besides certain multi-stakeholder organizations or non-governmental organizations, such non-governmental/private entities may also include, inter alia, companies and industry organizations[60] whose main activity is manufacturing rather than setting standards even if self-developed standards are aimed at products they produce. Private standards are generally voluntary in nature (albeit de facto mandatory in some cases), mostly focus on PPMs and pursue a wide array of (societal) objectives, such as environmental protection and conservation.[61] For instance, the Hydropower Sustainability Standard – launched by a multi-stakeholder body of representatives from energy companies and non-governmental organizations, among others – helps hydropower operators and developers demonstrate the environmental, social and governance performance of their projects around the world.[62] As another example, the Sustainable Biomass Program is a private certification scheme that provides assurance that woody biomass is both legally and sustainably sourced. Its governance structure includes members from biomass producers and end-users and civil society.[63]

Unless private standards are made part of technical regulations by incorporation or otherwise, the TBT Agreement's provisions on standards seem most relevant to private standards. In particular, Article 4.1 of the TBT Agreement obliges members to 'take such reasonable measures as may be available to them to ensure that ... *non-governmental standardizing bodies* within their territories ... accept and comply with this Code of Good Practice' (emphasis added). The Code of Good Practice is 'open to acceptance by any standardizing body within the territory of a Member of the WTO' (Annex 3:B). Article 4.2 adds that standardizing

(2021), p. 10; Petros C. Mavroidis and Robert Wolfe, 'Private Standards and the WTO: Reclusive No More', 16 *World Trade Review* 1 (2017), p. 13.

59 See, for example, some definitions of 'private standards' provided by international organizations, in WTO, Committee on SPS Measures – Existing Definitions of Private Standards in Other International Organizations – Note by the Secretariat – Revision, G/SPS/GEN/1334/Rev.1 (5 August 2014).

60 See G/SPS/GEN/1334/Rev.1, ibid.

61 Ming Du, 'WTO Regulation of Transnational Private Authority in Global Governance', 67 *International and Comparative Law Quarterly* 867 (2018), pp. 872–873.

62 See Hydropower Sustainability Council, 'Hydropower Sustainability Standard', www.hydrosustainability.org/standard-overview.

63 See Sustainable Biomass Program, https://sbp-cert.org.

bodies accepting and complying with the Code of Good Practice are acknowledged as complying with the principles of the TBT Agreement. As specified in Annex 3 on the Code of Good Practice, the term 'standardizing bodies'/'standardizing body' refers to

> a central government body, a local government body, or a *non-governmental body*; ... any governmental regional standardizing body one or more members of which are Members of the WTO; and ... any *non-governmental regional standardizing body* one or more members of which are situated within the territory of a Member of the WTO [emphasis added].

Annex 1:8, albeit omitting the word 'standardizing', defines '[n]on-governmental body' as '[b]ody other than a central government body or a local government body, including a non-governmental body which has legal power to enforce a technical regulation'.

In the light of their wording, the provisions above are not likely to apply to company- or industry-set private standards as these provisions seem to cover standards of non-governmental *standardizing* bodies.[64]

To make the WTO regime fully applicable to private standards, some authors suggest that a critical mass of interested members should adopt Reference Papers, modelled on the telecoms Reference Paper, inscribing members' commitments regarding private standards.[65] But given the above lack of progress in the SPS Committee, political feasibility of this approach is uncertain.[66]

Outside the multilateral trading system, private standards are exposed to so-called meta-regulation that consists in some oversight or control of such standards, standardization of private standard-setters, certification of private certifiers, awareness-raising about private standards' quality and so on.[67] The underlying idea here is to subject private standardization to some minimum requirements or steering mechanisms in private

[64] For the opposite view, see Enrico Partiti, '*What Use Is an Unloaded Gun*? The Substantive Discipline of the WTO TBT Code of Good Practice and Its Application to Private Standards Pursuing Public Objectives', 20 *Journal of International Economic Law* 829 (2017), p. 836 (arguing that because the TBT Agreement did not expressly exclude company standards from its scope of application – in contrast to the Tokyo Round TBT Code which had made such exclusion explicitly – this indicates 'the intention of WTO Members to subject also company standards under TBT discipline').

[65] Mavroidis and Wolfe, supra note 58, p. 18.

[66] See also Eva van der Zee, 'Disciplining Private Standards under the SPS and TBT Agreement: A Plea for Market-State Procedural Guidelines', 52 *Journal of World Trade* 393 (2018), p. 413; Du, supra note 61, p. 901.

[67] See, for example, Naiki, supra note 58, pp. 7, 13–23.

and/or public domains. In the private domain, the ISEAL Alliance, for example, represents an international association of private sustainability systems that requires its members to comply with the ISEAL's three Codes of Good Practice for: setting social and environmental standards; assuring compliance with social and environmental standards; and assessing the impacts of social and environmental standards systems.[68] Some of the ISEAL community members deal with hydropower, sustainable steel as well as bioenergy and related materials (biofuels, biomass and sustainable palm oil).[69]

In the public domain, meta-regulation can take place where national authorities accept validity of qualified private standards.[70] Under the EU renewable energy framework, the European Commission officially recognizes privately run voluntary schemes (including some ISEAL-related schemes, like the Sustainable Biomass Program above), meeting certain conditions, that help verify compliance of biofuels, bioliquids and biomass fuels with the EU's sustainability and GHG emissions saving criteria.[71] The European Commission's recognition is valid for up to five years, with the recognized schemes being obliged to provide annual reports.[72] Depending on the nature of such public–private 'co-regulation', private standards may fall within the WTO's jurisdiction. The panel in *Japan – Film* acknowledged that certain private actions could be attributed to a WTO member in the existence of 'some governmental connection to or endorsement of those actions',[73] provided that such governmental engagement with private conduct is *sufficient*:

> [P]ast GATT cases demonstrate that the fact that an action is taken by private parties does not rule out the possibility that it may be deemed to be governmental if there is sufficient government involvement with it. It is difficult to establish bright-line rules in this regard, however. Thus, that possibility will need to be examined on a case-by-case basis.[74]

[68] ISEAL Alliance, 'ISEAL Codes of Good Practice', www.isealalliance.org/defining-credible-practice/iseal-codes-good-practice.

[69] ISEAL Alliance, 'ISEAL Community Members', www.isealalliance.org/iseal-community-members.

[70] Naiki, supra note 58, pp. 13–15.

[71] European Commission, 'Voluntary Schemes', https://energy.ec.europa.eu/topics/renewable-energy/bioenergy/voluntary-schemes_en.

[72] Articles 30.4 and 30.5 of the Directive (EU) 2018/2001 of the European Parliament and of the Council of 11 December 2018 on the promotion of the use of energy from renewable sources (recast), OJ L 328, 21 December 2018.

[73] *Japan – Film*, WTO Panel Report, para. 10.52.

[74] Ibid., para. 10.56.

In addition, some RTAs have served to support meta-regulation(-like) activities regarding private standards. For example, the Trade and Sustainable Development Chapter of some EU FTAs sets forth best-endeavour commitments of the parties to:

- 'encourag[e] the development and use of *voluntary schemes* relating to the sustainable production of goods and services, such as eco-labelling and fair trade schemes';[75]
- 'promote trade and investment in goods that contribute to enhanced social conditions and environmentally sound practices, including goods that are the subject of labelling schemes, and recognise the contribution of other *voluntary initiatives*, including *private ones*, to sustainability';[76] or
- initiate cooperative activities on 'the exchange of information and cooperation on *private* and public certification and labelling schemes, including eco-labelling'.[77]

The United States–Mexico–Canada Agreement (USMCA) (2018) and the CPTTP (2018) provide more details. USMCA Article 12.D.5 ('Voluntary Approaches to Promote Energy Efficiency') recognizes the role of 'voluntary programs and voluntary mechanisms' in improving energy efficiency and that they should be open, transparent and designed to maximize environmental benefits and not to create unnecessary trade barriers. Article 12.D.5 urges the parties to encourage their use and cooperate to facilitate greater transparency and compatibility among these schemes. Similar to the USMCA, CPTTP Article 20.11 ('Voluntary Mechanisms to Enhance Environmental Performance') acknowledges the environmental contribution of 'voluntary mechanisms' and stresses maximization of environmental benefits and avoidance of unnecessary barriers to trade. Article 20.11.2(b) of the CPTPP calls on the parties to encourage relevant 'businesses and business organisations, non-governmental organisations', among others, to continuously develop and improve environmental performance evaluation criteria with respect to voluntary mechanisms. Remarkably, Article 20.11.3 of the CPTPP envisages what can become the best practice in this sphere:

[75] Article 22.3.2(a) of the EU–Canada CETA (2016) (emphasis added).

[76] Article 16.5(d) of the EU–Japan Economic Partnership Agreement (2018) (emphasis added).

[77] Article 12.10(d) of the EU–Singapore FTA (2018) (emphasis added).

3. Further, if private sector entities or non-governmental organisations develop voluntary mechanisms for the promotion of products based on their environmental qualities, each Party should encourage those entities and organisations to develop voluntary mechanisms that, among other things:

   (a) are truthful, are not misleading and take into account scientific and technical information;
   (b) if applicable and available, are based on relevant international standards, recommendations or guidelines, and best practices;
   (c) promote competition and innovation; and
   (d) do not treat a product less favourably on the basis of origin.

These RTAs are generally positive about private standards, and this attitude will likely spread across the parties' RTA networks. The particular reference to sustainability, energy efficiency and other environmental dimensions enables public–private interactions over energy–environment standards. At this point, RTAs still seem to be in the exploratory stage as the provisions considered above are largely of encouraging nature. But with the passage of time with more private standards becoming publicly engaged, RTAs will probably introduce more detailed meta-regulatory guidelines. Last but not least, the ACCTS – currently being negotiated within a small group of countries – is also expected to adopt guidelines for voluntary eco-labelling programmes and associated mechanisms.[78]

4.2.3 *Development and S&D Treatment*

Many producers in developing countries have difficulty in entering foreign markets with strict environmental requirements in place. They are not motivated to invest in more eco-friendly production when environmental standards at home are poor. They often lack the necessary skills for obtaining and utilizing required information about export markets, suffer from inadequate capacity in adapting to foreign standards and have to bear prohibitive costs of conformity assessment abroad. Thus, developing country exporters of unsustainable energy and energy-intensive products may face capacity constraints for meeting green standards.

[78] New Zealand Foreign Affairs and Trade, 'Agreement on Climate Change, Trade and Sustainability (ACCTS) Negotiations', www.mfat.govt.nz/en/trade/free-trade-agreements/trade-and-climate/agreement-on-climate-change-trade-and-sustainability-accts-negotiations/.

The TBT Agreement contains twenty-five provisions concerning technical assistance and S&D treatment, with the majority contained in Articles 11 and 12.[79] In some STCs and TBT disputes, certain developing countries raised development-related concerns about energy measures of developed countries. For example, with respect to the EU eco-design rules on energy-using products (*ID 123*), China insisted that the EU should conduct an impact assessment of those rules on developing countries, provide them technical assistance and take into account special needs and difficulties of developing countries as per Article 12 of the TBT Agreement.[80] In another STC on Spain's biodiesel measures (*ID 346*), Argentina argued that a de facto prohibition against non-EU biodiesel imports violated Article 12.[81] In *EU – Palm Oil (Indonesia)* and *EU and Certain Member States – Palm Oil (Malaysia)*, Indonesia and Malaysia complained about restrictions on the use of oil palm crop-based biofuels for meeting EU renewable energy targets and criticized the EU for ignoring developing country circumstances contrary to Articles 12.1 and 12.3 of the TBT Agreement.[82]

Article 11 of the TBT Agreement obligates members to provide, upon request, advice and/or technical assistance to other members, especially developing countries, with respect to, inter alia, the establishment of national standardizing or conformity assessment bodies, preparation of technical regulations and participation in international standardizing bodies. Article 12.1 of the TBT Agreement states that members must provide S&D treatment to developing country members as prescribed by the remaining provisions of Article 12 and other relevant provisions of the TBT Agreement. Article 12 concerns, inter alia:

- members' obligation to take account of 'the special development, financial and trade needs' of developing countries in the implementation of this agreement (Article 12.2);

[79] WTO, Committee on Trade and Development – Special and Differential Treatment Provisions in WTO Agreements and Decisions – Note by the Secretariat, WT/COMTD/W/271 (16 March 2023), p. 41, para. 2.38.

[80] G/TBT/M/37, supra note 13, para. 12; G/TBT/M/42, supra note 21, para. 82; G/TBT/M/50, supra note 15, paras. 177, 179.

[81] G/TBT/M/57, supra note 27, paras. 18, 20.

[82] WTO, *European Union – Certain Measures Concerning Palm Oil and Oil Palm Crop-Based Biofuels* – Request for the Establishment of a Panel by Indonesia, WT/DS593/9 (24 March 2020); WTO, *European Union and Certain Member States – Certain Measures Concerning Palm Oil and Oil Palm Crop-Based Biofuels* – Request for Consultations by Malaysia, WT/DS600/1, G/L/1384, G/TBT/D/54, G/SCM/D131/1 (19 January 2021).

- non-expectation from developing countries to use international standards that are inappropriate to those needs (Article 12.4);
- the facilitation of 'active and representative participation' in international bodies and systems (Article 12.5);
- the possibility of preparing international standards on products of special interest to developing countries (Article 12.6); and
- the provision of technical assistance, as per Article 11, to ensure avoidance of unnecessary obstacles to the expansion and diversification of exports from developing countries (Article 12.7).

WTO jurisprudence on the S&D provisions has centred on Article 12.3 of the TBT Agreement which states:

> Members shall, in the preparation and application of technical regulations, standards and conformity assessment procedures, take account of the special development, financial and trade needs of developing country Members, with a view to ensuring that such technical regulations, standards and conformity assessment procedures do not create unnecessary obstacles to exports from developing country Members.

WTO panels clarified that Article 12.3 contained only one obligation, articulated in the first part of the sentence, that is to 'take account of' developing country needs. The second part ('with a view to ensuring . . .') simply defines the objective of that obligation or provides guidance on how and why the subject member must 'take account of' the special needs.[83] The expression 'special development, financial and trade needs' seems to be left 'deliberately vague' and requires a case-by-case consideration of various factors, such as, for example, the importance of the affected product to a developing country's economy, producers and people.[84] Despite the mandatory language, Article 12.3 is actually worded in such a loose way that the panels in *US – COOL* and *US – Clove Cigarettes* unsurprisingly rejected the claims of, respectively, Mexico and Indonesia that the United States had failed to comply with this provision.[85] Indeed, the term 'take account of' merely requires 'to accord active and meaningful consideration to the special development, financial and trade needs of developing countr[ies]'. It does not obligate the

[83] *US – COOL*, WTO Panel Reports, para. 7.762; *US – Clove Cigarettes*, WTO Panel Report, para. 7.614.

[84] *US – Clove Cigarettes*, WTO Panel Report, paras. 7.627–7.628.

[85] *US – COOL*, WTO Panel Reports, para. 7.799; *US – Clove Cigarettes*, WTO Panel Report, para. 7.649.

subject members to document specifically in their rule-making process how actively they considered those needs or to accept a developing country's position and desired outcome.[86]

Development-related concerns extend to international standards as well. Thus, the principle of development dimension, adopted by the TBT Committee, acknowledges that developing countries cannot be excluded de facto from international standardization processes and calls for provision of technical assistance, including within international standardizing bodies.[87] Presumably in response to this, the ISO runs a five-year action plan for providing assistance to developing countries and furthering their integration into international standardization process.[88]

As regards specific international standards, one commentator argues that because developing countries were not adequately represented in the drafting of the ISO 14000 series on environmental management, these standards could act as a de facto trade barrier against these countries.[89] This family of standards aims to help companies and organizations integrate environmental considerations into their business processes and deals with, inter alia, environmental management systems, environmental auditing, environmental labelling, environmental performance evaluation and life cycle assessment. In the WTO Committee on Trade and Environment, China, Venezuela, Saudi Arabia, South Africa, El Salvador and Egypt contended that ISO 14067 on quantification of carbon footprint of products should take into account special needs of, and trade impacts on, developing countries.[90]

[86] *US – COOL*, WTO Panel Reports, paras. 7.786–7.787; *US – Clove Cigarettes*, WTO Panel Report, para. 7.646.

[87] WTO, Committee on TBT – Second Triennial Review of the Operation and Implementation of the Agreement on Technical Barriers to Trade, G/TBT/9 (13 November 2000), Annex 4, para. 13.

[88] See ISO, 'A Committee to Support Developing Countries: DEVCO', www.iso.org/devco .html. For some other international organizations' actions, see WTO, Committee on TBT – Actions to Increase Participation of Developing Country Members in the Work of Relevant International Standard Setting Organizations – Information from International Organizations – Report of the Director-General, G/TBT/W/172 (27 February 2002).

[89] Christine Mikulich, 'ISO 14000–14001, The Developing World's Perspective', 17 *Tulane Environmental Law Journal* 117 (2003), pp. 120, 127, 140, 149, 150.

[90] WTO, Committee on Trade and Environment – Report of the Meeting Held on 5 June 2013 – Note by the Secretariat, WT/CTE/M/55 (16 August 2013), paras. 1.13, 1.15, 1.19, 1.20, 1.22; WTO, Committee on Trade and Environment – Report of the Meeting Held on 20 June 2017 – Note by the Secretariat, WT/CTE/M/63 (27 September 2017), paras. 1.84, 1.87, 1.88.

Notwithstanding the relatively high number of the technical assistance and S&D provisions of the TBT Agreement, the real practice here does not appear to fully meet developing countries' expectations and needs.[91] In order to diagnose any gaps and problems currently faced by developing countries and seek solutions accordingly, the WTO could, for example, organize thematic TBT sessions on, say, energy–environment issues specific to developing countries. While thematic sessions are not new to the WTO's committee process,[92] the focus on the energy–environment nexus and developing countries here could explore more customized approaches to helping developing countries improve their technical capacity. As mentioned in Chapters 1 and 2,[93] without developing countries' ambitious decarbonization efforts, the global climate target is not likely to be met. Increased technical assistance for green standard-related measures could be part of solution, but the exact demand of developing countries requires a thorough examination.

4.2.4 *Regulatory Convergence*

A shift from regulatory divergence towards regulatory convergence across many jurisdictions without diminishing the underlying objectives of covered measures may have a positive impact on the environment. In particular, this reduces trade costs of (and hence increases the affordability of) clean energy and energy-efficient products, such as costs of adapting to requirements in export markets, conformity assessment costs and costs of identifying, collecting and processing of information on foreign TBT measures.[94] Furthermore, if domestic measures are aligned worldwide towards high sustainability standards on energy, this may bring about significant pro-environmental global outcomes. According to some estimates made in 2015, if all national minimum energy performance standards were commonly set at most stringent requirement

[91] This corresponds to the overall underperformance of the S&D regime of the WTO as noted in Section 1.2.1.2. For a comprehensive assessment of the WTO S&D provisions, see Sonia E. Rolland, *Development at the World Trade Organization* (Oxford: Oxford University Press, 2012), pp. 109–138.

[92] See, for example, WTO, Committee on TBT – Ninth Triennial Review of the Operation and Implementation of the Agreement on Technical Barriers to Trade under Article 15.4, G/TBT/46 (17 November 2021), paras. 1.1, 1.7(b), 2.11.

[93] See Sections 1.1.5 and 2.1.3.

[94] Martin von Lampe, Koen Deconinck and Véronique Bastien, 'Trade-Related International Regulatory Co-operation: A Theoretical Framework', OECD Trade Policy Paper No. 195, 2016, p. 4.

levels by 2020, this would generate gross global energy savings of 13 per cent in 2030.[95]

The divergence of national standards can be reduced through international regulatory cooperation, that is, any formal or informal engagements (with mandatory and/or voluntary elements) between countries to promote cooperation in the design, monitoring, enforcement or *ex post* management of regulation.[96] It typically includes inter-State regulatory partnerships, mutual recognition agreements, harmonization with international standards, regional agreements with regulatory provisions, dialogues or information exchanges on regulatory issues and so on.[97] International regulatory cooperation is instrumental for enhancing mutual understanding of regulatory systems, promoting regulatory convergence, disseminating good regulatory practices and lowering unnecessary trade barriers.[98] Some recent RTAs acknowledge the role of regulatory cooperation in narrowing regulatory differences, reducing duplicative requirements, promoting compatible regulatory approaches and improving the alignment of domestic regulations.[99]

The TBT Agreement encourages harmonization and equivalence of TBT measures and recognition of conformity assessment results across the board, hence encompassing the energy–environment nexus. While many RTAs follow suit, most recent agreements also tend to add horizontal chapters on these and other forms of regulatory cooperation and/or good regulatory practices, which indicates the growing interest of governments in raising the visibility and ambition of regulatory cooperation in the trade context.[100] As will be shown below, few RTAs contain certain energy-specific regulatory elements as well.

95 Edith Molenbroek et al., 'Savings and Benefits of Global Regulations for Energy Efficient Products: A "Cost of Non-World" Study, Final Report', European Commission, 2015, pp. 15, 59.

96 OECD, 'International Regulatory Co-operation: Addressing Global Challenges', 2013, p. 153.

97 Ibid., pp. 23–25.

98 G/TBT/26, supra note 54, para. 14; WTO, Committee on TBT – Fourth Triennial Review of the Operation and Implementation of the Agreement on Technical Barriers to Trade under Article 15.4, G/TBT/19 (14 November 2006), para. 18.

99 See Article 28.1 of the USMCA (2018); Article 18.1.1 of the EU–Japan Economic Partnership Agreement (2018); Article 13.2.2 of the Appendix, Protocol (2019) to Amend the Singapore–New Zealand Closer Economic Partnership Agreement.

100 Céline Kauffmann and Camila Saffirio, 'Good Regulatory Practices and Co-operation in Trade Agreements: A Historical Perspective and Stocktaking', OECD Regulatory Policy Working Paper No. 14, 2021, p. 36.

4.2.4.1 Harmonization with International Standards

International standards have been discussed in roughly half of the STCs (1995–2021) dealing with energy–environment TBT measures (see Figure 4.2). International standards on renewable energy, energy efficiency and carbon emissions are developed by the ISO and the IEC, among others.[101] For example, the ISO's portfolio includes more than 200 such standards (out of over 22,000 international standards), with many more being in the pipeline.[102] To name just a few, these are: ISO/IEC 13273 on energy efficiency and renewable energy sources; ISO 14067 on carbon footprint of products; ISO 14404 on CO_2 emission intensity from iron and steel production; ISO 8714 on reference energy consumption of electric passenger cars; ISO/IEC 30134 on energy-related aspects of information technology equipment; ISO 9459 on solar heating; and so on.[103]

The TBT Agreement encourages the development of international standards as it recognizes their importance in supporting regulatory harmonization and facilitating trade.[104] The preamble of the agreement also acknowledges the contribution of international standardization to technology transfer from developed to developing countries. While not defined in the agreement, the term 'international standard' was interpreted by the Appellate Body as a standard adopted by an international standardizing body – a body with 'recognized activities in standardization and whose membership is open to the relevant bodies of at least all Members' – for the purposes of the TBT Agreement.[105] In *US – Tuna II (Mexico)*, a 'dolphin-safe' definition and certification failed to qualify as a relevant international standard because membership in the related Agreement on the International Dolphin Conservation Program (1998) was not sufficiently open as an invitation to accede to this agreement was not issued automatically upon request.[106]

Standards that are developed in accordance with the TBT Committee's decision on principles for international standard-setting (2000)[107] are

[101] See IRENA, 'International Standardisation in the Field of Renewable Energy', 2013, pp. 10, 14; Table 4.1.

[102] ISO, 'ISO and Energy', 2018, p. 9, www.iso.org/publication/PUB100320.html.

[103] These and other standards can be searched at ISO, www.iso.org/standards.html.

[104] Preamble of the TBT Agreement; *EC – Sardines*, WTO Appellate Body Report, para. 214.

[105] *US – Tuna II (Mexico)*, WTO Appellate Body Report, paras. 356, 359.

[106] Ibid., paras. 398–399.

[107] WTO, Decision of the Committee on Principles for the Development of International Standards, Guides and Recommendations with Relation to Articles 2, 5 and Annex 3 of the Agreement. G/TBT/9, supra note 87, para. 20 and Annex 4.

likely to be recognized as relevant international standards for the purposes of the TBT Agreement.[108] Over forty RTAs make this point clear by using this decision as a benchmark for determining the existence of international standards within the meaning of the TBT Agreement.[109] The decision in question sets six principles concerning transparency, openness, impartiality and consensus, effectiveness and relevance, coherence, and development dimension.

The TBT Agreement mandates the use of relevant international standards or parts thereof 'as a basis' for domestic technical regulations or standards unless the international standards/parts are 'ineffective or inappropriate' for the fulfilment of the legitimate objectives due to, for example, 'fundamental climatic or geographical factors or fundamental technological problems' (Article 2.4 and Annex 3:F). According to judicial interpretation, there must be 'a very strong and very close relationship between two things' for one to be 'the basis for' the other;[110] and while it appears that domestic TBT measures do not need to 'conform to' relevant international standards,[111] the domestic measures, at a minimum, must not contradict international standards.[112] Further, (parts of) relevant guides or recommendations issued by international standardizing bodies must be used 'as a basis' for conformity assessment procedures except where such guides or recommendations are inappropriate for, inter alia, such reasons as 'protection of human health or safety, animal or plant life or health, or the environment; fundamental climatic or other geographical factors; fundamental technological or

[108] The Appellate Body (*US – Tuna II (Mexico)*, WTO Appellate Body Report, para. 372) considered the TBT Committee's decision in question as a 'subsequent agreement' within the meaning of Article 31(3)(a) of the VCLT for interpreting and applying the relevant provisions of the TBT Agreement. See also OECD/WTO, 'Facilitating Trade through Regulatory Cooperation: The Case of the WTO's TBT/SPS Agreements and Committees', 2019, p. 42.

[109] Devin McDaniels, Ana Cristina Molina and Erik Wijkström, 'How Does the Regular Work of WTO Influence Regional Trade Agreements? The Case of International Standards and the TBT Committee', WTO Staff Working Paper No. ERSD-2018-06, 2018, p. 9. See, for example, Articles 11.1.2 and 11.4.2 of the USMCA (2018).

[110] *EC – Sardines*, WTO Appellate Body Report, para. 245.

[111] See *EC – Hormones*, WTO Appellate Body Report, para. 163 cited in ibid., para. 242.

[112] *EC – Sardines*, WTO Appellate Body Report, paras. 248–249. In *EC – Sardines* (paras. 257–258), the Appellate Body confirmed a violation of Article 2.4 of the TBT Agreement by finding a contradiction between an EC technical regulation allowing only *Sardina pilchardus* fish products to be labeled as 'sardines' and Codex Stan 94 (an international standard adopted by the Codex Alimentarius Commission) that actually permits the use of the term 'sardines' for twenty species of fish in addition to *Sardina pilchardus*.

infrastructural problems' (Article 5.4). To harmonize TBT measures 'on as wide a basis as possible', WTO members/standardizing bodies must fully participate, 'within the limits of their resources', in the preparation of international standards, guides and recommendations by international standardizing bodies (Articles 2.6 and 5.5, Annex 3:G).

Article 2.5 of the TBT Agreement, and specifically its second sentence, states that a technical regulation pursuing one of the legitimate objectives listed in Article 2.2 and being 'in accordance with relevant international standards' is 'rebuttably presumed' as not creating an unnecessary obstacle to trade. Such rebuttable presumption is a 'privilege', so it requires 'a closer or higher degree of correspondence' between a technical regulation and a relevant international standard than that required under Article 2.4.[113] The panel in *Australia – Tobacco Plain Packaging* found that the term 'conform to' (international standards . . .) in Article 3.2 of the SPS Agreement[114] 'may constitute useful context for understanding' the term 'in accordance with' used in Article 2.5 of the TBT Agreement, which is 'the counterpart' of that SPS provision.[115]

Some RTAs support international standards that specifically affect energy production or use. In particular, the EU's FTAs with Singapore (2018) and Viet Nam (2019) contain separate chapters focusing on non-tariff barriers to trade and investment in renewable energy generation.[116] Whereas reiterating harmonization with international standards in this particular field, these chapters also explicitly recognize standards of the ISO and the IEC as being relevant for the harmonization purpose.[117] Under the EU–Canada Comprehensive and Economic Trade Agreement (CETA) (2016), the parties affirmed their joint commitment to improve vehicle environmental performance and promote harmonization efforts under the World Forum for Harmonization of Vehicle

[113] *Australia – Tobacco Plain Packaging*, WTO Panel Reports, paras. 7.272, 7.274.

[114] Article 3.2 of the SPS Agreement reads:

> Sanitary or phytosanitary measures which conform to international standards, guidelines or recommendations shall be deemed to be necessary to protect human, animal or plant life or health, and presumed to be consistent with the relevant provisions of this Agreement and of GATT 1994.

[115] *Australia – Tobacco Plain Packaging*, WTO Panel Reports, n. 959 to para. 7.274.

[116] Chapter 7 of the EU–Singapore FTA (2018); Chapter 7 of the EU–Viet Nam FTA (2019).

[117] Article 7.5.1 of the EU–Singapore FTA (2018); Article 7.5.2 of the EU–Viet Nam FTA (2019).

Regulations (WP.29) that deals with, inter alia, pollution and energy efficiency.[118] The Korea–EU FTA (2010) recognizes the WP.29 as 'the relevant international standard-setting body' for motor vehicles and parts and provides for harmonization with its regulations.[119]

4.2.4.2 Equivalence and Mutual Recognition

Article 2.7 of the TBT Agreement obliges members to 'give positive consideration' to accepting equivalence of foreign technical regulations even if the latter differ from their own, provided they are satisfied that these regulations adequately achieve the objectives of their own regulations. An STC in *ID 318* shows that equivalence may affect not only 'domestic vs. foreign' standards but also 'foreign vs. foreign' standards within a domestic regulatory domain. There, the United States invoked Colombia's earlier recognition of a 'temporary equivalence' between the European standard EURO IV and the US standard EPA 2004 and insisted on the permanent equivalence between these two in the context of Colombia's amended regulation on commercial truck diesel emissions.[120] But Colombia opted to eventually acknowledge only the European standard:

> In 2008, laws had been enacted with the effect that from 31 December 2012 onwards, diesel would have a maximum content of 50 ppm of sulphur when distributed in Colombia ... Colombia began to update its emission standards and the technology required for local and imported diesel vehicles in 2011. When determining the appropriate emission standards in Colombia, the decisive criterion was a standard which would allow for a more efficient use of the new 50 ppm sulphur diesel. Following a technical review and in accordance with international regulations in this area, the conclusion had been reached that the only standard which sufficiently met the legitimate policy objective to reduce particular emissions and where 50 ppm sulphur diesel could be used, was standard EURO 4. Vehicles that complied with standard EURO 4 emitted up to 87% less particular matter than those vehicles that comply with current standards used in Colombia, such as the EPA 4.[121]

[118] Article 1.2, Annex 4-A ('Cooperation in the Field of Motor Vehicle Regulations') of the EU–Canada CETA (2016). See also UN Economic Commission for Europe, 'Working Party on Pollution and Energy – Introduction', https://unece.org/transportvehicle-regulations/working-party-pollution-and-energy-introduction.

[119] Articles 2, 3 and 4 of Annex 2-C of the Korea–EU FTA (2010).

[120] G/TBT/M/59, supra note 22, para. 2.198.

[121] Ibid., para. 2.201.

Article 6.1 of the TBT Agreement provides for the recognition of the results of foreign conformity assessment procedures where members are satisfied that those foreign procedures assure conformity with technical regulations or standards equivalent to their own procedures. Further, members are encouraged to negotiate and conclude agreements for the mutual recognition of conformity assessment results (Article 6.3). A number of mutual recognition agreements notified to the WTO cover such energy-using products as electrical equipment, lighting devices, gas appliances, boilers, motor vehicles and others.[122] Agreements concluded by Ukraine with Korea and Sweden deal with energy labelling as well.[123]

Some RTAs oblige parties to provide explanation for refusing: equivalence of the other party's measure, conformity assessment results obtained in the other party and TBT harmonization with international standards.[124] Under the EU–Singapore FTA (2018), each party agreed to mutually recognize declarations of conformity with the other party's requirements for certain products related to renewable energy generation (boilers, machinery and mechanical appliances, wind-powered electric

[122] See, for example, WTO, Committee on TBT – Agreement Reached by a Member with Another Country or Countries on Issues Related to Technical Regulations, Standards or Conformity Assessment Procedures – Notification – The Separate Customs Territory of Taiwan, Penghu, Kinmen and Matsu, G/TBT/10.7/N/146 (8 February 2018); WTO, Committee on TBT – Agreement Reached by a Member with Another Country or Countries on Issues Related to Technical Regulations, Standards or Conformity Assessment Procedures – Notification – Japan and the Republic of Singapore, G/TBT/10.7/N/45 (17 July 2003); WTO, Committee on TBT – Agreement Reached by a Member with Another Country or Countries on Issues Related to Technical Regulations, Standards or Conformity Assessment Procedures – The European Communities and Switzerland – Notification, G/TBT/10.7/N/44 (29 January 2003); WTO, Committee on TBT – Agreement Reached by a Member with Another Country or Countries on Issues Related to Technical Regulations, Standards or Conformity Assessment Procedures – Notification – Japan and European Community – Telecommunications [. . .] Products and Medicinal Products, G/TBT/10.7/N/37 (31 May 2002).

[123] WTO, Committee on TBT – Agreement Reached by a Member with Another Country or Countries on Issues Related to Technical Regulations, Standards or Conformity Assessment Procedures – Notification – Ukraine, G/TBT/10.7/N/147 (23 February 2018); WTO, Committee on TBT – Agreement Reached by a Member with Another Country or Countries on Issues Related to Technical Regulations, Standards or Conformity Assessment Procedures – Notification – Ukraine, G/TBT/10.7/N/144 (30 March 2017).

[124] For horizontal TBT provisions, see, for example, Articles 11.5.3, 11.5.4 and 11.6.4 of the USMCA (2018). For TBT provisions related to renewable energy generation, see, for example, Article 7.5.2 of the EU–Viet Nam FTA (2019).

generators, solar panels and so on) listed in Harmonized System (HS) Chapter 84 (except 8401), HS 850231 and 854140.[125] As another example, the EU–Canada CETA (2016) provides for mutual acceptance of the results of conformity assessment for listed products (electrical and electronic equipment, machinery, hot water boilers and others) that may be subjected to energy performance standards in either party.[126]

4.2.4.3 Regional Harmonization and Collaboration

Regional harmonization of standards depends on the level of integration and trust among regulating countries as well as the degree of regulatory homogeneity. Therefore, developing single standards outside of highly integrated economic blocs is rather an exception in international practice.[127] With respect to the energy–environment nexus, some RTAs encourage certain forms of regulatory alignment.

The EU–Armenia Comprehensive and Enhanced Partnership Agreement (2017) exemplifies the case of non-reciprocal alignment of one party's regulatory policies with the other's. Under the cooperation chapter aimed at 'regulatory harmonisation' in the energy sector, Armenia committed to 'gradually approximate' its energy legislation to the listed pieces of EU law regarding, inter alia, energy efficiency, nuclear power and renewable energy within the stipulated timeframes.[128]

By contrast, regulatory alignment under the USMCA (2018) is not prescribed in such a one-way direction. Annex 12-D (titled 'Energy Performance Standards') of the USMCA encourages FTA-wide regulatory convergence on energy efficiency. Specifically, the USMCA obliges the parties to cooperate to enhance 'regulatory compatibility' with respect to central-government-mandated energy performance standards (specifications of energy efficiency or a product's maximum energy consumption amount) and related test procedures (methods of measuring energy use/efficiency).[129] In particular, the parties 'shall endeavor to harmonize' energy performance standards or test procedures that are already in

125 Article 7.5.3 of the EU–Singapore FTA (2018).

126 See the Protocol on the Mutual Acceptance of the Results of Conformity Assessment, included in the EU–Canada CETA (2016).

127 Christophe Bellmann and Colette van der Ven, 'Greening Regional Trade Agreements on Non-Tariff Measures through Technical Barriers to Trade and Regulatory Co-operation', OECD Trade and Environment Working Paper No. 2020/4, 2020, p. 24.

128 Articles 42.1 and 44 and Annex II of the EU–Armenia Comprehensive and Enhanced Partnership Agreement (2017).

129 For definitions, see Article 12.D.1 of the USMCA (2018).

place, provided that such harmonization 'should not diminish consumer welfare, consumer protection, or energy efficiency objectives' in the light of various factors, such as 'climate, geography, household purchasing power, and electricity infrastructure'.[130] This condition is important as it can prevent a race-to-the-bottom, or least ambitious, regional harmonization. When developing or modifying relevant standards or procedures, each party must 'give due consideration' to adopting another party's energy performance standards and test procedures or 'industry standards' developed by a standards organization accredited in the territory of another party.[131]

To ensure regulatory convergence at an environmentally optimal level, sustainable energy officials and experts should play a greater role under trade agreements through international collaboration platforms.[132] In this respect, the ECT (1994) provisions mention 'cooperation in the field of international environmental standards for the Energy Cycle'[133] as well as 'any appropriate form' of cooperation that may take place between contracting parties in relation to 'the development of energy labelling and efficiency standards', 'thermal insulation standards' in the building sector, 'motor vehicle performance standards' and so on.[134] Some RTAs define specific formats of communication and exchanges, including on research activities, namely:

- cooperation and communication on environmental performance research activities related to standard-setting on motor vehicles, information/research exchange on 'advanced emission reduction and electric vehicle technologies';[135]

[130] Article 12.D.4.2 and accompanying n. 9 of the USMCA (2018).

[131] Article 12.D.4.3 of the USMCA (2018).

[132] See Jurei Yada et al., 'Harmonization of Product Energy Efficiency Standards and Free Trade Agreements: The Role of International Cooperation', European Council for an Energy Efficient Economy, Summer Study Proceedings, 2017, www.eceee.org/library/conference_proceedings/eceee_Summer_Studies/2017/2-policy-governance-design-implementation-and-evaluation-challenges/harmonization-of-product-energy-efficiency-standards-and-free-trade-agreements-the-role-of-international-cooperation/.

[133] Article 19(1)(c) of the ECT (1994).

[134] Article 9 and the related Annex of the Energy Charter Protocol on Energy Efficiency and Related Environmental Aspects (1994).

[135] Articles 1.6 and 2(d), Annex 4-A ('Cooperation in the Field of Motor Vehicle Regulations') of the EU–Canada CETA (2016).

- exchanges of information, regulatory experiences and best practices regarding carbon capture and storage, smart grids, energy efficiency and TBT measures relating to grid code requirements;[136]
- information exchange on energy efficiency improvement and promotion of the use of alternative and renewable energy;[137]
- academic exchanges and exchanging views on policies on energy efficiency and climate change;[138]
- technical exchanges, exchanges of information and best practices, research projects, studies, reports, conferences and workshops on energy efficiency and renewable energy;[139] or
- dialogues, the sharing of best practices on policies and procedures, and the exchange of experts on energy efficiency, development of cost-effective, low emissions technologies and alternative, clean and renewable energy sources.[140]

The per se provisions of RTAs on such cooperation and communication frameworks hardly constitute concrete obligations for the sake of environmental protection. However, they may still be important for raising awareness of energy–environment concerns and addressing them in the regional trade context.

4.3 Sustainable Service Standards

Standard-setting for services is relatively sparse. Indeed, the ISO has so far published over 700 international standards for services, which makes up only about 3 per cent of the ISO portfolio.[141] As another example, despite the sheer size of services (70 per cent) in the EU economy, standards for services account for only 2 per cent of all European standards.[142] However, recent trends in many economies towards deregulation and privatization of public services, delocalization of supply, expansion of online services and 'servitization' in product manufacturing

[136] Article 7.7 of the EU–Singapore FTA (2018).
[137] Article 9.14 of the Malaysia–Turkey FTA (2014).
[138] Article 16.14 of the Korea–Australia FTA (2014).
[139] Article 24.12 of the EU–Canada CETA (2016).
[140] Articles 20.15.2 and 20.12.5 of the CPTPP (2018).
[141] Belinda Cleeland, 'ISO: International Standards for Services', UNCTAD Multi-Year Expert Meeting on Trade, Services and Development, 18–20 July 2017, https://unctad.org/system/files/non-official-document/c1mem5_2017_105_S1_Cleeland_2.pdf.
[142] European Commission, 'Service Standards', https://ec.europa.eu/growth/single-market/services/service-standards_en.

stimulate market demand for more service standards.[143] One survey (2014), commissioned by the European Commission to identify priority areas for developing EU service standards, reveals that over 30 per cent of respondents indicated the need for service standards in the cross-cutting area of 'Energy, environment and resource use'.[144]

Standards with the energy–environment link may have sectoral or horizontal applicability. At the sectoral level, they can apply to environmental services (e.g., cleaning services of exhaust gases, environmental impact assessment services or remediation and cleanup of soil and water)[145] and energy-related services (services incidental to mining, services incidental to energy distribution, transportation of fuels, services important to nuclear safety, construction and related engineering services, rail/road transport services and so on).[146] By contrast, standards for environmental management and energy management can apply across the board.

When energy products, like solar panels or wind turbines, are supplied as part of associated services (installation, maintenance, etc.), the WTO rules on goods standards would apply to such products. As for services per se, the GATS lacks details on standards and leaves specific regulatory issues for future negotiations to address. The text of the agreement mentions 'technical standards', without defining this term. The Reference Paper on Services Domestic Regulation,[147] adopted by a Joint Initiative on Services Domestic Regulation in 2021, does not define it either. This document provides that '[e]ach Member shall encourage its competent authorities, when adopting technical standards, to adopt technical standards developed through open and transparent processes, and shall encourage any body, including relevant international

143 ISO, 'ISO Strategy for Service Standardization', 2016, www.iso.org/files/live/sites/isoorg/files/store/en/PUB100393.pdf.

144 European Committee for Standardization, 'Mandate M/517 for the Programming and Development of Horizontal Service Standards: Phase I Final Report', 2015, pp. 166, 239, https://ftp.cencenelec.eu/CEN/WhatWeDo/Fields/Services/FinalReportPhase1-M517.pdf.

145 For the scope of environmental services, see WTO, Council for Trade in Services – Background Note on Environmental Services – Note by the Secretariat, S/C/W/320 (20 August 2010).

146 For the scope of energy services, see WTO, Council for Trade in Services – Energy Services – Background Note by the Secretariat, S/C/W/311 (12 January 2010).

147 WTO, Joint Initiative on Services Domestic Regulation – Reference Paper on Services Domestic Regulation, INF/SDR/2 (26 November 2021) annexed to WTO, Declaration on the Conclusion of Negotiations on Services Domestic Regulation, WT/L/1129 (2 December 2021).

organizations, designated to develop technical standards to use open and transparent processes'.[148]

From WTO discussions on accountancy disciplines, it can be inferred that technical standards in services refer to certain criteria or rules specifying the characteristics of a service and the manner in which it is performed or supplied, which is akin to the distinction between a product's characteristics and PPMs under the TBT Agreement.[149] Technical standards define, inter alia, a service's content, performance/process, frequency and format for service delivery and can also include specifications on service-related equipment, technology or infrastructure.[150] Conceptually, technical standards differ from 'qualification requirements' (and associated 'qualification procedures') and 'licensing requirements' (and associated 'licensing procedures') that relate to a service *supplier* rather than a service as such.[151]

Article VI of the GATS specifically deals with domestic regulations including technical standards. With respect to committed sectors, Article VI:1 mandates 'reasonable, objective and impartial' administration of 'all measures of general application affecting trade in services'. Article VI:4 envisages a negotiating agenda for developing new disciplines that would ensure that measures relating to 'qualification requirements and procedures, technical standards and licensing requirements' do not create unnecessary trade barriers. It states further:

> Such disciplines shall aim to ensure that such requirements are, inter alia:
>
> (a) based on objective and transparent criteria, such as competence and the ability to supply the service;
> (b) not more burdensome than necessary to ensure the quality of the service;
> (c) in the case of licensing procedures, not in themselves a restriction on the supply of the service.

148 INF/SDR/2, supra note 147, para. 21 (footnote omitted).

149 WTO, Working Party on Domestic Regulation – Technical Standards in Services – Note by the Secretariat, S/WPDR/W/49 (13 September 2012), paras. 20–21. See also WTO, Working Party on Domestic Regulation – Disciplines on Domestic Regulation Pursuant to GATS Article VI:4 – Chairman's Progress Report, S/WPDR/W/45 (14 April 2011), p. 55.

150 S/WPDR/W/49, supra note 149, paras. 22, 29, 86(c).

151 See WTO, Working Party on Professional Services – The Relevance of the Disciplines of the Agreement on Technical Barriers to Trade (TBT) and on Import Licensing Procedures to Article VI.4 of the General Agreement on Trade in Services – Note by the Secretariat, S/WPPS/W/9 (11 September 1996), para. 4.

Article VI:5 of the GATS provides two important details. In committed sectors, licensing and qualification requirements and technical standards must not nullify or impair scheduled commitments in a manner which does not comply with the criteria (a), (b) or (c) above and could not reasonably have been expected of a committing member at the time of commitment. Furthermore, when determining a member's compliance with this obligation, 'account shall be taken of international standards of relevant international organizations' – that is, 'international bodies whose membership is open to the relevant bodies of at least all Members of the WTO' – applied by that member.[152] This language does not go as far as the TBT Agreement that, as discussed above, generally mandates using the relevant international standards 'as a basis' for domestic TBT measures and creates a rebuttable presumption of the absence of unnecessary obstacles to international trade.[153] Therefore, during the WTO negotiations on domestic regulation, Switzerland and Mexico jointly proposed to introduce such TBT-like disciplines on technical standards on services.[154] However, this has not been reflected in the newly adopted Reference Paper on Services Domestic Regulation.

Nevertheless, international service standards should gain greater acceptance under the WTO services regime,[155] provided that they are developed in accordance with the TBT Committee's six principles on international standardization that can well be stretched to the services area as well. By way of illustration, Table 4.1 lists some areas where ISO

[152] See also the WTO disciplines on domestic regulation in the accountancy sector (WTO, Disciplines on Domestic Regulation in the Accountancy Sector – Adopted by the Council for Trade in Services on 14 December 1998, S/L/64, 17 December 1998):

> VIII. TECHNICAL STANDARDS
>
> 25. Members shall ensure that measures relating to technical standards are prepared, adopted and applied only to fulfil legitimate objectives.
> 26. In determining whether a measure is in conformity with the obligations under paragraph 2 [to not create unnecessary trade barriers and to avoid trade restrictiveness more than necessary to fulfil a legitimate objective], account shall be taken of internationally recognized standards of relevant international organizations applied by that Member [footnote omitted].

[153] S/WPDR/W/49, supra note 149, para. 25; Gabriel Gari, 'Is the WTO's Approach to International Standards on Services Outdated?', 19 *Journal of International Economic Law* 589 (2016), pp. 598–599.

[154] WTO, Working Party on Domestic Regulation – Communication from Switzerland – Proposal for Disciplines on Technical Standards in Services, S/WPDR/W/32/Rev.1 (28 October 2005).

[155] See also Gari, supra note 153, pp. 598–600, 605.

Table 4.1 *Examples of energy–environment areas in ISO standardization affecting services (as of 1 April 2023)*

ISO technical committee	Energy–environment areas of standardization	Number of published standards	Number of standards under development
Buildings and civil engineering works (ISO/TC 59)	General rules for performance requirements, including functional and user requirements related to service life, sustainability, accessibility and usability; general rules and guidelines for addressing the economic, environmental and social impacts and aspects related to sustainable development, etc.	135	20
Nuclear energy, nuclear technologies and radiological protection (ISO/TC 85)	Standardization in the field of peaceful applications of nuclear energy, nuclear technologies and in the field of the protection of individuals and the environment against all sources of ionizing radiations	257	50
Air quality (ISO/TC 146)	Standardization of tools for air quality characterization of emissions, workspace air, ambient air, indoor air, in particular measurement methods for air pollutants (particles, gases, odours, microorganisms) and for meteorological parameters, measurement planning, procedures for quality assurance/quality control and methods for the evaluation of results including the determination of uncertainty	198	28
Thermal performance and energy use in the built environment (ISO/TC 163)	Test and calculation methods for energy use in buildings, including the industrial built environment; test and calculation methods for heating and cooling loads in buildings; standardization of the holistic assessment of the energy performance of new and existing buildings as well as building retrofits, etc.	146	19
Solar energy (ISO/TC 180)	Standardization in the field of solar energy utilization in space and water heating, cooling, industrial process heating and air conditioning, which includes developing standards on the instrumentation and procedures used for measuring solar energy and solar measurement	20	5

Building environment design (ISO/TC 205)	Aspects of sustainability related to indoor environmental quality and energy that can be addressed in the design of buildings and the design of retrofits of existing buildings; design of energy-efficient buildings; design of heating and cooling systems including radiant; application of methods of testing and rating the performance of building environmental equipment in the design of new buildings and retrofits, etc.	40	16
Environmental management (ISO/TC 207)	Environmental management systems, auditing, verification/validation and related investigations, environmental labelling, environmental performance evaluation, life cycle assessment, climate change and its mitigation and adaptation, eco-design, material efficiency, environmental economics, environmental and climate finance	65	14
CO_2 capture, transportation and geological storage (ISO/TC 265)	Standardization of design, construction, operation, environmental planning and management, risk management, quantification, monitoring and verification, and related activities in the field of CO_2 capture, transportation and geological storage	12	7
Energy management and energy savings (ISO/TC 301)	Standardization in the field of energy management and energy savings	22	5
Sustainable finance (ISO/TC 322)	Standardization in the field of sustainable finance to integrate sustainability considerations including environmental, social and governance practices in the financing of economic activities	2	1

Source: Author's compilation from information at ISO, 'Technical Committees', www.iso.org/technical-committees.html.
Note: The number of standards corresponds to the total number of standards in both energy–environment and other areas covered by the respective ISO Technical Committee.

standardization of services affects the energy–environment link. To give some concrete examples of relevant standards, ISO 27913 concerns CO_2 capture, transportation and geological storage with particular focus on pipeline transportation systems; ISO 50001 encourages organizations in all sectors to improve energy use through the development of an energy management system; ISO 50007 on energy services covers energy efficiency; and ISO 15392 establishes general principles for sustainability in construction works throughout their entire life cycle.[156]

4.4 Green Procurement Standards

Green public procurement sends a signal to the market about the procuring government's eco-friendly consumption preferences, thereby (potentially) influencing the behaviour of market participants towards sustainable outcomes. According to national practices, governments of different jurisdictions procure, inter alia, energy-saving equipment, low-emission vehicles, renewable electricity or construction services dealing with energy-efficient public buildings.[157] Environmental criteria can be integrated into different stages of public procurement, such as the drafting of tendering requirements, selection of suppliers, the awarding of contracts or performance (execution) of contracts.[158]

On the basis of the mandate under Article XXII:8(a) of the revised WTO Government Procurement Agreement (GPA) 2012, the Government Procurement Committee of the WTO adopted a Work Programme on Sustainable Procurement to identify sustainable procurement measures and policies implemented consistently with the principle of 'best value for money' and international trade rules and to prepare a report listing best practices in this field.[159] Since the initiation of this work programme in 2014, the committee has worked in this direction, but in 2019 it agreed to temporarily suspend the work on the drafting of a

[156] ISO website, www.iso.org.

[157] See, for example, Harro van Asselt, Nicolien van der Grijp and Frans Oosterhuis, 'Greener Public Purchasing: Opportunities for Climate-Friendly Government Procurement under WTO and EU Rules', 6 *Climate Policy* 217 (2006), p. 220; OECD, 'Going Green: Best Practices for Sustainable Procurement', 2015.

[158] See Anja Wiesbrock, 'An Obligation for Sustainable Procurement? Gauging the Potential Impact of Article 11 TFEU on Public Contracting in the EU', 40 *Legal Issues of Economic Integration* 105 (2013), p. 117.

[159] Annex E to Appendix 2 of the Decision on the Outcomes of the Negotiations Under Article XXIV:7 of the Agreement on Government Procurement, adopted on 30 March 2012 (GPA/113, 2 April 2012, p. 444).

final report in order to further examine measures and policies concerning social considerations in government procurement.[160]

The GPA 2012 prohibits a procuring entity from using technical specifications and conformity assessment procedures that create unnecessary obstacles to trade (Article X:1). A 'technical specification' is 'a tendering requirement' that 'lays down the characteristics of goods or services to be procured, including quality, performance, safety and dimensions, or the processes and methods for their production or provision' or that 'addresses terminology, symbols, packaging, marking or labelling requirements, as they apply to a good or service' (Article I(u)). As this definition does not seem to exclude NPR-PPMs,[161] governments can include sustainable energy aspects of production or provision of procurable goods or services in technical specifications. Technical specifications must, where appropriate, be set out in terms of performance and functional requirements (rather than design or descriptive characteristics) and based on international standards 'where such exist' or otherwise on 'national technical regulations, recognized national standards or building codes' (Article X:2). Thus, technical specifications of goods or services can be presented in terms of environmental performance including energy consumption or GHG emission.

Unlike the GPA 1994, the GPA 2012 contains two provisions that explicitly incorporate environmental dimensions. First, Article X:6 of the GPA 2012 states that '[f]or greater certainty', a GPA party and its procuring entity 'may' use technical specifications 'to promote the conservation of natural resources or protect the environment'. While it is unclear whether this provision is completely new in the light of the words '[f]or greater certainty' that, according to one view, may indicate the continuation of what was implicit in the GPA 1994, this clarification may still serve as a basis or context for pro-environmental GPA interpretations in the future.[162]

Second, the GPA 2012 states that the notice of intended procurement or tender documentation must provide a complete description of 'all

[160] WTO, Committee on Government Procurement – Report (2022) of the Committee on Government Procurement, GPA/AR/5 (8 December 2022), p. 8, para. 35.

[161] Maria Anna Corvaglia, 'Public Procurement and Private Standards: Ensuring Sustainability under the WTO Agreement on Government Procurement', 19 *Journal of International Economic Law* 607 (2016), p. 623.

[162] Sue Arrowsmith, 'The Revised Agreement on Government Procurement: Changes to the Procedural Rules and Other Transparency Provisions', in Sue Arrowsmith and Robert D. Anderson (eds.), *The WTO Regime on Government Procurement: Challenge and Reform* (Cambridge: Cambridge University Press, 2011), p. 323.

evaluation criteria' that a procuring entity will apply in the awarding of a contract (Article X:7(c)). Such evaluation criteria 'may include, among others, price and other cost factors, quality, technical merit, *environmental characteristics* and terms of delivery' (Article X:9, emphasis added). The contract is awarded to a supplier that, inter alia, has submitted 'the lowest price' (where the price is the sole criterion) or 'the most advantageous tender' (Article XV:5). Thus, the aforementioned 'environmental characteristics' can well act as one of the evaluation criteria for determining the most advantageous tender.

To date, WTO adjudicators have not considered the GPA 2012 provisions yet, but EU jurisprudence on similar EU provisions implementing the GPA[163] is quite illuminating. In *Commission v. Netherlands* on public procurement for management and supply of ingredients for automatic coffee machines, the province of North Holland in the Netherlands required that coffee and tea to be supplied should carry the private labels EKO and MAX HAVELAAR. EKO certified the organic origin of ingredients, and MAX HAVELAAR certified that a product was purchased at fair trade terms. With respect to EKO, the Court of Justice of the EU found that by prescribing a specific ecolabel, rather than specifications underlying that label, the contracting authority used a technical specification that was inconsistent with Article 23(6) of EU Directive 2004/18/EC[164] on awarding public contracts.[165] According to Article 23(6) in question, where contracting authorities lay down environmental characteristics in terms of performance or functional requirements, they may use detailed specifications defined by ecolabels and may also indicate that products or services bearing ecolabels are presumed to comply with technical specifications in contract documents. Insisting on sufficient precision in technical specifications, the Court of Justice of the EU held that Article 23(6) allowed recourse to an ecolabel alone only indirectly and that the mere reference to an ecolabel itself would create uncertainties as, among other things, the criteria underlying the ecolabel could vary from time to time.[166] It also found that by awarding extra points in the tender evaluation for products' possession of specific labels, without

[163] See Recital 7 of Directive 2004/18/EC of the European Parliament and of the Council of 31 March 2004 on the coordination of procedures for the award of public works contracts, public supply contracts and public service contracts (OJ 2004 L 134, and corrigendum OJ 2004 L 351), as amended by Commission Regulation (EC) No. 1422/2007 of 4 December 2007, OJ 2007 L 317.

[164] Directive 2004/18/EC, ibid.

[165] *Commission v. Netherlands*, Judgment of the Court (EU), para. 70.

[166] Ibid., paras. 62–67.

listing the criteria underlying the labels and without allowing bidders to demonstrate compliance with those criteria 'by all appropriate means', the contracting authority established an award criterion that was incompatible with Article 53(1)(a) of EU Directive 2004/18/EC.[167] Similar to the GPA 2012, Article 53(1)(a) in question lists 'environmental characteristics' among possible criteria for the awarding of contracts. This provision expressly links these criteria to the 'most economically advantageous' tender. Overall, the EU ruling in *Commission v. Netherlands* is remarkable for widening the scope of the means of satisfying environmental standards in public procurement. Indeed, one cannot rule out that products or services being procured may well meet environmental criteria in different ways than just by carrying a specific ecolabel.

4.5 Concluding Remarks

From the analysis in this chapter, one can draw out some important implications for the energy–environment nexus. First, standardization regarding energy is increasingly incorporating environmental and sustainability elements impacting trade, which is indirectly indicated by the rising number of energy–environment STCs in the last ten years. The STC process has been useful in clarifying and revisiting concerned measures and thereby reducing the potential for energy–environment disputes. Second, although private standards may work to create de facto barriers to energy-related products, RTAs such as some EU FTAs, the USMCA and the CPTPP have a rather positive attitude and encourage governments to engage with voluntary environmental mechanisms, including private initiatives. Governments can use these public–private interaction formats as a means of identifying best private practices to attain optimal environmental results and discouraging inappropriate private standards. Third, international cooperation on standard-related issues should be intensified for reaching greater regulatory convergence. This will lessen trade frictions over pro-environmental standards. Finally, the international regime on government procurement gives State agencies certain leeway for making environmentally sound purchases and designing technical specifications accordingly. Such green procurement sends demand-side signals to the market about eco-friendly consumption preferences of the procuring agency, which may have a spillover effect for sustainable energy use in the public sector and beyond.

[167] Ibid., paras. 93–97.

5

Energy Investment Regulation and the Environment

Trade measures examined in the preceding analysis can be used in conjunction with investment policies. This chapter will focus on several investment-related aspects of the energy–environment nexus. In particular, State actions against fossil fuel investments often have an environmental cause, raising the issue of policy space under the investment regime. The doctrine of 'police powers' provides some grounds for qualifying certain pro-environmental interventions as non-compensable non-expropriatory measures. In addition to seeking policy flexibilities where needed, many States wish energy investors to voluntarily contribute to society by bearing social responsibility on the environmental front. As a result, a number of IIAs provide for responsible business conduct, bringing some changes to the 'investor vs. State' asymmetry in the investment legal system. Further, a surge in renewable energy ISDS cases in the last ten years is another noticeable trend. High upfront costs of renewable energy projects recoupable in the long run necessitate FIT or other long-term benefits to investors. However, when the government suddenly cancels or cuts promised incentives, this frustrates investors' legitimate expectations under IIAs but may also be welcomed under trade law as a way of getting rid of distortive subsidies. Thus, some discrepancy or tension between the trade and investment regimes can arise despite the complementarity of the two in many ways.

5.1 Environmental Control of Energy Investment

States can exert environmental 'control' over energy investments through the use of restrictions against eco-harmful activities or guidelines regarding investors' social responsibility. Because of expropriatory effects, some restrictions may call into question the legitimacy and environmental proportionality of such measures.

5.1.1 Restrictions on Environmentally Hazardous Energy Investment Activities

Environmental considerations often force governments to restrict energy investments at different stages of investors' activities. Such restrictions range from early permission denials to project suspensions or terminations and typically aim to alleviate environmental concerns and/or fulfil a pro-environmental election agenda. Internal and external factors may induce shifts in States' decision-making on energy investment, especially if it is necessary to maximize political expediency. Environment-related ISDS cases emerged mainly from the 1990s onwards, as the literature suggests.[1] A few recent disputes on the energy–environment nexus are noteworthy.

In 2016, TransCanada brought an investment complaint under the NAFTA (1992) after the Obama administration of the United States had denied to issue a presidential permit to construct the Keystone XL Pipeline that was supposed to transport crude oil from Alberta (Canada) to the United States. Criticizing the politicized approval process, the claimant asserted that the US president rejected the project to prove his government's environmental credentials to the constituents who worried that the consumption of pipeline-transported oil would increase GHG emissions.[2] The case ended following the Trump administration's issuance of the required permit but resurged after the Biden administration cancelled that permit in 2021.[3]

One ECT investment dispute over administrative delays pertained to the preservation of a water ecosystem. Specifically, *Vattenfall v. Germany (I)* centred on Germany's tardiness in authorizing the construction of a coal-fired power plant in Hamburg near the Elbe River as well as tightened requirements for using cooling water from the river. Aimed to protect fish stocks, these requirements were alleged to reduce the planned plant's capacity utilization to an 'uneconomical' level.[4] The case

[1] Jorge E. Viñuales, *Foreign Investment and the Environment in International Law* (Cambridge: Cambridge University Press 2012), p. 18.

[2] *TransCanada Corporation and TransCanada PipeLines Limited v. United States of America*, ICSID Case No. ARB/16/21, Request for Arbitration, 24 June 2016, pp. 6–10.

[3] Lisa Bohmer, '[Updated] Canadian Province of Alberta Files NAFTA/USMCA Notice of Intent in Relation to Keystone XL Pipeline Dispute with the USA', Investment Arbitration Reporter, 9 February 2022, www.iareporter.com.

[4] *Vattenfall AB, Vattenfall Europe AG, Vattenfall Europe Generation AG v. Federal Republic of Germany (I)*, ICSID Case No. ARB/09/6, Request for Arbitration, 30 March 2009, paras. 36–45.

was settled, with Germany agreeing to revise the water use restrictions and to issue the requisite permits for completing this project.[5] However, in response to the European Commission's subsequent challenge of the construction permit, the Court of Justice of the EU found that Germany had failed to appropriately assess environmental implications of the project, thereby violating Council Directive 92/43/EEC of 21 May 1992 on the Conservation of Natural Habitats and of Wild Fauna and Flora.[6]

Some disputes under the NAFTA (1992) deal with post-approval measures. In *Lone Pine v. Canada*, Quebec (Canada) passed a law revoking permits for shale gas exploration beneath the St. Lawrence River. The law was adopted after a strategic environmental study, commissioned by the government under public pressure, had concluded that the area in question was not suitable for hydrocarbon development activities. Other related studies also warned about certain risks of hydraulic fracturing for the biophysical and human environment. According to the investor, Quebec's 'arbitrary, capricious, and illegal revocation' of its mining right violated Article 1110 of the NAFTA on expropriation and Article 1105 of the NAFTA on the minimum standard of treatment.[7]

Further, *Windstream Energy v. Canada (I)* concerned a moratorium on an offshore construction of approximately 100 wind turbines in Lake Ontario – the source of drinking water for the local community.[8] Despite awarding a FIT contract to the claimant, the government of Ontario deferred offshore development because of the 'significant scientific uncertainty regarding the effects of offshore wind projects on human health, safety and the environment'.[9] Ironically, the underlying policy of promoting wind power was driven by health and environmental concerns related to the province's dependence on coal-fired power plants.[10] For Canada, the moratorium 'was grounded in the precautionary principle', which suggested waiting until sufficient research had been

[5] See *Vattenfall v. Germany (I)*, ICSID, Award Embodying the Parties' Settlement Agreement; ISDS Platform, 'Vattenfall vs. Germany I: Coal-Fired Electric Plant', April 2021, www.isds.bilaterals.org/vattenfall-vs-germany-i-coal-fired.

[6] *Commission v. Germany*, Judgment of the Court (EU), para. 74.

[7] See Government of Canada, 'Lone Pine Resources Inc. v. Government of Canada', 28 April 2021, www.international.gc.ca/trade-agreements-accords-commerciaux/topics-domaines/disp-diff/lone.aspx?lang=eng; *Lone Pine Resources Inc. v. Canada*, ICSID Case No. UNCT/15/2, Notice of Arbitration (6 September 2013).

[8] *Windstream Energy v. Canada (I)*, PCA, Award, para. 118.

[9] Ibid., paras. 5, 7.

[10] Ibid., para. 86.

conducted on noise emissions, water quality, disturbance on benthic life forms and so on.[11] For the claimant, the real reasons were the rising costs of renewable electricity and political expediency in the context of provincial elections.[12] The tribunal found that the moratorium was not an indirect expropriation because the FIT contract was formally in force, the claimant's security deposit remained untouched by the government and the claimant was not substantially deprived of the value of its investment.[13] Under the NAFTA's national treatment and MFN provisions, the tribunal concluded that other investors (TransCanada and Samsung), alleged to be treated more favourably than the claimant investor (Windstream), were not in 'like circumstances' as they operated under non-FIT schemes and in non-offshore energy segments.[14] However, the tribunal found Canada to violate the fair and equitable treatment (FET) rule by failing to properly address scientific and regulatory uncertainty after the imposition of the moratorium: many of the research plans did not progress, the already conducted studies did not lead to regulatory amendments and the investor remained in 'the legal and contractual limbo':[15]

> [T]he Government failed to clarify the situation, either by way of promptly completing the required scientific research and establishing the appropriate regulatory framework for offshore wind and reactivating Windstream's FIT Contract, or by amending the relevant regulations so as to exclude offshore wind altogether as a source of renewable energy and terminating Windstream's FIT Contract in accordance with the applicable law.[16]

Finally, some ECT and NAFTA disputes contested the phasing-out of energy plants in operation. Driven mainly by the GHG-reducing rationale, government decisions to close coal-fired power plants in the Netherlands and Canada by 2030 prompted compensation demands by investors vis-à-vis the Sate concerned.[17] In a different factual situation, energy safety concerns led to a German law amendment about the

[11] Ibid., para. 207.
[12] Ibid., para. 173.
[13] Ibid., paras. 290–291.
[14] Ibid., paras. 413–416.
[15] Ibid., paras. 378–379.
[16] Ibid., para. 379.
[17] See *Uniper SE, Uniper Benelux Holding B.V. and Uniper Benelux N.V. v. Kingdom of the Netherlands*, ICSID Case No. ARB/21/22; *RWE AG and RWE Eemshaven Holding II BV v. Kingdom of the Netherlands*, ICSID Case No. ARB/21/4; *Westmoreland Mining Holdings LLC v. Canada (II)*, ICSID Case No. UNCT/20/3.

shutdown and phase-out of nuclear power plants in the country by 2022 (later extended until mid-April 2023 because of the energy crisis following the war in Ukraine[18]). This policy change was provoked by the 2011 accident at the Fukushima Dai-ichi Nuclear Power Plant in Japan. In *Vattenfall v. Germany (II)*, foreign shareholders of three nuclear power plants in Germany, affected by the amendment, complained that the respondent unlawfully expropriated their investments, ignored the FET standard and acted in a discriminatory manner.[19] As the tribunal noted, this case was not about the dilemma per se whether or not to sustain nuclear power plants in Germany but rather about 'compensation for shutting down plants prior to the end of their economic life once a democratic decision has been made to end nuclear power generation'.[20] In March 2021, the disputing parties reached an agreement about compensation and discontinuation of the investor–State proceeding, without affecting Germany's commitment to phase out all nuclear power plants.[21] As a result, in November 2021, the tribunal issued its discontinuance order.[22]

As seen above, the energy–environment policy tension can arise from the industrialization or commercialization of both fossil fuels and clean energy. Slow administrative review procedures, cancellations of early permits or reconsideration of ongoing projects can be attributed to the scientific uncertainty about investments' ecological repercussions, to political events, accidental environmental calamities and so on. The termination of energy projects being otherwise in progress is perhaps the most radical restriction against investors. But *Vattenfall v. Germany (II)* suggests that the anti-State sentiment can subside in the presence of solid environmental grounds and the readiness of the government to compensate for losses. The next section will discuss whether governments are actually obliged to *always* pay compensation in the case of public-purpose regulations that end or limit investment activities.

[18] Guy Chazan, 'Germany Extends Life of Nuclear Power Plants until Next April', *Financial Times*, 18 October 2022, www.ft.com/content/3f48c18f-0348-46b0-a082-3bf07e14e589.

[19] *Vattenfall v. Germany (II)*, ICSID, Order of the Tribunal Taking Note of the Discontinuance of the Proceeding, paras. 5–7.

[20] Ibid., para. 9.

[21] Lisa Bohmer, 'Breaking: Germany and Vattenfall Settle Long-Running Arbitration Dispute Arising from Nuclear Phase-Out', Investment Arbitration Reporter, 5 March 2021, www.iareporter.com.

[22] *Vattenfall v. Germany (II)*, ICSID, Order of the Tribunal Taking Note of the Discontinuance of the Proceeding, para. 317; Lisa Bohmer, '[Updated] Vattenfall Asks for Discontinuance of ICSID Arbitration against Germany, after Settlement Enters into Force', Investment Arbitration Reporter, 2 November 2021, www.iareporter.com.

5.1.2 Environmental Expropriation

Investment treaties typically proscribe expropriatory measures except for lawful (or legitimate) expropriation such as compensable takings in the public interest. For example, Article 13(1) of the ECT (1994) prohibits nationalization, expropriation or measures with 'equivalent' effects except where such actions are in the public interest, non-discriminatory, carried out under due process of law and accompanied by 'prompt, adequate and effective compensation'. Direct seizures of foreign assets are rare today, and governmental interference with property rights occurs mainly indirectly, often through 'regulatory takings'. Depending on their nature, gravity and economic impacts, environmental measures devaluing energy investments can constitute an indirect expropriation. Many anti-expropriation provisions are explicit in forbidding not only direct but also indirect expropriation.

After the *Metalclad v. Mexico* ruling, many feared that international investment law would create serious obstacles to the implementation of domestic environmental policies.[23] In that dispute, a US company obtained the Mexican central government's permit to develop a hazardous waste landfill, but the local authorities of the area where the project was planned subsequently refused to issue a necessary construction permit due to environmental risks and instead declared that territory an ecological preserve. Under Article 1110 of the NAFTA (1992) that bans the parties from 'directly or indirectly' expropriating investments, the tribunal found the denial of the construction permit to be an indirect expropriation.[24] In so doing, the tribunal essentially endorsed the 'sole effects' doctrine, which considers only the measure's effect on investments regardless of its underlying purpose.[25] Specifically, the tribunal held:

> [E]xpropriation under NAFTA includes not only open, deliberate and acknowledged takings of property, such as outright seizure or formal or obligatory transfer of title in favour of the host State, but also covert or

[23] Anatole Boute, 'The Potential Contribution of International Investment Protection Law to Combat Climate Change', 27 *Journal of Energy & Natural Resources Law* 333 (2009), pp. 365–366.

[24] *Metalclad v. Mexico*, ICSID, Award, paras. 106–107.

[25] Stephan W. Schill, 'Do Investment Treaties Chill Unilateral State Regulation to Mitigate Climate Change?', 24 *Journal of International Arbitration* 469 (2007), p. 471. See also *Vivendi v. Argentina (I)*, ICSID, Award, para. 7.5.20 (finding in the expropriation context that '[t]here is extensive authority for the proposition that the state's intent, or its subjective motives are at most a secondary consideration' and that 'the *effect* of the measure on the investor, not the state's intent, is the critical factor' (emphasis added)).

> incidental interference with the use of property which has *the effect* of depriving the owner, in whole or in significant part, of the use or reasonably-to-be-expected economic benefit of property even if not necessarily to the obvious benefit of the host State.[26]

In contrast, ECT jurisprudence on the retraction of energy support schemes is more cautious in addressing expropriation claims. In *Nykomb v. Latvia*, the tribunal rejected the claim that the non-payment of a promised double tariff for electricity produced by a cogeneration plant constituted 'indirect' or 'creeping' expropriation under Article 13(1) of the ECT (1994). While accepting 'regulatory takings' as possible forms of expropriation, the tribunal said that '[t]he decisive factor for drawing the border line towards expropriation must primarily be the degree of possession taking or control over the enterprise the disputed measures entail'.[27] Similarly, the tribunal in *Charanne and Construction Investments v. Spain* held that a simple decrease in the investment's value (like the reduction in profitability at issue) not causing a deprivation of property was not an indirect expropriation.[28] In *Isolux v. Spain*, the expropriation claim failed because the current rate of profitability (7.11 per cent) turned out to be even higher than that (6.19 per cent or less) at the date of investment.[29] In other cases against Spain, it was found that the claimants were not deprived of legal title to PV facilities[30] or remained the 'untouched' owner of the plants.[31] Likewise, the claimants in *Blusun v. Italy* 'never lost title to the land' for building PV plants.[32] In *Eskosol v. Italy*, the claimant could not demonstrate the existence of a valid property right, so the government's conduct frustrating a company business plan did not constitute expropriation even if it led to the company's bankruptcy.[33]

Some past rulings acknowledged the relevance of legitimate expectations to expropriation-related considerations.[34] However, this may blur

[26] *Metalclad v. Mexico*, ICSID, Award, para. 103 (emphasis added).
[27] *Nykomb v. Latvia*, Arbitral Award, p. 33, section 4.3.1.
[28] *Charanne and Construction Investments v. Spain*, Stockholm Chamber of Commerce (SCC), Final Award (unofficial English translation by Mena Chambers), paras. 465–466.
[29] *Isolux v. Spain*, SCC, Award (unofficial English translation), para. 852.
[30] *Foresight and others v. Spain*, SCC, Final Award, para. 427.
[31] *Novenergia v. Spain*, SCC, Final Arbitral Award, para. 762.
[32] *Blusun v. Italy*, ICSID, Award, para. 407.
[33] *Eskosol v. Italy*, ICSID, Award, para. 472.
[34] See Rudolf Dolzer and Christoph Schreuer, *Principles of International Investment Law* (Oxford: Oxford University Press, 2008), pp. 104–106.

the distinction with the FET concept.[35] Therefore, the tribunal in the recent *Eurus Energy v. Spain* dispute found that the ECT expropriation clause was meant to protect investors' property interests but not reasonable or legitimate expectations as '[s]uch expectations can be frustrated or denied, but they cannot be expropriated'.[36]

In addition to non-grievous environmental regulatory takings (found to not constitute indirect expropriation in the ECT cases above), lawful (or legitimate) expropriations and non-compensable regulations are tolerated under international investment law of expropriation as well. As mentioned in the beginning of this section, lawful expropriation for a public purpose must be against the prompt payment of adequate and effective compensation. The *Santa Elena v. Costa Rica* ruling stressed a State's obligation to compensate for environmental expropriations:

> Expropriatory environmental measures – no matter how laudable and beneficial to society as a whole – are, in this respect, similar to any other expropriatory measures that a state may take in order to implement its policies: where property is expropriated, even for environmental purposes, whether domestic or international, the state's obligation to pay compensation remains.[37]

By contrast, the 'police powers' doctrine argues that States are free from paying compensation in the case of bona fide public interest regulations as a natural expression of sovereign powers. Such non-compensable regulations are a priori not considered to constitute expropriation. This school of thought has been gaining wide acceptance[38] and dispels the perception that expropriation law chills unilateral State regulation to serve public purposes.[39] Indeed, recent IIAs tend to carve out non-discriminatory legitimate regulations affecting, inter alia, public

[35] For critical comments, see Anna De Luca, 'Indirect Expropriations and Regulatory Takings: What Role for the "Legitimate Expectations" of Foreign Investors?', in Giorgio Sacerdoti (eds.), *General Interests of Host States in International Investment Law* (Cambridge: Cambridge University Press, 2014), pp. 58, 71–74.

[36] *Eurus Energy v. Spain*, ICSID, Decision on Jurisdiction and Liability, para. 256.

[37] *Santa Elena v. Costa Rica*, ICSID, Final Award, para. 72. Although the amount of compensation, rather than the lawfulness of expropriation, was at issue here (paras. 54–56), the tribunal stressed that the very fact of legitimacy of a taking for environmental reasons, and hence for a public purpose, 'does not affect either the nature or the measure of the compensation to be paid for the taking' (para. 71).

[38] See, for example, UNCTAD, 'Expropriation', UNCTAD Series on Issues in International Investment Agreements II, 2012, p. 85; M. Sornarajah, *The International Law on Foreign Investment* (New York: Cambridge University Press, 2010), 3rd edn, pp. 388–389.

[39] See Schill, supra note 25, pp. 472–474.

health and the environment from the scope of indirect expropriations.[40] Yet, some treaties attach reservations. The EU–Canada CETA (2016), for example, insists on proportionality by stating that such carve-out does not apply 'in the rare circumstance when the impact of a measure or series of measures is so severe in light of its purpose that it appears manifestly excessive'.[41] Recent jurisprudence confirms that such carve-outs from indirect expropriation reflect police powers of States.[42]

The passage below from the *Saluka v. Czech Republic* ruling is remarkable:

> In the opinion of the Tribunal, the principle that a State does not commit an expropriation and is thus not liable to pay compensation to a dispossessed alien investor when it adopts general regulations that are 'commonly accepted as within the police power of States' forms part of customary international law today. There is ample case law in support of this proposition. As the tribunal in *Methanex Corp. v. USA* said recently in its final award, '[i]t is a principle of customary international law that, where economic injury results from a *bona fide* regulation within the police powers of a State, compensation is not required'.[43]

From this finding, it follows that even if an investment treaty is silent on non-compensable regulations, the latter can still be accommodated by customary international law, which remains applicable between treaty parties unless agreed otherwise.[44] However, as the tribunal itself

[40] Annex 13B (para. 3(b)) of the Australia–UK FTA (2021) reads that '[n]on-discriminatory regulatory actions by a Party that are designed and applied to protect legitimate public welfare objectives, such as public health, [footnote omitted] safety, and the environment, do not constitute indirect expropriations, except in rare circumstances'. A similar provision is included in the CPTPP (2018) (Annex 9-B, para. 3(b)), the USMCA (2018) (Annex 14-B, para. 3(b)), the RCEP Agreement (2020) (Annex 10B, para. 4) and so on. Article 20.8 of the Investment Agreement for the COMESA Common Investment Area (2007) creates such regulatory carve-out '[c]onsistent with the right of states to regulate and the customary international law principles on police powers'.

[41] Annex 8-A (para. 3) of the EU–Canada CETA (2016).

[42] See, for example, *Eco Oro v. Colombia*, ICSID, Decision on Jurisdiction, Liability and Directions on Quantum, paras. 625–626, 642, 698–699.

[43] *Saluka v. Czech Republic*, Partial Award, para. 262.

[44] In *Philip Morris v. Uruguay* (ICSID, Award, paras. 289–290), the claimants argued that the police powers did not constitute a legal defence against expropriation or exempt the State from the obligation to pay compensation as the Switzerland–Uruguay BIT (1988) at issue did not provide for the State's police powers explicitly. But the tribunal disagreed, observing that the BIT's expropriation clause 'must be interpreted in accordance with Article 31(3)(c) of the VCLT requiring that treaty provisions be interpreted in the light of "[a]ny relevant rules of international law applicable to the relations between the parties," a reference "which includes . . . customary international law"'.

acknowledged, 'international law has yet to identify in a comprehensive and definitive fashion precisely what regulations are considered "permissible" and "commonly accepted" as falling within the police or regulatory power of States and, thus, non-compensable'.[45] Thus, an important but difficult task here is how to distinguish between lawful but compensable expropriation and non-compensable non-expropriatory regulations, as the two overlap in having the public interest, non-discrimination and due process of law in common.[46] In drawing a borderline between the two, one recent study suggests that compensable expropriatory regulations impose *new* limits on investors' property rights to *improve* public welfare (so society should pay to the 'victimized' investor for the better welfare) while non-compensable regulations merely clarify the *existing* inherent limits of such rights (e.g., investors' property rights as limited by the right of others to the clean environment) in the light of *newly emerging/discovered circumstances*.[47] Therefore, it is contended that bona fide climate regulations do not entail compensation because they prevent the worsening of the environmental situation by climate change – an emergent threat, not fully grasped by science yet.[48] On the basis of this approach, one could argue that such energy-related measures as carbon taxes, emission standards or ETS requirements, imposed by States in response to the emerging climate threats, would constitute a non-compensable measure provided that they are applied in a non-discriminatory way, with due process and proportionately to the climate mitigation goal. By the same token, such environmental measures should avoid unjustifiable differentiations between polluting sectors or activities.[49]

45 *Saluka v. Czech Republic*, Partial Award, para. 263.

46 See David Khachvani, 'Non-Compensable Regulation versus Regulatory Expropriation: Are Climate Change Regulations Compensable?', 35 *ICSID Review* 154 (2020), pp. 155, 158–159, 161. See also *Azurix v. Argentina (I)*, ICSID, Award, para. 311 (criticizing the public powers doctrine, defended by the *Myers v. Canada* tribunal, for being contradictory: 'the BIT would require that investments not be expropriated except for a public purpose and that there be compensation if such expropriation takes place and, at the same time, regulatory measures that may be tantamount to expropriation would not give rise to a claim for compensation if taken for a public purpose'); UNCTAD, supra note 38, p. 78 ('The task of distinguishing between non-compensable regulation, on the one hand, and indirect expropriation, on the other, is one of the key issues in modern international investment law.').

47 See Khachvani, supra note 46, pp. 163–170.

48 See ibid., pp. 170–173. See also Valentina Vadi, 'Beyond Known Worlds: Climate Change Governance by Arbitral Tribunals?', 48 *Vanderbilt Journal of Transnational Law* 1285 (2015), pp. 1327–1329.

49 See, for example, *Arcelor v. Parliament and Council*, Judgment of the General Court (EU), paras. 161–171.

5.1.3 *Environmental Accountability of Energy Investors*

The preceding sections have discussed the energy–environment issues with particular reference to government restrictions against foreign investments. International investment law has traditionally protected foreign investors from unwarranted government interventions and thus created obligations primarily for States rather than investors. However, an increasing pressure from society to raise investors' corporate social responsibility (CSR) can rectify such 'investor vs. State' asymmetry in the investment law system. While lacking a uniform definition, the concept of CSR revolves around the notion that investors should behave in a societally acceptable way, meeting public expectations and needs.[50]

CSR has an environmental dimension. As a widely recognized international instrument on CSR, the OECD Guidelines for Multinational Enterprises (1976) recommend in the Environment Chapter that enterprises should establish an environmental management system, notify about the potential environmental or health and safety impacts of their activities, conduct environmental impact assessments, maintain contingency plans in case of ecological accidents and improve corporate environmental performance and so on. Adhering countries must set up national contact points with the mandate to, inter alia, facilitate the resolution of cases (or 'specific instances') regarding corporate non-observance of the OECD guidelines in question.[51] Roughly 20–25 per cent of such cases handled worldwide have referenced the Environment Chapter of the OECD Guidelines for Multinational Enterprises, and the majority of those environmental cases have dealt with business operations in the mining, manufacturing and energy sectors.[52]

Since the 1990s, the clash between investment protection and investors' CSR has intensified following the proliferation of investment disputes involving human rights and environmental issues.[53]

[50] See UNEP, 'Corporate Social Responsibility and Regional Trade and Investment Agreements', 2011, pp. 13–15; Peter Muchlinski, 'Corporate Social Responsibility', in Peter Muchlinski, Federico Ortino and Christoph Schreuer (eds.), *The Oxford Handbook of International Investment Law* (Oxford: Oxford University Press, 2008), pp. 643–645.

[51] See OECD, 'OECD Guidelines for Multinational Enterprises: 2011 Edition', 2011.

[52] See OECD, 'Cases Handled by the National Contact Points for Responsible Business Conduct', https://mneguidelines.oecd.org/Flyer-OECD-National-Contact-Points.pdf; OECD, 'The Role of OECD Instruments on Responsible Business Conduct in Progressing Environmental Objectives', 2021, pp. 14–15.

[53] Ying Zhu, 'Corporate Social Responsibility and International Investment Law: Tension and Reconciliation', 2017 *Nordic Journal of Commercial Law* 90 (2017), p. 96.

Unsurprisingly, CSR today is being actively incorporated into the domestic and international 'legalization' processes.[54] The inclusion of CSR in the investment treaty-making is a noticeable trend for a minimum of the past fifteen years or so.[55] As of 1 January 2023, at least seventy-nine IIAs[56] contain provisions explicitly referencing CSR, which appear mostly in the treaty's body but some[57] in the preamble. Many of such IIAs speak of CSR in general. But several agreements specifically mention the OECD Guidelines for Multinational Enterprises (1976), the International Labour Organization's Tripartite Declaration of Principles Concerning Multinational Enterprises and Social Policy (1977), the UN Global Compact (2000), the OECD Principles of Corporate Governance (1999) and the UN Guiding Principles on Business and Human Rights (2011).[58]

The seventy-nine IIAs mentioned above impose CSR-related duties typically on a State and rarely directly on investors, but they are common in (implicitly) acknowledging the generally voluntary nature of CSR commitments for investors. With respect to the State duties, the vast majority of the IIAs merely calls upon the State to encourage investors to accept CSR standards, like in the following passage:

> The Parties affirm the importance of each Party encouraging enterprises operating within its Area or subject to its jurisdiction to voluntarily incorporate into their internal policies those internationally recognised standards, guidelines and principles of corporate social responsibility that have been endorsed or are supported by that Party.[59]

[54] Rafael Peels et al., 'Corporate Social Responsibility in International Trade and Investment Agreements: Implications for States, Business, and Workers', ILO Research Paper No. 13, 2016, pp. 6, 18.

[55] See the next footnote. Relatedly, the European Parliament's 2011 resolution calls for the inclusion of CSR clauses in every EU FTA with regard to the investment chapters. See European Parliament Resolution of 6 April 2011 on the future European international investment policy (2010/2203(INI)), OJ C 296 E, 2 October 2012, para. 28.

[56] Author's search at the UNCTAD's database (as of 1 April 2023) on 'International Investment Agreements Navigator', https://investmentpolicy.unctad.org/international-investment-agreements. The earliest agreement mentioning CSR as such in our search result list was the Canada–Peru FTA (2008).

[57] See, for example, the preambles of the Hungary–Oman BIT (2022), the Lithuania–Turkey BIT (2018) and the Switzerland–Georgia BIT (2014).

[58] See, for example, Article 13.19 of the Australia–UK FTA (2021); Article 8.10.2 of the EU–UK Trade and Cooperation Agreement (2020); the preamble of the European Free Trade Association–Indonesia Comprehensive Economic Partnership Agreement (2018); Article 17 of the Argentina–UAE BIT (2018).

[59] Article 16 of the Australia–Hong Kong BIT (2019).

In addition, a number of IIAs provide for inter-governmental cooperation to promote CSR, often mentioning environmental protection or sustainable development in this context.[60] The CSR cooperation between the EU and Kazakhstan specifically concerns 'raw materials and energy goods'.[61]

In contrast to such IIAs with the State duties on CSR, ten IIAs, all signed between developing countries, directly appeal to investors to assume soft law[62] commitments regarding CSR.[63] Among them, six IIAs concluded by Brazil contain detailed CSR clauses. By way of illustration, the BIT between Brazil and the United Arab Emirates (UAE) states in relevant part:[64]

> 1. Investors and their investment shall strive to achieve the highest possible level of contribution to the sustainable development of the Host State and the local community, through the adoption of a high degree of socially responsible practices, based on the voluntary principles, and standards set out in the OECD Guidelines for Multinational Enterprises.
> 2. The investors and their investment shall endeavor to comply with the following voluntary principles and standards for a responsible business conduct and consistent with the laws adopted by the Host State receiving the investment:
>
> a) Contribute to the economic, social and environmental progress, aiming at achieving sustainable development;
>
> . . .

[60] See, for example, Article 16.2(e) of the Japan–UK Comprehensive Economic Partnership Agreement (2020); Annex 13 of the Korea–EU FTA (2010); Article 11.3(c) of the Southern African Customs Union and Mozambique–UK Economic Partnership Agreement (2019).

[61] Article 148.3 of the EU–Kazakhstan Enhanced Partnership and Cooperation Agreement (2015).

[62] The focus here is on IIA provisions dedicated to CSR per se. There may be stronger language in other IIA provisions not mentioning CSR but still dealing with responsible business conducts. For example, while Article 24 (titled 'Corporate Social Responsibility') of the Morocco–Nigeria BIT (2016) is formulated in a soft law manner (using the words 'should strive' or 'should apply'), some other provisions of this treaty impose hard law obligations on investors regarding environmental and social impact assessments (Article 14), anti-corruption (Article 17), environmental management, human rights and labour standards (Article 18).

[63] See Article 12 of the Brazil–India BIT (2020); Article 12 of the India–Kyrgyz Republic BIT (2019); Article 15 of the Brazil–UAE BIT (2019); Article 15 of the Brazil–Guyana BIT (2018); Article 12 of the India–Belarus BIT (2018); Article 15 of the Brazil–Suriname BIT (2018); Article 14 of the Brazil–Ethiopia BIT (2018); Article 24 of the Morocco–Nigeria BIT (2016); Article 12 of the Argentina–Qatar BIT (2016); Article 9 of the Brazil–Malawi BIT (2015).

[64] Article 15 of the Brazil–UAE BIT (2019).

e) Refrain from seeking or accepting exemptions that are not established in the legal or regulatory framework relating to human rights, environment, health, security, work, tax system, financial incentives, or other issues;

...

Interestingly, Brazil proposed including CSR duties directed at investors and their investments in ongoing WTO talks on Investment Facilitation for Development that may result in adopting a new WTO agreement in this field.[65]

Some IIAs creating CSR duties for a State or investors exclude the provisions on CSR from the scope of arbitral reviews in dispute settlement proceedings.[66] Nevertheless, subject to the legal and factual contexts, CSR clauses may play some role in helping States obtain favourable results in investment disputes, including on energy–environment matters.

First, when tribunals consider environmental counterclaims of a responding State in relation to an ISDS claim, they may give some weight to the complaining investor's failure to abide by the CSR rules, depending on the specific circumstances of the case at hand. Being recently discussed in international deliberations on investment dispute settlement reforms and in the literature,[67] environmental counterclaims, albeit still controversial, will likely expand in the future.[68] Reportedly, States' counterclaims to date have been ultimately upheld in only two out of twenty-five investment arbitration cases where such counterclaims were at

[65] WTO, Structured Discussions on Investment Facilitation – Communication from Brazil, INF/IFD/W/1 (26 March 2019). See also WTO, 'Investment Facilitation for Development in the WTO', January 2023, www.wto.org/english/tratop_e/invfac_public_e/factsheet_ifd.pdf.

[66] See, for example, Article 13, footnote 5 of the Hong Kong–Mexico BIT (2020); Article 21.1(b)(i) of the Argentina–UAE BIT (2018); Article 23 of Canada–Benin BIT (2013); Article 25.3 of the Brazil–UAE BIT (2019); Article 24.3 of the Brazil–Ethiopia BIT (2018).

[67] See UNCITRAL Working Group III, 'Possible Reform of Investor–State Dispute Settlement (ISDS): Multiple Proceedings and Counterclaims', Note by the Secretariat, Thirty-ninth Session, New York, 30 March–3 April 2020, A/CN.9/WG.III/WP.193 (22 January 2020), paras. 32–45; Maxi Scherer, Stuart Bruce and Juliane Reschke, 'Environmental Counterclaims in Investment Treaty Arbitration', 36 *ICSID Review* 413 (2021); Xuan Shao, 'Environmental and Human Rights Counterclaims in International Investment Arbitration: At the Crossroads of Domestic and International Law', 24 *Journal of International Economic Law* 157 (2021); James Harrison, 'Environmental Counterclaims in Investor–State Arbitration', 17 *The Journal of World Investment & Trade* 479 (2016).

[68] See Scherer et al., supra note 67, pp. 439–440. While not linking to the environment per se, Article 9.19.2 of the CPTPP (2018), for example, allows for counterclaims in investment disputes under certain terms.

issue.[69] In particular, the tribunals in *Burlington v. Ecuador* and *Perenco v. Ecuador* found Ecuador's environmental counterclaims admissible and ordered the claimants – belonging to the same consortium – to pay compensation to Ecuador for the soil and groundwater contamination caused by their oil drilling activities.[70] Two other cases – *Urbaser and CABB v. Argentina* and *Aven and others v. Costa Rica* – are also noteworthy in that the tribunal accepted its jurisdiction over human rights/ environmental counterclaims in principle, although it eventually rejected them on certain grounds.[71]

Second, with respect to substantive issues, a tribunal may dismiss the allegations of IIA violations by a host country in the light of an investor's anti-CSR conduct. For instance, governmental restrictions against a socially irresponsible investor could be found to be FET-compliant if it is determined that CSR was actually part of the host country's regulatory framework (for example, because of the implementation of the IIA's CSR provisions) that the investor overlooked at the time of investing. Such oversight by the investor (and hence its 'distorted' legitimate expectations) could be due to its failure to properly conduct due diligence and regulatory risk assessments.[72]

Finally, an investor's environmental misbehaviour, contrary to CSR standards, may provide legal grounds for cutting the amount of compensation awarded for investment losses caused by a host country. The Dutch Model BIT (2019) foresees this possibility by stating that a tribunal 'in deciding on the amount of compensation, is expected to take into account non-compliance by the investor with its commitments under the UN Guiding Principles on Business and Human Rights, and the OECD Guidelines for Multinational Enterprises'.[73]

[69] Anna De Luca and Crina Baltag, 'Counterclaims in Investment Arbitration: Reflections on UNCITRAL WG III Reform', Kluwer Arbitration Blog, 5 November 2021, http://arbitrationblog.kluwerarbitration.com/2021/11/05/counterclaims-in-investment-arbitration-reflections-on-uncitral-wg-iii-reform/.

[70] *Burlington v. Ecuador*, ICSID, Decision on Counterclaims, paras. 60–62, 1099; *Perenco v. Ecuador*, ICSID, Decision on Perenco's Application for Dismissal of Ecuador's Counterclaims, paras. 35, 43–44, 51; *Perenco v. Ecuador*, ICSID, Award, para. 1023(b).

[71] See *Urbaser and CABB v. Argentina*, ICSID, Award, paras. 1155, 1221; *Aven and others v. Costa Rica*, ICSID, Final Award, paras. 742, 747.

[72] See Yulia Levashova, 'The Accountability and Corporate Social Responsibility of Multinational Corporations for Transgressions in Host States through International Investment Law', 14 *Ultrecht Law Review* 40 (2018), pp. 51–53.

[73] Article 23 of the Netherlands Model BIT (2019), https://investmentpolicy.unctad.org/international-investment-agreements/treaty-files/5832/download.

5.2 Regulatory Changes in Renewable Energy Support

In addition to environmentally driven restrictions on energy investments discussed in the previous sections, renewable energy support amendments have emerged as another noticeable pattern of energy–environment State conduct challenged in investment disputes. Since 2011, there have been ninety ISDS cases concerning renewable energy brought predominantly under the ECT (1994) (Figure 5.1),[74] and most of them were about the scaling-back or cancellation of incentives otherwise promised for investments in renewable energy. These cases are common in scrutinizing such regulatory changes under the FET standard – the most frequently cited standard in all ISDS cases.[75] The following sections will focus on ECT case law involving some EU members as host countries.

5.2.1 *The Contours of FET*

Most investment treaties provide for FET and have similarities in defining the FET contours.[76] Article 10(1) of the ECT (1994), the second sentence suggests reading FET in conjunction with the conditions envisaged in the first sentence:[77]

> Each Contracting Party shall, in accordance with the provisions of this Treaty, encourage and create stable, equitable, favourable and transparent conditions for Investors of other Contracting Parties to make Investments in its Area. Such conditions shall include a commitment to accord at all times to Investments of Investors of other Contracting Parties fair and equitable treatment.

ECT case law identified several elements of FET, such as stability and predictability including legitimate expectations; transparency; justice

[74] See also Appendix B.

[75] Breaches of the fair and equitable treatment (FET) standard have been alleged in 86 per cent and found in 65 per cent of all ISDS cases with available data. Author's calculation from data at UNCTAD Investment Dispute Settlement Navigator, 'Breaches of IIA Provisions Alleged and Found', https://investmentpolicy.unctad.org/investment-dispute-settlement (database updated 31 July 2022).

[76] Roland Kläger, *'Fair and Equitable Treatment' in International Investment Law* (Cambridge: Cambridge University Press, 2011), p. 9.

[77] One tribunal interpreted the first-sentence obligation regarding 'stable, equitable, favourable and transparent conditions' as part of the FET commitment in the second sentence. See *Hydro Energy 1 and Hydroxana v. Spain*, ICSID, Decision on Jurisdiction, Liability and Directions on Quantum, paras. 548–549.

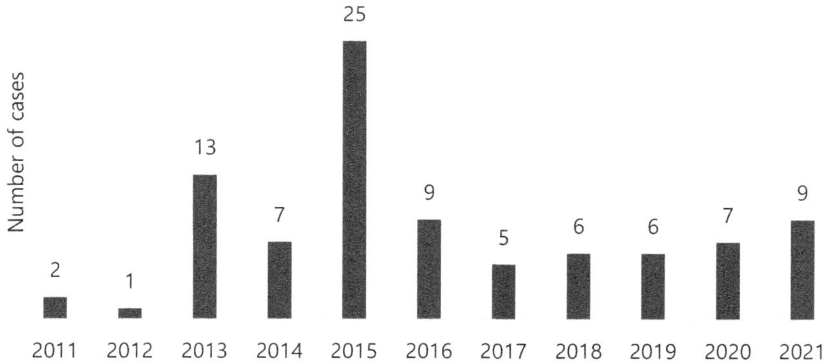

Figure 5.1 Renewable energy ISDS cases by year of initiation (2011–2021).
Source: Author's compilation from data at the UNCTAD's database, as arranged in Appendix B.

and due process; and freedom from harassment and discrimination.[78] FET-related disputes on renewable energy support revisions have mainly centred on whether investors could have legitimately expected that the regulatory framework at the time of investment would remain stable and predictable and if so, whether State measures at issue defeated their expectations. According to the *SunReserve v. Italy* ruling, this is a multi-element test:

> [T]here are broadly three questions to be answered as part of this examination: (a) whether the investors in the case had any expectations based on any conduct of the host State, and if so, whether these expectations were legitimate; (b) whether the investors relied on these expectations to make their investments in the host State; and (c) whether the host State by its subsequent conduct frustrated these expectations. If any of these three questions is answered in the negative, the investors' claim for breach of the FET obligation fails.[79]

It is generally acknowledged that legitimate expectations of investors are not unfettered and must be balanced against the host State's sovereign right to regulate in the public interest.[80] Legitimate expectations

[78] Kaj Hobér, *The Energy Charter Treaty: A Commentary* (Oxford: Oxford University Press, 2020), p. 191.
[79] *SunReserve v. Italy*, SCC, Final Award, para. 695.
[80] See, for example, *Electrabel v. Hungary*, ICSID, Award, para. 165. See also Kläger, supra note 76, p. 159.

derive from the legal framework – existing at the time of making investment – which includes the host State's domestic laws and regulations, international obligations, investor–State contractual arrangements and the State's specific representations or undertakings.[81] Broadly speaking, such legal framework can encompass (i) the State's specific commitments vis-à-vis an individual investor or (ii) rules that, albeit not investor-specific, have a particular aim to induce foreign investments and are relied upon by a foreign investor in making its investment.[82] The specific commitments in the first category are typically embodied in stabilization clauses that freeze the domestic legislation during a certain term or guarantee the restoration of an economic equilibrium disturbed by regulatory changes.[83] In the second category above, the role of general laws or regulations in creating legitimate expectations is less clear.[84] National law-making practice shows that general legislation can include stabilization clauses for unspecified investors.[85] Case law requires that the investor exercise due diligence to explore regulatory stability or potential risks under general legislation.[86] In this connection, the tribunal in *Masdar v. Spain* approved of due diligence because the claimant, prior to its solar power investment, had commissioned external reports, held multiple discussions with its joint venture partner and consulted with the capital-lending banks and law firms with respect to regulatory issues.[87] By contrast, due diligence regarding solely the economics of an investment project rather than regulatory risks will likely fail in this context.[88]

5.2.2 Renewable Energy Jurisprudence and Policy Lessons

Spain, Italy and the Czech Republic have been among most frequent targets of renewable energy investment disputes (Figure 5.2). These three

[81] *ESPF and others v. Italy*, ICSID, Award, para. 513.
[82] UNCTAD, 'Fair and Equitable Treatment', 2012, p. 69.
[83] See Athina Fouchard Papaefstratiou, 'Stabilisation Clauses in Long-Term Investment Contracts: Their Evolution and Their Application by Investment Tribunals', in Elena Cima and Makane Moïse Mbengue (eds.), *A Multifaceted Approach to Trade Liberalisation and Investment Protection in the Energy Sector* (Leiden and Boston: Brill, Nijhoff, 2021), pp. 43–57.
[84] See *Masdar v. Spain*, ICSID, Award, paras. 490–495, 504–510.
[85] Papaefstratiou, supra note 83, p. 46.
[86] *Masdar v. Spain*, ICSID, Award, para. 494; *Stadtwerke München and others v. Spain*, ICSID, Award, para. 264.
[87] *Masdar v. Spain*, ICSID, Award, para. 497.
[88] *RWE Innogy v. Spain*, ICSID, Decision on Jurisdiction, Liability and Certain Issues of Quantum, paras. 508–513.

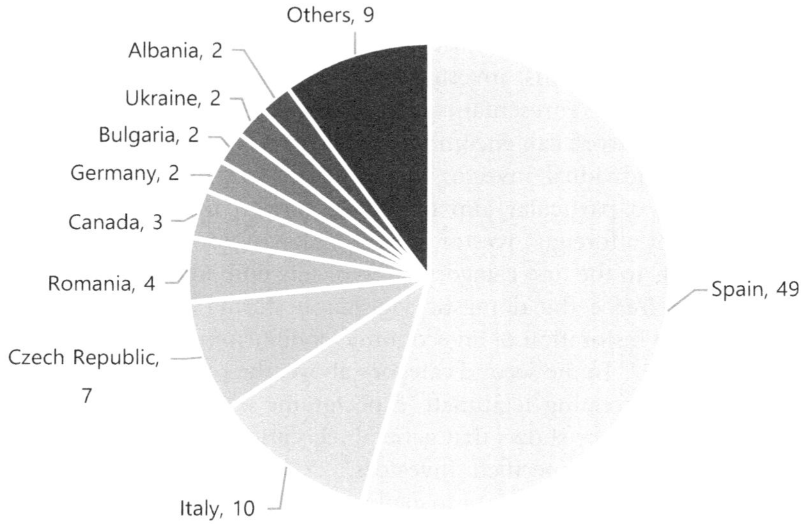

Figure 5.2 Renewable energy ISDS cases by targeted country (2011–2021).
Notes: Ninety renewable energy ISDS cases in total. Numbers indicate the number of cases per country. 'Others' includes nine countries (one case per country).
Source: Author's compilation from data at the UNCTAD's database, as arranged in Appendix B.

countries adopted renewable energy support programmes to meet their international and EU climate obligations and national decarbonization goals. However, the global financial crisis of 2008 caused huge budget deficits and deteriorated the economic position of many energy consumers there. Meanwhile, the falling costs of renewable energy production created a sentiment of 'over-subsidization' by the existing support schemes. As a result, the domestic authorities opted to scale back the existing bounties. Given that these actions were taken by developed countries, the risk of regulatory changes regarding the energy–environment nexus can no longer be ascribed mainly to developing and transition economies as was opined in the previous literature.[89]

The sections below discuss the relevant case law involving Spain, Italy and the Czech Republic as the host country and investors typically from another EU member country. Although the validity of such intra-EU investor–State cases under EU law is beyond the scope of this analysis, it

[89] Cf. Boute, supra note 23, pp. 337–338.

is worth noting in brief that the EU judiciary has been hostile to intra-EU arbitrations under BITs or the ECT on the grounds that EU law precludes such arbitrations as they vitiate the autonomy of the EU legal system.[90] By contrast, investment tribunals have confirmed their intra-EU jurisdiction and considered these cases despite the opposition from the EU side.[91]

5.2.2.1 ISDS Cases against Spain

Spain's FIT regime, launched in 2007, offered high tariffs for the first twenty-five years and lower tariffs for the remaining lifetime of electricity-generating facilities. But the 2010 legal amendments eliminated the lower tariffs, limited the FIT-eligible operating hours of the facilities and imposed special charges for access to the transport and distribution networks.[92] In 2012, the government introduced a 7 per cent tax on electricity generation. In 2013–2014, it replaced the FIT scheme with substantially less generous incentives. The authorities justified the regulatory changes with the need to respond to a growing shortfall of revenues (or 'tariff deficit') in the country's electricity system.[93]

A series of ISDS cases against Spain have produced inconsistent results[94] partly due to the differences in the facts and claims raised before tribunals.[95] The factual differences pertained to (i) the scope of the challenged measures, (ii) the timing of investment and (iii) the existence or lack of specific assurances given to investors. As regards the first

[90] See *Achmea*, Judgment of the Court (EU), para. 62; *République de Moldavie*, Judgment of the Court (EU), paras. 47, 60–66; *PL Holdings*, Judgment of the Court (EU), para. 70; *Commission v. European Food and Others*, Judgment of the Court (EU), paras. 138–145.

[91] See Szilárd Gáspár-Szilágyi and Maxim Usynin, 'The Uneasy Relationship between Intra-EU Investment Tribunals and the Court of Justice's *Achmea* Judgment', 4 *European Investment Law and Arbitration Review* 29 (2019).

[92] *Charanne and Construction Investments v. Spain*, Final Award (unofficial English translation by Mena Chambers), paras. 149, 158, 452. For the FIT regime relied upon by the investors, see para. 516.

[93] The information in this paragraph summarizes the relevant facts elucidated in various arbitral cases. See, for example, *Stadtwerke München and others v. Spain*, ICSID, Award, paras. 50–78, 89–95; *The PV Investors v. Spain*, PCA, Final Award, paras. 182–212; *Cube Infrastructure and others v. Spain*, ICSID, Decision on Jurisdiction, Liability and Partial Decision on Quantum, paras. 241–272, 315–328, 361–379. See also Carmen Otero García-Castrillón, 'Spain and Investment Arbitration: The Renewable Energy Explosion', Centre for International Governance Innovation, Investor–State Arbitration Series, Paper No. 17, 2016, pp. 2–6.

[94] See Appendix B.

[95] See *The PV Investors v. Spain*, PCA, Final Award, paras. 553–555.

factor, the tribunal in *Charanne and Construction Investments v. Spain* sided with the State because the 2010 amendments, albeit having lowered profitability of solar projects, did not eliminate such key features of the FIT scheme as a guaranteed tariff and preferential access to the power grid.[96] By contrast, *Eiser and Energía Solar v. Spain*, ending in the investor's favour, additionally reviewed the post-2010 regulatory changes. These were more 'dramatic' and 'sweeping' changes than the 2010 measures as they created a new 'profoundly unfair and inequitable' system, which led to a significant devaluation of the claimants' investment from €125 million to €4 million.[97]

As for the second factor concerning investment's timing, the tribunal in *Isolux v. Spain* rejected the claim about FET violations by concluding that at the time of investment (i.e., on 29 October 2012), the then regulatory framework could not have created a legitimate expectation that it would not be modified, as it was, by the 2012 and 2013 rules.[98] The tribunal found that prior to the claimant's investment, the regulatory framework had already changed and that the claimant was 'perfectly aware' of the Spanish Supreme Court's decisions that had confirmed the government's right to amend the remuneration system at issue.[99] This aspect contrasts with the factual circumstances in some other cases, won by the claimants, where investments were made far before the 2013 regulatory changes.[100]

Regarding the third factor concerning government assurances, the *Charanne and Construction Investments v. Spain* tribunal held that the Spanish renewable energy regime was general in nature and did not create a 'specific commitment' to ensure regulatory stability vis-à-vis the investors concerned.[101] By contrast, some other tribunals found that Spain had in fact given specific assurances that the investors would obtain FIT payments across the lifespan of their solar power plants.[102] For example, the *Masdar v. Spain* ruling observed:

[96] *Charanne and Construction Investments v. Spain*, Final Award (unofficial English translation by Mena Chambers), paras. 518–519, 533, 539.

[97] *Eiser and Energía Solar v. Spain*, ICSID, Award, paras. 365, 368–370, 418.

[98] *Isolux v. Spain*, SCC, Award (unofficial English translation), paras. 784–785, 815.

[99] Ibid., paras. 789–795.

[100] See, for example, *Novenergia v. Spain*, SCC, Final Arbitral Award, paras. 539, 695–697.

[101] *Charanne and Construction Investments v. Spain*, SCC, Final Award (unofficial English translation by Mena Chambers), paras. 490–494, 499, 503–504.

[102] See, for example, *Masdar v. Spain*, ICSID, Award, paras. 511–520; *NextEra v. Spain*, ICSID, Decision on Jurisdiction, Liability and Quantum Principles, paras. 587–592.

> It would be difficult to conceive of a more specific commitment than a Resolution issued by Spain addressed specifically to each of the Operating Companies, confirming that each of the Plants qualified under the RD661/2007 economic regime for their '*operational lifetime*'.[103]

With respect to the claim-related differences, unlike general claims of FET violations in some cases, the FET claims in *The PV Investors v. Spain* were more nuanced and bifurcated as the 'primary' and 'alternative' claims regarding legitimate expectations of, respectively, the FIT's immutability and a reasonable return on investments.[104] The tribunal rejected the primary claim but agreed with the alternative one that '[i]f changes cross the "reasonable return" line, that is if they deprive investors of a reasonable return, the State conduct transgresses the [FET] standards contained in Article 10(1) of the ECT'. The focus of the FET examination on the guarantee of a reasonable rate of return would strike, the tribunal said, a right balance between the protection of clean energy investors and the State's right to regulate as exercised in a 'proportionate, reasonable, and non-arbitrary' manner.[105]

Governments can draw out several lessons from the cases above. First, while the State's power to adapt the existing regulatory framework to changing circumstances is generally accepted, dramatic and sweeping changes (like those considered in *Eiser and Energía Solar v. Spain*) should be avoided. If needed, regulatory changes should be introduced gradually to lessen destructive effects on investments and the legitimate expectations of the existing investors. Arguably, such gradual policy revisions may not frighten new investors and will encourage them to 'readjust' their expectations by changing their investment plans accordingly. Second, when new restrictions are imposed, keeping essential features of the early incentive package is important. For example, the modification of the FIT (e.g., reducing tariffs or shortening the terms of benefits) is more tolerable than its cancellation or replacement with less attractive incentives. Third, prior to regulatory changes, governments should take genuine efforts in assessing the possible extent of loss of the value of investment and returns that such changes may cause. Policy alterations with insignificant devaluation impacts are likely to survive FET challenges.

[103] *Masdar v. Spain*, ICSID, Award, para. 520 (emphasis in original).

[104] *The PV Investors v. Spain*, PCA, Final Award, para. 550.

[105] Ibid., paras. 638–639.

5.2.2.2 ISDS Cases against Italy

In 2005–2012, Italy adopted a series of energy account (or *Conto Energia*) ministerial decrees that explicitly guaranteed the payment of feed-in premiums (as an addition to the electricity market prices) to PV operators for a period of twenty years. The costs of incentives were passed on to consumers through electricity bills. Qualified operators were awarded 'Tariff Recognition Letters' that verified their right to a specific tariff for twenty years as well as agreements that specified the incentive rates and the twenty-year duration dates. Such letters and agreements were issued by GSE, a State company managing renewables support schemes. In addition, an 'off-take regime' envisaged purchasing electricity from small-scale renewable energy plants at minimum guaranteed prices. Starting from 2011, Italy revised the system by replacing the premiums with less generous incentives, delaying payments, modifying guaranteed prices under the 'off-take regime', imposing an annual administrative fee to cover management costs of the incentive-paying agency, revoking an exemption of renewables from the energy windfall profits tax and reclassifying PV plants from movable to immovable property to impose higher taxes.[106]

With respect to FET claims, the tribunals commonly referred to clear-cut wordings in the related documents that suggested unchangeableness of the *Conto Energia* regime. Indeed, the *Conto Energia* decrees expressly provided for twenty-year tariff premiums, and the GSE letters and agreements vis-à-vis specific investors stated that the tariff of a defined amount was 'constant' throughout the twenty-year term.[107] Therefore, the tribunal in *ESPF and others v. Italy* observed:

> In the majority of the Tribunal's view, the Claimants' interpretation and understanding of the incentive regime established under the *Conto Energia* Decrees and, in particular, the understanding that the specific tariff rates granted to qualifying production facilities would remain unchanged for the term of 20 years, was objectively reasonable and justified on the basis of the language of the *Conto Energia* Decrees, the GSE Letters and the GSE Agreements. In the absence of any mention in those instruments that the tariffs were subject to adjustment, the Claimants' understanding was well founded.[108]

106 The factual information on Italy's system here derives from *Greentech and NovEnergia v. Italy*, SCC, Final Award, paras. 109–130, 143–170.

107 See, for example, ibid., paras. 109–128; *ESPF and others v. Italy*, ICSID, Award, paras. 76–120, 568.

108 *ESPF and others v. Italy*, ICSID, Award, para. 529.

In *Greentech and NovEnergia v. Italy*, the tribunal determined that the tariff reductions defeated investors' legitimate expectations, contrary to Italy's 'repeated and precise assurances to specific investors' – recorded in the decrees, letters and agreements – that the tariffs would remain fixed for twenty years. These assurances amounted to 'a stabilization clause or otherwise' and 'non-waivable guarantees' of the State. The tribunal concluded that the fact of Italy being in 'a situation of economic difficulty' did not reach the level of force majeure to justify the tariff reductions.[109]

By contrast, *Blusun v. Italy* ended in the State's favour partly because of factual differences and less dramatic changes.[110] In the Italian region of Puglia, investors acquired local companies and land for constructing solar plants and signed contracts to build substations and transmission lines to connect to the grid. However, the project eventually failed due to the lack of financing. The claimants attributed this failure to 'legal instability' (or 'legal insecurity') caused by a series of measures adopted between 2010 and 2012, notably a constitutional court decision (that invalidated a regional law relied upon by the investors), the restriction of agricultural land use for solar plants, tariff reductions and a temporary 'stop-work order' preventing the progress of some PV plants.[111] The claimants argued that 'during the two years between permissible and legally impossible, the legal framework for the project constantly changed, leaving no period of stability in which the requisite capital investment for a project of this size could be realised'.[112] But all FET claims were rejected. The tribunal noted that the claimants proceeded with the project despite the pending constitutional challenge, thus taking the risk that the eventual decision might cause delays in the project's financing.[113] The reduction in tariffs, albeit 'quite substantial', was not 'crippling or disabling' and addressed 'a genuine fiscal need, given the large take-up' of incentives, while the principle of tariff guarantees for twenty years was still maintained.[114] The restrictions on the agricultural

[109] *Greentech and NovEnergia v. Italy*, SCC, Final Award, paras. 450–453.

[110] Jarrod Hepburn, 'ANALYSIS: In New Award, Italian Renewables Changes Appear Less Dramatic Than Those in Recent Spain Case, Thus Leading to Failure of Blusun's FET Claim; Arbitrators Disagree on Expropriation Assessment', *Investment Arbitration Reporter*, 7 June 2017, www.iareporter.com.

[111] For the factual background and the claims on the merits, see *Blusun v. Italy*, ICSID, Award, paras. 52–124, 310.

[112] Ibid., para. 320.

[113] Ibid., para. 329.

[114] Ibid., para. 342.

land use responded to 'valid rural planning concerns'.[115] As for the stop-work order issued by the local authorities but annulled by an administrative court two months later, the tribunal found that this short-term measure was neither arbitrary nor discriminatory.[116]

In conclusion, under Italy's renewable energy system, investors were assured of regulatory stability through a combination of general law (the *Conto Energia* decrees) and investor-specific State commitments (the GSE letters and agreements). These instruments were clear enough in defining the amount and duration of tariff premiums and did not envisage the possibility of modifications. Therefore, Italy's case teaches one policy lesson: when the government enters into long-term arrangements (like twenty-year contracts here) with an investor, the related document should explicitly provide for regulatory changeability in appropriate situations going beyond conceivable force majeure.

5.2.2.3 ISDS Cases against the Czech Republic

The Czech Republic provided solar energy producers an income tax exemption (under a 1992 Act) and a FIT (under a 2005 Act) that could not be lowered by more than 5 per cent of the tariff's value in the previous year. Since 2010, the authorities amended the existing regime. They abolished the 5 per cent rule for the PV plants that were connected to the grid from 2011 onwards, repealed the income tax exemption and introduced a solar levy (initially at 26 per cent and later at 10 per cent) on the revenues of PV plants. These regulatory changes aimed to address negative effects of a 'solar boom' caused by a sharp fall in solar capital costs and, as a result, unusually increasing investments.[117] Specifically, between 2008 and 2010, the price of PV panels decreased by more than 40 per cent, leading to the FIT overcompensation by some 30 per cent vis-à-vis the originally anticipated level.[118] The number of solar power plants in the country increased from just 28 in 2007 to 2,230 in August 2009.[119] The Czech Energy Regulatory Office noted that under these circumstances,

> an uncontrolled increase in solar energy would be highly undesirable because (1) it would increase the price of RES [renewable energy sources]

[115] Ibid.

[116] Ibid., para. 360.

[117] For factual details, see, for example, *Antaris and Göde v. Czech Republic*, PCA, Award, paras. 81–253; *Europa Nova v. Czechia*, PCA, Award, paras. 130–151, 158–183.

[118] *Europa Nova v. Czechia*, PCA, Award, para. 554.

[119] *Antaris and Göde v. Czech Republic*, PCA, Award, para. 376.

> support paid by consumers; (2) it would lead to significantly higher profits for solar investors compared with other RES producers; and (3) it would threaten the stability of the grid because of the unpredictable and volatile nature of solar electricity production.[120]

The Czech Republic prevailed in most investment cases.[121] Specifically, it was found that the Czech legislation did not contain any guarantee about a stable FIT and that the regulatory revisions maintained the commitment under the original support scheme that the investors would be able to recoup their investments in fifteen years and receive a minimum annual return of 7 per cent.[122] By contrast, one tribunal reportedly noted that even in the absence of an explicit stabilization guarantee in the relevant legislation, 'a legislative provision [could] guarantee stabilization intrinsically' and reportedly found such guarantee in the statutory provision which stated that 'the amount of [FIT] revenues' was 'maintained as the minimum [amount of revenue]' for a specified period.[123]

The *Antaris and Göde v. Czech Republic* ruling is remarkable for its critical stance towards investors exploiting last-minute opportunities prior to the imminent policy rectification. There, the tribunal dismissed the FET claim on the grounds that the claimant 'was essentially an opportunistic investor . . . who was aware, or should have been aware, that dealing with the solar boom was a fast-moving and controversial political issue'.[124] In particular, 'the investment protection regime was never intended to promote and safeguard those who . . . "pile in" to take advantage of laws which they must know may be in a state of flux caused essentially by investors of that type'.[125] The tribunal agreed with the respondent that the solar power market was a 'bubble' and that the FIT

[120] Ibid., para. 120.

[121] Florian Stefan, 'A Reflection on the Czech Republic's Solar Investment Arbitration Successes', PSL LexisNexis News Analysis, 1 October 2019, www.lexisnexis.com/uk/lexispsl/energy/document/412012/5X5P-71G3-CGXG-01J7-00000-00/A_reflection_on_the_Czech_Republic_s_solar_investment_arbitration_successes.

[122] See Lisa Bohmer, 'Revealed: Reasons Why Van Houtte, Beechey, and Landau Saw No Legitimate Expectation to Stabilization of Czech Solar Feed-In-Tariffs; Newly-Seen Award also Deemed Intra-EU Objection Untimely', *Investment Arbitration Reporter*, 23 June 2019, www.iareporter.com.

[123] Damien Charlotin, '*Natland v. Czech Republic* (Part 2 of 2): On the Merits, Tribunal Finds Stabilisation Commitment in Czech Legislation and Breach of That Commitment with Introduction of Solar Levy', Investment Arbitration Reporter, 26 July 2018, www.iareporter.com.

[124] *Antaris and Göde v. Czech Republic*, PCA, Award, para. 431.

[125] Ibid., para. 435.

regime was 'out of balance', which was 'obvious' to any participant in the market.[126] In addition:

> The Tribunal accepts that the Respondent had the rational objective of reducing excessive profits and sheltering consumers from excessive electricity price rises, and that its actions were not arbitrary or irrational. There was an appropriate correlation between the Respondent's objectives and the measures it took. There is nothing irrational or unreasonable about the imposition of a charge to regulate what the Respondent reasonably regarded as windfall profits and to reduce the impact on consumers, and the measures, which applied only to the most recent installations and therefore the ones able to earn the profits as a result of the decline in PV costs, were not disproportionate.[127]

As seen, the Czech Republic's regulatory changes were adopted under the extraordinary circumstances of the solar energy boom. The measures were introduced to address the obvious FIT imbalance and mitigate undesirable socio-economic impacts of the bubble in the country's solar market. Despite a burning need for an urgent solution, the 2010 FIT changes cancelling the 5 per cent rule were importantly *prospective* in affecting only latecomer PV plants from 2011 onwards. As retroactive modifications by nature retract the policy promised to the existing investors, they are more likely to fail the tribunal's scrutiny. Therefore, to be on a safer footing, it is desirable that regulatory changes, if adopted, are future-oriented.

5.2.2.4 Overall Implications for the Energy–Environment Nexus

Since renewable energy costs are often recoupable over a long run, it is not fair to place all burden of regulatory changes on investors' shoulders alone. Indeed, the State is responsible for properly designing and implementing its support policies and duly communicating with investors. At the same time, it is not reasonable for investors to not expect any sort of alteration of the promised incentives, especially in the case of long-term projects where no government assurances to maintain the legal status quo have been clearly spelled out.

The recent surge of investment disputes and case law concerning the cutting or rolling-back of renewable energy benefits suggest that regulatory flexibility should be directly envisaged in the pertinent legal texts on

[126] Ibid., para. 434.
[127] Ibid., para. 444.

foreign investment, whether general frameworks or specific regimes. This will reduce ISDS frictions. Otherwise, unexpected regulatory changes would undermine investor confidence and discourage green investments, and the arbitral rulings denying regulatory flexibility under the existing schemes would discourage the affected host States from offering new support measures in clean energy.

Where policy flexibility is envisaged and recognized, regulatory changes must still be reasonable, non-discriminatory and proportional to the underlying public purpose. Procedurally, investors should be treated in full respect of due process. As noted in case law, 'an investor's legitimate expectations might be breached not only by a substantive change in policy, but also by the treatment of the investor during the process of the change of policy'.[128] But one study asserts that unless investment treaties provide otherwise, consulting with investors about new laws and amendments affecting their activities does not constitute the host State's duty under the FET obligation, customary international law or general principles of law.[129] Nevertheless, proactive engagements with investors regarding forthcoming policy developments can enhance transparency in the government's decision-making process and relieve the investor–State tension. Planned changes duly communicated to investors beforehand can eventually take into account their comments and concerns and preclude arbitrariness in the State's conduct.

5.3 Trade and Investment Interplay in Clean Energy

In the energy–environment context, the trade and investment regimes are mutually complementary in restricting unnecessary obstacles to economic operators in the respective field. Both provide for non-discrimination in terms of national treatment and MFN. A number of IIAs reaffirm their parties' WTO obligations not to apply illegal TRIMs, such as LCRs, trade-balancing requirements and so on.[130] Like the WTO, IIAs can make some exemptions for LCRs qualifying as a government procurement. But differences in the trade and investment texts may lead

[128] *Arif v. Moldova*, ICSID, Award, para. 538.

[129] Caroline Henckels, 'A Duty to Consult Foreign Investors When Changing the Regulatory Framework? Implications for Non-Communicable Disease Prevention and Beyond', 21 *Journal of World Investment & Trade* 698 (2020), pp. 698, 722–723.

[130] See, for example, Article 12.6 of the Malaysia–Australia FTA (2012); Article 6 of the Jordan–Singapore BIT (2004).

to dissimilar outcomes. In *Mesa Power v. Canada* dealing with the Canadian province of Ontario's FIT programme, the tribunal determined that the LCR at issue was covered by the NAFTA's government procurement exception to national treatment and MFN on investment.[131] This is in sharp contrast to the WTO findings in *Canada – Renewable Energy / Canada – Feed-in Tariff Program* on essentially the same FIT programme where the LCR was found to be unqualified for the government procurement derogation because the good being procured (electricity) and the good being discriminated against (electricity-generating equipment) were not alike to be 'in a competitive relationship'.[132] In fact, the NAFTA's investment provisions do not replicate the government procurement criteria articulated in Article III:8(a) of the GATT.[133] As a result, the *Mesa Power v. Canada* tribunal found:

> The final submission put forward by the Claimant is that Canada cannot rely on the procurement exception since it has not demonstrated that there is a 'nexus' between the FIT Contract and the measures challenged by the Claimant under Articles 1102 [national treatment] and 1103 [MFN] of the NAFTA. The Tribunal does not accept this submission. First, the Claimant's view appears to arise from arguments put before the WTO Panel and Appellate Body in the context of Article III:8(a) of the GATT, which, as mentioned earlier, is of limited use in the present analysis. *There, the finding of a nexus between the good being procured and the good subject to domestic content was fundamental. The existence of a nexus is irrelevant here, because Article 1108(7)(a) [government procurement exception] of the NAFTA is broader than Article III:8(a) of the GATT*. Once it is established that there has been 'procurement' by a Party or state enterprise, Article 1108(7)(a) excludes all claims of NT [national treatment], MFN and domestic content in connection with such procurement.[134]

Further, investment treaties may prohibit certain trade-related performance requirements that are not outlawed in WTO agreements explicitly. Such prohibition applies, for example, to a State's requirement for

[131] *Mesa Power v. Canada*, PCA, Award, paras. 396, 465–466.

[132] *Canada – Renewable Energy / Canada – Feed-in Tariff Program*, WTO Appellate Body Reports, paras. 5.63, 5.75, 5.79. See Sections 2.2.1.2 and 3.2.3.

[133] Article III:8(a) of the GATT reads that Article III on national treatment 'shall not apply to laws, regulations or requirements governing the procurement by governmental agencies of products purchased for governmental purposes and not with a view to commercial resale or with a view to use in the production of goods for commercial sale'.

[134] *Mesa Power v. Canada*, PCA, Award, para. 459 (emphasis added).

investors 'to export a given level or percentage of goods or services'.[135] By contrast, the GATT panel in *Canada – FIRA* found that 'there is no provision in the General Agreement [on Tariffs and Trade] which forbids requirements to sell goods in foreign markets in preference to the domestic market'.[136] Nonetheless, a State complying with the investment treaty's ban on the exportation requirement does not violate the GATT.

The EU's FTAs with Singapore (2018) and Viet Nam (2019) are remarkable for *holistically* addressing non-tariff barriers to trade and investment *specifically in the renewable energy sector*. With respect to renewable energy generation, the agreements urge the parties to 'refrain from adopting measures providing for local content requirements or any other offset affecting the other Party's products, service suppliers, investors or enterprises'.[137] The term 'local content requirement' in this context means:[138]

> (i) with respect to goods, a requirement for an enterprise to purchase or use goods of domestic origin or from a domestic source, whether specified in terms of particular products, in terms of volume or value of products, or in terms of a proportion of volume or value of its local production;
> (ii) with respect to services, a requirement which restricts the choice of the service supplier or the service supplied to the detriment of services or service suppliers from the other Party.

The EU FTAs with Singapore and Viet Nam also disallow requirements to establish 'partnerships' (joint legal entities) with local companies unless they are otherwise necessary for 'technical reasons' to be demonstrated by the imposing party upon request.[139] These anti-localization provisions seem to apply at the investment's pre-establishment stage, while relevant protection standards of the respective investment treaties apply post-establishment.[140] Another merit of the

[135] See, for example, Article 8(a) of the US Model BIT (2012); Article 5.1(a) of the Colombia–Japan BIT (2011); Article 9.1.1 of the Burkina Faso–Canada BIT (2015).

[136] *Canada – FIRA*, GATT Panel Report, para 5.18.

[137] Article 7.4(a) of the EU–Singapore FTA (2018); Article 7.4(a) of the EU–Viet Nam FTA (2019).

[138] Article 7.2(a) of the EU–Singapore FTA (2018); Article 7.2(a) of the EU–Viet Nam FTA (2019).

[139] Article 7.4(b) of the EU–Singapore FTA (2018); Article 7.4(b) of the EU–Viet Nam FTA (2019).

[140] Articles 2.3.1 (national treatment) and 2.4.1 (most-favoured nation (MFN)) of the EU–Viet Nam Investment Protection Agreement (2019) apply with respect to the 'operation' of the covered investments, with 'operation' meaning 'the conduct, management, maintenance, use, enjoyment, sale or other forms of disposal of the investment' (Article 1.2

RTA-inserted localization bans for renewable energy investment projects is the possibility for the investor's home State (if foreseen by the text) to rely on the RTA's dispute settlement remedies, including trade sanctions if applicable, against a wrongdoing host State, something which is normally not available under BITs.

The trade and investment regimes may get into some tension in the field of governmental subsidies. A conceivable scenario of such tension is when subsidies relied upon by investors have to be terminated or modified due to the subsidizing State's trade obligations. If a WTO ruling finds an investment-promoting measure to be a 'prohibited' subsidy[141] or 'actionable' subsidy, the responding member must 'withdraw the subsidy without delay' (in the case of the prohibited subsidy) or 'remove the adverse effects or ... withdraw the subsidy' (in the case of the actionable subsidy).[142] A subsidy's discontinuation or revision, unexpected by the benefiting investor, may trigger an investor–State dispute with the claim about an FET violation, among other things. Some developments pertaining to the EU State aid rules show that a trade–investment clash of this kind is realistic. As the EU State aid rules are comparable, albeit not necessarily alike, to the WTO subsidy rules,[143] the EU-related developments here may have some implications for the multilateral trading system.

EU law generally prevents Member States from granting aid that distorts competition in the internal market by favouring certain undertakings or the production of certain goods.[144] If an EU Member State has granted an illegal aid, the European Commission orders it to recover the aid with interest from the beneficiaries. The purpose of recovery is to remove the improper advantage that the beneficiary enjoyed over its competitors, so as to restore the situation in the market that existed before such aid was granted.[145] For example, the European Commission's

(f)). Likewise, Articles 2.3.1 (national treatment) and 2.4.1 (FET), footnote 8 of the EU–Singapore Investment Protection Agreement (2018) apply with respect to the 'operation, management, conduct, maintenance, use, enjoyment and sale or other disposal' of the covered investments.

141 In the future, prohibited subsidies may also include harmful fossil fuel subsidies if they are banned by new WTO rules.

142 Articles 4.7 and 7.8 of the SCM Agreement.

143 See, for example, Gracia Marín Durán, 'Sheltering Government Support to "Green" Electricity: The European Union and the World Trade Organization', 67 *International and Comparative Law Quarterly* 129 (2018), pp. 140–150.

144 Article 107 of the Treaty on the Functioning of the European Union.

145 European Commission, 'Commission Notice on the Recovery of Unlawful and Incompatible State Aid (2019/C 247/01)', OJ C 247/1, 23 July 2019, para. 16.

past decisions required partial or full recovery of State aid in the case of Germany's electricity surcharge reductions for energy-intensive companies under a renewable energy scheme, Italy's preferential electricity tariffs and Sweden's energy tax exemption.[146] EU recovery decisions may potentially be challenged in investment disputes. Furthermore, retrospective remedies, like recovery (repayment) of State aid here, are not typical of the WTO system but not completely ruled out thereunder.[147] For instance, the panel in *Australia – Automotive Leather II (Article 21.5 – US)* found that the subsidy at issue must be fully repaid in the light of Article 4.7 of the SCM Agreement that calls for the withdrawal of prohibited subsidies, which, the panel said, 'is not limited to prospective action only but may encompass repayment of the prohibited subsidy'.[148] Even when the withdrawal is not retrospective, a potential investor–State dispute may still arise concerning the WTO-induced discontinuation or reduction of a prospective allocation of a subsidy (e.g., tax benefits) to an investor that is found to be WTO-inconsistent.

Another scenario of the trade–investment tension can unfold in relation to the enforcement of an investor–State arbitral ruling that orders a responding State to pay compensation to a complaining investor. So far, this has been controversial under the EU legal system,[149] but not the WTO regime. In 2021, the European Commission made a preliminary determination that the award in *Antin v. Spain* to be paid by Spain for the amendment of its 2007 renewable electricity support scheme would

[146] See European Commission, 'State Aid: Commission Approves German Aid Scheme for Renewable Energy (EEG 2012); Orders Partial Recovery', 25 November 2014, https://ec.europa.eu/commission/presscorner/detail/en/IP_14_2122; European Commission, 'State Aid: Commission Requires Italy to Recover around €18 Million Incompatible State Aid from Metal Producers Portovesme, ILA and Eurallumina', 23 February 2011, https://ec.europa.eu/commission/presscorner/detail/en/IP_11_215; Commission Decision of 30 June 2004 on the Aid Scheme Implemented by Sweden for an Exemption from the Tax on Energy from 1 January 2002 to 30 June 2004 (2005/468/EC), OJ L 165, 25 June 2005.

[147] See Sherzod Shadikhodjaev and Nohyoung Park, 'Cessation and Reparation in the GATT/WTO Legal System: A View from the Law of State Responsibility', 41 *Journal of World Trade* 1237 (2007), pp. 1243–1256.

[148] *Australia – Automotive Leather II (Article 21.5 – US)*, WTO Panel Report, paras. 6.22, 6.39, 6.43–6.45.

[149] See, for example, Pietro Ortolani, 'Intra-EU Arbitral Awards vis-à-vis Article 107 TFEU: State Aid Law as a Limit to Compliance', 6 *Journal of International Dispute Settlement* 118 (2015), pp. 125–134; Kai Struckmann, Genevra Forwood and Aqeel Kadri, 'Investor-State Arbitrations and EU State Aid Rules: Conflict or Co-existence?', 15 *European State Aid Law Quarterly* 258 (2016), pp. 264–269.

constitute State aid because of granting an undue advantage to the beneficiary – the investor from Luxembourg and the Netherlands. In the Commission's view, the arbitral award could cause discrimination based on investors' nationality and ability to access international arbitration as Spanish investors, unlike those from the countries above, were prevented from resorting to an arbitration tribunal over the modification of the 2007 scheme.[150] At the time of writing, no EU final determination has been issued on this matter yet.[151]

More insights into the enforcement issue can be drawn from the developments around *Micula v. Romania (I)* that dealt with Romania's premature abolishment of ten-year fiscal incentives for investors, which was aimed to comply with the EU State aid rules as part of the country's EU accession process. Romania's act led to the breach of the Sweden–Romania BIT's FET provision.[152] In the ruling issued in 2013, the tribunal acknowledged that the revocation of the incentives was 'reasonably tailored to the pursuit of a rational policy (specifically, EU accession)'. But it found unreasonable for Romania 'to maintain as a whole the investors' obligations while at the same time eliminating virtually all of their benefits'.[153] Romania partially executed the award and has faced enforcement procedures commenced in multiple national jurisdictions.[154] However, the European Commission's 2015 decision determined that the payment of the compensation awarded by this arbitral tribunal constituted State aid incompatible with the EU internal market and that Romania must thus recover the already paid-out portion of the compensation.[155] In particular, the Commission took into account the tribunal's explanation that 'damages had to be awarded on the basis of the principle that "the claimant must be placed back in the position it

[150] European Commission, 'State Aid: Commission Opens In-Depth Investigation into Arbitration Award in Favour of Antin to Be Paid by Spain', 19 July 2021, https://ec.europa.eu/commission/presscorner/detail/en/IP_21_3783.

[151] For the investigation materials for 'Arbitration Award to Antin – Spain' (State aid, SA.54155), see the EU State aid register at https://ec.europa.eu/competition/elojade/isef/index.cfm?clear=1&policy_area_id=3.

[152] *Micula v. Romania (I)*, ICSID, Award, para. 872.

[153] Ibid., paras. 825–826.

[154] Aikaterini Florou, 'The UK Supreme Court Judgment in *Micula v. Romania*: A Landmark Judgment for the Relationship between EU Law and International Investment Law?', 36 *ICSID Review* 295 (2021), p. 296.

[155] Commission Decision (EU) 2015/1470 of 30 March 2015 on State aid SA.38517 (2014/C) (ex 2014/NN) implemented by Romania – Arbitral Award *Micula v. Romania* of 11 December 2013, OJ L 232, 4 September 2015, Articles 1 and 2.

would have been 'in all probability' but for the international wrong'".[156] Therefore, the Commission said, the execution of the award granted the claimants 'an amount corresponding exactly to the advantages' under the abolished scheme from the moment the scheme was repealed on 22 February 2005 until its scheduled expiry on 1 April 2009.[157] By re-establishing the advantageous situation that would have existed if the scheme had remained, the award, according to the Commission, granted a 'selective' economic 'advantage' – otherwise not available on the market – to the claimants in *Micula v. Romania (I)*.[158] This aspect is in a sense analogous to the WTO's concept of enterprise-specific subsidy.

But in 2019, the General Court of the Court of Justice of the EU invalidated the Commission's decision in question on the grounds that its State aid assessments referred to the relevant events predating Romania's accession to the EU in 2007, and the claimants' right to compensation arose in 2005 when the incentive scheme was repealed.[159] On appeal, the Court of Justice of the EU, however, disagreed and found that the right to compensation actually arose from the 2013 investment arbitral award, that is, *after* Romania's EU accession, so the General Court erred in law in holding that the Commission lacked competence *ratione temporis* to adopt its decision on State aid. But the very question as to whether the compensation granted by the arbitral award constituted State aid was not within the Court of Justice's appeal jurisdiction.[160] Importantly, in the finding not reviewed on appeal,[161] the General Court noted that 'compensation for damage suffered cannot be regarded as aid *unless* it has the effect of compensating for the withdrawal of *unlawful* or *incompatible* aid'.[162] From this statement, it follows that the payment of

[156] Ibid., recital 94.

[157] Ibid., recital 95.

[158] Ibid., recitals 95–96, 110.

[159] *European Food and Others v. Commission*, Judgment of the General Court (EU), paras. 71–80, 108–111.

[160] *Commission v. European Food and Others*, Judgment of the Court (EU), paras. 123–136, 151, 154–155.

[161] Ibid., para. 131.

[162] *European Food and Others v. Commission*, Judgment of the General Court (EU), para. 103 (emphasis added). The court cited the interpretation in *Asteris and Others v. Greece and EEC*, Judgment of the Court (EU), paras. 23–24:

> It follows that State aid, that is to say measures of the public authorities favouring certain undertakings or certain products, is fundamentally different in its legal nature from damages which the competent national

damages to investors constitutes State aid when it serves to compensate them for the repeal of an illegal State aid.

As seen above, government support for clean energy investments can fall within the scope of the investment promotion/protection regime but face legal constraints under the subsidy/State aid rules. Greater policy coherence on green incentives is important for maintaining investor confidence and pursuing environmental goals. In order to minimize the trade and investment friction, States can undertake regulatory re-framings. For example, investment treaties could (and some indeed do[163,164]) envisage carve-outs for withdrawals or modifications of government support that are necessitated by, and/or consistent with, applicable international trade rules. Trade agreements could exclude relevant awards/compensation ordered by investment tribunals from the scope of trade disputes.[165] Further, legislative reforms towards greening the subsidy rules as discussed in Chapter 3[166] could put qualified clean energy

> authorities may be ordered to pay to individuals in compensation for the damage they have caused to those individuals.
>
> It must therefore be stated . . . that damages which the national authorities may be ordered to pay to individuals in compensation for damage they have caused to those individuals do not constitute aid within the meaning of Articles 92 and 93 of the EEC Treaty.

163 For example, the EU–Viet Nam Investment Protection Agreement (2019) excludes a party's refusal to subsidize from the scope of violations of investment protection standards (Article 2.2.3) and does not prevent either party from 'discontinuing the granting of a subsidy [footnote omitted] or requesting its reimbursement', or does not 'requir[e] that Party to compensate the investor therefor, where such action has been ordered by one of its competent authorities listed in Annex 1 (Competent Authorities)' (Article 2.2.4). The listed EU competent authorities include, inter alia, the European Commission and the European Court of Justice. The term 'subsidy' here includes State aid under EU law – for the EU party – and 'investment incentives', 'investment assistance' and 'human resources training and competitiveness strengthening activities' – for Viet Nam. See also proposed Article 17 *bis* ('Subsidies') of the modernized ECT draft (dated 24 June 2022), www.bilaterals.org/IMG/pdf/reformed_ect_text.pdf.

164 Articles 9.6.5 and 9.8.6 of the CPTPP (2018), in the investment chapter, carve out a subsidy's non-payment, modification or reduction from the FET and expropriation provisions, even without explicitly stating that these subsidy-related actions should be necessitated by trade rules.

165 See, for example, Ana Mercedes López-Rodríguez, 'The Sun Behind the Clouds? Enforcement of Renewable Energy Awards in the EU', 8 *Transnational Environmental Law* 279 (2019), p. 302 (arguing: 'The [European] Commission, in particular, should review its policy on state aid rules and avoid untested extensions to the realm of arbitration. It should monitor the proper functioning of the internal market, while avoiding any unnecessary infliction of further damage on investor confidence').

166 See Section 3.2.4.

schemes on a safer footing in the trade domain and hence obviate the need for trade-law-induced and investor-irritating subsidy withdrawals or modifications. Finally, placing the trade and investment regimes under a single international framework would arguably strengthen their harmonious co-existence within that framework. While the ECT (1994) already covers the energy trade and investment parts, RTAs may also fully or partially 'absorb' existing investment treaties between the parties concerned. In Conclusion of this book, we also advocate negotiating a Sustainable Energy Trade and Investment Agreement.

5.4 Concluding Remarks

The preceding analysis has shown that the mere existence of a State's genuine intention to protect legitimate public policy objectives is not sufficient to vindicate energy investment restrictions or regulatory changes. In addition to this, proportionality of measures, their impact on the value of investment and reasonable returns as well as compliance with due process standards are among main factors that determine their legality under IIAs. Furthermore, an assessment of the validity of policy changes detrimental to investors' economic interests will also check whether the host country has actually assured regulatory stability to investors. As the EU State aid practice demonstrates, the trade and investment regimes need greater harmony with respect to subsidy issues.

The energy–environment nexus considered in this chapter is not confined to State conduct only. The fact that the CSR standards are being increasingly incorporated into IIAs is indicative of the growing public sentiment that investors should pay back to the society where they are making profits. This naturally places communal pressure on investors as environmentally irresponsible behaviour may negatively affect their reputation. Despite the largely soft law nature, the CSR provisions may add some value to the rebalancing of the investment law system, complementing the attempts, discussed in Chapter 1, towards expanding regulatory space under IIAs.

6

Energy and Green Technologies

Energy technologies refer to 'the combination of hardware, techniques, skills, methods and processes' involved in 'producing, transforming, storing, transporting and using energy'.[1] The IEA database captures over 500 mature and immature 'clean energy' technologies worldwide that contribute to achieving the goal of net-zero emissions in such areas as buildings, energy transformation, transport, CO_2 management and industries.[2] In the previous chapters, we have seen that green technologies used in the energy chain may become the object of LCRs, subsidies, TBT measures and investment policies. This chapter will show that international economic law is applicable to government interventions in even the early stages of technology development. For example, State-imposed R&D investment obligations may be banned by IIA provisions on performance requirements, and public incentives for R&D may be disciplined by WTO subsidy rules. Once commercialized, green technologies can reach foreign markets thanks to international trade and technology transfers that fall within the scope of international economic rules. Reducing trade barriers to environmental goods and services could give a further boost to the international movement of energy-related green technologies. While the importance of green technology transfers between countries is widely recognized, trade and investment rules must be consulted when imposing technology transfer measures.

6.1 Developing Green Technologies Related to Energy

Floating offshore wind turbines, technologies of producing non-food biofuels, low-impact hydropower dams and new drilling technologies to access geothermal energy are among emergent advancements related to

1 IEA, 'Energy Technology Perspectives 2020', 2020, p. 27.
2 IEA, 'ETP Clean Energy Technology Guide', 21 September 2022, www.iea.org/articles/etp-clean-energy-technology-guide.

energy today. Currently, work is ongoing on the third-generation solar cells (the earlier two generations include silicon and thin film cells) that would have low cost and high efficiency features. Under exploration are also new technologies concerning marine energy, hydrogen and microbial fuel cells. Artificial photosynthesis represents a promising technology of capturing and storing solar energy, converting it into a usable fuel. An emerging vehicle-to-grid technology is expected to enable drawing unused power from electric cars into the smart grid. The technology of utilizing thorium, a more abundant alternative to uranium, in nuclear energy production shows some promise in generating carbon-free energy while enhancing nuclear safety, reducing radioactive waste and lowering proliferation risks associated with the unauthorized spread or use of nuclear materials for the development of nuclear weapons. In addition to technologies of producing clean energy, digital technologies optimize energy supply systems, foster smart infrastructure and increase energy efficiency in households and elsewhere. These are only few examples, and the list of novel or improved green technologies will expand with the passage of time.[3]

Energy technologies are developed in the process of privately and/or publicly funded R&D activities. The following sections will examine the legal issues in trade and investment arising from government interventions in the form of R&D performance requirements and R&D subsidies.

6.1.1 R&D Spending Requirements

The IEA reports that global corporate R&D spending in energy-technology-dependent sectors has increased by around 40 per cent over the last decade since 2010. Most of such spending is concentrated in the automotive industry, and the rest in the categories of oil and gas, electricity generation and networks, renewables, nuclear energy, thermal power and combustion equipment and others.[4] Public policies can definitely

[3] The examples of technologies in this paragraph are mainly taken from UNCTAD, 'The Role of Science, Technology and Innovation in Promoting Renewable Energy by 2030', 2019, pp. 7–8; IAEA, 'Near Term and Promising Long Term Options for the Deployment of Thorium Based Nuclear Energy', Final Report of a Coordinated Research Project No. IAEA-TECDOC-2009, 2022; IAEA, 'Thorium's Long-Term Potential in Nuclear Energy: New IAEA Analysis', 13 March 2023, www.iaea.org/newscenter/news/thoriums-long-term-potential-in-nuclear-energy-new-iaea-analysis.

[4] IEA, 'World Energy Investment 2020', 2020, pp. 185–186, www.iea.org/reports/world-energy-investment-2020.

influence corporate expenditures. For example, compliance with an R&D requirement can be made a condition for companies to obtain approvals or incentives from the government. But this may raise trade and investment issues.

With respect to trade, WTO jurisprudence confirms that the fact that governments' R&D measures affect production stages before a subject product enters the marketplace does not make these measures immune from WTO disciplines.[5] In *Brazil – Taxation*, companies were required to invest in R&D in Brazil in order to qualify for certain tax exemptions and reductions. Tax beneficiaries had to invest annually in R&D activities in Brazil a certain percentage of their gross sales on the domestic market, but the value of their purchases of certain domestic products in Brazil was deducted from the calculation of that percentage. Because this essentially incentivized companies to buy more domestic products concerned to invest less in R&D, such calculation mechanism was found to treat imported products less favourably in violation of Article III:4 of the GATT on national treatment.[6]

With respect to investment protection, compelling foreign investors into R&D spending may constitute an illegal performance requirement under IIAs. In *Mobil and Murphy v. Canada (I)*, the tribunal found that an R&D expenditure obligation imposed on US oil companies violated Article 1106 ('Performance Requirements') of the NAFTA (1992). The tribunal held that R&D was a 'service' and hence fell within the scope of the Article 1106(1)(c) prohibition against a contracting party's investment requirement 'to purchase, use or accord a preference to goods produced or services provided in its territory, or to purchase goods or services from persons in its territory'.[7] Such prohibition was unaffected by Article 1106(4) under which a party was not prevented 'from conditioning the receipt or continued receipt of an advantage . . . on [investors'] compliance with a requirement to . . . carry out research and development, in its territory':

> In the view of the Tribunal, the specific mention of R&D in Article 1106 (4) may be seen as a means of indicating the NAFTA drafters' view that they intended to exclude R&D for the purposes of investment incentives

[5] See *Brazil – Taxation*, WTO Panel Reports, paras. 7.61, 7.70; *Brazil – Taxation*, WTO Appellate Body Reports, paras. 5.14–5.16.

[6] *Brazil – Taxation*, WTO Panel Reports, paras. 7.231–7.243. See also paras. 7.766–7.771.

[7] *Mobil and Murphy v. Canada (I)*, ICSID, Decision on Liability and Principles of Quantum, paras. 216, 219, 246.

enumerated in Article 1106(4), but that they did not explicitly do so, for purposes of Article 1106(1).[8]

Like Article 1106(4) of the NAFTA (1992), some later IIAs also provide that the performance requirements ban does not prevent a host country from giving foreign investors an 'advantage' conditional upon their R&D performance in its territory.[9] Granting R&D advantages lies within a discretionary power of the host country. Under the GATS, a number of WTO members – both developed and developing, original and acceded members – have 'unbound', or no, commitments for national treatment in relation to R&D subsidies for mode 3 (or commercial presence) services.[10] Thus, they are free to provide R&D subsidies to domestic firms to the exclusion of FDIs. However, such subsidizing right under an investment treaty and the GATS is not unfettered under other legal contexts. For example, as noted below, the SCM Agreement does not treat certain R&D subsidies as 'non-actionable' any longer.

6.1.2 R&D Subsidies

Low-carbon energy technologies receive the largest portion of governments' energy R&D funding.[11] In 2019, public spending on energy R&D stood at $30 billion globally, and around 80 per cent of it was directed to low-carbon energy technologies.[12]

From an economic perspective, R&D subsidies are desirable to stimulate the generation and spillover of knowledge – a public good – which is otherwise uncompensated or undercompensated in the market. Without government support, firms are inclined to underinvest in R&D as 'the

[8] Ibid., para. 224.

[9] See, for example, Article 6.3 of the Japan–Peru BIT (2008); Article 9.10.3(a) of the CPTPP (2018); Article 14.10.3(a) of the USMCA (2018).

[10] See the GATS schedules of specific commitments of: Australia (GATS/SC/6, 15 April 1994); Brazil (GATS/SC/13, 15 April 1994); Cambodia (GATS/SC/140, 25 October 2005); Canada (GATS/SC/16, 15 April 1994); the EU (GATS/SC/157, 7 May 2019); Iceland (GATS/SC/41, 15 April 1994); Japan (GATS/SC/46, 15 April 1994); Kazakhstan (GATS/SC/154, 15 February 2016); Korea (GATS/SC/48, 15 April 1994); Mexico (GATS/SC/56, 15 April 1994); Montenegro (GATS/SC/146, 5 June 2012); Norway (GATS/SC/66, 15 April 1994); Russia (GATS/SC/149, 5 November 2012); Tajikistan (GATS/SC/151, 22 April 2013); the United States (GATS/SC/90, 15 April 1994); Viet Nam (GATS/SC/142, 19 March 2007).

[11] For the dynamics in R&D spending in IEA member countries in 1974–2020, see IEA, 'Low-Carbon RD&D', www.iea.org/reports/energy-technology-rdd-budgets-overview/low-carbon-rdd#abstract.

[12] IEA, supra note 1, p. 318.

private rate of return to R&D is less than the social return'.[13] In response to this market failure, Part IV of the SCM Agreement exempted certain R&D (and other 'non-actionable') subsidies from WTO dispute complaints and countervailing measures, but members failed to extend such non-actionable treatment beyond the agreed five-year period. Now-defunct Article 8.2, included in Part IV of the SCM Agreement, treated governmental 'assistance for research activities' of firms or qualified research entities as non-actionable subsidies if the assistance did not exceed certain caps (i.e., 75 per cent of the costs of industrial research or 50 per cent of the costs of pre-competitive development activity) and covered specified costs only. In addition, a qualified R&D subsidy had to be notified in advance of its implementation and was subject to the prescribed WTO review procedures. Although Part IV of the SCM Agreement is not in operation any longer, India, Canada and perhaps some other countries maintain provisions on non-actionable treatment for Article 8.2-like subsidies under their respective countervailing duty laws.[14]

Notwithstanding the fact that the WTO subsidy regime is not lenient towards R&D subsidies any more, recourse to R&D subsidies will likely increase in many countries to further technological advancements for mitigating and adapting to the environmental degradation.[15] It is thus

[13] IMF, OECD, World Bank and WTO, 'Subsidies, Trade, and International Cooperation', 2022, p. 7. See also WTO, 'Exploring the Links between Subsidies, Trade and the WTO', World Trade Report 2006, 2006, p. 61 (stating: 'if the benefits of R&D investments spill over to others, while the costs are borne privately by those carrying out R&D, markets will not generate the socially optimal level of R&D', so an R&D subsidy 'that generates spillovers to other firms in the industry could help stimulate productivity and growth in a socially optimal way'); Alan O. Sykes, 'The Economics of WTO Rules on Subsidies and Countervailing Measures', John M. Olin Program in Law and Economics Working Paper No. 186 (2003), University of Chicago, p. 6.

[14] See Section 9 of India's 1975 Customs Tariff Act and Rule 11 of India's 1995 Customs Tariff (Identification, Assessment and Collection of Countervailing Duty on Subsidized Articles and for Determination of Injury) Rules (as updated on 1 August 2018 at Ministry of Commerce and Industry, www.dgtr.gov.in/sites/default/files/Compendium_of_Law%26Regulations_for-mail%281%29.pdf) as explained in Radhika Sharma, 'Countervailing Duty Laws in India', 11 December 2015, www.lakshmisri.com/insights/articles/countervailing-duty-laws-in-india/#; Article 2(1) ('Definitions') and Article 30.4(3) of Canada's Special Import Measures Act, R.S.C., 1985, c. S-15 (last amended 1 July 2020), https://laws-lois.justice.gc.ca/eng/acts/S-15/FullText.html as explained in Bennett Johns, 'Canadian Anti-dumping and Countervailing Duty Measures', 2019, p. 17, www.bennettjones.com/Publications-Section/Guides/Canadian-AntiDumping-and-Countervailing-Duty-Measures.

[15] Keith Maskus, 'Research and Development Subsidies: A Need for WTO Disciplines?', International Centre for Trade and Sustainable Development and World Economic Forum, 2015, pp. 1, 5–6.

not surprising that several WTO members have recently proposed that the SCM Agreement provisions on non-actionable subsidies should be reinstated with modified terms and coverage to allow for greater flexibility in relation to, inter alia, (green) R&D subsidies. They argue that this could be especially beneficial for developing countries that were largely unable to fully utilize these provisions during the initial five-year transitional period.[16] The question of whether to reintroduce the category of non-actionable subsidies, including for R&D subsidies, remains controversial as discussed in the literature.[17] In Chapter 3, we have explored some options for WTO law reforms to accommodate green energy subsidies, which could also apply to relevant R&D subsidies.[18]

In 2009–2021, WTO members submitted fifty-seven notifications covering 179 R&D subsidy measures (predominantly grants and tax incentives) in the energy sector as related to the environment (Figure 6.1). The notified R&D subsidies concerned renewable/alternative energy technologies or fossil fuel technologies aimed at the environmental protection (energy conservation, air pollution/emission reduction and so on). About 92 per cent of the notified subsidies in Figure 6.1 were adopted by

[16] See WTO, General Council – Committee on SCM – Committee on Trade and Development – A Case for Rebalancing the Agreement on Subsidies and Countervailing Measures (ASCM) – Policy Space to Promote Industrialisation in Developing Countries – Communication from the African Group (Angola; Benin; [. . .]; Uganda; Zambia and Zimbabwe), WT/GC/W/880, G/SCM/W/589, WT/COMTD/W/274 (26 May 2023), para. 3.2; WTO, General Council – 28 February and 1 March 2019 – The Continued Relevance of Special and Differential Treatment in Favour of Developing Members to Promote Development and Ensure Inclusiveness – Communication from China, India, South Africa and the Bolivarian Republic of Venezuela, [. . .] and Pakistan – Revision, WT/GC/W/765/Rev.2 (4 March 2019), para. 5.8; WTO, General Council – China's Proposal on WTO Reform – Communication from China, WT/GC/W/773 (13 May 2019), para. 2.16.

[17] See, for example, Sadeq Z. Bigdeli, 'Resurrecting the Dead – The Expired Non-Actionable Subsidies and the Lingering Question of "Green Space"', 8(2) *Manchester Journal of International Economic Law* 2 (2011); Aaron Cosbey and Petros C. Mavroidis, 'A Turquoise Mess: Green Subsidies, Blue Industrial Policy and Renewable Energy: The Case for Redrafting the Subsidies Agreement of the WTO', 17 *Journal of International Economic Law* 11 (2014), pp. 42–43, 45–46; Sherzod Shadikhodjaev, 'Renewable Energy and Government Support: Time to "Green" the SCM Agreement?', 14 *World Trade Review* 479 (2015), pp. 494–495; Ilaria Espa and Sonia E. Rolland, 'Subsidies, Clean Energy, and Climate Change', International Centre for Trade and Sustainable Development and World Economic Forum, 2015, p. 12; Robert Howse, 'Climate Mitigation Subsidies and the WTO Legal Framework: A Policy Analysis', International Institute for Sustainable Development, 2010, pp. 20–21.

[18] See Section 3.2.4.

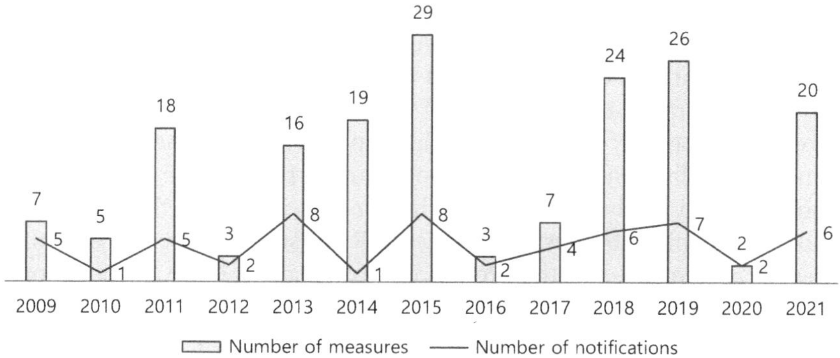

Figure 6.1 Environment-related R&D subsidy notifications in energy sector (2009–2021).

Source: Author's compilation from data (as of 1 April 2023) in WTO Environmental Database, https://edb.wto.org.

Notes: Subsidies were notified by members under Article 25 of the SCM Agreement, but one notification was made under Article 27.4 of the SCM Agreement. The notifying members were the United States, the EU (notifying its Member States' subsidy programmes), Canada, Israel, Japan, Mexico, China, Chinese Taipei, Australia, Norway, Costa Rica and Tunisia. The number of measures captures R&D subsidies in each notification in this dataset. Thus, the same subsidy notified, for example, twice was counted as two measures.

developed country members, especially the United States (57 per cent of the notified total) and EU Member States (17 per cent). Given the practice of 'chronic' non-notification of subsidies in the WTO,[19] many energy–environment R&D subsidies are likely to remain under-notified.

WTO litigation on R&D subsidies concentrated mainly on relevant government subsidies for the aircraft industry (related to Canada's Bombardier, the United States' Boeing and the EU's Airbus) that traditionally requires high entry costs and huge investments in R&D.[20] Among other things, WTO jurisprudence admits that by helping local companies produce technologically superior competitive goods, R&D subsidies may cause 'adverse effects' on foreign rivals. In *US – Large Civil Aircraft (2nd complaint)*, 'technology effects' – the impact of US

[19] WTO, 'Chair Cites "Chronic" Low Compliance with Subsidy Notification Requirements', 27 October 2020, www.wto.org/english/news_e/news20_e/scm_27oct20_e.htm.

[20] Maskus, supra note 15, pp. 4–5.

aeronautics R&D subsidies on the development of aircraft technologies dealing with, inter alia, low fuel consumption[21] – were considered as part of an overall assessment of 'serious prejudice' to EU commercial interests under Articles 5 and 6 of the SCM Agreement. It was found that the R&D subsidies greatly contributed to Boeing's development of technologies and enabled it to quickly launch and commercialize the aircraft incorporating all of the relevant technologies.[22] In addition, it was determined that but for the R&D subsidies' effects, Airbus would have obtained additional orders for its aircraft, made additional sales of it and would not have suffered significant price suppression.[23] Being critical of these findings, one commentator suggests that the concept of 'serious prejudice' should be interpreted (or reformulated in the future subsidy rules) narrowly to exclude technology effects. He argues that only financial effects of R&D subsidies on production costs and prices should be accepted for the purpose of multilateral remedies so as to leave more policy space for promoting societally desirable technological innovations.[24]

WTO anti-subsidy complaints are substantially outnumbered by countervailing duty investigations and measures.[25] In line with this trend, members' infrequent recourse to the multilateral anti-subsidy track vis-à-vis R&D subsidies is contrasted with their higher activism in countervailing those subsidies, including in the energy–environment context. By way of illustration, in subsidy determinations not reviewed by WTO adjudicators, EU, US, Canadian and Indian countervailing duty investigations on solar/wind power equipment from China commonly confirmed countervailibility of certain R&D subsidies. These investigations found that China's tax law entitled enterprises of approved R&D projects to a corporate income tax reduction by 50 per cent of the actual research expenditures incurred in the development of new technologies. This scheme was determined to provide a subsidy in the form of forgone

21 For the description of aircraft technologies linked to R&D subsidies, see *US – Large Civil Aircraft (2nd complaint)*, WTO Panel Report, Appendix VII.F.1; *US – Large Civil Aircraft (2nd complaint) (Article 21.5 – EU)*, WTO Panel Report, paras. 9.179, 9.187.

22 *US – Large Civil Aircraft (2nd complaint)*, WTO Panel Report, paras. 7.1773, 7.1775; *US – Large Civil Aircraft (2nd complaint)*, WTO Appellate Body Report, para. 1030.

23 *US – Large Civil Aircraft (2nd complaint)*, WTO Panel Report, para. 7.1794; *US – Large Civil Aircraft (2nd complaint)*, WTO Appellate Body Report, paras. 1040, 1126–1127.

24 See Matthew Kennedy, 'The Adverse Effects of Technological Innovation under WTO Subsidy Rules', 19 *World Trade Review* 511 (2020), pp. 521–529.

25 See Sherzod Shadikhodjaev, *Industrial Policy and the World Trade Organization: Between Legal Constraints and Flexibilities* (Cambridge: Cambridge University Press, 2018), pp. 91–92.

government revenue, specific to certain enterprises with R&D in eligible high technology sectors.[26] In addition, affirmative determinations were also made for China's R&D grants.[27] Interestingly, one of the parties in the Indian investigation contended that the R&D support at issue constituted a 'non-actionable subsidy' within the meaning of Article 8 of the SCM Agreement as presently replicated in India's countervailing duty law, but the investigating authority made affirmative subsidy findings without directly addressing this assertion.[28]

As another example, US investigations on refrigerators and washing machines from Korea reviewed an R&D scheme that was used, inter alia, to improve energy efficiency of home appliances. The USDOC determined that countervailable grants were provided under Korea's Green Technology R&D programme described as follows:[29]

> According to the GOK [Government of Korea], technology is a crucial factor in promoting and achieving green growth in all economic sectors

[26] See Council Implementing Regulation (EU) No. 1239/2013 of 2 December 2013 imposing a definitive countervailing duty on imports of crystalline silicon photovoltaic modules and key components (i.e. cells) originating in or consigned from the People's Republic of China, OJ L 325, 5 December 2013, paras. 306–317; Commission Implementing Regulation (EU) No. 471/2014 of 13 May 2014 imposing definitive countervailing duties on imports of solar glass originating in the People's Republic of China, OJ L 142, 14 May 2014, paras. 161–169; USDOC, Issues and Decision Memorandum for the Final Determination in the Countervailing Duty Investigation of Crystalline Silicon Photovoltaic Cells, Whether or Not Assembled Into Modules, from the People's Republic of China [C-570-980], 9 October 2012, p. 17; USDOC, Issues and Decision Memorandum for the Final Determination in the Countervailing Duty Investigation of Utility Scale Wind Towers (Wind Towers) from the People's Republic of China [C-570-982], 17 December 2012, pp. 18–19; Canada Border Services Agency, Statement of Reasons Concerning the Final Determinations with Respect to the Dumping and the Subsidizing of Certain Photovoltaic Modules and Laminates Originating in or Exported from the People's Republic of China, 18 June 2015, pp. 79–80; Ministry of Commerce and Industry (India), Final Findings: Anti-subsidy/Countervailing Duty Investigation Concerning Imports of Castings for Wind Operated Electricity Generators, Whether or Not Machined, in Raw, Finished or Sub-assembled Form, or as a Part of a Sub-Assembly, or as a Part of an Equipment/Component Meant for Wind-Operated Electricity Generators, Originating in or Exported from China PR, 27 November 2015, pp. 129–135.

[27] Canada Border Services Agency, supra note 26, pp. 45–78; Ministry of Commerce and Industry (India), supra note 26, pp. 100–102.

[28] Ministry of Commerce and Industry (India), supra note 26, pp. 100–102, 130–134.

[29] USDOC, Issues and Decision Memorandum for the Final Determination in the Countervailing Duty Investigation of Bottom Mount Combination Refrigerator-Freezers from the Republic of Korea [C-580-866], 16 March 2012, pp. 26–28; USDOC, Issues and Decision Memorandum for the Final Determination in the Countervailing Duty Investigation of Large Residential Washers from the Republic of Korea [C-580-869], 18 December 2012, pp. 17–19.

> and, thus, the development of relevant green technology has been regarded as the main pillar of the country's Green Growth policy. The technology development component is one of the important factors of the government's five-year Green Growth Plan, which was adopted by the GOK in January 2009. Under the plan, the GOK has selected 27 core technologies for support. The MKE [Ministry of Knowledge Economy] is involved in this program and provides support to Green Technology R&D. This program provides for the establishment and enforcement of measures to facilitate research, development and commercialization of green technology, including financial support for these activities. Support is provided to approved applicants in the form of grants . . .. The GOK reported that the approval of the applicants is based on the merits of each application, which must be in accordance with the requirements set by the law and MKE's internal guidelines. According to the GOK, the provision of support under the program is automatic as long as the budgets earmarked for this program are available.[30]

During the investigation, the Korean government submitted that the Green Technology R&D programme was designed to establish 'general infrastructure' (for attaining green growth across all sectors), which was excluded from the scope of 'financial contribution' (one of the elements of 'subsidy') and that the programme was not 'specific' because the subject twenty-seven technologies covered 'almost all conceivable technologies' regarding green growth, GHG reduction and renewable energy. But the USDOC disagreed saying that this programme did not fit the concept of 'general infrastructure' as exemplified by 'interstate highways, schools, health care facilities, sewage systems and the provision of police protection' and that the R&D programme was expressly limited by Korea's law to the twenty-seven technologies making it de jure specific.[31] Pursuant to Article 1.1(a)(1)(iii) of the SCM Agreement, a subsidy is deemed to exist if 'a government provides goods or services other than general infrastructure'. While the concept of 'general infrastructure' is not limited to the 'conventional' public goods exemplified by the USDOC,[32] providing public

[30] USDOC, Issues and Decision Memorandum [C-580-869], supra note 29, p. 17; Similarly worded in USDOC, Issues and Decision Memorandum [C-580-866], supra note 29, p. 26.

[31] USDOC, Issues and Decision Memorandum [C-580-866], supra note 29, pp. 71–73; USDOC, Issues and Decision Memorandum [C-580-869], supra note 29, pp. 47–49.

[32] One WTO panel considered that no type of infrastructure was 'inherently "general" *per se*' and held (*EC and certain member States – Large Civil Aircraft*, WTO Panel Report, para. 7.1039):

> For instance, in our view, such things as railroads or electrical distribution systems do not necessarily constitute 'general infrastructure'. Rather, the determination whether the provision of the good or service in question is 'general infrastructure' or not must be made on a case-by-case basis, taking

R&D grants for green technologies is arguably not the same as providing general infrastructure simply because what is provided here is R&D financial support rather than infrastructure. Moreover, R&D-covered green technologies – even if they may qualify as 'green' general infrastructure – are typically not mature yet (as they are under development) to be provided. But the idea about the provision of green general infrastructure could matter when the government provides such green technologies, or makes them accessible, across the board after they are ready for use.

In the subsequent WTO case on *US – Washing Machines*, Korea did not challenge the USDOC's finding on the Green Technology R&D programme with respect to washing machines but contested its findings in the same investigation on tax credits for Samsung under the Tax Deduction for Research and Manpower Development programme.[33] The Appellate Body held that the USDOC miscalculated by attributing the tax credits to all of Samsung's products instead of tying a relevant portion of the tax credits to Samsung's digital appliances (including washing machines),[34] consequently imposing excessive countervailing duties.[35]

Since it takes time for a new technology to be developed and commercialized, governments can provide R&D subsidies for decarbonization and clean energy technologies without fear of triggering foreign anti-subsidy measures at the stage when technology is under development. Even though the SCM Agreement is applicable to R&D subsidies provided at that stage in principle (for example, these subsidies, if caught, can be countervailed later once the technology product is traded), until

> into account the existence or absence of *de jure* or *de facto* limitations on access or use, and any other factors that tend to demonstrate that the infrastructure was or was not provided to or for the use of only a single entity or a limited group of entities . . .. If an evaluation of relevant facts concerning such factors demonstrates that the infrastructure was provided to a single entity or a limited group of entities, then we believe it cannot properly be considered 'general' infrastructure, and consequently falls within the scope of Article 1.1(a)(1) of the SCM Agreement, necessitating further analysis to determine whether a subsidy exists.

33 *US – Washing Machines*, WTO Appellate Body Report, para. 5.205.

34 Among Samsung's different units, it was its digital appliance business unit that was producing washing machines investigated by the USDOC. But in calculating Samsung's subsidization rate, the USDOC considered the tax credits received by Samsung across all its products, rather than focusing on the tax credits earned by the digital appliance business unit as tied to the products made by that business unit (*US – Washing Machines*, WTO Appellate Body Report, paras. 5.248–5.250).

35 *US – Washing Machines*, WTO Appellate Body Report, paras. 5.274, 5.284–5.285, 6.14.

technologies enter the marketplace and as long as related R&D subsidies do not have LCR or export promotion elements (which may lead to successful challenges against prohibited subsidies even if the technology is not mature), no one is likely to challenge the legality of such subsidies in advance. Indeed, in this case, proving the existence of adverse effects by actionable subsidies and material injury by not-yet imported technologies is hardly possible. At the technology development stage, subsidies are important in promoting positive externalities (or societal benefits) that these technologies can create. By sharing the risk of failure in R&D projects, such subsidies encourage developers to explore or experiment with (even risky) innovative solutions that, depending on the outcome, may eventually become technological breakthroughs in case of success.

6.2 Facilitation of Green Technology Use in Energy Trade and Investment

R&D policies help create new energy technologies. Because the market has yet to absorb these technologies, governments may additionally employ various other tools, such as consumption subsidies or standards (including in green public procurement) discussed in Chapter 4. Besides, market opening and technology transfer policies can facilitate international technology dissemination as considered in the next sections.

6.2.1 Trade Liberalization

Clean energy technologies have both hardware and software components, integrated into relevant goods and services. Pressing environmental problems, like climate change, are expected to significantly increase demand for environmental goods and services, including green technologies, in any country in the near future.[36] The lowering of barriers to trade in environmental goods and services can help meet such demand, expand green trade and assist developing countries in satisfying environmental priorities in their development path. In other words, this can create triple wins for the environment, trade and development.[37]

[36] WTO, 'The Future of Services Trade', World Trade Report 2019, 2019, p. 121.

[37] WTO, 'Eliminating Trade Barriers on Environmental Goods and Services', www.wto.org/English/tratop_e/envir_e/envir_neg_serv_e.htm.

6.2.1.1 The Goods Sector

According to a joint report of the World Bank and the WTO (2022), average tariffs on environmental goods, including clean and renewable energy and energy efficiency goods, are lower in high-income countries than other countries. In contrast, high- and upper-middle-income countries apply more non-tariff measures on these goods than lower-income countries.[38] Thus, reducing both tariff and non-tariff barriers to green trade could create balanced export opportunities for both developed and developing countries. Furthermore, the WTO estimates that eliminating tariffs and lowering non-tariff barriers on energy-related environmental goods could boost global exports of these goods by 5 per cent by 2030 and cut global emissions by 0.6 per cent through the resulting increases in energy efficiency and renewable uptake.[39]

To date, a few multi-party initiatives on environmental trade liberalization have been carried out. In the WTO, multilateral negotiations on the reduction or elimination of tariff and non-tariff barriers to environmental goods and services took place as part of the 2001 Doha Development Agenda (DDA),[40] but they failed to conclude. In 2014–2016, a group of (eventually forty-six) WTO members conducted negotiations under a plurilateral Environmental Goods Agreement (EGA) with a purpose to eliminate tariffs on an MFN basis but could not reach consensus.[41] The stalemate in the DDA and EGA initiatives, caused, inter alia, by the lack of agreement on the product coverage, contrasts with the success of the APEC in clinching a deal in 2012 for the voluntary reduction of tariffs on certain environmental goods.[42] In addition, the ongoing WTO environmental initiatives may show some promise.[43] Specifically, the TESSD

[38] World Bank and WTO, 'The Role of Trade in Developing Countries' Road to Recovery', Joint Policy Note, 2022, pp. 22, 23 (figure 8). The environmental goods in question are some 177 low-carbon goods, including clean and renewable energy and energy efficiency goods (WTO, Trade and Environmental Sustainability Structured Discussions (TESSD) – Experiences in the Promotion and Facilitation of Environmental Goods and Services – Note by the Secretariat, INF/TE/SSD/W/18 (23 March 2022), para. 3.3).

[39] WTO, 'Climate Change and International Trade', World Trade Report 2022, 2022, pp. 8, 117.

[40] WTO, 'Negotiations on Trade and the Environment', www.wto.org/English/tratop_e/envir_e/envir_negotiations_e.htm.

[41] WTO, 'Environmental Goods Agreement (EGA)', www.wto.org/english/tratop_e/envir_e/ega_e.htm.

[42] APEC, '2012 Leaders' Declaration', Vladivostok (Russia), 8–9 September 2012, www.apec.org/Meeting-Papers/Leaders-Declarations/2012/2012_aelm.

[43] See Section 1.2.1.

explores the ways of promoting and facilitating trade in environmental goods and services and access to new and emerging climate-friendly technologies.[44] The IDP discusses how to promote trade in goods and services including the use of technologies that can reduce plastics pollution.[45]

Negotiations on environmental tariff eliminations or reductions require specifying target products. Negotiators may first agree to one definition and then select products that would fit it. However, in a large-group setting, this approach has turned out to be nearly infeasible because of divergent views on environmental friendliness or relevance of products and other definitional aspects.[46] Instead, negotiators have focused on identifying relevant products or activities, without adopting a blanket definition. For example, the DDA negotiations explored a variety of techniques. In particular, a 'list-based approach' defines a common list of goods that are deemed to fulfil certain environmental objectives. A 'request and offer approach' is about the selection of environmental goods of interest to each negotiating party through a bilateral request–offer process. Alternatively, parties can list environmental activities or projects for which any utilized imported product will be given tariff preferences. Such a 'project approach' is meritorious for tackling a multiple-use issue (see below) as any product becomes environmental only when used for environmental activities, but this approach may cause customs control and monitoring difficulties. In addition, a mixture of these approaches can be used to negotiate a common core list of environmental goods and a complimentary self-selected list with some flexibilities for developing countries.[47]

[44] See WTO, Committee on Trade and Environment – Communication on Trade and Environmental Sustainability – Communication from Australia; Canada; Chad; Chile; Costa Rica; EU; The Gambia; Fiji; Iceland; Japan; Korea; [. . .]; and the UK, WT/CTE/W/249 (17 November 2020); WTO, Ministerial Conference – [Twelfth Session – Geneva, 30 November–3 December 2021] – TESSD – Ministerial Statement on Trade and Environmental Sustainability – Revision, WT/MIN(21)/6/Rev.2 (14 December 2021).

[45] See WTO, Ministerial Conference – [Twelfth Session – Geneva, 30 November–3 December 2021] – Informal Dialogue on Plastic Pollution and Environmentally Sustainable Plastics Trade (IDP) – MC12 Ministerial Statement on Plastic Pollution and Environmentally Sustainable Plastics Trade – Revision, WT/MIN(21)/8/Rev.2 (10 December 2021).

[46] See, for example, WTO, Committee on Trade and Environment – Special Session – Statement by the Chairperson of the Special Session of the Committee on Trade and Environment to the Trade Negotiations Committee, TN/TE/2 (4 July 2002), para. 11.

[47] The explanation of the negotiation approaches in this paragraph is based on INF/TE/SSD/W/18, supra note 38, paras. 2.15–2.28, 2.39; WTO, Committee on Trade and

Table 6.1 compares environmental goods categories in the three negotiation initiatives – the DDA, the EGA and the APEC – and the OECD statistical database. These classification lists are said to broadly reflect the OECD's working definition below:[48]

> The environmental goods and services industry consists of activities which produce goods and services to measure, prevent, limit, minimise or correct environmental damage to water, air and soil, as well as problems related to waste, noise and eco-systems. This includes cleaner technologies, products and services that reduce environmental risk and minimise pollution and resource use.[49]

Among the negotiation lists, the DDA's is the longest (411 goods), followed by the EGA's (about 300 goods) and the APEC's (54 goods).[50] The OECD's list (about 250 goods)[51] is used for analytical and statistical, rather than negotiation, purposes. With respect to the energy–environment nexus, all four lists contain low-emission and clean energy technologies and have the overlapping categories regarding air pollution control, renewable energy, waste management and environmental monitoring, among others.

In 2012, APEC members adopted a non-binding commitment to reduce their applied tariffs to 5 per cent or less on fifty-four environmental goods by the end of 2015 with a view to enhancing accessibility and the deployment of 'important environmental technologies'.[52] As of March 2021, nineteen out of twenty-one APEC members were able to fully implement this commitment.[53] The largest portion of the environmental goods in the APEC list is made up by renewable energy

Environment – Special Session – Report by the Chairman, Ambassador Manuel A. J. Teehankee, to the Trade Negotiations Committee, TN/TE/20 (21 April 2011), pp. 14–17.

48 INF/TE/SSD/W/18, supra note 38, para. 2.25.

49 OECD, 'The Environmental Goods and Services Industry: Manual for Data Collection and Analysis', 1999, p. 9, https://unstats.un.org/unsd/envaccounting/ceea/archive/EPEA/EnvIndustry_Manual_for_data_collection.PDF.

50 INF/TE/SSD/W/18, supra note 38, para. 2.24.

51 The 2014 OECD list of environmental goods contained 248 goods. See Jehan Sauvage, 'The Stringency of Environmental Regulations and Trade in Environmental Goods', OECD Trade and Environment Working Paper, COM/TAD/ENV/JWPTE(2013)33/FINAL, 2014, pp. 20–21, 51–56.

52 APEC, supra note 42; APEC, 'Annex C – APEC List of Environmental Goods', 2012, www.apec.org/Meeting-Papers/Leaders-Declarations/2012/2012_aelm/2012_aelm_annexC.

53 APEC, 'APEC Advances Environmental Goods Tariffs Cut', 11 March 2021, www.apec.org/press/news-releases/2021/0311_mag.

Table 6.1 *Comparative classification of environmental goods categories*

DDA	EGA	APEC	OECD
Air pollution control	Air pollution control	Air pollution control	Air pollution control
Renewable energy	Cleaner and renewable energy	Renewable energy	Renewable energy plant
Waste management and water treatment • Clean-up or remediation of soil and water • Management of solid and hazardous waste and recycling systems • Waste management, recycling and remediation • Wastewater management and potable water treatment	Wastewater management and water treatment Environmental remediation and clean-up Solid and hazardous waste management	Wastewater management and potable water treatment Management of solid and hazardous waste and recycling systems	Wastewater management and potable water treatment Management of solid and hazardous waste and recycling systems Clean-up or remediation of soil and water
Environmental technologies • Gas flaring emission reduction • Efficient consumption of energy technologies • Cleaner or more resource efficient technologies and products • Energy efficiency	Environmental monitoring, analysis and assessment Resource efficiency Energy efficiency Noise and vibration abatement	Environmental monitoring analysis and assessment equipment Natural risk management	Environmental monitoring, analysis and assessment equipment Heat and energy management Cleaner or more resource efficient technologies and products Noise and vibration abatement

Table 6.1 (*cont.*)

DDA	EGA	APEC	OECD
• Environmental monitoring, analysis and assessment equipment • Heat and energy management • Natural risk management • Noise and vibration abatement Carbon capture and storage			
Others • Environmentally preferable products • Natural resources protection • Renewable products and energy sources • Resource and pollution management	Environmentally preferable products	Environmentally preferable products	Environmentally preferable products based on end use or disposal characteristics Natural resources protection

Source: Author's compilation from WTO, Trade and Environmental Sustainability Structured Discussions (TESSD) – Experiences in the Promotion and Facilitation of Environmental Goods and Services – Note by the Secretariat, INF/TE/SSD/W/18 (23 March 2022), p. 8 (citing WTO, JOB/TE/3/Rev.1; Reinsch et al. (2021); and APEC Policy Support Unit, Policy Brief No. 41 (October 2021)); OECD, 'Trade in Environmentally Related Goods', https://stats.oecd.org/Index.aspx?DataSetCode=TRADEENV_IND10.

products (28 per cent), environmental monitoring analysis and assessment equipment (28 per cent) and management of solid and hazardous waste and recycling systems (22 per cent).[54] Since 2012, trade in the APEC-listed environmental goods has increased significantly compared to overall merchandise trade, and this is partly attributable to the tariff reductions endorsed by the APEC commitment.[55] Given new technological developments and innovations since 2012, the APEC list is likely to expand in the future.[56] In this regard, the APEC Market Access Group recommends the inclusion of twenty-one additional environmental goods related to renewable energy sources/carriers (solar energy, wind energy, hydrogen and ammonia), energy storage and integration (cell and accumulators and cell recycling) as well as transport and other end use (electric vehicles, hydrogen internal combustion engine vehicles and hydrogen fuel cell vehicles).[57]

The existing international product nomenclature does not necessarily reflect the eco-friendliness of goods. The WTO and APEC lists above classify environmental goods at the six-digit HS sub-heading levels. But where HS sub-headings are considered to cover goods with a dual (environmental and non-environmental) use or to be broad otherwise, those sub-headings also contain 'ex-outs' to capture only 'environmental goods' of interest. Each of the APEC, DDA and EGA lists has ex-outs for more than half of the covered environmental goods.[58] For instance, HS 903289 (automatic regulating or controlling instruments, other) under the APEC list is accompanied by the ex-out limiting this category to heliostats, temperature sensor for solar boiler/water heaters and

[54] Carlos Kuriyama, 'The APEC List of Environmental Goods', APEC Policy Support Unit, Policy Brief No. 5, 2012, p. 1, www.apec.org/publications/2012/11/the-apec-list-of-environmental-goods.

[55] Carlos Kuriyama, 'A Review of the APEC List of Environmental Goods', APEC Policy Support Unit, Policy Brief No. 41, 2021, p. 1, www.apec.org/publications/2021/10/a-review-of-the-apec-list-of-environmental-goods.

[56] See APEC, 'APEC Ministers Responsible for Trade Meeting Joint Statement 2021', Wellington (New Zealand), 5 June 2021, section 2, www.apec.org/Meeting-Papers/Sectoral-Ministerial-Meetings/Trade/2021_MRT; APEC, '2021 APEC Ministerial Meeting', Wellington (New Zealand), 9 November 2021, para. 32, www.apec.org/meeting-papers/annual-ministerial-meetings/2021/2021-apec-ministerial-meeting.

[57] APEC Market Access Group, 'Scoping Study on New and Emerging Environmental Goods', 2021, pp. 22–27, www.apec.org/publications/2021/12/scoping-study-on-new-and-emerging-environmental-goods.

[58] INF/TE/SSD/W/18, supra note 38, paras. 2.40–2.41; 'Annex C – APEC List of Environmental Goods', supra note 52.

differential temperature controllers for solar boiler/water heaters.[59] As another example, the DDA list included HS 730820 (towers and lattice masts) with the corresponding ex-out for wind turbine towers.[60] In theory, tariff preferences given to environmental ex-outs but not the remainder of the corresponding HS sub-heading may arouse MFN claims where the ex-outs and the remainder originate from different WTO members.[61] However, if properly incorporated into the WTO system and applied to all eligible goods alike, the environmental ex-outs per se – just like the existing ex-outs under the (Expanded) Information Technology Agreement and the Agreement on Trade in Civil Aircraft[62] – seem to be at low risk of facing WTO legal challenges concerning MFN. It is noteworthy that the preferential treatment of the ex-outs in the APEC list has, so far, not been challenged in the WTO.

Unlike the multi-party forums above, RTAs and small-group initiatives represent less challenging paths for freeing trade in environmental goods. Under most RTAs, across-the-board tariff removals already affect environmental goods even without categorizing them as such. Few agreements, however, make it explicit that they eliminate duties on the agreed list of environmental goods, thereby accentuating the environmental agenda of bilateral trade.[63] Besides RTAs, in 2022, the parties to the ongoing negotiations on the ACCTS announced 'good progress ... in

[59] 'Annex C – APEC List of Environmental Goods', supra note 52. See also Rene Vossenaar, 'The APEC List of Environmental Goods: An Analysis of the Outcome & Expected Impact', ICTSD Issue Paper No. 18, 2013, pp. 3–4.

[60] WTO, Committee on Trade and Environment – Special Session – Report by the Chairman, Ambassador Manuel A. J. Teehankee, to the Trade Negotiations Committee for the Purpose of the TNC Stocktaking Exercise, TN/TE/19 (22 March 2010), p. 19.

[61] See Petros C. Mavroidis and Damien J. Neven, 'Greening the WTO Environmental Goods Agreement, Tariff Concessions, and Policy Likeness', 22 *Journal of International Economic Law* 373 (2019), pp. 383–386.

[62] Partially covered sub-headings were identified by the symbol 'ex' in: WTO, Ministerial Conference – Tenth Session – Nairobi, 15–18 December 2015 – Ministerial Declaration on the Expansion of Trade in Information Technology Products – Nairobi, 16 December 2015, WT/MIN(15)/25 (16 December 2015); WTO, Ministerial Conference, Singapore – Ministerial Declaration on Trade in Information Technology Products – Singapore, 13 December 1996, WT/MIN(96)/16 (13 December 1996); the Annex to the Agreement on Trade in Civil Aircraft, www.wto.org/english/docs_e/legal_e/air-79_e .htm. See also Dayong Yu, 'The Harmonized System – Amendments and Their Impact on WTO Members' Schedules', WTO Staff Working Paper No. ERSD-2008-02, 2008, pp. 16–17.

[63] See, for example, Article 22.7.2 and Annex 22A of the New Zealand–UK FTA (2022); Article 3.2 of chapter 17 and Annex 7 of the New Zealand–Chinese Taipei Economic Cooperation Agreement (2013).

expanding the prospective list of environmental goods for tariff elimination'.[64]

In addition to tariffs, green trade is also affected by such non-tariff barriers as quotas, import/export bans, non-automatic import licensing, trade remedies, LCRs and so on. One study identifies over 200 such non-tariff measures in the APEC region affecting the APEC-listed environmental goods.[65] The number becomes higher if wider geography is taken into account. Compared to tariffs, non-tariff barriers are normally harder to track and handle in a product-specific way. Perhaps for this reason, the DDA negotiations carried out only limited work here even though non-tariff barriers were included in the agenda on environmental goods.[66] The APEC and EGA talks have focused on tariffs only. However, tariff liberalization outcomes can be undermined by non-tariff barriers, which will necessitate negotiating efforts in this direction probably after tariffs have been lowered.

Some RTAs specifically regulate environmental non-tariff barriers. The EU's FTAs with Singapore (2018) and Viet Nam (2019) have a separate chapter on 'Non-Tariff Barriers to Trade and Investment in Renewable Energy Generation'. This chapter discourages LCRs and forced partnerships with local companies and requires that TBT measures be based on international standards and that authorization and licensing procedures for equipment and related transmission network infrastructures be objective, non-arbitrary, transparent and non-discriminatory.[67] Many other agreements are less specific. For example, New Zealand's FTAs with the UK (2022) and Chinese Taipei (2013) remain open to address any potential non-tariff barriers, identified by a party, to trade and investment in environmental goods and services.[68]

While RTAs (and IIAs) are certainly meritorious for advancing intra-regional green trade and investment, they cannot substitute for big-group forums. Among the multi-party initiatives discussed above, the APEC has so far been most successful mainly because of the unbinding nature of the tariff reduction commitment and the shortness of the subject list.

64 New Zealand Government, 'Joint Statement: Agreement on Climate Change, Trade and Sustainability (ACCTS) at MC12', 15 June 2022, www.beehive.govt.nz/release/joint-statement-agreement-climate-change-trade-and-sustainability-accts-mc12.

65 Kuriyama, supra note 55, p. 6.

66 See INF/TE/SSD/W/18, supra note 38, paras. 2.60–2.62.

67 See Articles 7.4 and 7.5 of the EU–Singapore FTA (2018); Articles 7.4 and 7.5 of the EU–Viet Nam FTA (2019).

68 See Article 22.7.2(b) of New Zealand–UK FTA (2022); Article 3.2(c) of chapter 17 of the New Zealand–Chinese Taipei Economic Cooperation Agreement (2013).

Since the APEC's soft law normative framework enables smooth consensus-building among its member economies, the APEC should continue its work on furthering green trade liberalization. In addition to the potential expansion of the list of environmental goods, the APEC could also explore the ways of constraining non-tariff barriers to trade and investment in environmental goods and services. Any progress achieved here could then pass through to other forums to evolve to hard law.[69] Indeed, the APEC's 2012 list and related tariff reduction commitment informed the non-APEC discussions and negotiations on environmental goods in the past. The APEC's follow-up activities on promoting green trade could help create necessary momentum for what some suggest: the reactivation of the stalled WTO negotiations on environmental goods[70] or their reframing towards more focus on direct climate change mitigation.[71]

6.2.1.2 The Services Sector

Trade liberalization on environmental goods should proceed in parallel with market openings in relevant services. Indeed, environmental goods and services are mutually complementary: environmental goods often incorporate environmental services content or involve installation, maintenance, monitoring or other services, and the provision of many environmental services necessitates the use of corresponding environmental goods.[72] Moreover, environmental services account for over 65 per cent of the global environmental industry's market value.[73] Thus, the omission of this largest component of the environment industry from the lowering of trade barriers would slow down the adoption and diffusion of environmental goods and technologies.

[69] In the past, some APEC soft law rules contributed to the development of international hard law rules outside the APEC. See Pasha L. Hsieh, 'Reassessing APEC's Role as a Trans-Regional Economic Architecture: Legal and Policy Dimensions', 16 *Journal of International Economic Law* 119 (2013), p. 133.

[70] See, for example, James Bacchus and Inu Manak, 'Free Trade in Environmental Goods Will Increase Access to Green Tech', *Free Trade Bulletin* No. 80, Cato Institute, 2021, pp. 6–8.

[71] See William A. Reinsch, Emily Benson and Catherine Puga, 'Environmental Goods Agreement: A New Frontier or an Old Stalemate?', Centre for Strategic and International Studies, 2021, pp. 15–22.

[72] See WTO, supra note 36, p. 121; Hildegunn Kyvik Nordås and Ronald Steenblik, 'Environmental Services in the APEC Region: Definition, Challenges and Opportunities', APEC Group on Services, 2021, pp. 6–7.

[73] Nora Carina Dihel, 'Understanding Trade in Environmental Services: Key Issues and Prospects', in Olivier Cattaneo et al. (eds.), *International Trade in Services: New Trends and Opportunities for Developing Countries* (Washington, DC: World Bank, 2010), p. 323.

The WTO services classification system (hereinafter 'W/120' as part of the related document's code) distinguishes 'Environmental Services' as a separate sector consisting of 'Sewage services' (Central Product Classification (CPC) 9401), 'Refuse disposal services' (CPC 9402), 'Sanitation and similar services' (CPC 9403) and 'Other' (no CPC code provided).[74] Under CPC Provisional on which the WTO services classification is based, the 'Other' category refers to four sub-sectors (CPC 9404, 9405, 9406 and 9409) as shown in Table 6.2. Among environmental services, so-called infrastructure services (in general, CPC 9401, 9402 and 9403) typically have the characteristics of public goods and are provided mainly by public suppliers to local communities while non-infrastructure services (in general, CPC 9404, 9405, 9406 and 9409) are often supplied on a business-to-business basis to firms that need to comply with environmental standards.[75]

Only 59 (out of 164) WTO members have specific commitments in at least one environmental service (Table 6.2), which makes environmental services one of the least-committed sectors under the GATS.[76] Conversely, 64 per cent of the members remain uncommitted, or essentially free to regulate, under the multilateral trading system. This probably explains why environmental services are among least-traded services in the world,[77] putting additional pressure for greater openness in this segment.

Among environmental service categories, CPC 9402, 9404, 9406 and 9409 appear most relevant to the energy–environment nexus. According to the CPC Provisional description, refuse disposal services (CPC 9402) deal with the collection and disposal of, inter alia, waste from industrial establishments,[78] which can include waste generated by mining and energy processing industries, among others.[79] Cleaning services of exhaust gases (CPC 9404) deal with air pollution control and include

[74] GATT, Uruguay Round – Group of Negotiations on Services – Services Sectoral Classification List – Note by the Secretariat, MTN.GNS/W/120 (10 July 1991).

[75] See WTO, Council for Trade in Services – Background Note on Environmental Services – Note by the Secretariat, S/C/W/320 (20 August 2010), paras. 5–6; WTO, 'Environmental Services', www.wto.org/english/tratop_e/serv_e/environment_e/environment_e.htm.

[76] S/C/W/320, supra note 75, para. 85; WTO, 'Trade in Services: The Most Dynamic Segment of International Trade', 2015, p. 5, www.wto.org/english/thewto_e/20y_e/services_brochure2015_e.pdf.

[77] See WTO, supra note 36, p. 25.

[78] UN Department of International Economic and Social Affairs, 'Provisional Central Product Classification', Statistical Papers, ST/ESA/STAT/SER.M/77, 1991, p. 277.

[79] See S/C/W/320, supra note 75, paras. 13–17.

Table 6.2 *State of play in WTO commitments on environmental services (as of 1 April 2023)*

				Other			
WTO members	Sewage services (CPC 9401)	Refuse disposal services (CPC 9402)	Sanitation and similar services (CPC 9403)	Cleaning services of exhaust gases (CPC 9404)	Noise abatement services (CPC 9405)	Nature and landscape protection services (CPC 9406)	Other environmental protection services not elsewhere classified (CPC 9409)
Afghanistan	X	X	X	X	X	X	
Albania	X	X	X	X	X		
Armenia	X	X	X	X	X	X	
Australia	X	X	X				
Bulgaria	X	X	X	X	X	X	
Cabo Verde	X	X	X	X	X	X	X
Cambodia	X	X	X	X	X	X	X
Canada	X	X	X	X	X	X	X
Central African Republic							X
China	X	X	X	X	X	X	X
Colombia							X
Croatia	X	X	X	X	X	X	X
EU 25	X	X	X	X	X	X	X
Ecuador	X	X	X	X	X	X	X
El Salvador				X	X	X	X
Gambia	X		X				
Georgia	X	X	X	X	X	X	X
Guinea	X		X				
Iceland	X	X	X	X	X	X	X

Israel	X	X	X	X	X		
Japan	X	X	X	X	X	X	X
Jordan			X	X	X		X
Kazakhstan	X	X	X	X	X	X	X
Korea	X	X		X	X	X	X
Kuwait	X	X	X				
Kyrgyz Republic	X	X	X	X	X	X	X
Lao PDR	X	X	X	X	X	X	
Lesotho	X	X	X	X	X	X	
Liberia	X	X	X	X	X	X	X
Liechtenstein	X	X	X	X	X	X	X
Moldova	X	X	X	X	X	X	X
Montenegro	X	X	X	X	X	X	X
Morocco	X	X	X	X	X	X	X
Nepal	X	X	X				
North Macedonia	X	X	X	X	X	X	
Norway	X	X	X	X	X	X	X
Oman	X	X	X	X	X	X	X
Panama				X	X	X	
Qatar	X	X	X	X	X	X	X
Romania				X	X	X	X
Russia	X	X	X	X	X	X	X
Rwanda			X				
Samoa	X	X	X	X	X	X	
Saudi Arabia	X	X	X	X	X	X	X
Seychelles	X	X			X		X
Sierra Leone	X	X	X	X	X	X	X

Table 6.2 (*cont.*)

WTO members	Sewage services (CPC 9401)	Refuse disposal services (CPC 9402)	Sanitation and similar services (CPC 9403)	Other: Cleaning services of exhaust gases (CPC 9404)	Other: Noise abatement services (CPC 9405)	Other: Nature and landscape protection services (CPC 9406)	Other: Other environmental protection services not elsewhere classified (CPC 9409)
South Africa	X	X	X	X	X	X	
Switzerland	X	X	X	X	X	X	X
Chinese Taipei	X	X	X	X	X	X	X
Tajikistan	X	X	X	X	X		X
Thailand	X	X	X	X	X	X	X
Tonga	X	X	X	X	X	X	X
Türkiye	X	X	X				
Ukraine	X	X	X	X	X	X	X
UAE	X	X	X	X	X	X	X
United States	X	X	X	X	X	X	X
Vanuatu	X	X	X				
Viet Nam	X	X		X	X		X
Yemen	X	X	X	X	X	X	
TOTAL (59 members)	52	50	51	48	49	43	39

Source: Author's compilation from data (as of 1 April 2023) at WTO and World Bank, 'I-TIP Services', https://i-tip.wto.org/services/default.aspx.

Note: CPC codes are the codes appearing in the WTO Services Sectoral Classification List (MTN.GNS/W/120, 10 July 1991) and CPC Provisional.

'[e]mission monitoring and control services of pollutants into the air, whether from mobile or stationary sources, mostly caused by the burning of fossil fuels' as well as '[c]oncentration monitoring, control and reduction services of pollutants in ambient air, especially in urban areas'.[80] Nature and landscape protection services (CPC 9406), as explained in CPC Provisional, include, inter alia, ecosystem protection services and services consisting in studies on the environment–climate interrelationship. For example, these could be services of restoring former mining sites after remediation to revive the surrounding biodiversity and landscape.[81] As for remediation services per se, they are not separately categorized in the W/120 list and CPC Provisional[82] and may fall within CPC 9409 if national schedules of commitments do not provide otherwise.[83]

Since its adoption in 1991, the W/120 classification system has never been updated, inviting sound criticism about the obsoleteness of the environmental services list.[84] For example, the up-to-date CPC Ver. 2.1 classification explicitly distinguishes remediation services (and their subclasses) – services aimed to 'eliminate or contain any existing contamination of the soil, water or air' caused by operation of facilities or accidents – as a sub-sector of environmental services (CPC Ver. 2.1, 944).[85] It also segregates waste management services (CPC Ver. 2.1, 942 and 943) into various sub-classes, making distinction between hazardous and non-hazardous waste.[86] Moreover, there is a separate category of 'environmental consulting services' (CPC Ver. 2.1, 83931) comprising environmental assessments, environmental audits, site remediation planning services, evaluation of environmental studies and so on.[87] Ideally, regular adjustments to services classification in GATS national schedules in line with UN CPC updates and without changing the inscribed commitments would bring more certainty to traders and investors. But such

80 ST/ESA/STAT/SER.M/77, supra note 78, p. 277.

81 S/C/W/320, supra note 75, para. 39.

82 Ibid., para. 42.

83 In some WTO members' schedules, remediation and clean-up of soil and water is included in CPC 9406. See, for example, GATS/SC/154 (Kazakhstan), supra note 10; WTO, Trade in Services – Lao PDR – Schedule of Specific Commitments, GATS/SC/150 (22 April 2013).

84 S/C/W/320, supra note 75, para. 49.

85 UN Department of Economic and Social Affairs, 'Central Product Classification (CPC) Version 2.1', Statistical Papers, ST/ESA/STAT/SER.M/77/Ver.2.1, 2015, pp. 559–560.

86 Ibid., pp. 556–559.

87 Ibid., p. 491.

adjustments in services schedules have never happened, which contrasts with the periodic HS modification in WTO goods schedules based on HS updates. The outdated W/120 classification can, of course, be stretched to changing realities via 'adaptive' interpretation techniques, but this would essentially require case-by-case clarification through adjudication.[88]

As the W/120 list remains 'frozen' in the early 1990s, technological advances affecting services can give rise to a highly controversial issue of proper classification of services under the WTO system.[89] It is not always clear-cut whether a recently emerged service is a completely 'new' service uncaptured by W/120 or just a modified version of an 'old' service. Take smart grid services as an example. According to the IEA, a smart grid is 'an electricity network that uses digital and other advanced technologies to monitor and manage the transport of electricity from all generation sources to meet the varying electricity demands of end-users'. It improves demand response and energy efficiency, integrates variable renewable energy resources and electric vehicle recharging services, reduces peak demand and stabilizes the electricity system.[90] Smart grid services cut across several W/120 sectors, such as telecommunication services, computer services and services incidental to energy distribution.[91] Another example is carbon capture, utilization and storage that consists of: capturing CO_2 from power stations, industrial facilities or directly from the air; transporting compressed CO_2 from the point of capture to the point of use or storage; using captured CO_2 as an input to create products or services; and storing CO_2 into underground geological formations (e.g., depleted oil and gas reservoirs).[92] These activities include certain business services and transport services at least.[93] None of these examples of 'complex' services is listed in W/120.

88 See Sherzod Shadikhodjaev, 'Technological Neutrality and Regulation of Digital Trade: How Far Can We Go?', 32 *European Journal of International Law* 1221 (2021), pp. 1226–1229, 1244–1245.

89 See UN Department of Economic and Social Affairs, 'New Issues Requiring Guidance in the Central Product Classification (CPC)', Meeting of the Expert Group on International Statistical Classifications, New York, 19–22 May 2015, ESA/STAT/AC.289/20 (12 May 2015).

90 IEA, 'Technology Roadmap: Smart Grids', 2011, pp. 5–6, www.iea.org/reports/technology-roadmap-smart-grids.

91 ESA/STAT/AC.289/20, supra note 89, para. 1.21.

92 IEA, 'Legal and Regulatory Frameworks for CCUS: An IEA CCUS Handbook', 2022, pp. 9–10.

93 See ESA/STAT/AC.289/20, supra note 89, para. 1.17.

WTO case law provides some guidance on the legal characterization of services with controversial status. First, the fact that an already existing service is being supplied through new technology-enabled ways will not necessarily make it a 'new' service. Indeed, the panel in *US – Gambling* held that mode 1 (cross-border supply) under the GATS encompassed 'all possible means of supplying services' (whether offline or online) in accordance with the principle of 'technological neutrality' that 'seems to be largely shared among WTO Members'.[94] Second, from the panel decision in *China – Electronic Payment Services* it follows that where component services, as combined together, result in 'a new and distinct service' being supplied and consumed as such, such an 'integrated service' should be classified under a relevant single service sub-sector.[95] It could be a sub-sector to which none of the component services belongs or a sub-sector of one of the component services. In this connection, CPC Provisional, which has 'potential value in assisting the interpretation of GATS schedules',[96] suggests selecting a sub-sector that gives the service at issue its 'essential character'.[97] However, if a sub-sector to which an integrated service can be linked does not exist yet, the integrated service can qualify as a genuinely 'new' service.

Among four modes of supply, mode 3 (commercial presence) is the predominant way of supplying foreign environmental services in the host country.[98] Mode 3 has not been left totally unbound in environmental services listed in the GATS schedules. On average, 57 per cent of mode 3 commitments in this sector are full commitments, meaning that there are no limitations inscribed on market access and national treatment.[99] The remaining commitments here envisage partial restrictions on FDIs, such as certain numerical quotas, joint-venture and incorporation requirements, economic needs tests, licensing requirements, foreign capital limitations and so on.[100] Some members have reserved room for

[94] *US – Gambling*, WTO Panel Report, para. 6.285. See Shadikhodjaev, supra note 88.

[95] *China – Electronic Payment Services*, WTO Panel Report, paras. 7.188, 7.198.

[96] *China – Publications and Audiovisual Products*, WTO Panel Report, para. 7.923.

[97] ST/ESA/STAT/SER.M/77, supra note 78, p. 20 (stating '[c]omposite services consisting of a combination of different services which cannot be classified by reference to 1(a) shall be classified as if they consisted of the service which gives them their essential character, in so far as this criterion is applicable'). Almost the same remark on composite services appears in ST/ESA/STAT/SER.M/77/Ver.2.1, supra note 85, p. 15 (para. 56).

[98] INF/TE/SSD/W/18, supra note 38, para. 2.74.

[99] Ibid., para. 2.90.

[100] S/C/W/320, supra note 75, paras. 100–101.

monopolies. For instance, Norway's schedule states that the '[g]overnment owned monopoly for control services of exhaust-gas from cars and trucks', and such services 'must be offered on a non-profit basis'.[101] These are the examples of restrictions that the relevant committing members can legally impose as per their schedule of commitments. In addition, since most WTO members did not include environmental services in their schedules, they secured substantial leeway for regulating this sector and its FDIs.

The WTO negotiations on environmental services have taken place since 2000 as part of the original GATS built-in agenda and then the DDA, but with no result finalized. Environmental services are also part of the ongoing TESSD and IDP discussions.[102] Since 2019, the Special Session of the Council for Trade in Services has conducted 'exploratory discussions' on members' current areas of interest in relation to environmental services without prejudice to their negotiating positions.[103] In this context, a communication (2022) of a group of members reiterated the idea (known since 2000) of broadening the scope of negotiations to also include so-called *environment-related* services so as to better capture all services dealing with climate change, carbon emissions and other environmental issues.[104] Environment-related services are not necessarily environmental in nature but have environmental end-uses or serve environmental purposes.[105] They are scattered across the board, unlike environmental services that are categorized as a single sector. The 2022 communication above identified such environment-related services as professional (engineering and architectural) services; construction services; distribution services; consulting services; maintenance, repair and recycling services; and other services (transportation, storage, R&D, technical testing and analysis services and so on).[106] For example, the

[101] GATS/SC/66 (Norway), supra note 10.

[102] See WT/MIN(21)/6/Rev.2, supra note 44; WT/MIN(21)/8/Rev.2, supra note 45.

[103] WTO, 'WTO Members Engage in Exploratory Talks on Market Access for Environmental Services', 30 September 2019, www.wto.org/english/news_e/news19_e/serv_30sep19_e.htm. For the proposal to launch WTO exploratory discussions on market access across services, see WTO, Council for Trade in Services – Special Session – Communication from Chile, Mexico, New Zealand and Panama – Exploratory Discussions on Market Access, JOB/SERV/282 (13 June 2018).

[104] WTO, Council for Trade in Services – Special Session – Communication from Australia, Canada, the EU, the Republic of Korea, Mexico, New Zealand, Norway, Switzerland and the UK – Exploratory Discussions on Market Access: Environmental Services – Revision, JOB/SERV/299/Rev.4 (21 July 2022), section 1.

[105] See S/C/W/320, supra note 75, paras. 50–51.

[106] JOB/SERV/299/Rev.4, supra note 104, section 2.

generation, transmission, distribution and sale of renewable electricity is associated with services related to the financing, planning, design, engineering, construction, operation and maintenance of equipment, energy distribution, training and others.[107] Typical barriers here include LCRs (e.g., use of local labour), investment restrictions (e.g., prescribed forms of legal entities, ownership restrictions, foreign equity limits or economic needs tests), technology transfer obligations and cumbersome or opaque approval and licensing procedures, among others.[108]

Because of the broad scope of environment-related services, not all members would wish to undertake market openings across several sectors. In order to focus on environmentally desirable activities of otherwise 'multi-use' services, members could include, say, sectoral headnotes, footnotes or reservations in their schedules limiting their commitments to such activities.[109] Similar to the project approach for environmental goods above, they could also negotiate lists of specific environmental projects or activities so as to lower trade barriers to associated services supplied. Alternatively, they may also include environmental ex-outs for scheduled services. In 2021, the APEC ministers endorsed a non-binding and non-exhaustive 'reference list' of environmental and environment-related services which already adopts this approach by adding ex-outs where necessary.[110]

With respect to preferential trade rules, at least 16 RTAs contain provisions on environmental services (typically best endeavour provisions on promoting trade and investment in environmental services), and at least 101 RTAs include specific commitments on trade liberalization in environmental services, with some also containing reservations (i.e., secured trade restrictions) for maintaining a public monopoly, nationality requirements, concession requirements or a commercial presence obligation.[111] Interestingly, 'environmental services' under the New

107 See US International Trade Commission, 'Renewable Energy and Related Services: Recent Developments', Investigation No. 332-534, USITC Publication 4421, 2013, pp. 2-12–2-13.

108 See ibid., pp. 2-21–2-22, 4-26.

109 For the GATS scheduling practice of limiting the scope of environmental (sub-)services or related commitments, see S/C/W/320, supra note 75, paras. 89–93.

110 APEC, 'Annex 2 – Reference List of Environmental and Environmentally Related Services', endorsed by the '2021 APEC Ministerial Meeting', supra note 56. See also Nordås and Steenblik, supra note 72, pp. 68–71.

111 José-Antonio Monteiro, 'Typology of Environment-Related Provisions in Regional Trade Agreements', WTO Working Paper No. ERSD-2016-13, 2016, pp. 57, 59–60. See also Christophe Bellmann and Alena Bulatnikova, 'Incorporating Environmental Provisions in Regional Trade Agreements in Chapters and Articles Dealing with Trade

Zealand–Chinese Taipei Economic Cooperation Agreement (2013) are not limited to the W/120 or the CPC Provisional classification but also include services 'directly related to the investment, sale, delivery or installation' of 132 environmental goods listed in the annex.[112] In other words, this definition, accompanying the parties' commitment to facilitate the movement of business persons involved in the supply of environmental services, determines environmental services based on, inter alia, how closely they are linked to environmental goods, thereby reinforcing mutual complementarity of goods and services in this field.

6.2.2 *Technology Transfer*

In the WTO negotiations above, developing country members have stressed the importance of transfer of technology as a means of enhancing their environmental industries.[113] One may expect that freer trade in environmental goods and services would improve access to embedded technologies and create a more conducive climate for technology transfer.

Broadly speaking, technology transfer represents a series of processes of sharing and acquisition of certain ideas, knowledge, technology and skills between a provider and a recipient.[114] International technology transfers occur roughly in four stages: (i) a cross-border passage of a technology, (ii) the recipient's learning of the know-how and know-why of the technology, (iii) adaptation of the foreign technology to local conditions and (iv) diffusion, or spread, of the new technology within the receiving country.[115] Technologies cross countries through technology owners' sales abroad against licensing fees or royalties, trade in technology-embedding goods and services, FDIs and movements of

in Services', OECD Trade and Environment Working Paper No. 2022/01, OECD, 2022, pp. 29–31.

[112] Article 3.2(b), footnote 14, of chapter 17 and Annex 7 of the New Zealand–Chinese Taipei Economic Cooperation Agreement (2013).

[113] INF/TE/SSD/W/18, supra note 38, para. 2.69.

[114] See WIPO, 'Transfer of Technology', Standing Committee on the Law of Patents, Fourteenth Session (Geneva, 25–29 January 2010), SCP/14/4 REV.2 (26 October 2011), para. 19.

[115] WTO, Working Group on Trade and Transfer of Technology – A Taxonomy on Country Experiences on International Technology Transfers – Note by the Secretariat, WT/WGTTT/W/3 (11 November 2002), para. 4.

people with technology-related knowledge and skills.[116] The transfer of green technologies is similar to 'general' technology transfers in many aspects, but it is more dependent on public funding.[117]

In *Indonesia – Autos*, Indonesia said that to develop a national car under a government-promoted programme, a local automobile company chose to partner with Korea's Kia for 'one reason only': Kia, unlike other foreign companies, was 'willing to transfer technology (including production technology and training)'. The local company had also a technical services arrangement with Kia.[118] Indonesia's case here largely echoes what the literature suggests: trade and foreign investments (especially FDIs) can facilitate not only the cross-border movement of 'hardware' technologies and equipment but also the delivery of a 'package' of such hardware elements together with the related 'software' components, notably services, know-how, skills and experience.[119]

6.2.2.1 International Rule-Making Developments

The issue of transferring green technologies has been on the world policymaking agenda since the 1970s. The beginning of international discussions on this issue coincides with the time when developing countries pushed for creating a New International Economic Order to ensure, inter alia, the equitable sharing of the benefits of technological progress within the global community.[120]

The 1972 Declaration of the UN Conference on the Human Environment sets out twenty-six principles for addressing environmental issues.[121] Principle 20 states that scientific research and development on environmental problems 'must be promoted in all countries, especially the developing countries', and 'environmental technologies should be made available to developing countries on terms which would encourage

116 Sébastien Miroudot, 'The Linkages between Open Services Markets and Technology Transfer', OECD Trade Policy Working Paper No. 29, TD/TC/WP(2005)9/FINAL, 2006, para. 11 (pp. 8–9).

117 Cristina Tébar Less and Steven McMillan, 'Achieving the Successful Transfer of Environmentally Sound Technologies: Trade-Related Aspects', OECD Trade and Environment Working Paper No. 2005-2, COM/ENV/TD(2004)33/FINAL, 2005, pp. 7–8.

118 *Indonesia – Autos*, WTO Panel Report, paras. 7.94, 7.97–7.98.

119 Less and McMillan, supra note 117, pp. 9–13.

120 See UN, 'Declaration on the Establishment of a New International Economic Order', UN General Assembly Resolution A/RES/S-6/3201 (1 May 1974).

121 See UN, 'United Nations Conference on the Human Environment, 5–16 June 1972, Stockholm', www.un.org/en/conferences/environment/stockholm1972.

their wide dissemination without constituting an economic burden on the developing countries'.

As a next important development, international negotiations (1976–1985) under the auspices of the UNCTAD produced, but failed to adopt, a Draft International Code of Conduct on the Transfer of Technology.[122] In pursuit of the objective to 'establish general and equitable standards' as a basis of the relationships among technology-transfer parties and governments concerned, the draft code contained detailed provisions on the guiding principles, national regulation of transfer of technology transactions, restrictive business practices, responsibilities and obligations of technology-transfer parties, special treatment of developing countries, international collaboration and the institutional machinery.[123] The scope was comprehensive enough to extend to the environmental domain. The draft code eventually could not garner broad support because developed countries opposed the very idea of controlling external commercial activities of their multinational companies. Even developing countries became less insistent as they relaxed investor performance requirements in response to the debt crisis and a sharp decline in foreign investment in the late 1970s and early 1980s.[124] Despite its non-adoption, the draft code set a 'high benchmark for a model of provisions espousing the "regulatory" approach to technology transfer'[125] that could be taken into account in subsequent international rule-making on this matter.

Further, chapter 34 of Agenda 21 (1992) calls for the transfer of 'environmentally sound technologies', that is, those that 'protect the environment, are less polluting, use all resources in a more sustainable manner, recycle more of their wastes and products, and handle residual wastes in a more acceptable manner than the technologies for which they

[122] See, for example, Pedro Roffe, 'UNCTAD: Code of Conduct for the Transfer of Technology – Progress and Issues under Negotiation', 14 *Journal of World Trade Law* 160 (1980).

[123] For the 1985 version, see WTO, Working Group on the Relationship between Trade and Investment – Communication from UNCTAD – The Draft United Nations Code of Conduct on Transnational Corporations and the OECD Guidelines for Multinational Enterprises, WT/WGTI/W/52 (21 August 1998), Annex 4.

[124] Wei Zhuang, *Intellectual Property Rights and Climate Change: Interpreting the TRIPS Agreement for Environmentally Sound Technologies* (Cambridge: Cambridge University Press, 2017), p. 59.

[125] UNCTAD, 'Transfer of Technology', UNCTAD Series on Issues in International Investment Agreement, 2001, p. 52.

were substitutes'.[126] In the context of pollution, such technologies are '"process and product technologies" that generate low or no waste, for the prevention of pollution' and also include '"end of the pipe" technologies for treatment of pollution after it has been generated'.[127] Importantly, environmentally sound technologies are not confined to 'individual technologies' only but also cover 'total systems which include know-how, procedures, goods and services, and equipment as well as organizational and managerial procedures'.[128]

Under the UNFCCC (1992), contracting parties committed to promote and cooperate in technology transfer regarding emission control (Article 4.1(c)) and fully consider 'the specific needs and special situations' of LDCs in their technology transfer actions (Article 4.9). Developed countries committed to promote, facilitate and finance the transfer of green technologies to developing countries (Articles 4.3 and 4.5). The Paris Agreement (2015) urges the parties to 'strengthen cooperative action on technology development and transfer' (Article 10.2). The UNFCCC Technology Mechanism, established in 2010 and currently guided by the Paris Agreement's Technology Framework, has addressed policy issues and implementation actions (such as technical assistance to developing countries) related to climate technology development and transfer.[129] Apart from the climate treaties, technology transfer provisions are also scattered across other multilateral environmental agreements regarding the ozone layer, transboundary movements of hazardous wastes, biological diversity and so on.[130]

It is not a mere coincidence that the international rule-making above has sought to address the technological divide between the Global North and the Global South. Empirical studies suggest that the development of green technologies is largely concentrated in developed countries and that such technologies are transferred mainly between developed countries and relatively rarely to developing countries, especially LDCs.[131]

126 UN Conference on Environment & Development (1992), Agenda 21, para. 34.1.

127 Ibid., para. 34.2.

128 Ibid., para. 34.3.

129 See UNFCCC, 'What Is Technology Development and Transfer?', https://unfccc.int/topics/climate-technology/the-big-picture/what-is-technology-development-and-transfer; Stephen Minas, 'The Paris Agreement's Technology Framework and the Need for "Transformational Change"', 2020(4) *Carbon & Climate Law Review* 241 (2020).

130 See UNCTAD, 'Compendium of International Arrangements on Transfer of Technology: Selected Instruments', UNCTAD/ITE/IPC/Misc.5 (2001).

131 See Zhuang, supra note 124, pp. 32–38.

Such asymmetry in cross-border movements can be explained with different North–South portions in the sectoral composition of trade. Compared to inter-industry trade, intra-industry trade plays a greater role in transferring technology because countries tend to absorb foreign technologies more willingly when imports of technologies are from the same sectors as their production and export sectors.[132] But intra-industry trade is more pervasive among developed countries while inter-industry trade is more prominent between developed and developing countries.[133]

Under normal market conditions, technology transfers would occur on a voluntary basis. But if foreign firms are compelled to share their proprietary technologies in exchange for market access or business opportunities, this may run counter to international economic law as discussed below. Ideally, the rigidity of trade and investment law restrictions on forced technology transfers should correspond to the level of technological development of a technology-receiving country, by being strict towards technologically competitive countries and lenient towards less advanced countries.[134] Such a customized approach seems realizable under bilateral/regional trade and investment treaties in principle but more difficult in the WTO mainly because of its current general practice of treating developing countries (other than LDCs) as one group without further segregation.

6.2.2.2 WTO Law

WTO rules on technology transfer apply to energy and non-energy sectors alike although accession documents and market access schedules can introduce energy-specific elements. The technology transfer rules are especially discernible in the fields of product standards, services and intellectual property rights. Most of them are development-oriented, albeit largely 'best endeavours',[135] provisions that:

[132] Dalia Hakura and Florence Jaumotte, 'The Role of Inter- and Intraindustry Trade in Technology Diffusion', IMF Working Paper No. WP/99/58 (1999).

[133] Less and McMillan, supra note 117, p. 9.

[134] See Julia Ya Qin, 'Forced Technology Transfer and the US–China Trade War: Implications for International Economic Law', 22 *Journal of International Economic Law* 743 (2019), pp. 758–759.

[135] WTO, Working Group on Trade and Transfer of Technology – Provisions Relating to Transfer of Technology in WTO Agreements – Communication from Cuba, Egypt, Honduras, India, Indonesia, Jamaica, Kenya, Mauritius, Pakistan and Zimbabwe – Revision, WT/WGTTT/3/Rev.1 (21 October 2002).

- recognize international standardization's contribution to 'the transfer of technology from developed to developing countries' (preamble of the TBT Agreement);
- concern technical assistance on standards (Article 9 of the SPS Agreement; Article 11 of the TBT Agreement);
- call for technical cooperation on technology transfer to LDCs in telecommunications services (paragraph 6(d) of the GATS Annex on Telecommunications);
- encourage increasing participation of developing countries in services trade 'through access to technology on a commercial basis' (Article IV:1 of the GATS) and access to certain technology-related information via developed countries' contact points (Article IV:2 of the GATS);
- oblige developed countries to 'provide incentives to enterprises and institutions in their territories for the purpose of promoting and encouraging technology transfer to least-developed country Members in order to enable them to create a sound and viable technological base' (Article 66.2 of the TRIPS Agreement).[136]

Article 66.2 of the TRIPS Agreement on incentives for technology transfer to LDCs is supplemented by developed countries' obligation, introduced in 2003, to annually report on their actions of implementing Article 66.2 by providing new detailed reports every third year and updates in the intervening years to be reviewed by the WTO Council for TRIPS.[137] Since 2003, an average of seventeen members have reported their actions each year.[138] Among other things, the reported measures included financial incentives and non-financial incentives (e.g., advisory services, training and technical assistance) channelled from governments directly or through international institutions, for example, as part of official development assistance and concerned, inter alia, renewable energy, energy efficiency, energy conservation, emission control and nuclear technologies.[139] While being a positive step towards

[136] This commitment of developed country members was reaffirmed in WTO, Ministerial Conference – Fourth Session – Doha, 9–14 November 2001 – Declaration on the TRIPS Agreement and Public Health – Adopted on 14 November 2001, WT/MIN(01)/DEC/2 (20 November 2001), para. 7.

[137] WTO, Council for TRIPS – Implementation of Article 66.2 of the TRIPS Agreement – Decision of the Council for TRIPS of 19 February 2003, IP/C/28 (20 February 2003).

[138] WTO, Council for TRIPS – Annual Report on Notifications and Other Information Flows – Note by the Secretariat – Revision, IP/C/W/687/Rev.1 (7 March 2022), para. 46.

[139] See, for example, WTO, Council for TRIPS – Report on the Implementation of Article 66.2 of the TRIPS Agreement – EU – Addendum, IP/C/W/656/Add.5 (6 February 2020);

increasing transparency, this mechanism of monitoring the implementation of Article 66.2, albeit evolving, is yet far from effectively showing the level of compliance by developed countries with their Article 66.2 obligation.[140] It could be said that the absence of a clear definition of 'incentives' and 'technology transfer' under Article 66.2 gives developed countries some room to avoid providing substantive incentives and concrete details in their reports.[141] However, such a definitional gap in the text of Article 66.2 may also give them discretion in providing relevant incentives in a way not violating the SCM Agreement and especially the ban of export subsidies. Indeed, the SCM Agreement does not make an exception for the Article 66.2 incentives,[142] so developed country members have to simultaneously comply with their SCM and TRIPS obligations in a mutually harmonious manner.

In addition, the TRIPS Agreement references technology transfer in a broader, not development-specific, context. Article 7 specifying the objectives of the agreement says that the intellectual property regime 'should contribute to the promotion of technological innovation and to the transfer and dissemination of technology, to the mutual advantage of producers and users of technological knowledge and in a manner conducive to social and economic welfare, and to a balance of rights and

WTO, Council for TRIPS – Report on the Implementation of Article 66.2 of the TRIPS Agreement – New Zealand – Addendum, IP/C/W/656/Add.7 (4 February 2020); WTO, Council for TRIPS – Report on the Implementation of Article 66.2 of the TRIPS Agreement – Australia – Addendum, IP/C/W/656/Add.3 (10 October 2019); WTO, Council for TRIPS – Report on the Implementation of Article 66.2 of the TRIPS Agreement – Canada – Addendum, IP/C/W/656/Add.4 (10 October 2019); WTO, Council for TRIPS – Report on the Implementation of Article 66.2 of the TRIPS Agreement – Norway – Addendum, IP/C/W/656/Add.6 (10 October 2019); WTO, Council for TRIPS – Report on the Implementation of Article 66.2 of the TRIPS Agreement – Switzerland, IP/C/W/656 (27 September 2019). The most recent reports use the code 'IP/C/R/TTI/[Member]/'.

140 See Jayashree Watal and Leticia Caminero, 'Least-Developed Countries, Transfer of Technology and the TRIPS Agreement', WTO Staff Working Paper No. ERSD-2018-01 (2018), pp. 12–25.

141 See ibid., p. 23 (citing the absence of a common understanding of 'transfer of technology' and 'incentives' and noting in this context that developed countries' Article 66.2 reports in 2003–2004 focused on capacity building programmes for LDC government officials (rather than incentives to their domestic enterprises) as the developed countries considered these programmes to be an instrument of improving the enabling environment in LDCs for technology transfer).

142 See Matthew Kennedy, *WTO Dispute Settlement and the TRIPS Agreement: Applying Intellectual Property Standards in a Trade Law Framework* (Cambridge: Cambridge University Press, 2016), p. 275. See also Section 3.2.4.2.

obligations'. Article 8.2 on principles admits that appropriate measures 'may be needed to prevent the abuse of intellectual property rights by right holders or the resort to practices which unreasonably restrain trade or adversely affect the international transfer of technology'. Similarly, Article 40 acknowledges that some anti-competitive licensing practices and conditions concerning intellectual property rights 'may impede the transfer and dissemination of technology' and allows members to take preventive or controlling measures.

When China acceded to the WTO, it committed not to force foreign technology to be transferred into the country. The EU in the non-adjudicated *China – Certain Measures on the Transfer of Technology* case took issue with China's alleged practices of conditioning the approval of foreign investments upon compliance with performance requirements regarding technology transfer and the conduct of R&D in China. The EU complained that China's new energy vehicle regulation mandated 'the transfer of technology, software, tools and equipment to the joint ventures in China' in violation of its WTO Accession Protocol that states in relevant part:[143]

> Without prejudice to the relevant provisions of this Protocol, China shall ensure that the distribution of import licences, quotas, tariff-rate quotas, or any other means of approval for importation, the right of importation or investment by national and sub-national authorities, is not conditioned on: whether competing domestic suppliers of such products exist; or performance requirements of *any* kind, such as local content, offsets, the *transfer of technology*, export performance or the conduct of research and development in China.[144]

China subsequently promulgated a new Foreign Investment Law, effective as of 1 January 2020, to explicitly prohibit forced technology transfer,[145] which may be the reason for this dispute not to proceed to the panel stage.

Further, the *US – Tariff Measures (China)* case checked whether trade restrictions imposed in reaction to forced technology transfer abroad

143 WTO, *China – Certain Measures on the Transfer of Technology* – Request for Consultations by the EU – Revision, WT/DS549/1/Rev.1, G/L/1244/Rev.1, IP/D/39/Rev.1 (8 January 2019), pp. 1, 6–7.

144 WTO, Accession of the People's Republic of China – Decision of 10 November 2001, WT/L/432 (23 November 2001), section 7.3 in part I (emphasis added). See also WTO, Working Party on the Accession of China – Report of the Working Party on the Accession of China, WT/ACC/CHN/49 (1 October 2001), para. 203.

145 Qin, supra note 134, p. 750.

could avail the WTO public morals exception. There, the United States contended that its discriminatory additional duties on Chinese products addressed China's 'state-sanctioned theft and misappropriation of U.S. technology, intellectual properly, and commercial secrets'.[146] Invoking Article XX(a) of the GATT, it also claimed that the duties at issue protected the 'public morals' prevailing in the United States, namely US standards of right and wrong, by countering China's practices of 'coercion and subterfuge to steal or otherwise improperly acquire intellectual property, trade secrets, technology, and confidential business information from U.S. companies with the aim of advantaging Chinese companies'.[147] While agreeing that such standards of right and wrong could fall within 'public morals' at least conceptually, the panel concluded that the United States had failed to substantiate how the additional duties contributed to the protection of the public morals claimed.[148] Although the panel opted not to consider a controversial issue of whether Article XX(a) defence was available to illegal trade measures pertaining to only morally offensive products (rather than products of choice), it noted:

> In the Panel's view, the scope of Article XX(a) is intrinsically limited and is circumscribed, *first*, by the determination of the specific content of the public morals that the responding Member wishes to protect, and, *second*, by the requirement that the measure a Member has chosen can be demonstrated to be *necessary* to the achievement of this public morals objective. In other words, even assuming, *arguendo*, that a measure does not have to only apply to products that are considered to embody morally offensive conduct to be justified under Article XX(a), the respondent still has to demonstrate that the measure it chose (in this case, additional duties on a wide range of products from China) is apt to contribute to protecting public morals concerns, by establishing the relevant nexus, and also that such measures do not go beyond what is necessary within the meaning of Article XX(a).[149]

Given Article XX(a)'s silence on the product coverage and varying public moral contexts in each case, the statement above seems to admit justifiability of measures that counter 'immoral' technology transfers through limiting trade even in products unrelated to this 'immoral' conduct. But for this, the imposing member must persuasively explain

[146] *US – Tariff Measures (China)*, WTO Panel Report, paras. 7.98, 7.100.
[147] Ibid., para. 7.128.
[148] Ibid., paras. 7.215, 7.227, 7.229–7.231.
[149] Ibid., para. 7.179 (emphasis in original).

how the selection of such unrelated products serves the Article XX (a) purpose.

Institutionally, the WTO Working Group on Trade and Transfer of Technology, established by the 2001 Doha Ministerial Declaration, has served as an avenue for the examination of 'the relationship between trade and transfer of technology, and of any possible recommendations on steps that might be taken within the mandate of the WTO to increase flows of technology to developing countries'.[150] While this has been a useful channel for discussing the existing practices, studies and members' submissions regarding technology transfer, the progress on improving the status quo is rather limited. At a minimum, the WTO Secretariat should create a dedicated webpage on technology transfer and relevant data.[151] The inclusion of detailed information on low-carbon and clean energy technologies and related practices could provide a clearer picture of the current state of play. In turn, this could further discussions on how to better promote the transfer of green technologies through the available resources (e.g., technical assistance and the Aid for Trade system) or possible legal reforms. In the DDA negotiations on environmental goods and services, some developing country members even proposed creating a financing mechanism for the transfer of green technologies.[152]

6.2.2.3 Non-WTO Trade Agreements

With respect to technology transfer in general, RTA provisions mostly concern the protection of intellectual property rights and bilateral cooperation and exchanges.[153] The intellectual property chapter of the

[150] WTO, Ministerial Conference – Fourth Session – Doha, 9–14 November 2001 – Ministerial Declaration – Adopted on 14 November 2001, WT/MIN(01)/DEC/1 (20 November 2001), para. 37; WTO, Ministerial Conference – Sixth Session – Hong Kong, 13–18 December 2005 – Doha Work Programme – Ministerial Declaration – Adopted on 18 December 2005, WT/MIN(05)/DEC (22 December 2005), para. 43.

[151] See, for example, WTO, Working Group on Trade and Transfer of Technology – Report 2021 of the Working Group on Trade and Transfer of Technology to the General Council, WT/WGTTT/23 (5 November 2021), para. 3.2; WTO, Report (2008) of the Working Group on Trade and Transfer of Technology to the General Council, WT/WGTTT/10 (11 December 2008), para. 19.

[152] See, for example, WTO, Committee on Trade and Environment – Special Session – WTO Negotiations on Environmental Goods and Services – Addressing the Development Dimension for a 'Triple-Win' Outcome – Communication from China and India, TN/TE/W/79 (15 April 2011), paras. 13–15.

[153] See, for example, Articles 15.5.6 and 15.10 of the Korea–Colombia FTA (2013); Articles 196.3, 197.6 and 255 of the EU–Colombia–Peru Trade Agreement (2012); Articles

Korea–China FTA (2015) is noteworthy for urging cooperation specifically on 'technology transfer on energy-saving and green technologies'.[154]

Relevant provisions of the ECT (1994) are contained in Parts II ('Commerce') and IV ('Miscellaneous Provisions'). Article 8 ('Transfer of Technology') in Part II spells out the agreement of parties to 'promote access to and transfer of energy technology on a commercial and non-discriminatory basis' and their corresponding obligation to 'eliminate existing and create no new obstacles to the transfer of technology in the field of Energy Materials and Products and related equipment and services, subject to non-proliferation and other international obligations'. Further, Article 19(1)(h) in Part IV states that the parties 'shall … encourage favourable conditions for the transfer and dissemination of [energy efficient and environmentally sound] technologies consistent with the adequate and effective protection of Intellectual Property rights'.[155]

In addition, the Energy Charter Protocol on Energy Efficiency and Related Environmental Aspects (1994) introduces a 'principle' that the parties must establish energy efficiency policies and legal frameworks promoting 'dissemination and transfer of technologies' (Article 3(2)(e) of the protocol). It also provides for international cooperation on technology transfer (Article 9 and the Annex).

6.2.2.4 International Investment Regulation

Like the trade rules above, international investment law acknowledges (or at least does not deny) the importance of technology transfer for host countries and is generally negative towards forced technology transfers. The international instruments on CSR, such as the UN Global Compact (2000) and the OECD Guidelines for Multinational Enterprises (1976), referenced in many IIAs, encourage (but do not compel) the transfer and diffusion by enterprises of environmentally friendly technologies.[156] Many IIAs qualify State-imposed technology transfer obligations as an illegal performance requirement. By way of illustration, Article 10.6 ('Prohibition of Performance Requirements') of the Regional Comprehensive Economic Partnership Agreement (2020) reads:

12.10.4(d) and 13.3(m) of the Korea–Viet Nam FTA (2015); Article 54(h) of the EU–Armenia Comprehensive and Enhanced Partnership Agreement (2017).

154 Article 15.30(d)(iii) of the Korea–China FTA (2015).

155 A similar provision is also included in the energy chapter, notably Article 93.2(b), of the Japan–Brunei Economic Partnership Agreement (2007).

156 See Principle 9 of the UN Global Compact (2000); chapter IX ('Science and Technology') of the OECD Guidelines for Multinational Enterprises (1976).

1. No Party shall impose or enforce, as a condition for establishment, acquisition, expansion, management, conduct, operation, or sale or other disposition of an investment in its territory of an investor of any other Party, any of the following requirements: [footnote omitted]

...

(f) to transfer a particular technology, a production process, or other proprietary knowledge to a person in its territory;

However, unlike many IIAs, the USMCA (2018) excludes measures 'necessary to protect human, animal or plant life or health' or 'related to the conservation of living or non-living exhaustible natural resources' from the prohibition on forced technology transfer, subject to the *chapeau* requirements formulated similarly to Article XX of the GATT.[157] The NAFTA (1992), the predecessor of the USMCA, stated that a 'measure that requires an investment to use a technology to meet generally applicable health, safety or environmental requirements shall not be construed to be inconsistent with' the ban on forced technology transfer.[158] This language was not carried over to the USMCA but was incorporated into the Canada–Guinea BIT (2015),[159] for instance.

As part of approval conditions, host countries may require FDIs to be established in the form of joint ventures. An underlying rationale is to facilitate the transfer of (green) technologies and know-how from foreign investors to domestic partners. However, economists caution that a joint venture requirement may actually induce the transfer of out-of-date (rather than advanced) technologies, put joint enterprises at a higher risk of failure than wholly owned subsidiaries, discourage new investments or expel the already established foreign investments from the market.[160] By limiting investors' discretion, this measure can restrict their investment activities in the host country. Thus, the WTO rules on trade in services (and some IIAs[161]) oppose any joint venture requirement in committed sectors as a principle unless there are member-specific reservations to the contrary. In particular, such requirement is

157 Article 14.10.3(c) of the USMCA (2018).

158 Article 1106.2 of the NAFTA (1992).

159 Article 9.2 of the Canada–Guinea BIT (2015).

160 Przemyslaw Kowalski, Daniel Rabaioli and Sebastian Vallejo, 'International Technology Transfer Measures in an Interconnected World: Lessons and Policy Implications', OECD Trade Policy Paper No. 206, 2017, p. 46.

161 See, for example, Article 14.5(b) of the New Zealand–UK FTA (2022); Article 13.4.1(b) of the Australia–UK FTA (2021); Article SERVIN.2.2(b) of the EU–UK Trade and Cooperation Agreement (2020).

considered illegal under Article XVI:2(e) of the GATS unless it is expressly inscribed in a member's schedule of specific commitments. In practice, some national schedules contain entries for keeping joint ventures in the sectors of environmental services (e.g., cleaning services of exhaust gases or other environmental protection services)[162] and energy services (e.g., services incidental to mining or services incidental to energy distribution),[163] among other things. Croatia's GATS schedule requires in-country collaboration for foreign scientific and technical consulting services (CPC 8675), specifically stating that 'services of basic geological, geodetic and mining research as well as related environment protection research services on the territory of Croatia can be carried out only jointly with/or through domestic legal persons'.[164]

The GATS schedules of several WTO members have direct references to the technology transfer. Kuwait and Qatar have conditioned market access for FDIs, or mode 3 services, in all scheduled sectors (including environmental services) upon the creation by investors of benefits in the form of 'technology transfer, research and development programs, technical or marketing assistance and educational or training of local manpower'.[165] India's or Sri Lanka's horizontal commitments in its respective schedule suggest that in the case of joint ventures partnering with public sector enterprises or government undertakings, preferential access will be given to foreign entities that offer 'the best terms for transfer of technology'.[166] Tunisia issues trader's licences across all listed sectors '[w]hen the proposed activities will generate technology transfer and jobs and/or may

162 See, for example, WTO, Trade in Services – The People's Republic of China – Schedule of Specific Commitments, GATS/SC/135 (14 February 2002); WTO, Trade in Services – Samoa – Schedule of Specific Commitments, GATS/SC/147 (5 June 2012); WTO, Trade in Services – Georgia – Schedule of Specific Commitments, GATS/SC/129 (20 December 2000).

163 See, for example, GATS/SC/142 (Viet Nam), supra note 10; WTO, Communication from Sierra Leone – General Agreement on Trade in Services – Schedule of Specific Commitments, GATS/SC/105 (30 August 1995) (the scheduled category of 'F. Other Business Services', relevant to our context, is not specified further, so it may include 'services incidental to mining' and 'services incidental to energy distribution' as per the WTO's classification of services in MTN.GNS/W/120, supra note 74).

164 WTO, Trade in Services – The Republic of Croatia – Schedule of Specific Commitments, GATS/SC/130 (22 December 2000).

165 WTO, Kuwait – Schedule of Specific Commitments, GATS/SC/49 (15 April 1994); WTO, Qatar – Schedule of Specific Commitments, GATS/SC/120 (10 November 1995).

166 WTO, India – Schedule of Specific Commitments, GATS/SC/42 (15 April 1994); WTO, Sri Lanka – Schedule of Specific Commitments, GATS/SC/79 (15 April 1994).

help to promote exports in the services sector'.[167] In Thailand, foreign intra-corporate transferees may work in the area of services incidental to mining at oil and gas fields, environmental and other scheduled sectors, subject to certain criteria of management needs including the transfer of technology.[168] When authorizing the commercial presence of foreign financial institutions, the Philippines considers, inter alia, their potential contribution to technology transfer.[169]

6.2.2.5 Training of Local Personnel

A technology-receiving country should have enough capacity to absorb the acquired technology so as to maximize positive spillovers from the technological diffusion.[170] National policies for fostering such 'absorptive capacity' should create and maintain an environment that would encourage local firms to assimilate knowledge gained from external sources.[171] For this, supporting an enabling climate for firms' technical training (e.g., education of local staff and attraction of foreign talents) may contribute to the nurturing of highly skilled workforce without compromising international trade obligations. Furthermore, the prohibition of performance requirements under certain IIAs does not prevent the host country from obliging foreign investors to train local workers as long as this does not require the transfer of a technology, a production process or other proprietary knowledge to a local person.[172]

The design of technical training is likely to be affected by government priorities. For example, the literature suggests that China's wind energy policy initially focused on promoting the production of wind turbines (rather than wind power), which prompted domestic firms to apply

[167] WTO, Tunisia – Schedule of Specific Commitments, GATS/SC/87 (15 April 1994).

[168] WTO, Thailand – Schedule of Specific Commitments, GATS/SC/85 (15 April 1994).

[169] WTO, Trade in Services – Philippines – Schedule of Specific Commitments – Supplement 3, GATS/SC/70/Suppl.3 (26 February 1998).

[170] See Bernard M. Hoekman, Keith E. Maskus and Kamal Saggi, 'Transfer of Technology to Developing Countries: Unilateral and Multilateral Policy Options', 33 *World Development* 1587 (2005), pp. 1588, 1591.

[171] See Wesley M. Cohen and Daniel A. Levinthal, 'Absorptive Capacity: A New Perspective on Learning and Innovation', 35 *Administrative Science Quarterly* 128 (1990), p. 129; Kowalski et al., supra note 160, pp. 20–22.

[172] See, for example, Article 807.1(f), footnote 4 of the Canada–Colombia FTA (2008); Article 9.10.4 of the CPTPP (2018). By contrast, a government-imposed obligation for a foreign investor to provide education and training of locals was found to be an impermissible performance requirement under Article 1106 of the NAFTA (1992) (see *Mobil and Murphy v. Canada (I)*, ICSID, Decision on Liability and Principles of Quantum, paras. 212, 216, 221, 246).

international learning networks only to wind turbine R&D and manufacturing. As wind turbine maintenance suffered from poor quality due to the lack of training regarding the turbines' post-installation operation, the Chinese government took additional steps to increase wind power output and improve grid connections.[173] Such expansion of the policy's target from the production of wind turbines to their utilization in electricity generation can motivate firms to add maintenance of installed capacity to their training package.

6.3 Concluding Remarks

Energy-related green technologies should be disseminated worldwide to accelerate global decarbonization. Government interventions may make this happen but must comply with international economic law. Forcing firms to invest in environmental R&D or transfer green technologies through joint ventures or otherwise is probably one of the most radical ways of directing private conduct towards greening ends. But as considered in this chapter, this may generally act as impermissible market access restrictions for foreign investments and services.

By contrast, creating a conducive climate through, inter alia, lowering trade barriers, encouraging technical cooperation and technical training is what provides a legally safer footing for low-carbon and clean energy technology policies. Even R&D subsidies, not conditional upon import substitution or export performance, are less constrained by the WTO disciplines than prohibited subsidies. In addition, giving the Global South wider access to green technologies from the Global North in line with international economic law will not only bridge the North–South technological divide but also help developing countries decarbonize and meet environmental requirements in export markets.

[173] Jennifer F. Sklarew, 'How Can China and India Serve as Models for Developing Nations Striving to Build Absorption Capacity for Renewable Energy Technologies?', 2 *Renewable Energy Law and Policy Review* 181 (2011), p. 189.

Conclusion

Sovereignty and sustainable development are among important factors that define environmentally conscious energy-related policies (Chapter 1). On the one hand, States have sovereign powers in regulating their energy system. They are sovereign in utilizing their natural resources in the energy chain. On the other hand, unsustainable exploitation of the existing resources may cause energy supply disruptions and ecological problems. Achieving environmental sustainability requires conservation efforts and lesser combustion of fossil fuels, with the residual energy demand to be met with clean energy sources.

As shown throughout this book, the interface between energy and the environment gains importance under international economic law. The data in our analysis indicate that the period from 2010 onwards is characterized by an evident upward trend in raising energy–environment STCs and initiating trade and investment disputes and countervailing actions in the renewable energy segment.

The energy–environment nexus is multi-faceted. From a factual perspective, policies that discourage the use of fossil fuels and encourage the adoption of clean energy are based on the general belief that fossil fuels have negative environmental impacts while clean energy creates environmental benefits. However, some STC and ISDS cases suggest that government restrictions on renewable and nuclear energy may also be motivated by environmental concerns (Chapters 4 and 5), highlighting the complexity of this issue. By the same token, discussions on reforming fossil fuel subsidies (Chapter 3) focus on 'inefficient' and 'wasteful consumption' subsidies deemed to be environmentally harmful rather than all subsidies for fossil fuels. The difficulty of classifying environmental products (Chapter 6) presents another challenge for properly situating the energy–environment nexus. Thus, the energy–environment factual context suggests that any energy source, whether dirty or clean, must undergo environmentally sound activities for associated measures to be accepted on environmental grounds.

From a legal perspective, the energy–environment nexus has raised a multitude of issues often crossing both trade and investment law domains. Given the purpose of this book to examine the current extent of, and gaps in, international economic law in regulating this nexus (Introduction), the following overall observations can be made.

First, in order for many economic restrictions and regulatory actions to be justified, the mere existence of an underlying environmental motive itself is not enough. Trade law and investment law commonly require that these measures should be supported by a demonstrable environmental link, employ means that are proportional to the ends sought and be applied in an even-handed manner. On the trade front (Chapter 2), market-distortive measures, like LCRs or export quotas, camouflaged with environmental rationales are not only unhelpful but may even be counter-productive in solving environmental problems. Arbitrary distinctions based on NPR-PPMs in support of protectionism or unjustified discrimination question the genuineness of underlying environmental purposes. On the investment front (Chapter 5), restrictions on investment activities imposed to protect legitimate public welfare objectives must be applied on a bona fide and non-discriminatory basis to be considered as acceptable exercises of police power. Regulatory changes to the detriment of investors' interests must be reasonable, non-discriminatory, proportional to the intended public purpose and consistent with the due process of law.

Second, with respect to the government's promotive role in developing the energy sector, the main message from Chapter 3 is that trade law should give different treatment to fossil fuel subsidies and renewable energy subsidies to lead the energy–environment nexus towards better environmental outcomes. At the same time, we have also seen in Chapter 5 that the trade and investment regimes need greater harmony with respect to energy subsidies to avoid legal conflicts in the case of discontinued or reduced subsidies for investors and State compensation to investors under ISDS rulings.

Third, as regards green technologies discussed in Chapter 6, governments should provide a conducive environment for international technology movements and transfers through lower trade barriers, extensive technical cooperation and technical training for the decarbonization and clean energy purposes. By contrast, forcing technology transfers through joint ventures or otherwise can restrict investment and trade flows. Thus, trade and investment rules are generally against such coercive State practices.

Fourth, private environmental standards and CSR duties represent the examples where international economic law shows some signs of greater engagement with private conduct at the energy–environment intersection. As considered in Chapter 4, some recent RTAs lay down foundations for public–private interactions through which governments can make good use of private environmental standards by identifying environmentally best practices and discouraging inappropriate private standards. In Chapter 5, we have seen that the CSR standards are being increasingly incorporated into recent IIAs. Responding to public pressure for greater social contribution by investors, this trend may add some value to the rebalancing of the investment legal system by, for example, helping States advance their position in energy–environment investment disputes in the case of irresponsible business behaviour.

Fifth, notwithstanding its economic orientation, international economic law is becoming greener in addressing energy–environment issues. This is what green rule-making in RTAs and IIAs and some 'environmentally friendly' interpretations in energy-related trade and investment disputes are showing. This is what can potentially be bolstered by the new WTO initiatives on trade and sustainability, fossil fuel subsidies and plastics pollution as well as the ACCTS negotiations. These developments create a positive momentum for taking further actions to ensure that the pace and scope of greening efforts correspond to the pace and scale of environmental degradation. Considering this factor and our book's purpose, we can distinguish three groups of trade and investment rules named, for the sake of simplicity, as 'permissions', 'restrictions' and 'commands' and, based on our analysis, highlight some areas needing improvements in each of these categories.

Many energy–environment rules are seated within the category of permissions that allow governments to take illegal action in the light of environmental policy needs. These provisions accept the right of States to regulate in the public interest. Like in trade law, new-generation IIAs follow the text-based approach in doing so. Besides the provisions with the direct recognition of this right, permissions are often found in exception or carve-out clauses. As we have observed in Chapter 1, general exceptions for environmental protection are a comparatively new trend in IIAs aimed to rebalance investor–State interests under investment law. Unlike general exceptions in trade law that prevent legal remedies against qualified energy–environment restrictions, IIA general exceptions do not necessarily preclude adverse consequences for violating States and may thus provide rather limited environmental policy space under investment law. But trade law's general exceptions have their limitations too. As discussed in Chapter 3 (and Chapter 2), WTO general exceptions seem inapplicable across the board and, in particular, to renewable energy subsidies under the SCM Agreement. Thus, general exceptions in both fields are in need of reform.

Because permissions leave it to a State to decide whether or not to take environment-protective measures, international economic law should additionally adopt a more proactive stance by strengthening its role in curtailing environmentally harmful, and ordering environmentally sound, behaviour or effects. This can be explored under the categories of restrictions and commands, respectively.

The category of restrictions typically prevents States from racing to the bottom so that, inter alia, the attractiveness of an investment climate is not increased at environmental sacrifice (Chapter 1). In trade law, a similar restrictive effect is reachable, for example, through regulatory convergence among States towards highest environmental standards (Chapter 4). Perhaps the currently most pressing issue in the restrictions basket is how to curtail harmful fossil fuel subsidies (Chapter 3). Similarly, investment law can introduce rules to stop providing legal protection to certain fossil fuel investments as explored by the modernized ECT text. Another type of conduct that could also be discouraged is government counteractions against environmentally friendly practice or behaviour. Here, this book has suggested constraining anti-subsidy measures vis-à-vis qualified renewable energy promotion schemes.

The third category is about commanding States to take pro-environmental action. It includes, inter alia, IIA clauses requiring governments to encourage investors to accept CSR standards, RTAs with carbon pricing obligations and provisions on regulatory cooperation. Furthermore, climate clubs have the potential to create greening commands for their members in the future. In the commands basket, international economic law could improve by, for instance, mandating environmental impact assessments for international rule-making (Chapter 1) and compelling trade liberalization for environmental goods and services (Chapter 6). Importantly, ordering more technical and financial assistance for developing countries is imperative in the global fight against climate change. Just as unequal vaccine availability between developed and developing countries prolonged and expanded virus spread and mutation across the globe during the COVID-19 pandemic,[1]

[1] See, for example, Richard L. Oehler and Vivian R. Vega, 'Worldwide Vaccine Inequality Threatens to Unleash the Next COVID-19 Variant', 123 *International Journal of Infectious Diseases* 133 (2022).

unequal climate capacity between the North and South will only delay if not disable the process of limiting global warming to a controllable level. Thus, ensuring the accessibility of green technologies all over the world will not only address the imbalance of climate capacity between developed and developing countries but also enable global carbon neutrality without compromising economic growth. It is better to make costly investments in green infrastructure everywhere today than to pass on a more costly burden of climate change to future generations who have nothing to do with the current climate crisis.

These and other improvements can be undertaken within each regime – whether the WTO, the ECT, IIAs, RTAs and others – accordingly. It would already be a success if each or some of these regimes make proper energy–environment adjustments to become more responsive to environmental challenges. The fact that the WTO was able to deliver a global environmental agreement on fisheries subsidies despite all hardship is a telling example indicating that it is realistic to make progress on environmental issues under international economic law.

Another probably more difficult approach to incorporating greening improvements would be to give a holistic energy–environment consideration within a single trade and investment framework. The ECT has already proved that international regulation of energy trade and investment under the same umbrella is possible. But several countries have recently announced their withdrawals from this system, and the EU is also considering the exit scenario, so the status of the modernized ECT text at the moment remains unclear. In 2011, the International Centre for Trade and Sustainable Development, the Global Green Growth Institute and the Peterson Institute for International Economics made a joint proposal for States to launch a Sustainable Energy Trade Agreement based on comprehensive research findings.[2] Although this initiative was not realized, it could serve – together with the (modernized) ECT – as a prototype for, say, another 'Sustainable Energy Trade and Investment Agreement' that could be negotiated among all interested jurisdictions in the future. Albeit beyond the scope of this book, the rough idea here is about developing a new multi-party trade *and* investment treaty with the focus on all important aspects of the energy–environment nexus.

[2] See Gary C. Hufbauer, Ricardo Meléndez-Ortiz and Richard Samans (eds.), *The Law and Economics of a Sustainable Energy Trade Agreement* (Cambridge: Cambridge University Press, 2016).

Appendix A

Energy–Environment STCs Raised in TBT Committee (1995–2021)

IMS ID	STC title	Member(s) responding to STC	Member(s) raising STC	First date raised	Last date raised	Number of times raised
726	United States – Energy efficiency requirements for general service lamps (GSL) (ID 726)	United States	China	10/11/2021	10/11/2021	1
716	United States – Energy Conservation Program: Test Procedure for Metal Halide Lamp Fixtures (ID 716)	United States	China	10/11/2021	10/11/2021	1
710	India – Important Instruction regarding Voluntary Star Labelling Programme for UHD (4 K, 8 K) Televisions (ID 710)	India	Korea	10/11/2021	10/11/2021	1
709	United States – Energy Conservation Program: Test Procedures for Residential and Commercial Clothes Washers (ID 709)	United States	China	10/11/2021	10/11/2021	1
708	European Union – Draft Commission Regulation laying down ecodesign requirements for light sources and separate control gears pursuant to Directive 2009/125/EC of the European Parliament and of the Council and repealing Commission Regulation(EC) No. 244/2009, (EC) No. 245/2009 and (EU) No. 1194/2012 (ID 708)	EU	Korea	10/11/2021	10/11/2021	1
707	Viet Nam – Draft National Technical Regulation on the fifth level of gaseous pollutants emissions for new assembled, manufactured and imported automobiles (ID 707)	Viet Nam	Thailand	10/11/2021	10/11/2021	1
695	Colombia – Biofuels Decree – Resolution No. 40111 of 9 April 2021 (ID 695)	Colombia	EU	02/06/2021	02/06/2021	1

(*cont.*)

IMS ID	STC title	Member(s) responding to STC	Member(s) raising STC	First date raised	Last date raised	Number of times raised
685	European Union – Draft EU Batteries Regulation (implementation of the European Green Deal) (ID 685)	EU	China, Korea, Russia	02/06/2021	16/11/2022	5
684	Turkey – Eco-design regulation (ID 684)	Türkiye	Korea	24/02/2021	24/02/2021	1
673	Oman – Water heaters-energy performance requirements; Electrical Clothes Washing Machines Energy and Water performance requirements and Refrigerators, Refrigerator-Freezers and Freezers-Energy Performance, Testing and Labeling Requirements (ID 673)	Oman	Korea	24/02/2021	24/02/2021	1
670	United States – Energy Conservation Program: Energy conservation standards for residential dishwashers (ID 670)	United States	China	24/02/2021	02/06/2021	2
668	Kingdom of Saudi Arabia – Air Conditioners – Minimum Energy Performance, Labelling and Testing Requirements for Low Capacity Window Type and Single-Split (ID 668)	Saudi Arabia	Korea	24/02/2021	02/06/2021	2
654	Chile – Technical specifications for the design of energy efficiency labels for washing machines	Chile	Korea	28/10/2020	02/06/2021	3
647	Zimbabwe – Electricity (Minimum Energy Efficiency Performance of Domestic Electrical Appliances) Regulations, 2020	Zimbabwe	Korea	28/10/2020	28/10/2020	1
635	Kingdom of Saudi Arabia – SASO 2663 Air conditioner Minimum Energy, Performance, Labelling and Testing requirements for Low Capacity Window type and single-split, and related certifications (IMS ID 635)	Saudi Arabia	China	13/05/2020	13/05/2020	1

634	European Union – EU Commission Regulation (EU) 2019/2013 for Energy Labelling of Electronic Displays (IMS ID 634)	EU	China	13/05/2020	28/10/2020	2
624	Russian Federation; Kazakhstan; Kyrgyz Republic; Armenia – Requirements for energy efficiency of energy related devices (IMS ID 624)	Armenia, Kazakhstan, Kyrgyz Republic, Russia	Korea	13/05/2020	13/05/2020	1
623	Colombia – Issuing the Technical Regulation on rational energy-use labelling for certain types of electrical and gas end-use equipment, for marketing in Colombia (IMS ID 623)	Colombia	Korea, United States	13/05/2020	13/05/2020	1
619	Kingdom of Saudi Arabia – Electrical Clothes Washing Machines – Energy and Water performance requirements and labelling	Saudi Arabia	Korea, Mexico	26/02/2020	28/10/2020	3
605	Kingdom of Saudi Arabia – Electrical Clothes Dryers Energy Performance Requirements and Labelling (IMS ID 605)	Saudi Arabia	Korea	13/11/2019	28/10/2020	4
599	Ecuador – Energy Efficiency Requirements for Clothes Dryers for Domestic Use (IMS ID 599)	Ecuador	Korea	13/11/2019	13/05/2020	3
592	European Union – Concerns on regulations with regard to eco-design requirements for various products in EU (ID 592)	EU	China	20/06/2019	24/02/2021	6
582	Republic of Korea – Regulation on Energy Efficiency Management Equipment (ID 582)	Korea	China	06/03/2019	06/03/2019	1
575	European Union – Draft Commission Regulation laying down eco-design requirements for electronic displays pursuant to Directive 2009/125/EC of the European Parliament and of the Council, amending Commission Regulation (EC) No. 1275/2008 and repealing Commission Regulation (EC) 642/2009 (and its accompanying annexes) (ID 575)	EU	China, United States, Japan, Brazil, Israel, Korea	06/03/2019	16/11/2022	9

(cont.)

IMS ID	STC title	Member(s) responding to STC	Member(s) raising STC	First date raised	Last date raised	Number of times raised
560	United States – Energy Conservation Program: Energy Conservation Standards for Compressors (ID 560)	United States	China	20/06/2018	20/06/2018	1
553	European Union – Amendments to the Directive 2009/28/EC, Renewable Energy Directive (ID 553)	EU	Malaysia, Thailand, Indonesia, Colombia, Costa Rica, Guatemala, Nigeria, Honduras, Ecuador, Argentina	21/03/2018	24/02/2021	10
536	China – Limits and Measurement Methods for Emissions of Light-duty Vehicles (China 6) (ID 536)	China	Japan	14/06/2017	15/06/2017	1
527	China – Tentative Administrative Rules on Enterprises Average Fuel Consumption and New Energy Vehicle Credits and Administration Regulation on the Access of New Energy Vehicle Manufactures and Products (ID 527)	China	United States, EU, Japan	29/03/2017	21/03/2018	4
508	China – Chinese Standards of Exhaust Emissions (China 6, Beijing VI) (ID 508)	China	Korea	15/06/2016	15/06/2016	1
485	Kingdom of Bahrain, State of Kuwait, Kingdom of Saudi Arabia, Qatar – Motor Vehicles: General Requirements "No. GSO 42:2003" (ID 485)	Bahrain, Kuwait, Qatar, Saudi Arabia	EU	04/11/2015	04/11/2015	1

481	United Arab Emirates – Labelling – Energy efficiency label for electrical appliances (ID 481)	UAE	Korea	04/11/2015	04/11/2015	1
477	China – Interim Measures for Quality Management of Commercial Coal (ID 477)	China	Australia, Canada	04/11/2015	26/02/2020	14
455	Ecuador – (PRTE INEN) No. 111: Energy efficiency. Clothes dryers. Labelling (ID 455)	Ecuador	Mexico, United States	05/11/2014	09/03/2016	5
410	United States – Energy Conservation Program: Test Procedure for Commercial Refrigeration Equipment (ID 410)	United States	China	19/03/2014	19/03/2014	1
408	United States – EPA Palm Oil Biofuels Regulatory Program (ID 408)	United States	Indonesia, Malaysia	30/10/2013	19/03/2014	2
406	Mexico – Draft Mexican Official Standard PROY-NOM-032-ENER-2013: Maximum electrical power limits for equipment and appliances requiring stand-by power. Test methods and labelling (ID 406)	Mexico	Korea, United States	30/10/2013	19/03/2014	2
405	European Union – Fuel Quality Directive (ID 405)	EU	Canada, United States	30/10/2013	30/10/2013	1
403	Chile – Safety for Printers and Energy Efficiency for Printers (ID 403)	Chile	United States	30/10/2013	19/03/2014	2
396	European Union – Draft Commission Regulation implementing Directive 2009/125/EC of the European Parliament and of the Council with regard to ecodesign requirements for vacuum cleaners (ID 396)	EU	China	30/10/2013	30/10/2013	1
391	European Union – Proposal for a Regulation on Fluorinated Greenhouse Gases (ID 391)	EU	Japan, Korea, United States	17/06/2013	19/03/2014	3
384	US – Energy Conservation Program for Consumer Products: various products (ID 384)	United States	China	17/06/2013	17/06/2013	1

(cont.)

IMS ID	STC title	Member(s) responding to STC	Member(s) raising STC	First date raised	Last date raised	Number of times raised
365	European Union – Draft Commission Regulation implementing Directive 2009/125/EC of the European Parliament and of the Council with regard to ecodesign requirements for directional lamps, light emitting diode lamps and related equipment (ID 365)	EU	Korea	27/11/2012	06/03/2013	2
357	Korea – Windows Energy Efficiency, Ministry of Knowledge Economy (MKE) Notification 2011–263, December 2011 (ID 357)	Korea	United States	13/06/2012	13/06/2012	1
355	United States – Energy conservation program: energy conservation standards for residential refrigerators, refrigerator-freezers, and freezers (ID 355)	United States	China	13/06/2012	13/06/2012	1
352	European Union – Air conditioners, liquid chilling packages and heat pumps, with electrically driven compressors, for space heating and cooling. Testing and rating at part load conditions and calculation of seasonal performance (EN 14825) (ID 352)	EU	China	13/06/2012	13/06/2012	1
348	Korea – A Draft of Regulation for Measurement of Energy Efficiency of Tyres for Motor Vehicles, and Its Rating and Identification (ID 348)	Korea	Japan, EU	13/06/2012	27/11/2012	2
346	Spain – Ministerial Order of the Government of Spain IET/822/2012, published on 21 April 2012 and in force as of 22 April 2012 (ID 346)	EU, Spain	Argentina	13/06/2012	13/06/2012	1
342	European Union – Regulation (EC) No. 1222/2009 Labelling of Tyres, Commission Regulation (EC) No. 228/2011, No. 1235/2011 (ID 342)	EU	Korea	20/03/2012	20/03/2012	1

341	United States – Test procedures for high density discharge lamps (ID 341)	United States	China	20/03/2012	20/03/2012	1
323	United States – ENERGYSTAR 6.0 Draft 2 Program Requirements for Displays-Draft Partner Commitments (ID 323)	United States	Korea	10/11/2011	10/11/2011	1
321	European Union – Draft Commission Regulation implementing Directive 2009/125/EC of the European Parliament and of the Council with regard to ecodesign requirements for air conditioners and comfort fans (ID 321)	EU	China	10/11/2011	20/03/2012	2
318	Colombia – Commercial Truck Diesel Emissions Regulation (Resolution 2604, 24 December 2009) (ID 318)	Colombia	Canada, Mexico, United States	15/06/2011	17/06/2013	6
314	Mexico – Energy Labelling Measures (Law for Sustainable Use of Energy, 28 November 2008; Regulation of the Law for Sustainable Use of Energy, 11 September 2009; National Program for Sustainable Use of Energy 2009–2012, 27 November 2009; and Catalogue of equipment and appliances used by manufacturers, importers, distributors and marketers that require mandatory inclusion of energy consumption information, 10 September 2010) (ID 314)	Mexico	Argentina, Japan, Korea, United States, EU	15/06/2011	20/03/2012	3
307	European Union – Directive 2009/28/CE, Renewable Energy Directive (EU – RED) (ID 307)	EU	Argentina, Indonesia, Malaysia, United States	15/06/2011	19/03/2014	7
306	France – Loi No. 2010–788: The National Commitment for the Environment (Grenelle 2 Law) (ID 306)	France, EU	Argentina, Brazil, Cuba, India, Korea, South Africa, Uruguay	15/06/2011	30/10/2013	8

(*cont.*)

IMS ID	STC title	Member(s) responding to STC	Member(s) raising STC	First date raised	Last date raised	Number of times raised
286	European Union – Directive on eco-design requirements for household dishwashers, Directive on eco-design requirement for fans (ID 286)	EU	China	03/11/2010	03/11/2010	2
282	Canada – Proposed Amendment to the Energy Efficiency Regulations (ID 282)	Canada	Korea	03/11/2010	03/11/2010	1
281	Korea – Automobile standards of the efficiency of average energy consumption and allowable emission of greenhouse gases (ID 281)	Korea	United States, EU	03/11/2010	03/11/2010	1
271	Korea – KS C IEC61646:2007 Standard for Thin-film Solar Panels (IMS ID 271)	Korea	United States, EU	23/06/2010	19/03/2014	11
268	United States – Conditions and Criteria for Recognition of Accreditation Bodies & Laboratories for the Energy Star Program (ID 268)	United States	Korea, EU	23/06/2010	03/11/2010	2
248	United States – Test Procedures for Fluorescent Lamp Ballasts in stand-by mode (ID 248)	United States	China	25/06/2009	25/06/2009	1
216	Colombia – Draft Decree Establishing Provisions to Promote the Use of Biofuels (ID 216)	Colombia	Argentina, Mexico, EU	18/03/2009	20/03/2012	10
195	China – Energy Efficiency and Energy Efficiency Grades for Copy Machines (ID 195)	China	Japan	01/07/2008	18/03/2009	3
166	Hong Kong – Energy Efficiency Labelling Scheme (ID 166)	Hong Kong (China)	EU	05/07/2007	05/07/2007	1
156	India – Electrical products (ID 156)	India	EU	21/03/2007	21/03/2007	1
150	United States – Energy Conservation Program for Consumer Products: Test Procedure for Residential Central Air Conditioners and Heat Pumps; Proposed Rule (ID 150)	United States	China	09/11/2006	09/11/2006	1

148	Japan – Revision to Enforcement Regulation for the Law Concerning the Rational Use of Energy and Ministerial Notification of the Ministry of Economy, Trade and Industry (ID 148)	Japan	China	09/11/2006	09/11/2006	1
140	United States – Energy Conservation Standards for Certain Consumer Products and Commercial and Industrial Equipment (ID 140)	United States	China	17/03/2006	07/06/2006	2
123	European Communities – Ecodesign requirements for energy-using products ('EuP Directive') (ID 123)	EU	China, Japan, Malaysia, United States	02/11/2005	24/03/2010	6
110	Switzerland – Measures to Reduce Particle Emissions from Diesel Engine (ID 110)	Switzerland	United States, EU	01/07/2004	05/07/2007	7
105	Korea – Average Fuel Economy Standards for Passenger Cars (ID 105)	Korea	Japan, United States, EU	23/03/2004	01/07/2004	2
72	Korea – Emission Standards for Automobiles (ID 72)	Korea	EU	15/03/2002	21/06/2002	2
71	Japan Partial Amendment to the Safety Regulations for Road Vehicles Establishing Standards of Vehicle Emission (ID 71)	Japan	EU	15/03/2002	21/06/2002	2
32	European Communities – Regulation on Aircrafts (ID 32)	EU	Japan, United States	20/11/1998	11/06/1999	3

Source: Author's compilation from data (as of 1 April 2023) at WTO, 'SPS & TBT Platform', https://epingalert.org.

Appendix B

Renewable Energy ISDS Cases (2011–2021)

Year of initiation	Case name	Respondent state	Investor's home state	Applicable IIA	Status
2021	*Enel, S.p.A. v. Republic of Turkey (ICSID Case No. ARB/21/61)*	Türkiye	Italy	Italy–Turkey BIT (1995)	Pending
2021	*Energía y Renovación Holding, S.A. v. Republic of Guatemala (ICSID Case No. ARB/21/56)*	Guatemala	Panama	Central America–Panama FTA (2002)	Pending
2021	*ESSA2 SpA and Enel Green Power Costa Rica S.A. v. Republic of Costa Rica (ICSID Case No. ARB/21/49)*	Costa Rica	Chile	Chile–Costa Rica BIT (1996)	Pending
2021	*KELAG-Kärntner Elektrizitäts-Aktiengesellschaft and others v. Romania (ICSID Case No. ARB/21/54)*	Romania	Austria	ECT (1994)	Pending
2021	*Mainstream Renewable Power Ltd and others v. Federal Republic of Germany (ICSID Case No. ARB/21/26)*	Germany	Ireland	ECT (1994)	Pending
2021	*Modus Energy International B.V. v. Ukraine*	Ukraine	Netherlands	ECT (1994)	Pending
2021	*Spanish Solar 1 Limited and Spanish Solar 2 Limited v. Kingdom of Spain (ICSID Case No. ARB/21/39)*	Spain	Ireland	ECT (1994)	Pending
2021	*SREW N.V. v. Ukraine (ICSID Case No. ARB/21/52)*	Ukraine	Belgium	BLEU (Belgium–Luxembourg Economic Union)–Ukraine BIT (1996)	Pending
2021	*TS Villalba GmbH and others v. Kingdom of Spain (ICSID Case No. ARB/21/43)*	Spain	Germany	ECT (1994)	Pending

(*cont.*)

Year of initiation	Case name	Respondent state	Investor's home state	Applicable IIA	Status
2020	*Arka Energy B.V. v. Republic of Albania (ICSID Case No. ARB/20/54)*	Albania	Netherlands	Albania–Netherlands BIT (1994)	Discontinued
2020	*Campos de Pesé, S.A. v. Republic of Panama (ICSID Case No. ARB/20/19)*	Panama	Italy	Italy–Panama BIT (2009)	Pending
2020	*Encavis AG, Fano Solar 1 S.r.l., DE Stern 10 S.r.l. and others v. Italian Republic (ICSID Case No. ARB/20/39)*	Italy	Germany	ECT (1994)	Pending
2020	*EP Wind Project (Rom) Six Ltd. v. Romania (ICSID Case No. ARB/20/15)*	Romania	Cyprus	ECT (1994)	Pending
2020	*Fin.Doc S.r.l., Domenica Gazineo, En.Doc S. r.l. and others v. Romania (ICSID Case No. ARB/20/35)*	Romania	Cyprus, Czech Republic, Germany, Greece, Italy, Luxembourg, Türkiye	ECT (1994)	Pending
2020	*Mitsui & Co., Ltd. v. Kingdom of Spain (ICSID Case No. ARB/20/47)*	Spain	Japan	ECT (1994)	Pending
2020	*Shift Energy Japan KK v. Japan*	Japan	Hong Kong (China's Special Administrative Region)	Hong Kong–Japan BIT (1997)	Pending
2019	*Canepa Green Energy Opportunities I, S.á r.l. and Canepa Green Energy Opportunities II, S.á r.l. v. Kingdom of Spain (ICSID Case No. ARB/19/4)*	Spain	Luxembourg	ECT (1994)	Pending

2019	*Jetion Solar Co. Ltd and Wuxi T-Hertz Co. Ltd. v. Hellenic Republic*	Greece	China	China–Greece BIT (1992)	Discontinued
2019	*CH Mamacocha S.R.L. and Latam Hydro LLC v. Republic of Peru (ICSID Case No. ARB/19/28)*	Peru	United States	Peru–United States FTA (2006)	Pending
2019	*Sapec, S.A. v. Kingdom of Spain (ICSID Case No. ARB/19/23)*	Spain	Belgium	ECT (1994)	Pending
2019	*Erste Nordsee-Offshore Holding GmbH, Strabag SE, Zweite Nordsee-Offshore Holding GmbH v. Federal Republic of Germany (ICSID Case No. ARB/19/29)*	Germany	Austria	ECT (1994)	Pending
2019	*M Solar GmbH & Co. KG, M Solar Verwaltungs GmbH, Solarizz Holding GmbH & Co. KG and others v. Kingdom of Spain (ICSID Case No. ARB/19/30)*	Spain	Germany	ECT (1994)	Pending
2018	*EBL (Genossenschaft Elektra Baselland) and Tubo Sol PE2 S.L. v. Kingdom of Spain (ICSID Case No. ARB/18/42)*	Spain	Switzerland	ECT (1994)	Pending
2018	*European Solar Farms A/S v. Kingdom of Spain (ICSID Case No. ARB/18/45)*	Spain	Denmark	ECT (1994)	Pending
2018	*Invenergy LLC v. Republic of Poland (PCA Case No. 2018-40)*	Poland	United States	Poland–United States BIT (1990)	Pending
2018	*Itochu Corporation v. Kingdom of Spain (ICSID Case No. ARB/18/25)*	Spain	Japan	ECT (1994)	Pending
2018	*KLS Energy Lanka Sdn. Bhd. v. Democratic Socialist Republic of Sri Lanka (ICSID Case No. ARB/18/39)*	Sri Lanka	Malaysia	Malaysia–Sri Lanka BIT (1982)	Pending
2018	*Anina Pro Invest Ltd, Core Value Capital GmbH, Core Value Investments GmbH & Co KG Gamma and others v. Romania (ICSID Case No. ARB/18/19)*	Romania	Austria, Cyprus, Germany, Netherlands	ECT (1994)	Pending

(*cont.*)

Year of initiation	Case name	Respondent state	Investor's home state	Applicable IIA	Status
2017	*DCM Energy GmbH & Co. Solar 1 KG, DCM Energy GmbH & Co. Solar 2 KG, Edisun Power Europe A.G., Hannover Leasing Sun Invest 2 Spanien Beteiligungs GmbH, and Hannover Leasing Sun Invest 2 Spanien GmbH & Co. KG v. Kingdom of Spain (ICSID Case No. ARB/17/41)*	Spain	Germany, Switzerland	ECT (1994)	Pending
2017	*FREIF Eurowind Holdings Ltd. v. Kingdom of Spain (SCC Case No. 2017/060)*	Spain	UK	ECT (1994)	Decided in favour of the State
2017	*Portigon AG v. Kingdom of Spain (ICSID Case No. ARB/17/15)*	Spain	Germany	ECT (1994)	Pending
2017	*Tennant Energy, LLC. v. Canada (PCA Case No. 2018-54)*	Canada	United States	NAFTA (1992)	Pending
2017	*Triodos SICAV II v. Kingdom of Spain (SCC Case No. 2017-194)*	Spain	Luxembourg	ECT (1994)	Pending
2016	*Aharon Naftali Biram, Gilatz Spain SL, Redmill Holdings Ltd and Sun-Flower Olmeda GmbH v. Kingdom of Spain (ICSID Case No. ARB/16/17)*	Spain	Germany, UK	ECT (1994)	Decided in favour of the investor
2016	*CIC Renewable Energies Italy GmbH, Enernovum Asset 1 GmbH & Co. KG, Enernovum GmbH & Co. KG and others v. Italian Republic (ICSID Case No. ARB/16/39)*	Italy	Germany, UK, Luxembourg	ECT (1994)	Pending

2016	*Cordoba Beheer B.V., Cross Retail S.L., Sevilla Beheer B.V., Spanish project companies v. Kingdom of Spain (ICSID Case No. ARB/16/27)*	Spain	Netherlands	ECT (1994)	Pending
2016	*EDF Energies Nouvelles S.A. v. Kingdom of Spain*	Spain	France	ECT (1994)	Pending
2016	*ESPF Beteiligungs GmbH, ESPF Nr. 2 Austria Beteiligungs GmbH, and InfraClass Energie 5 GmbH & Co. KG v. Italian Republic (ICSID Case No. ARB/16/5)*	Italy	Austria, Germany	ECT (1994)	Decided in favour of the investor
2016	*Eurus Energy Holdings Corporation and Eurus Energy Europe B.V. v. Kingdom of Spain (ICSID Case No. ARB/16/4)*	Spain	Japan, Netherlands	ECT (1994)	Pending
2016	*Green Power Partners K/S and SCE Solar Don Benito APS v. Kingdom of Spain (SCC Case No. 2016/135)*	Spain	Denmark	ECT (1994)	Decided in favour of the State
2016	*Infracapital F1 S.à r.l. and Infracapital Solar B.V. v. Kingdom of Spain (ICSID Case No. ARB/16/18)*	Spain	Luxembourg, Netherlands	ECT (1994)	Pending
2016	*SunReserve Luxco Holdings v. Italy (SCC Case No. 2016/32)*	Italy	Luxembourg	ECT (1994)	Decided in favour of the State
2015	*9REN Holding S.a.r.l v. Kingdom of Spain (ICSID Case No. ARB/15/15)*	Spain	Luxembourg	ECT (1994)	Decided in favour of the investor
2015	*Alten Renewable Energy Developments BV v. Kingdom of Spain (SCC Case No. 2015/036)*	Spain	Netherlands	ECT (1994)	Pending

(*cont.*)

Year of initiation	Case name	Respondent state	Investor's home state	Applicable IIA	Status
2015	*BayWa r.e. Renewable Energy GmbH and BayWa r.e. Asset Holding GmbH v. Kingdom of Spain (ICSID Case No. ARB/15/16)*	Spain	Germany	ECT (1994)	Decided in favour of the investor
2015	*Belenergia S.A. v. Italian Republic (ICSID Case No. ARB/15/40)*	Italy	Luxembourg	ECT (1994)	Decided in favour of the State
2015	*Cavalum SGPS, S.A. v. Kingdom of Spain (ICSID Case No. ARB/15/34)*	Spain	Portugal	ECT (1994)	Pending
2015	*CEF Energia BV v. Italian Republic (SCC Case No. 158/2015)*	Italy	Netherlands	ECT (1994)	Decided in favour of the investor
2015	*Cube Infrastructure Fund SICAV and others v. Kingdom of Spain (ICSID Case No. ARB/15/20)*	Spain	France, Luxembourg	ECT (1994)	Decided in favour of the investor
2015	*E.ON SE, E.ON Finanzanlagen GmbH and E.ON Iberia Holding GmbH v. Kingdom of Spain (ICSID Case No. ARB/15/35)*	Spain	Germany	ECT (1994)	Pending
2015	*ENERGO-PRO a.s. v. Republic of Bulgaria (ICSID Case No. ARB/15/19)*	Bulgaria	Czech Republic	ECT (1994), Bulgaria–Czech Republic BIT (1999)	Data not available
2015	*Eskosol S.p.A. in liquidazione v. Italian Republic (ICSID Case No. ARB/15/50)*	Italy	Italy	ECT (1994)	Decided in favour of the State

2015	*Foresight Luxembourg Solar 1 S.Á.R.L., Foresight Luxembourg Solar 2 S.Á.R.L., Greentech Energy System A/S, GWM Renewable Energy I S.P.A and GWM Renewable Energy II S.P.A v. Kingdom of Spain (SCC Case No. 2015/150)*	Spain	Luxembourg, Denmark, Italy	ECT (1994)	Decided in favour of the investor
2015	*Greentech Energy Systems A/S, NovEnergia II Energy & Environment (SCA) SICAR, and NovEnergia II Italian Portfolio SA v. Italian Republic (SCC Case No. 2015/095)*	Italy	Denmark, Luxembourg	ECT (1994)	Decided in favour of the investor
2015	*Hydro Energy 1 S.à r.l. and Hydroxana Sweden AB v. Kingdom of Spain (ICSID Case No. ARB/15/42)*	Spain	Luxembourg, Sweden	ECT (1994)	Decided in favour of the investor
2015	*JGC Holdings Corporation (formerly JGC Corporation) v. Kingdom of Spain (ICSID Case No. ARB/15/27)*	Spain	Japan	ECT (1994)	Decided in favour of the investor
2015	*Frank Schumm, Joachim Kruck, Jürgen Reiss and others v. Kingdom of Spain (ICSID Case No. ARB/15/23)*	Spain	Germany	ECT (1994)	Pending
2015	*KS Invest GmbH and TLS Invest GmbH v. Kingdom of Spain (ICSID Case No. ARB/15/25)*	Spain	Germany	ECT (1994)	Pending
2015	*Landesbank Baden-Württemberg, HSH Nordbank AG, Landesbank Hessen-Thüringen Girozentrale and Norddeutsche Landesbank-Girozentrale v. Kingdom of Spain (ICSID Case No. ARB/15/45)*	Spain	Germany	ECT (1994)	Pending

(*cont.*)

Year of initiation	Case name	Respondent state	Investor's home state	Applicable IIA	Status
2015	*Novenergia II - Energy & Environment (SCA), SICAR v. Kingdom of Spain (SCC Case No. 063/2015)*	Spain	Luxembourg	ECT (1994)	Decided in favour of the investor
2015	*OperaFund Eco-Invest SICAV PLC and Schwab Holding AG v. Kingdom of Spain (ICSID Case No. ARB/15/36)*	Spain	Malta, Switzerland	ECT (1994)	Decided in favour of the investor
2015	*Silver Ridge Power BV v. Italian Republic (ICSID Case No. ARB/15/37)*	Italy	Netherlands	ECT (1994)	Decided in favour of the State
2015	*Solarpark Management GmbH & Co. Atum I KG v. Kingdom of Spain (SCC Case No. 2015/163)*	Spain	Germany	ECT (1994)	Discontinued
2015	*SolEs Badajoz GmbH v. Kingdom of Spain (ICSID Case No. ARB/15/38)*	Spain	Germany	ECT (1994)	Decided in favour of the investor
2015	*Stadtwerke München GmbH and others v. Kingdom of Spain (ICSID Case No. ARB/15/1)*	Spain	Germany	ECT (1994)	Decided in favour of the State
2015	*STEAG GmbH v. Kingdom of Spain (ICSID Case No. ARB/15/4)*	Spain	Germany	ECT (1994)	Decided in favour of the investor
2015	*Watkins Holdings S.à r.l. and others v. Kingdom of Spain (ICSID Case No. ARB/15/44)*	Spain	Luxembourg, Netherlands	ECT (1994)	Decided in favour of the investor
2014	*Albaniabeg Ambient Sh.p.k, M. Angelo Novelli and Costruzioni S.r.l. v. Republic of Albania (ICSID Case No. ARB/14/26)*	Albania	Italy	ECT (1994)	Data not available

2014	*Blusun S.A., Jean-Pierre Lecorcier and Michael Stein v. Italian Republic (ICSID Case No. ARB/14/3)*	Italy	Belgium, France, Germany	ECT (1994)	Decided in favour of the State
2014	*InfraRed Environmental Infrastructure GP Limited and others v. Kingdom of Spain (ICSID Case No. ARB/14/12)*	Spain	UK	ECT (1994)	Decided in favour of the investor
2014	*Masdar Solar & Wind Cooperatief U.A. v. Kingdom of Spain (ICSID Case No. ARB/14/1)*	Spain	Netherlands	ECT (1994)	Decided in favour of the investor
2014	*NextEra Energy Global Holdings B.V. and NextEra Energy Spain Holdings B.V. v. Kingdom of Spain (ICSID Case No. ARB/14/11)*	Spain	Netherlands	ECT (1994)	Decided in favour of the investor
2014	*RENERGY S.à r.l. v. Kingdom of Spain (ICSID Case No. ARB/14/18)*	Spain	Luxembourg	ECT (1994)	Decided in favour of the investor
2014	*RWE Innogy GmbH and RWE Innogy Aersa S.A.U. v. Kingdom of Spain (ICSID Case No. ARB/14/34)*	Spain	Germany	ECT (1994)	Decided in favour of the investor
2013	*Antaris Solar GmbH and Dr. Michael Göde v. The Czech Republic (PCA Case No. 2014-01)*	Czech Republic	Germany	Germany–Slovakia BIT (1990), ECT (1994)	Decided in favour of the State
2013	*CSP Equity Investment Sarl v. Kingdom of Spain (SCC Case No. 094/2013)*	Spain	Luxembourg	ECT (1994)	Pending
2013	*WA Investments-Europa Nova Limited v. The Czech Republic (PCA Case No. 2014-19)*	Czech Republic	Cyprus	Cyprus–Czech Republic BIT (2001), ECT (1994)	Decided in favour of the State
2013	*EVN AG v. Republic of Bulgaria (ICSID Case No. ARB/13/17)*	Bulgaria	Austria	Austria–Bulgaria BIT (1997), ECT (1994)	Decided in favour of the State

(*cont.*)

Year of initiation	Case name	Respondent state	Investor's home state	Applicable IIA	Status
2013	*I.C.W. Europe Investments Limited v. The Czech Republic (PCA Case No. 2014-22)*	Czech Republic	UK	Czech Republic–UK BIT (1990), ECT (1994)	Decided in favour of the State
2013	*Infrastructure Services Luxembourg S.à.r.l. and Energia Termosolar B.V. (formerly Antin Infrastructure Services Luxembourg S.à.r.l. and Antin Energia Termosolar B.V.) v. Kingdom of Spain (ICSID Case No. ARB/13/31)*	Spain	Luxembourg, Netherlands	ECT (1994)	Decided in favour of the investor
2013	*Isolux Infrastructure Netherlands B.V. v. Kingdom of Spain (SCC Case No. 2013/153)*	Spain	Netherlands	ECT (1994)	Decided in favour of the State
2013	*JSW Solar (zwei) GmbH & Co.KG, Gisela Wirtgen, Jürgen Wirtgen, and Stefan Wirtgen v. Czech Republic (PCA Case No. 2014-03)*	Czech Republic	Germany	Czech Republic–Germany BIT (1990)	Decided in favour of the State
2013	*G.I.H.G. Limited, Natland Group Limited, Natland Investment Group NV, and Radiance Energy Holding S.A.R.L. v. The Czech Republic (PCA Case No. 2013-35)*	Czech Republic	Cyprus, Luxembourg, Netherlands	Czech Republic–Netherlands BIT (1991), Cyprus–Czech Republic BIT (2001), BLEU (Belgium–Luxembourg Economic Union)–Czech Republic BIT (1989), ECT (1994)	Pending

2013	*Photovoltaik Knopf Betriebs-GmbH v. The Czech Republic (PCA Case No. 2014-21)*	Czech Republic	Germany	Czech Republic–Germany BIT (1990), ECT (1994)	Decided in favour of the State
2013	*RREEF Infrastructure (G.P.) Limited and RREEF Pan-European Infrastructure Two Lux S.à.r.l. v. Kingdom of Spain (ICSID Case No. ARB/13/30)*	Spain	Luxembourg, UK	ECT (1994)	Decided in favour of the investor
2013	*Voltaic Network GmbH v. The Czech Republic (PCA Case No. 2014-20)*	Czech Republic	Germany	Czech Republic–Germany BIT (1990), ECT (1994)	Decided in favour of the State
2013	*Windstream Energy LLC v. The Government of Canada (I) (PCA Case No. 2013-22)*	Canada	United States	NAFTA (1992)	Decided in favour of the investor
2012	*Charanne B.V. and Construction Investments S.à.r.l. v. Spain (SCC Case No. 062/2012)*	Spain	Luxembourg, Netherlands	ECT (1994)	Decided in favour of the State
2011	*Mesa Power Group LLC v. Government of Canada (PCA Case No. 2012-17)*	Canada	United States	NAFTA (1992)	Decided in favour of the State
2011	*The PV Investors v. Spain (PCA Case No. 2012-14)*	Spain	Germany, Luxembourg, Netherlands	ECT (1994)	Decided in favour of the investor

Source: Author's compilation from data at the UNCTAD's database (database updated as of 31 July 2022 when accessed on 1 April 2023), 'Investment Dispute Settlement Navigator', https://investmentpolicy.unctad.org/investment-dispute-settlement.

Note: Ninety ISDS cases in total.

BIBLIOGRAPHY

African Union, 'Africa Speaks with Unified Voice as AU Executive Council Adopts African Common Position on Energy Access and Just Energy Transition', 22 July 2022, https://au.int/en/pressreleases/20220722/africa-speaks-unified-voice-au-executive-council-adopts-african-common.

'African Union Launches World's Largest Single Electricity Market (AFSEM)', 4 June 2021, https://au.int/en/pressreleases/20210604/african-union-launches-worlds-largest-single-electricity-market-afsem.

Alschner, Wolfgang, Joost Pauwelyn and Sergio Puig, 'The Data-Driven Future of International Economic Law', 20 *Journal of International Economic Law* 217 (2017).

APEC, '2021 APEC Ministerial Meeting', Wellington (New Zealand), 9 November 2021, www.apec.org/meeting-papers/annual-ministerial-meetings/2021/2021-apec-ministerial-meeting.

'Annex C – APEC List of Environmental Goods', 2012, www.apec.org/Meeting-Papers/Leaders-Declarations/2012/2012_aelm/2012_aelm_annexC.

'APEC Advances Environmental Goods Tariffs Cut', 11 March 2021, www.apec.org/press/news-releases/2021/0311_mag.

'APEC Ministers Responsible for Trade Meeting Joint Statement 2021', Wellington (New Zealand), 5 June 2021, www.apec.org/Meeting-Papers/Sectoral-Ministerial-Meetings/Trade/2021_MRT.

APEC Market Access Group, 'Scoping Study on New and Emerging Environmental Goods', 2021, www.apec.org/publications/2021/12/scoping-study-on-new-and-emerging-environmental-goods.

Arrowsmith, Sue, 'The Revised Agreement on Government Procurement: Changes to the Procedural Rules and Other Transparency Provisions', in Sue Arrowsmith and Robert D. Anderson (eds.), *The WTO Regime on Government Procurement: Challenge and Reform* (Cambridge: Cambridge University Press, 2011), pp. 285–336.

ASEAN Centre for Energy, 'ASEAN Plan of Action for Energy Cooperation (APAEC) 2016–2025, Phase II: 2021–2025', 2020, https://aseanenergy.org/asean-plan-of-action-for-energy-cooperation-apaec-phase-ii-2021-2025/.

Asmelash, Henok Birhanu, 'Energy Subsidies and WTO Dispute Settlement: Why Only Renewable Energy Subsidies Are Challenged', 18 *Journal of International Economic Law* 261 (2015).

'Phasing Out Fossil Fuel Subsidies in the G20: Progress, Challenges, and Ways Forward', International Centre for Trade and Sustainable Development, 2017.

'The Regulation of Environmentally Harmful Fossil Fuel Subsidies: From Obscurity to Prominence in the Multilateral Trading System', 33 *European Journal of International Law* 993 (2022).

Asselt, Harro van and Kati Kulovesi, 'Seizing the Opportunity: Tackling Fossil Fuel Subsidies under the UNFCCC', 17 *International Environmental Agreements: Politics, Law and Economics* 357 (2017).

Asselt, Harro van, Laura Merrill and Kati Kulovesi, 'Fossil Fuel Subsidies and the Global Climate Regime', in Jakob Skovgaard and Harro van Asselt (eds.), *The Politics of Fossil Fuel Subsidies and Their Reform* (Cambridge: Cambridge University Press, 2018), pp. 140–155.

Asselt, Harro van, Nicolien van der Grijp and Frans Oosterhuis, 'Greener Public Purchasing: Opportunities for Climate-Friendly Government Procurement under WTO and EU Rules', 6 *Climate Policy* 217 (2006).

Azaria, Danae, *Treaties on Transit of Energy via Pipelines and Countermeasures* (Oxford: Oxford University Press, 2015).

Bacchus, James, 'The Case for a WTO Climate Waiver', Centre for International Governance Innovation, Special Report, 2017.

'Legal Issues with the European Carbon Border Adjustment Mechanism', CATO Briefing Paper No. 125, CATO, 2021.

The Willing World: Shaping and Sharing a Sustainable Global Prosperity (Cambridge: Cambridge University Press, 2018).

Bacchus, James and Inu Manak, 'Free Trade in Environmental Goods Will Increase Access to Green Tech', Free Trade Bulletin No. 80, Cato Institute, 2021.

Bartels, Lorand, 'The WTO Legality of the Application of the EU's Emission Trading System to Aviation', 23 *European Journal of International Law* 429 (2012).

Bartenhagen, Erik P., 'The Intersection of Trade and the Environment: An Examination of the Impact of the TBT Agreement on Ecolabelling Programs', 17 *Virginia Environmental Law Journal* 51 (1997).

Bast, Elizabeth et al., 'Empty Promises: G20 Subsidies to Oil, Gas and Coal Production', Overseas Development Institute and Oil Change International, 2015.

Bazilian, Morgan, Victoria Cuming and Thomas Kenyon, 'Local-Content Rules for Renewables Projects Do Not Always Work', 32 *Energy Strategy Reviews* (2020) 100569.

Bellmann, Christophe and Alena Bulatnikova, 'Incorporating Environmental Provisions in Regional Trade Agreements in Chapters and Articles Dealing with Trade in Services', OECD Trade and Environment Working Paper No. 2022/01, OECD, 2022.

Bellmann, Christophe and Colette van der Ven, 'Greening Regional Trade Agreements on Non-Tariff Measures through Technical Barriers to Trade and Regulatory Co-operation', OECD Trade and Environment Working Paper No. 2020/4, 2020.

Benton, Tim G., Antony Froggatt and Laura Wellesley, 'The Ukraine War and Threats to Food and Energy Security: Cascading Risks from Rising Prices and Supply Disruptions', Research Paper, Royal Institute of International Affairs, 2022.

Bigdeli, Sadeq Z., 'Resurrecting the Dead – The Expired Non-actionable Subsidies and the Lingering Question of "Green Space"', 8(2) *Manchester Journal of International Economic Law* 2 (2011).

Bohmer, Lisa, 'Breaking: Germany and Vattenfall Settle Long-Running Arbitration Dispute Arising from Nuclear Phase-Out', Investment Arbitration Reporter, 5 March 2021, www.iareporter.com.

'Revealed: Reasons Why Van Houtte, Beechey, and Landau Saw No Legitimate Expectation to Stabilization of Czech Solar Feed-In-Tariffs; Newly-Seen Award also Deemed Intra-EU Objection Untimely', Investment Arbitration Reporter, 23 June 2019, www.iareporter.com.

'[Updated] Canadian Province of Alberta Files NAFTA/USMCA Notice of Intent in Relation to Keystone XL Pipeline Dispute with the USA', Investment Arbitration Reporter, 9 February 2022, www.iareporter.com.

'[Updated] Vattenfall Asks for Discontinuance of ICSID Arbitration against Germany, after Settlement Enters Into Force', Investment Arbitration Reporter, 2 November 2021, www.iareporter.com.

Böhringer, Christoph, Jared C. Carbone and Thomas F. Rutherford, 'Embodied Carbon Tariffs', 120 *Scandinavian Journal of Economics* 183 (2018).

Boute, Anatole, 'The Potential Contribution of International Investment Protection Law to Combat Climate Change', 27 *Journal of Energy & Natural Resources Law* 333 (2009).

Bronckers, Marco and Giovanni Gruni, 'Retooling the Sustainability Standards in EU Free Trade Agreements', 24 *Journal of International Economic Law* 25 (2021).

Cameron, Peter D., *International Energy Investment Law: The Pursuit of Stability* (Oxford: Oxford University Press, 2010).

Canada Border Services Agency, Statement of Reasons Concerning the Final Determinations with Respect to the Dumping and the Subsidizing of Certain Photovoltaic Modules and Laminates Originating in or Exported from the People's Republic of China, 18 June 2015.

Capobianco, Antonio and Hans Christiansen, 'Competitive Neutrality and State-Owned Enterprises: Challenges and Policy Options', OECD Corporate Governance Working Papers No. 1, 2011.

Carbon Tracker Initiative, 'Carbon Supply Cost Curves: Evaluating Financial Risk to Coal Capital Expenditures', 2014, www.carbontracker.org/wp-content/uploads/2014/09/CTI-Coal-report-Sept-2014-WEB1.pdf.

Casier, Liesbeth et al., 'Shining a Light on Fossil Fuel Subsidies at the WTO: How NGOs Can Contribute to WTO Notification and Surveillance', 13 *World Trade Review* 603 (2014).

Cendra, Javier de, 'Can Emissions Trading Schemes Be Coupled with Border Tax Adjustments? An Analysis vis-à-vis WTO Law', 15 *RECIEL* 131 (2006).

Centre for Global Development, 'Developed Countries Are Responsible for 79 Percent of Historical Carbon Emissions', 2015, www.cgdev.org/media/who-caused-climate-change-historically#:~:text=Developed%20Countries%20Are%20Responsible%20for,Global%20Development%20%7C%20Ideas%20to%20Action.

'Developing Countries Are Responsible for 63 Percent of Current Carbon Emissions', 2015, www.cgdev.org/media/developing-countries-are-responsible-63-percent-current-carbon-emissions.

Centre for International Environmental Law, 'Plastic & Climate: The Hidden Costs of a Plastic Planet', 2019.

Chang, Seung Wha, 'GATTing a Green Trade Barrier: Eco-Labelling and the WTO Agreement on Technical Barriers to Trade', 31 *Journal of World Trade* 137 (1997).

Charlotin, Damien, '*Natland v. Czech Republic* (Part 2 of 2): On the Merits, Tribunal Finds Stabilisation Commitment in Czech Legislation and Breach of That Commitment with Introduction of Solar Levy', Investment Arbitration Reporter, 26 July 2018, www.iareporter.com.

Charnovitz, Steve, 'The Law of Environmental "PPMs" in the WTO: Debunking the Myth of Illegality', 27 *Yale Journal of International Law* 59 (2002).

Chatzivasileiadis, Spyros, Damien Ernst and Göran Andersson, 'The Global Grid', 57 *Renewable Energy* 372 (2013).

Chazan, Guy, 'Germany Extends Life of Nuclear Power Plants until Next April', *Financial Times*, 18 October 2022, www.ft.com/content/3f48c18f-0348-46b0-a082-3bf07e14e589.

Chelminski, Kathryn, 'Fossil Fuel Subsidy Reform in Indonesia: The Struggle for Successful Reform', in Jakob Skovgaard and Harro van Asselt (eds.), *The Politics of Fossil Fuel Subsidies and Their Reform* (Cambridge: Cambridge University Press, 2018), pp. 193–211.

Chi, Manjiao, 'Sustainable Development Provisions in Investment Treaties', UN Economic and Social Commission for Asia and the Pacific, 2018.

China, 'Outline of the People's Republic of China 14th Five-Year Plan for National Economic and Social Development and Long-Range Objectives for 2035', 12 March 2021 (English translation at Centre for Security and Emerging Technology, https://cset.georgetown.edu/publication/china-14th-five-year-plan/).

Cleeland, Belinda, 'ISO: International Standards for Services', UNCTAD Multi-year Expert Meeting on Trade, Services and Development, 18–20 July 2017, https://unctad.org/system/files/non-official-document/c1mem5_2017_105_S1_Cleeland_2.pdf.

Coady, David et al., 'How Large Are Global Energy Subsidies?', IMF Working Paper No. WP/15/105, 2015.

Coady, David, Valentina Flamini and Louis Sears, 'The Unequal Benefits of Fuel Subsidies Revisited: Evidence for Developing Countries', IMF Working Paper No. WP/15/250, 2015.

Cohen, Wesley M. and Daniel A. Levinthal, 'Absorptive Capacity: A New Perspective on Learning and Innovation', 35 *Administrative Science Quarterly* 128 (1990).

Commission Decision (EU) 2015/1470 of 30 March 2015 on State aid SA.38517 (2014/C) (ex 2014/NN) Implemented by Romania – Arbitral Award *Micula v. Romania* of 11 December 2013, OJ L 232, 4 September 2015.

Commission Decision of 30 June 2004 on the Aid Scheme Implemented by Sweden for an Exemption from the Tax on Energy from 1 January 2002 to 30 June 2004 (2005/468/EC), OJ L 165, 25 June 2005.

Commission Implementing Regulation (EU) No. 471/2014 of 13 May 2014 Imposing Definitive Countervailing Duties on Imports of Solar Glass Originating in the People's Republic of China, OJ L 142, 14 May 2014.

Condon, Bradly J. and Tapen Sinha, *The Role of Climate Change in Global Economic Governance* (Oxford: Oxford University Press, 2013).

Conrad, Christiane R., *Processes and Production Methods (PPMs) in WTO Law: Interfacing Trade and Social Goals* (Cambridge: Cambridge University Press, 2011).

Coppens, Dominic, *WTO Disciplines on Subsidies and Countervailing Measures: Balancing Policy Space and Legal Constraints* (Cambridge: Cambridge University Press, 2014).

Corvaglia, Maria Anna, 'Public Procurement and Private Standards: Ensuring Sustainability under the WTO Agreement on Government Procurement', 19 *Journal of International Economic Law* 607 (2016).

Cosbey, Aaron and Petros C. Mavroidis, 'A Turquoise Mess: Green Subsidies, Blue Industrial Policy and Renewable Energy: The Case for Redrafting the Subsidies Agreement of the WTO', 17 *Journal of International Economic Law* 11 (2014).

Cosbey, Aaron, Michael Bernstein and Seton Stiebert, 'Enabling Climate Ambition: Border Carbon Adjustment in Canada and Abroad', International Institute for Sustainable Development and Clean Prosperity, 2021.

Cottier, Thomas and Ilaria Espa (eds.), *International Trade in Sustainable Electricity: Regulatory Challenges in International Economic Law* (Cambridge: Cambridge University Press 2017).

Council Implementing Regulation (EU) No. 1239/2013 of 2 December 2013 Imposing a Definitive Countervailing Duty on Imports of Crystalline Silicon Photovoltaic Modules and Key Components (i.e. Cells) Originating in or Consigned from the People's Republic of China, OJ L 325, 5 December 2013.

Council of European Energy Regulators, 'Key Support Elements of RES in Europe: Moving towards Market Integration', C15-SDE-49-03, 2016.

Cox, Sadie and Sean Esterly, 'Renewable Electricity Standards: Good Practices and Design Considerations', Technical Report No. NREL/TP-6A20-65507, National Renewable Energy Laboratory, 2016.

De Luca, Anna and Crina Baltag, 'Counterclaims in Investment Arbitration: Reflections on UNCITRAL WG III Reform', Kluwer Arbitration Blog, 5 November 2021, http://arbitrationblog.kluwerarbitration.com/2021/11/05/counterclaims-in-investment-arbitration-reflections-on-uncitral-wg-iii-reform/.

Deane, Felicity, *Emissions Trading and WTO Law: A Global Analysis* (Cheltenham and Northampton: Edward Elgar, 2015).

Dihel, Nora Carina, 'Understanding Trade in Environmental Services: Key Issues and Prospects', in Olivier Cattaneo et al. (eds.), *International Trade in Services: New Trends and Opportunities for Developing Countries* (Washington, DC: World Bank, 2010), pp. 319–348.

DiMascio, Nicholas and Joost Pauwelyn, 'Nondiscrimination in Trade and Investment Treaties: Worlds Apart or Two Sides of the Same Coin?', 102 *American Journal of International Law* 48 (2008).

Dolzer, Rudolf and Christoph Schreuer, *Principles of International Investment Law* (Oxford: Oxford University Press, 2008).

Du, Ming, 'WTO Regulation of Transnational Private Authority in Global Governance', 67 *International and Comparative Law Quarterly* 867 (2018).

Dufo-López, Rodolfo and José L. Bernal-Agustín, 'A Comparative Assessment of Net Metering and Net Billing Policies. Study Cases for Spain', 84 *Energy* 684 (2015).

Durán, Gracia Marín, 'Sheltering Government Support to "Green" Electricity: The European Union and the World Trade Organization', 67 *International and Comparative Law Quarterly* 129 (2018).

Energy Charter Secretariat, 'Energy Efficiency Group', 14 December 2016, www.energycharter.org/who-we-are/subsidiary-bodies/energy-efficiency-group/.

'Finalisation of the Negotiations on the Modernisation of the Energy Charter Treaty', Public Communication approved by the Energy Charter Conference on 24 June 2022, www.energycharter.org/fileadmin/DocumentsMedia/CCDECS/2022/CCDEC202210.pdf.

'Statistics of ECT Cases (as of 01/06/2022)', www.energychartertreaty.org/fileadmin/user_upload/All_statistics_-_1_June_2022.pdf.

Energypedia, 'Feed-in Premiums (FIP)', https://energypedia.info/wiki/Feed-in_Premiums_(FIP).

'Feed-in Tariffs (FIT)', https://energypedia.info/wiki/Feed-in_Tariffs_(FIT).

Epps, Tracey and Andrew Green, *Reconciling Trade and Climate: How the WTO Can Help Address Climate Change* (Cheltenham and Northampton: Edward Elgar, 2010).

Espa, Ilaria and Gracia Marín Durán, 'Renewable Energy Subsidies and WTO Law: Time to Rethink the Case for Reform Beyond *Canada – Renewable Energy / Fit Program*', 21 *Journal of International Economic Law* 621 (2018).

Espa, Ilaria and Sonia E. Rolland, 'Subsidies, Clean Energy, and Climate Change', International Centre for Trade and Sustainable Development and World Economic Forum, 2015.

EU, Commission Decision of 20 December 2012 Terminating the Anti-subsidy Proceeding Concerning Imports of Bioethanol Originating in the United States of America and Terminating the Registration of Such Imports Imposed by Regulation (EU) No. 771/2012, OJ L 352, 21 December 2012.

EU's Concept Paper on WTO Modernization, 18 September 2018, http://trade.ec.europa.eu/doclib/docs/2018/september/tradoc_157331.pdf.

Euractive, 'LEAK: Exit from Energy Charter Treaty "unavoidable", EU Commission Says', 9 February 2023, www.euractiv.com/section/energy/news/exit-from-energy-charter-treaty-unavoidable-eu-commission-says/.

European Commission, 'Carbon Border Adjustment Mechanism: Questions and Answers', 14 July 2021, https://ec.europa.eu/commission/presscorner/detail/en/qanda_21_3661.

'Commission Notice on the Recovery of Unlawful and Incompatible State Aid (2019/C 247/01)', OJ C 247/1, 23 July 2019.

'Commission Services Position Paper on the Trade Sustainability Impact Assessment for the FTA between the EU and the Republic of India', March 2010, https://policy.trade.ec.europa.eu/analysis-and-assessment/sustainability-impact-assessments_en.

'Electricity Market Design', https://energy.ec.europa.eu/topics/markets-and-consumers/market-legislation/electricity-market-design_en.

'European Commission Services' Position Paper on the Sustainability Impact Assessment in Support of Negotiations on a Trade Agreement between the European Union and Indonesia', 26 June 2020, https://policy.trade.ec.europa.eu/analysis-and-assessment/sustainability-impact-assessments_en.

'European Commission Services' Position Paper on the Trade Sustainability Impact Assessment in Support of Negotiations of a Deep and Comprehensive Free Trade Agreement between the European Union and

Morocco', April 2015, https://policy.trade.ec.europa.eu/analysis-and-assessment/sustainability-impact-assessments_en.

'European Commission Services' Position Paper on the Trade Sustainability Impact Assessment in Support of Negotiations of a Deep and Comprehensive Free Trade Area between the European Union and Jordan', December 2016, https://policy.trade.ec.europa.eu/analysis-and-assessment/sustainability-impact-assessments_en.

'European Green Deal: Agreement Reached on the Carbon Border Adjustment Mechanism (CBAM)', 13 December 2022, https://ec.europa.eu/commission/presscorner/detail/en/ip_22_7719.

'The European Green Deal', Communication to the European Parliament, the European Council, the Council, the European Economic and Social Committee and the Committee of the Regions, COM(2019) 640 final, 11 December 2019.

'Impact Assessment Report Accompanying the Document: Proposal for a Regulation of the European Parliament and of the Council Establishing a Carbon Border Adjustment Mechanism', Commission Staff Working Document, SWD(2021) 643 final, 14 July 2021.

'Non-paper from the European Commission: Next Steps as Regards the EU, Euratom and Member States' Membership in the Energy Charter Treaty', 2023, www.euractiv.com/wp-content/uploads/sites/2/2023/02/Non-paper_ECT_nextsteps.pdf.

'Service Standards', https://ec.europa.eu/growth/single-market/services/service-standards_en.

'State Aid: Commission Adopts Temporary Crisis and Transition Framework to Further Support Transition towards Net-Zero Economy', 9 March 2023, https://ec.europa.eu/commission/presscorner/detail/en/ip_23_1563.

'State Aid: Commission Approves German Aid Scheme for Renewable Energy (EEG 2012); Orders Partial Recovery', 25 November 2014, https://ec.europa.eu/commission/presscorner/detail/en/IP_14_2122.

'State Aid: Commission Opens In-Depth Investigation into Arbitration Award in Favour of Antin to Be Paid by Spain', 19 July 2021, https://ec.europa.eu/commission/presscorner/detail/en/IP_21_3783.

'State Aid: Commission Requires Italy to Recover around €18 Million Incompatible State Aid from Metal Producers Portovesme, ILA and Eurallumina', 23 February 2011, https://ec.europa.eu/commission/presscorner/detail/en/IP_11_215.

'Temporary Crisis and Transition Framework' (applicable as of 9 March 2023), https://competition-policy.ec.europa.eu/state-aid/ukraine_en.

'Trade and Climate: EU and Partner Countries Launch the "Coalition of Trade Ministers on Climate"', 19 January 2023, https://ec.europa.eu/commission/presscorner/detail/en/IP_23_248.

'Voluntary Schemes', https://energy.ec.europa.eu/topics/renewable-energy/bioenergy/voluntary-schemes_en.

European Committee for Standardization, 'Mandate M/517 for the Programming and Development of Horizontal Service Standards: Phase I Final Report', 2015, https://ftp.cencenelec.eu/CEN/WhatWeDo/Fields/Services/FinalReportPhase1-M517.pdf.

Falcão, Tatiana, 'Toward Carbon Tax Internationalism: The EU Border Carbon Adjustment Proposal', 98 *Tax Notes International* 1047 (2020).

Farah, Paolo D. and Elena Cima, 'Energy Trade and the WTO: Implications for Renewable Energy and the OPEC Cartel', 16 *Journal of International Economic Law* 707 (2013).

Feichtner, Isabel, *The Law and Politics of WTO Waivers: Stability and Flexibility in Public International Law* (New York: Cambridge University Press, 2011).

Fleury, Julien Sylvestre and Jean-Michel Marcoux, 'The US Shaping of State-Owned Enterprise Disciplines in the Trans-Pacific Partnership', 19 *Journal of International Economic Law* 445 (2016).

Florou, Aikaterini, 'The UK Supreme Court Judgment in *Micula v. Romania*: A Landmark Judgment for the Relationship between EU Law and International Investment Law?', 36 *ICSID Review* 295 (2021).

Fowlie, Meredith and Mar Reguant, 'Challenges in the Measurement of Leakage Risk', 108 *AEA Papers and Proceedings* 124 (2018).

Fung, K. C. and Jane Korinek, 'Economics of Export Restrictions as Applied to Industrial Raw Materials', OECD Trade Policy Paper No. 155, 2013.

G7, 'Terms of Reference for the Climate Club', 12 December 2022, www.g7germany.de/resource/blob/974430/2153140/a04dde2adecf0ddd38cb9829a99c322d/2022-12-12-g7-erklaerung-data.pdf?download=1.

García-Castrillón, Carmen Otero, 'Spain and Investment Arbitration: The Renewable Energy Explosion', Centre for International Governance Innovation, Investor-State Arbitration Series, Paper No. 17, 2016.

Gari, Gabriel, 'Is the WTO's Approach to International Standards on Services Outdated?', 19 *Journal of International Economic Law* 589 (2016).

Gáspár-Szilágyi, Szilárd and Maxim Usynin, 'The Uneasy Relationship between Intra-EU Investment Tribunals and the Court of Justice's *Achmea* Judgment', 4 *European Investment Law and Arbitration Review* 29 (2019).

GATT, 'Report by the Working Party on Border Tax Adjustments', L/3464, 20 November 1970.

Council – Minutes of Meeting – Held in the Centre William Rappard on 22 May 1986, GATT Doc., C/M/198, 12 June 1986.

Uruguay Round – Group of Negotiations on Services – Services Sectoral Classification List – Note by the Secretariat, MTN.GNS/W/120, 10 July 1991.

Gerasimchuk, Ivetta et al., 'A Guidebook to Reviews of Fossil Fuel Subsidies: From Self-Reports to Peer Learning', International Institute for Sustainable Development, 2017.

Global Ecolabelling Network, 'All Ecolabels on Energy', www.ecolabelindex.com/ecolabels/?st=category,energy.

Gordon, Kathryn and Joachim Pohl, 'Environmental Concerns in International Investment Agreements: A Survey', OECD Working Papers on International Investment No. 2011/01, 2011.

Government of Canada, 'Consultation on Border Carbon Adjustments', 1 February 2022, www.canada.ca/en/department-finance/programs/consultations/2021/border-carbon-adjustments.html.

'Lone Pine Resources Inc. v. Government of Canada', 28 April 2021, www.international.gc.ca/trade-agreements-accords-commerciaux/topics-domaines/disp-diff/lone.aspx?lang=eng.

Gruère, Guillaume, 'A Characterization of Environmental Labelling and Information Schemes', OECD Environment Working Paper No. 62, ENV/WKP(2013)9, 2013.

Hakura, Dalia and Florence Jaumotte, 'The Role of Inter- and Intraindustry Trade in Technology Diffusion', IMF Working Paper No. WP/99/58 (1999).

Harrison, James, 'Environmental Counterclaims in Investor–State Arbitration', 17 *The Journal of World Investment & Trade* 479 (2016).

Hegde, Vineet and Jan Wouters, 'Special and Differential Treatment under the World Trade Organization: A Legal Typology', 24 *Journal of International Economic Law* 551 (2021).

Heine, Dirk, Michael G. Faure and Goran Dominioni, 'The Polluter-Pays Principle in Climate Change Law: An Economic Appraisal', 10 *Climate Law* 94 (2020).

Henckels, Caroline, 'A Duty to Consult Foreign Investors When Changing the Regulatory Framework? Implications for Non-Communicable Disease Prevention and Beyond', 21 *Journal of World Investment & Trade* 698 (2020).

Hepburn, Jarrod, 'ANALYSIS: In New Award, Italian Renewables Changes Appear Less Dramatic Than Those in Recent Spain Case, Thus Leading to Failure of Blusun's FET Claim; Arbitrators Disagree on Expropriation Assessment', Investment Arbitration Reporter, 7 June 2017, www.iareporter.com.

Hobér, Kaj, *The Energy Charter Treaty: A Commentary* (Oxford: Oxford University Press, 2020).

Hoekman, Bernard M., Keith E. Maskus and Kamal Saggi, 'Transfer of Technology to Developing Countries: Unilateral and Multilateral Policy Options', 33 *World Development* 1587 (2005).

Hogan, Megan, 'Local Content Requirements Threaten Renewable Energy Uptake: Featuring a List of Local Content Requirements in Wind and Solar Industries', Peterson Institute for International Economics, 6 December

2021, www.piie.com/blogs/trade-and-investment-policy-watch/local-content-requirements-threaten-renewable-energy-uptake.

Holzer, Kateryna, 'Addressing Tensions and Avoiding Disputes: Specific Trade Concerns in the TBT Committee', WTO Staff Working Paper No. ERSD-2018–11, 31 October 2018.

Carbon-Related Border Adjustment and WTO Law (Cheltenham and Northampton: Edward Elgar, 2014).

'Proposals on Carbon-Related Border Adjustments: Prospects for WTO Compliance', 1 *Carbon & Climate Law Review* 51 (2010).

Horlick, Gary and Peggy A. Clarke, 'Rethinking Subsidy Disciplines for the Future: Policy Options for Reform', 20 *Journal of International Economic Law* 673 (2017).

Horn, Henrik and Petros C. Mavroidis, 'To B(TA) or Not to B(TA)? On the Legality and Desirability of Border Tax Adjustments from a Trade Perspective', 34 *The World Economy* 1911 (2011).

Horn, Henrik and André Sapir, 'Can Border Carbon Taxes Fit into the Global Trade Regime?', Policy Brief No. 2013/06, Bruegel, 2013.

Horn, Henrik, Petros C. Mavroidis and Erik N. Wijkström, 'In the Shadow of the DSU: Addressing Specific Trade Concerns in the WTO SPS and TBT Committees', 47 *Journal of World Trade* 729 (2013).

Howse, Robert, 'Climate Mitigation Subsidies and the WTO Legal Framework: A Policy Analysis', International Institute for Sustainable Development, 2010.

Howse, Robert and Antonia L. Eliason, 'Domestic and International Strategies to Address Climate Change: An Overview of the WTO Legal Issues', in Thomas Cottier, Olga Nartova and Sadeq Z. Bigdeli (eds.), *International Trade Regulation and the Mitigation of Climate Change* (New York: Cambridge University Press, 2009), pp. 48–93.

Howse, Robert and Donald Regan, 'The Product/Process Distinction – An Illusory Basis for Disciplining "Unilateralism" in Trade Policy', 11 *European Journal of International Law* 249 (2000).

Hsieh, Pasha L., 'Reassessing APEC's Role as a Trans-Regional Economic Architecture: Legal and Policy Dimensions', 16 *Journal of International Economic Law* 119 (2013).

Hufbauer, Gary Clyde, Ricardo Meléndez-Ortiz and Richard Samans (eds.), *The Law and Economics of a Sustainable Energy Trade Agreement* (Cambridge: Cambridge University Press, 2016).

Hufbauer, Gary Clyde et al., *Local Content Requirements: A Global Problem* (Washington, DC: Peterson Institute for International Economics, 2013).

Hufbauer, Gary Clyde, Steve Charnovitz and Jisun Kim, *Global Warming and the World Trading System* (Washington, DC: Peterson Institute for International Economics, 2009).

Hydropower Sustainability Council, 'Hydropower Sustainability Standard', www.hydrosustainability.org/standard-overview.

IAEA, 'IAEA Nuclear Safety and Security Glossary', 2022 (Interim) Edition, 2022.

'Near Term and Promising Long Term Options for the Deployment of Thorium Based Nuclear Energy', Final Report of a Coordinated Research Project No. IAEA-TECDOC-2009, 2022.

'Nuclear Safety Conventions', www.iaea.org/topics/nuclear-safety-conventions.

'Thorium's Long-Term Potential in Nuclear Energy: New IAEA Analysis', 13 March 2023, www.iaea.org/newscenter/news/thoriums-long-term-potential-in-nuclear-energy-new-iaea-analysis.

IEA, 'Carrots and Sticks: Taxing and Subsidising Energy', Note on Energy Subsidies and Taxes, 17 January 2006, www.iea.org/publications/freepublica tions/publication/oil_subsidies.pdf.

'Energy Security: Ensuring the Uninterrupted Availability of Energy Sources at an Affordable Price', www.iea.org/areas-of-work/ensuring-energy-security.

'Energy Subsidies: Tracking the Impact of Fossil-Fuel Subsidies', www.iea.org/topics/energy-subsidies.

'Energy Technology Perspectives 2020', 2020.

'ETP Clean Energy Technology Guide', 21 September 2022, www.iea.org/art icles/etp-clean-energy-technology-guide.

'Legal and Regulatory Frameworks for CCUS: An IEA CCUS Handbook', 2022.

'Low-Carbon RD&D', www.iea.org/reports/energy-technology-rdd-budgets-overview/low-carbon-rdd#abstract.

'Technology Roadmap: Smart Grids', 2011, www.iea.org/reports/technology-roadmap-smart-grids.

'World Energy Investment 2020', 2020, www.iea.org/reports/world-energy-investment-2020.

IEA–RETD, 'Driving Renewable Energy for Transport: Next Generation Policy Instruments for Renewable Transport (Res-T-Next)', 2015.

IMF, OECD, World Bank and WTO, 'Subsidies, Trade, and International Cooperation', 2022.

Intergovernmental Panel on Climate Change, 'The Evidence Is Clear: The Time for Action Is Now. We Can Halve Emissions by 2030', 4 April 2022, www.ipcc .ch/2022/04/04/ipcc-ar6-wgiii-pressrelease/.

International Laboratory Accreditation Cooperation, 'ILAC MRA and Signatories', https://ilac.org/ilac-mra-and-signatories/.

IRENA, 'Global Energy Transformation: A Roadmap to 2050', 2018.

'International Standardisation in the Field of Renewable Energy', 2013.

'Renewable Power Generation Costs in 2018', 2019.

IRENA, IEA and REN21, 'Renewable Energy Policies in a Time of Transition', 2018.

ISDS Platform, 'Vattenfall vs. Germany I: Coal-fired Electric Plant', April 2021, www.isds.bilaterals.org/vattenfall-vs-germany-i-coal-fired.

ISEAL Alliance, 'ISEAL Codes of Good Practice', www.isealalliance.org/defining-credible-practice/iseal-codes-good-practice.

'ISEAL Community Members', www.isealalliance.org/iseal-community-members.

Ishikawa, Tomoko, 'The Role of the Precautionary and Polluter Pays Principles in Assessing Compensation', RIETI Discussion Paper Series No. 15-E-107, 2015.

Ismer, R. and K. Neuhoff, 'Border Tax Adjustments: A Feasible Way to Address Nonparticipation in Emission Trading', CMI Working Paper No. 36, 2004.

ISO, 'A Committee to Support Developing Countries: DEVCO', www.iso.org/devco.html.

'Environmental Labels and Declarations: How ISO Standards Help', 2012.

'Environmental Labels', 2019.

'ISO and Energy', 2018, www.iso.org/publication/PUB100320.html.

'ISO Strategy for Service Standardization', 2016, www.iso.org/files/live/sites/isoorg/files/store/en/PUB100393.pdf.

Jackson, John H., *World Trade and the Law of GATT* (Indianapolis: Bobbs-Merrill Company, 1969).

Jain, Abhishek, Shalu Agrawal and Karthik Ganesan, 'Lessons from the World's Largest Subsidy Benefit Transfer Scheme: The Case of Liquefied Petroleum Gas Subsidy Reform in India', in Jakob Skovgaard and Harro van Asselt (eds.), *The Politics of Fossil Fuel Subsidies and Their Reform* (Cambridge: Cambridge University Press, 2018), pp. 212–228.

Johns, Bennett, 'Canadian Anti-dumping and Countervailing Duty Measures', 2019, www.bennettjones.com/Publications-Section/Guides/Canadian-AntiDumping-and-Countervailing-Duty-Measures.

Karapinar, Baris, 'Export Restrictions and the WTO Law: How to Reform the "Regulatory Deficiency"', 45 *Journal of World Trade* 1139 (2011).

Karapinar, Baris and Kateryna Holzer, 'Legal Implications of the Use of Export Taxes in Addressing Carbon Leakage: Competing Border Adjustment Measures', 10 *New Zealand Journal of Public and International Law* 15 (2012).

Karttunen, Marianna B., *Transparency in the WTO SPS and TBT Agreements: The Real Jewel in the WTO's Crown* (Cambridge: Cambridge University Press, 2020).

Kauffmann, Céline and Camila Saffirio, 'Good Regulatory Practices and Co-operation in Trade Agreements: A Historical Perspective and Stocktaking', OECD Regulatory Policy Working Paper No. 14, 2021.

Kaufmann, Christine and Rolf H. Weber, 'Carbon-Related Border Tax Adjustment: Mitigating Climate Change or Restricting International Trade?', 10 *World Trade Review* 497 (2011).

Keene, Amelia, 'The Incorporation and Interpretation of WTO-Style Environmental Exceptions in International Investment Agreements', 18 *Journal of World Investment & Trade* 62 (2017).

Kennedy, Matthew, 'The Adverse Effects of Technological Innovation under WTO Subsidy Rules', 19 *World Trade Review* 511 (2020).

WTO Dispute Settlement and the TRIPS Agreement: Applying Intellectual Property Standards in a Trade Law Framework (Cambridge: Cambridge University Press, 2016).

Khachvani, David, 'Non-compensable Regulation versus Regulatory Expropriation: Are Climate Change Regulations Compensable?', 35 *ICSID Review* 154 (2020).

Kigali Communique, 'Ensuring a Just and Equitable Energy Transition in Africa: Seven Transformative Actions for SDG 7', 19 May 2022, www.mininfra.gov.rw/index.php?eID=dumpFile&t=f&f=44024&token=c9d8a3e4e9ad4d22aa3c3b883055c9426760c584.

Kim, Jeonghoi, 'Recent Trends in Export Restrictions on Raw Materials', in OECD, *The Economic Impact of Export Restrictions on Raw Materials* (OECD Trade Policy Studies, 2010), pp. 13–57.

Kläger, Roland, *'Fair and Equitable Treatment' in International Investment Law* (Cambridge: Cambridge University Press, 2011).

Kojima, Masami and Doug Koplow, 'Fossil Fuel Subsidies: Approaches and Valuation', Policy Research Working Paper No. WPS7220, World Bank, 2015.

Kowalski, Przemyslaw, Daniel Rabaioli and Sebastian Vallejo, 'International Technology Transfer Measures in an Interconnected World: Lessons and Policy Implications', OECD Trade Policy Paper No. 206, 2017.

Kuntze, Jan-Christoph and Tom Moerenhout, 'Local Content Requirements and the Renewable Energy Industry – A Good Match?', International Centre for Trade and Sustainable Development, 2013.

Kuriyama, Carlos, 'The APEC List of Environmental Goods', APEC Policy Support Unit, Policy Brief No. 5, 2012, www.apec.org/publications/2012/11/the-apec-list-of-environmental-goods.

'A Review of the APEC List of Environmental Goods', APEC Policy Support Unit, Policy Brief No. 41, 2021, www.apec.org/publications/2021/10/a-review-of-the-apec-list-of-environmental-goods.

Kurtz, Jürgen, *The WTO and International Investment Law: Converging Systems* (Cambridge: Cambridge University Press, 2016).

Lampe, Martin von, Koen Deconinck and Véronique Bastien, 'Trade-Related International Regulatory Co-operation: A Theoretical Framework', OECD Trade Policy Paper No. 195, 2016.

Lamy, Pascal, Geneviève Pons and Pierre Leturcq, 'Greening EU Trade 3: A European Border Carbon Adjustment Proposal', Policy Paper, Europe Jacques Delors, 2020.

Lawder, David, 'U.S. Floats New Steel, Aluminum Tariffs Based on Carbon Emissions', Reuters, 8 December 2022, www.reuters.com/business/sustainable-business/us-floats-new-steel-aluminum-tariffs-based-carbon-emissions-2022-12-08/.

Lee, Yong-Shik, 'Regulatory Autonomy under the WTO Agreement on Sanitary and Phytosanitary Measures: Implications of *Korea–Import Bans, and Testing and Certification Requirements for Radionuclides*', 20 *World Trade Review* 321 (2021).

Legum, Barton and Ioana Petculescu, 'GATT Article XX and International Investment Law', in Roberto Echandi and Pierre Sauvé (eds.), *Prospects in International Investment Law and Policy* (Cambridge: Cambridge University Press, 2013), pp. 340–362.

Less, Cristina Tébar and Steven McMillan, 'Achieving the Successful Transfer of Environmentally Sound Technologies: Trade-Related Aspects', OECD Trade and Environment Working Paper No. 2005-2, COM/ENV/TD(2004)33/FINAL, 2005.

Levashova, Yulia, 'The Accountability and Corporate Social Responsibility of Multinational Corporations for Transgressions in Host States through International Investment Law', 14 *Ultrecht Law Review* 40 (2018).

Lévesque, Céline, 'The Inclusion of GATT Article XX Exceptions in IIAs: A Potentially Risky Policy', in Roberto Echandi and Pierre Sauvé (eds.), *Prospects in International Investment Law and Policy* (Cambridge: Cambridge University Press, 2013), pp. 363–370.

Lone Pine Resources Inc. v. Canada, ICSID Case No. UNCT/15/2, Notice of Arbitration (6 September 2013).

López-Rodríguez, Ana Mercedes, 'The Sun behind the Clouds? Enforcement of Renewable Energy Awards in the EU', 8 *Transnational Environmental Law* 279 (2019).

Luca, Anna De, 'Indirect Expropriations and Regulatory Takings: What Role for the "Legitimate Expectations" of Foreign Investors?', in Giorgio Sacerdoti (ed.), *General Interests of Host States in International Investment Law* (Cambridge: Cambridge University Press, 2014), pp. 58–75.

Marceau, Gabrielle and Joel P. Trachtman, 'The Technical Barriers to Trade Agreement, the Sanitary and Phytosanitary Measures Agreement, and the General Agreement on Tariffs and Trade: *A Map of the World Trade Organization Law of Domestic Regulation of Goods*', 36 *Journal of World Trade* 811 (2002).

Marcu, Andrei et al., 'Carbon Leakage: An Overview', Centre for European Policy Studies, CEPS Special Report No. 79 (2013).

Marhold, Anna-Alexandra, *Energy in International Trade Law: Concepts, Regulations and Changing Markets* (Cambridge: Cambridge University Press, 2021).

'Fossil Fuel Subsidy Reform in the WTO: Options for Constraining Dual Pricing in the Multilateral Trading System', International Centre for Trade and Sustainable Development, 2017.

Maskus, Keith, 'Research and Development Subsidies: A Need for WTO Disciplines?', International Centre for Trade and Sustainable Development and World Economic Forum, 2015.

Matsumura, Wataru and Zakia Adam, 'Commentary: Fossil Fuel Consumption Subsidies Bounced Back Strongly in 2018', 13 June 2019, www.iea.org/newsroom/news/2019/june/fossil-fuel-consumption-subsidies-bounced-back-strongly-in-2018.html.

Mavroidis, Petros C. and Damien J. Neven, 'Greening the WTO Environmental Goods Agreement, Tariff Concessions, and Policy Likeness', 22 *Journal of International Economic Law* 373 (2019).

Mavroidis, Petros C. and Robert Wolfe, 'Private Standards and the WTO: Reclusive No More', 16 *World Trade Review* 1 (2017).

Mayeda, Graham, 'Integrating Environmental Impact Assessments into International Investment Agreements: Global Administrative Law and Transnational Cooperation', 18 *Journal of World Investment & Trade* 131 (2017).

Mayer, Benoit, *The International Law on Climate Change* (Cambridge: Cambridge University Press, 2018).

McDaniels, Devin, Ana Cristina Molina and Erik Wijkström, 'How Does the Regular Work of WTO Influence Regional Trade Agreements? The Case of International Standards and the TBT Committee', WTO Staff Working Paper No. ERSD-2018-06, 2018.

McDonald, Jan, 'Domestic Regulation, International Standards, and Technical Barriers to Trade', 4 *World Trade Review* 249 (2005).

McGlade, Christophe and Paul Ekins, 'The Geographical Distribution of Fossil Fuels Unused When Limiting Global Warming to 2°C', 517 *Nature* 187 (2015).

Mclntyre, Owen and Thomas Mosedale, 'The Precautionary Principle as a Norm of Customary International Law', 9 *Journal of Environmental Law* 221 (1997).

Mehling, Michael A. et al., 'Designing Border Carbon Adjustments for Enhanced Climate Action', 113 *American Journal of International Law* 433 (2019).

Meltzer, Joshua, 'Climate Change and Trade – The EU Aviation Directive and the WTO', 15 *Journal of International Economic Law* 111 (2012).

Merrill, Laura et al., 'Making the Switch: From Fossil Fuel Subsidies to Sustainable Energy', Nordic Council of Ministers, 2017.

'Tackling Fossil Fuel Subsidies and Climate Change: Levelling the Energy Playing Field', Nordic Council of Ministers, 2015.

Meyer, Timothy, 'Explaining Energy Disputes at the World Trade Organization', 17 *International Environmental Agreements: Politics, Law and Economics* 391 (2017).

Mikulich, Christine, 'ISO 14000–14001, The Developing World's Perspective', 17 *Tulane Environmental Law Journal* 117 (2003).

Miles, Kate, *The Origins of International Investment Law: Empire, Environment and the Safeguarding of Capital* (Cambridge: Cambridge University Press, 2013).

Minas, Stephen, 'The Paris Agreement's Technology Framework and the Need for "Transformational Change"', 2020(4) *Carbon & Climate Law Review* 241 (2020).

Ministry of Commerce and Industry (India), Final Findings: Anti-subsidy/Countervailing Duty Investigation Concerning Imports of Castings for Wind Operated Electricity Generators, Whether or Not Machined, in Raw, Finished or Sub-assembled Form, or as a Part of a Sub-Assembly, or as a Part of an Equipment/Component Meant for Wind-Operated Electricity Generators, Originating in or Exported from China PR, 27 November 2015.

Miroudot, Sébastien, 'The Linkages between Open Services Markets and Technology Transfer', OECD Trade Policy Working Paper No. 29, TD/TC/WP(2005)9/FINAL, 2006.

Moïsé, Evdokia and Stela Rubínová, 'Sustainability Impact Assessments of Free Trade Agreements: A Critical Review', OECD Trade Policy Paper No. 255, 2021.

Molenbroek, Edith et al., 'Savings and Benefits of Global Regulations for Energy Efficient Products: A "Cost of Non-World" Study, Final Report', European Commission, 2015.

Molina, Ana Cristina and Vira Khoroshavina, 'TBT Provisions in Regional Trade Agreements: To What Extent Do They Go beyond the WTO TBT Agreement?', WTO Staff Working Paper No. ERSD-2015-09, 2015.

Monteiro, José-Antonio, 'Typology of Environment-Related Provisions in Regional Trade Agreements', WTO Working Paper No. ERSD-2016-13, 2016.

Muchlinski, Peter, 'Corporate Social Responsibility', in Peter Muchlinski, Federico Ortino and Christoph Schreuer (eds.), *The Oxford Handbook of International Investment Law* (Oxford: Oxford University Press, 2008), pp. 637–687.

Munro, James, *Emissions Trading Schemes under International Economic Law* (Oxford: Oxford University Press, 2018).

Naiki, Yoshiko, 'Meta-Regulation of Private Standards: The Role of Regional and International Organizations in Comparison with the WTO', 20 *World Trade Review* 1 (2021).

Nelson, David et al., 'Moving to a Low-Carbon Economy: The Impact of Policy Pathways on Fossil Fuel Asset Values', Climate Policy Initiative, 2014.

New Zealand Foreign Affairs and Trade, 'Agreement on Climate Change, Trade and Sustainability (ACCTS) Negotiations', www.mfat.govt.nz/en/trade/free-trade-agreements/trade-and-climate/agreement-on-climate-change-trade-and-sustainability-accts-negotiations/.

'New Zealand with Costa Rica, Fiji, Iceland, Norway and Switzerland Have Launched a New Initiative – the Agreement on Climate Change, Trade and Sustainability (ACCTS)', www.mfat.govt.nz/en/trade/free-trade-agreements/trade-and-climate/agreement-on-climate-change-trade-and-sustainability-accts-negotiations/.

New Zealand Government, 'Joint Statement: Agreement on Climate Change, Trade and Sustainability (ACCTS) at MC12', 15 June 2022, www.beehive.govt.nz/release/joint-statement-agreement-climate-change-trade-and-sustainability-accts-mc12.

Nordås, Hildegunn Kyvik and Ronald Steenblik, 'Environmental Services in the APEC Region: Definition, Challenges and Opportunities', APEC Group on Services, 2021.

Nordhaus, William, 'Climate Clubs: Overcoming Free-Riding in International Climate Policy', 105 *American Economic Review* 1339 (2015).

OECD, 'Agreement Reached at OECD to End Export Credit Support for Unabated Coal-Fired Power Plants', 22 October 2021, www.oecd.org/newsroom/agreement-reached-at-oecd-to-end-export-credit-support-for-unabated-coal-fired-power-plants.htm.

'Cases Handled by the National Contact Points for Responsible Business Conduct', https://mneguidelines.oecd.org/Flyer-OECD-National-Contact-Points.pdf.

'The Climate Action Monitor 2022: Helping Countries Advance Towards Net Zero', OECD, 2022.

'Climate Finance and the USD 100 Billion Goal', www.oecd.org/climate-change/finance-usd-100-billion-goal/.

'Climate Policy Leadership in an Interconnected World: What Role for Border Carbon Adjustments?', 2020.

'Effects of Eco-Labelling Schemes: Compilation of Recent Studies', COM/ENV/TD(2004)34/FINAL, 2005.

'The Environmental Goods and Services Industry: Manual for Data Collection and Analysis', 1999, https://unstats.un.org/unsd/envaccounting/ceea/archive/EPEA/EnvIndustry_Manual_for_data_collection.PDF.

'Environmental Labelling and Information Schemes', Policy Perspectives: Synthesis Report, 2016.

'Going Green: Best Practices for Sustainable Procurement', 2015.

'International Regulatory Co-operation: Addressing Global Challenges', 2013.

'OECD Guidelines for Multinational Enterprises: 2011 Edition', 2011.

'OECD Inventory of Support Measures for Fossil Fuels: Database Brochure', 2019, www.oecd.org/fossil-fuels/data/OECD-Fossil-Fuels-Support-database-brochure-2019.pdf.

'OECD Work on Support for Fossil Fuels', www.oecd.org/fossil-fuels/.

'Overcoming Barriers to International Investment in Clean Energy', OECD, 2015.

'The Role of OECD Instruments on Responsible Business Conduct in Progressing Environmental Objectives', 2021.

'State-Owned Enterprises as Global Competitors: A Challenge or an Opportunity?', 2016.

'Support for Fossil Fuels Almost Doubled in 2021, Slowing Progress toward International Climate Goals, according to New Analysis from OECD and IEA', 29 August 2022, www.oecd.org/newsroom/support-for-fossil-fuels-almost-doubled-in-2021-slowing-progress-toward-international-climate-goals-according-to-new-analysis-from-oecd-and-iea.htm.OECD and IEA,

'Update on Recent Progress in Reform of Inefficient Fossil-Fuel Subsidies That Encourage Wasteful Consumption', 2019.

OECD/WTO, 'Facilitating Trade through Regulatory Cooperation: The Case of the WTO's TBT/SPS Agreements and Committees', 2019.

Oehler, Richard L. and Vivian R. Vega, 'Worldwide Vaccine Inequality Threatens to Unleash the Next COVID-19 Variant', 123 *International Journal of Infectious Diseases* 133 (2022).

Organization of the Petroleum Exporting Countries, OECD and World Bank, 'Analysis of the Scope of Energy Subsidies and Suggestions for the G-20 Initiative', Joint Report (prepared for submission to the G-20 Summit Meeting in Toronto (Canada), 26–27 June 2010), 2010.

Ortolani, Pietro, 'Intra-EU Arbitral Awards vis-à-vis Article 107 TFEU: State Aid Law as a Limit to Compliance', 6 *Journal of International Dispute Settlement* 118 (2015).

Osakwe, Chiedu, Dayong Yu and Petra Beslać, 'Export Duty Commitments: The Treaty Dialogue and the Pattern of Commitments', in Uri Dadush and Chiedu Osakwe (eds.), *WTO Accessions and Trade Multilateralism: Case Studies and Lessons from the WTO at Twenty* (Cambridge: Cambridge University Press, 2015), pp. 741–763.

Papaefstratiou, Athina Fouchard, 'Stabilisation Clauses in Long-Term Investment Contracts: Their Evolution and Their Application by Investment Tribunals', in Elena Cima and Makane Moïse Mbengue (eds.), *A Multifaceted Approach to Trade Liberalisation and Investment Protection in the Energy Sector* (Leiden and Boston: Brill, Nijhoff, 2021), pp. 43–67.

Parry, Ian, Simon Black and Nate Vernon, 'Still Not Getting Energy Prices Right: A Global and Country Update of Fossil Fuel Subsidies', IMF Working Paper No. WP/21/236, 2021.

Partiti, Enrico, '*What Use Is an Unloaded Gun*? The Substantive Discipline of the WTO TBT Code of Good Practice and Its Application to Private Standards Pursuing Public Objectives', 20 *Journal of International Economic Law* 829 (2017).

Pauer, Stefan U., 'Including Electricity Imports in California's Cap-And-Trade Program: A Case Study of a Border Carbon Adjustment in Practice', 31 *The Electricity Journal* 39 (2018).

Pauwelyn, Joost, 'U.S. Federal Climate Policy and Competitiveness Concerns: The Limits and Options of International Trade Law', Working Paper No. NI WP 07-02, Nicholas Institute for Environmental Policy Solutions at Duke University, 2007.

Pauwelyn, Joost and David Kleimann, 'Trade Related Aspects of a Carbon Border Adjustment Mechanism: A Legal Assessment', Briefing, European Parliament, 2020.

Peels, Rafael et al., 'Corporate Social Responsibility in International Trade and Investment Agreements: Implications for States, Business, and Workers', ILO Research Paper No. 13, 2016.

Pereira, Ricardo and Orla Gough, 'Permanent Sovereignty over Natural Resources in the Twenty-first Century: Natural Resource Governance and the Right to Self-Determination of Indigenous Peoples under International Law', 14 *Melbourne Journal of International Law* 451 (2013).

Perrez, Franz Xaver, 'The Relationship between "Permanent Sovereignty" and the Obligation Not to Cause Transboundary Environmental Damage', 25 *Environmental Law* 1187 (1996).

Petersmann, Ernst-Ulrich, *Transforming World Trade and Investment Law for Sustainable Development* (Oxford: Oxford University Press, 2022).

Pfeifer, Sylvia and Jim Pickard, 'UK to Propose Carbon Border Tax as Part of Steel Industry Aid Package', *Financial Times*, 24 January 2023, www.ft.com/content/94eab3e5-87dd-424f-9c5a-be0d79d7cb5c.

Pogoretskyy, Vitaliy, 'Energy Dual Pricing in International Trade: Subsidies and Anti-dumping Perspectives', in Yulia Selivanova (ed.), *Regulation of Energy in International Trade Law: WTO, NAFTA and Energy Charter* (Alphen aan den Rijn: Kluwer Law International, 2011), pp. 181–228.

Freedom of Transit and Access to Gas Pipeline Networks under WTO Law (Cambridge: Cambridge University Press, 2017).

Pomerleau, Shuting, 'What's in the Carbon Border Adjustment Bill Introduced by Senator Whitehouse?', 8 June 2022, Niskanen Center, www.niskanencenter.org/whats-in-the-carbon-border-adjustment-bill-introduced-by-senator-whitehouse.

Prag, Andrew, 'The Climate Challenge and Trade: Would Border Carbon Adjustments Accelerate or Hinder Climate Action?', OECD, 2020.

Prag, Andrew, Thomas Lyon and Aimée Russillo, 'Multiplication of Environmental Labelling and Information Schemes (ELIS): Implications for Environment and Trade', OECD Environment Working Paper No. 106, ENV/WKP(2016)8, 2016.

Probst, Benedict et al., 'The Short-Term Costs of Local Content Requirements in the Indian Solar Auctions', 5 *Nature Energy* 842 (2020).

Qin, Julia Ya, 'Forced Technology Transfer and the US–China Trade War: Implications for International Economic Law', 22 *Journal of International Economic Law* 743 (2019).

'Reforming WTO Discipline on Export Duties: Sovereignty over Natural Resources, Economic Development and Environmental Protection', 46 *Journal of World Trade* 1147 (2012).

Quick, Reinhard and Christian Lau, 'Environmentally Motivated Tax Distinctions and WTO Law: The European Commission's Green Paper on Integrated Product Policy in Light of the "Like Product-" and "PPM-" Debates', 6 *Journal of International Economic Law* 419 (2003).

Reinsch, William A., Emily Benson and Catherine Puga, 'Environmental Goods Agreement: A New Frontier or an Old Stalemate?', Centre for Strategic and International Studies, 2021.

REN21, 'Renewables 2019: Global Status Report', 2019.

Ripinsky, Sergey, 'The System of Gas Dual Pricing in Russia: Compatibility with WTO Rules', 3 *World Trade Review* 463 (2004).

Ritchie, Hannah, Max Roser and Pablo Rosado (2020), 'CO_2 and Greenhouse Gas Emissions', OurWorldInData.org, 2020, https://ourworldindata.org/co2-and-greenhouse-gas-emissions.

Rive, Vernon, 'Anatomy of an International Norm Entrepreneur: The Friends of Fossil Fuel Subsidy Reform', in Jakob Skovgaard and Harro van Asselt (eds.), *The Politics of Fossil Fuel Subsidies and Their Reform* (Cambridge: Cambridge University Press, 2018), pp. 156–172.

Roffe, Pedro, 'UNCTAD: Code of Conduct for the Transfer of Technology – Progress and Issues under Negotiation', 14 *Journal of World Trade Law* 160 (1980).

Rokadiya, Shikha and Zifei Yang, 'Overview of Global Zero-Emission Vehicle Mandate Programs', International Council on Clean Transportation, Briefing, 2019.

Rolland, Sonia E., *Development at the World Trade Organization* (Oxford: Oxford University Press, 2012).

Rubini, Luca, '*Ain't Wastin' Time No More*: Subsidies for Renewable Energy, The SCM Agreement, Policy Space, and Law Reform', 15 *Journal of International Economic Law* 525 (2012).

Sacerdoti, Giorgio, 'The Application of BITs in Time of Economic Crisis: Limits to Their Coverage, Necessity and the Relevance of WTO Law', in Giorgio Sacerdoti et al. (eds.), *General Interests of Host States in International Investment Law* (Cambridge: Cambridge University Press, 2014), pp. 3–25.

Salehi-Isfahani, Djavad, Bryce Wilson Stucki and Joshua Deutschmann, 'The Reform of Energy Subsidies in Iran: The Role of Cash Transfers', 51 *Emerging Markets Finance and Trade* 1144 (2015).

Sands, Philippe et al., *Principles of International Environmental Law* (Cambridge: Cambridge University Press, 2018), 4th ed.

Sauvage, Jehan, 'The Stringency of Environmental Regulations and Trade in Environmental Goods', OECD Trade and Environment Working Paper, COM/TAD/ENV/JWPTE(2013)33/FINAL, 2014.

Savatic, Filip, 'Fossil Fuel Subsidy Reform: Lessons from the Indonesian Case', Studies No. 06/16, IDDRI, 2016.

Scherer, Maxi (ed.), *International Arbitration in the Energy Sector* (Oxford: Oxford University Press, 2018).

Scherer, Maxi, Stuart Bruce and Juliane Reschke, 'Environmental Counterclaims in Investment Treaty Arbitration', 36 *ICSID Review* 413 (2021).

Schill, Stephan W., 'Do Investment Treaties Chill Unilateral State Regulation to Mitigate Climate Change?', 24 *Journal of International Arbitration* 469 (2007).

Schrijver, Nico J., 'Natural Resources, Permanent Sovereignty Over', in Rüdiger Wolfrum (ed.), *The Max Planck Encyclopedia of Public International Law* (Oxford: Oxford University Press, 2008), Vol. VII, pp. 535–544.

Schrijver, Nicolaas, 'Self-Determination of Peoples and Sovereignty over Natural Wealth and Resources', in UN Human Rights Office of the High Commissioner, *Realizing the Right to Development: Essays in Commemoration of 25 Years of the United Nations Declaration on the Right to Development* (New York and Geneva: UN, 2013), pp. 95–102.

Selivanova, Julia, 'World Trade Organization Rules and Energy Pricing: Russia's Case', 38 *Journal of World Trade* 559 (2004).

Selivanova, Yulia (ed.), *Regulation of Energy in International Trade Law: WTO, NAFTA and Energy Charter* (Alphen aan den Rijn: Kluwer Law International, 2011).

Shadikhodjaev, Sherzod, 'Checking RTA Compatibility with Global Trade Rules: WTO Litigation Practice and Implications from the Transparency Mechanism for RTAs', 45 *Journal of World Trade* 529 (2011).

'First WTO Judicial Review of Climate Change Subsidy Issues', 107 *American Journal of International Law* 864 (2013).

'How to Pass a Pass-through Test: The Case of Input Subsidies', 15 *Journal of International Economic Law* 621 (2012).

'India – Certain Measures Relating to Solar Cells and Solar Modules', 111 *American Journal of International Law* 139 (2017).

'Industrial Policy in Asia-Pacific Integration: Localization Measures and Subsidies in ASEAN Countries, 31 *Asia Pacific Law Review* 618 (2023).

Industrial Policy and the World Trade Organization: Between Legal Constraints and Flexibilities (Cambridge: Cambridge University Press, 2018).

'Input Cost Adjustments and WTO Anti-Dumping Law: A Closer Look at the EU Practice', 18 *World Trade Review* 81 (2019).

'Non-Market Economies, Significant Market Distortions, and the 2017 EU Anti-Dumping Amendment', 21 *Journal of International Economic Law* 885 (2018).

'Promotion of "Green" Electricity and International Dispute Settlement: Trade and Investment Issues', 49 *International Lawyer* 343 (2016).

'Renewable Energy and Government Support: Time to "Green" the SCM Agreement?', 14 *World Trade Review* 479 (2015).

'Russia and Energy Issues under the WTO System', 50 *Journal of World Trade* 705 (2016).

'Steel Overcapacity and the Global Trading System', 16 *Asian Journal of WTO & International Health Law and Policy* 179 (2021).

'Technological Neutrality and Regulation of Digital Trade: How Far Can We Go?', 32 *European Journal of International Law* 1221 (2021).

'United States – Safeguard Measure on Imports of Crystalline Silicon Photovoltaic Products', 116 *American Journal of International Law* 842 (2022).

Shadikhodjaev, Sherzod and Nohyoung Park, 'Cessation and Reparation in the GATT/WTO Legal System: A View from the Law of State Responsibility', 41 *Journal of World Trade* 1237 (2007).

Shao, Xuan, 'Environmental and Human Rights Counterclaims in International Investment Arbitration: At the Crossroads of Domestic and International Law', 24 *Journal of International Economic Law* 157 (2021).

Sharma, Radhika, 'Countervailing Duty Laws in India', 11 December 2015, www.lakshmisri.com/insights/articles/countervailing-duty-laws-in-india/#.

Sherlock, Molly F., 'Clean Vehicle Tax Credits in the Inflation Reduction Act of 2022', US Congressional Research Service, 2022, https://crsreports.congress.gov/product/pdf/IN/IN11996.

Sifonios, David, *Environmental Process and Production Methods (PPMs) in WTO Law* (Cham: Springer, 2018).

Sklarew, Jennifer F., 'How Can China and India Serve as Models for Developing Nations Striving to Build Absorption Capacity for Renewable Energy Technologies?', 2 *Renewable Energy Law and Policy Review* 181 (2011).

Sornarajah, M., *The International Law on Foreign Investment* (New York: Cambridge University Press, 2010), 3rd ed.

Spears, Suzanne A., 'The Quest for Policy Space in a New Generation of International Investment Agreements', 13 *Journal of International Economic Law* 1037 (2010).

Special Eurobarometer 492, 'Europeans' Attitudes on EU Energy Policy: Summary', May 2019, https://ec.europa.eu/commfrontoffice/publicopinion/index.cfm/survey/getsurveydetail/instruments/special/surveyky/2238.

Steenblik, Ronald, Jehan Sauvage and Christina Timiliotis, 'Fossil Fuel Subsidies and the Global Trade Regime', in Jakob Skovgaard and Harro van Asselt (eds.), *The Politics of Fossil Fuel Subsidies and Their Reform* (Cambridge: Cambridge University Press, 2018), pp. 121–139.

Stefan, Florian, 'A Reflection on the Czech Republic's Solar Investment Arbitration Successes', PSL LexisNexis News Analysis, 1 October 2019, www.lexisnexis.com/uk/lexispsl/energy/document/412012/5X5P-71G3-CGXG-01J7-00000–00/A_reflection_on_the_Czech_Republic_s_solar_investment_arbitration_successes.

Struckmann, Kai, Genevra Forwood and Aqeel Kadri, 'Investor-State Arbitrations and EU State Aid Rules: Conflict or Co-existence?', 15 *European State Aid Law Quarterly* 258 (2016).

Swanson, Ana, 'U.S. Proposes Green Steel Club That Would Levy Tariffs On Outliers', *The New York Times*, 7 December 2022, www.nytimes.com/2022/12/07/business/economy/steel-tariffs-climate-change.html.

Sykes, Alan O., 'The Economics of WTO Rules on Subsidies and Countervailing Measures', John M. Olin Program in Law and Economics Working Paper No. 186 (2003), University of Chicago.

Teehankee, Manuel A. J., *Trade and Environment Governance at the World Trade Organization Committee on Trade and Environment* (Alphen aan den Rijn: Kluwer Law International, 2020).

Tienhaara, Kyla, *The Expropriation of Environmental Governance: Protecting Foreign Investors at the Expense of Public Policy* (Cambridge: Cambridge University Press, 2009).

Titi, Aikaterini, *The Right to Regulate in International Investment Law* (Baden-Baden: Nomos, 2014).

Titievskaia, Jana, 'Sustainability Provisions in EU Free Trade Agreements: Review of the European Commission Action Plan', European Parliamentary Research Service, Briefing, 2021.

Tyagi, Yogesh, 'Permanent Sovereignty over Natural Resources', 4 *Cambridge Journal of International and Comparative Law* 588 (2015).

UN Department of Economic and Social Affairs, 'Central Product Classification (CPC) Version 2.1', Statistical Papers, ST/ESA/STAT/SER.M/77/Ver.2.1, 2015.

UN Department of Economic and Social Affairs, 'New Issues Requiring Guidance in the Central Product Classification (CPC)', Meeting of the Expert Group on International Statistical Classifications, New York, 19–22 May 2015, ESA/STAT/AC.289/20, 12 May 2015.

UN Department of International Economic and Social Affairs, 'Provisional Central Product Classification', Statistical Papers, ST/ESA/STAT/SER.M/77, 1991.

UN Economic Commission for Europe, 'Working Party on Pollution and Energy – Introduction', https://unece.org/transportvehicle-regulations/working-party-pollution-and-energy-introduction.

UN, '2020 United Nations Energy Statistics Yearbook', 2020, https://unstats.un.org/unsd/energystats/pubs/yearbook/2020/04d.pdf.

'Nationally Determined Contributions under the Paris Agreement: Synthesis Report by the Secretariat', Conference of the Parties Serving as the Meeting of the Parties to the Paris Agreement, FCCC/PA/CMA/2022/4, 26 October 2022.

'Report of the Conference of the Parties on Its Twenty-Seventh Session, Held in Sharm el-Sheikh from 6 to 20 November 2022', Decision 1/CP.27, FCCC/CP/2022/10/Add.1, 17 March 2023.

UNCITRAL Working Group III, 'Possible Reform of Investor-State Dispute Settlement (ISDS): Multiple Proceedings and Counterclaims', Note by the Secretariat, Thirty-ninth Session, New York, 30 March–3 April 2020, A/CN.9/WG.III/WP.193, 22 January 2020.

UNCTAD, 'Compendium of International Arrangements on Transfer of Technology: Selected Instruments', UNCTAD/ITE/IPC/Misc.5, 2001.

'A European Union Carbon Border Adjustment Mechanism: Implications for Developing Countries', 2021.

'Expropriation', UNCTAD Series on Issues in International Investment Agreements II, 2012.

'Fair and Equitable Treatment', 2012.

'International Investment Agreements Navigator', https://investmentpolicy.unctad.org/international-investment-agreements.

'International Investment Agreements Reform Accelerator', 2020.

'The International Investment Treaty Regime and Climate Action', IIA Issues Note: International Investment Agreements, Issue No. 3, 2022.

'Investment Dispute Settlement Navigator', https://investmentpolicy.unctad.org/investment-dispute-settlement. 'The Role of Science, Technology and Innovation in Promoting Renewable Energy by 2030', 2019.

'Transfer of Technology', UNCTAD Series on Issues in International Investment Agreement, 2001.

'Treaty-Based Investor–State Dispute Settlement Cases and Climate Action', IIA Issues Note: International Investment Agreements, Issue No. 4, 2022.

UNEP, 'Actions on Air Quality: A Global Summary of Policies and Programmes to Reduce Air Pollution', 2021.

'Corporate Social Responsibility and Regional Trade and Investment Agreements', 2011.

'Measuring Fossil Fuel Subsidies in the Context of the Sustainable Development Goals', 2019.

UNFCCC, 'What Is Technology Development and Transfer?', https://unfccc.int/topics/climate-technology/the-big-picture/what-is-technology-development-and-transfer.

US International Trade Commission, 'Renewable Energy and Related Services: Recent Developments', Investigation No. 332-534, USITC Publication 4421, 2013.

US Trade Representative, '2021 Trade Policy Agenda and 2020 Annual Report of the President of the United States on the Trade Agreements Program', 2021.

US Trade Representative, 'Report on the Appellate Body of the World Trade Organization', 2020.

US White House, 'Biden-Harris Administration Releases Inflation Reduction Act Guidebook for Clean Energy and Climate Programs', 15 December 2022, www.whitehouse.gov/briefing-room/statements-releases/2022/12/15/biden-harris-administration-releases-inflation-reduction-act-guidebook-for-clean-energy-and-climate-programs/.

'Statement on Indo-Pacific Economic Framework for Prosperity', 23 May 2022, www.whitehouse.gov/briefing-room/statements-releases/2022/05/23/statement-on-indo-pacific-economic-framework-for-prosperity.

USDOC, Issues and Decision Memorandum for the Final Affirmative Determination of the Countervailing Duty Investigation of Forged Steel Fluid End Blocks from the Federal Republic of Germany [C-428-848], 7 December 2020.

Issues and Decision Memorandum for the Final Determination in the Countervailing Duty Investigation of Forged Steel Fluid End Blocks from Italy [C-475-841], 7 December 2020.

Issues and Decision Memorandum for the Final Determination in the Countervailing Duty Investigation of Crystalline Silicon Photovoltaic Cells, Whether or Not Assembled Into Modules, from the People's Republic of China [C-570-980], 9 October 2012.

Issues and Decision Memorandum for the Final Determination in the Countervailing Duty Investigation of Utility Scale Wind Towers (Wind Towers) from the People's Republic of China [C-570-982], 17 December 2012.

Issues and Decision Memorandum for the Final Determination in the Countervailing Duty Investigation of Bottom Mount Combination Refrigerator-Freezers from the Republic of Korea [C-580-866], 16 March 2012.

Issues and Decision Memorandum for the Final Determination in the Countervailing Duty Investigation of Large Residential Washers from the Republic of Korea [C-580-869], 18 December 2012.

'Steel and Aluminum U.S.–EU Joint Statement', 31 October 2021, www.commerce.gov/news/fact-sheets/2021/10/steel-and-aluminum-us-eu-joint-statement.

Vadi, Valentina, 'Beyond Known Worlds: Climate Change Governance by Arbitral Tribunals?', 48 *Vanderbilt Journal of Transnational Law* 1285 (2015).

Veel, Paul-Erik, 'Carbon Tariffs and the WTO: An Evaluation of Feasible Policies', 12 *Journal of International Economic Law* 749 (2009).

Viñuales, Jorge E., *Foreign Investment and the Environment in International Law* (Cambridge: Cambridge University Press, 2012).

Vossenaar, Rene, 'The APEC List of Environmental Goods: An Analysis of the Outcome & Expected Impact', ICTSD Issue Paper No. 18, 2013.

Vranes, Erich, *Trade and the Environment: Fundamental Issues in International Law, WTO Law, and Legal Theory* (Oxford: Oxford University Press, 2009).

Watal, Jayashree and Leticia Caminero, 'Least-Developed Countries, Transfer of Technology and the TRIPS Agreement', WTO Staff Working Paper No. ERSD-2018-01, 2018.

Whitley, Shelagh and Laurie van der Burg, 'Fossil Fuel Subsidy Reform: From Rhetoric to Reality', Working Paper, New Climate Economy, 2015.

Wiesbrock, Anja, 'An Obligation for Sustainable Procurement? Gauging the Potential Impact of Article 11 TFEU on Public Contracting in the EU', 40 *Legal Issues of Economic Integration* 105 (2013).

WIPO, 'Transfer of Technology', Standing Committee on the Law of Patents, Fourteenth Session (Geneva, 25–29 January 2010), SCP/14/4 REV.2, 26 October 2011.

Wolfrum, Rüdiger, Peter-Tobias Stoll and Michael Koebele (eds.), *WTO – Trade Remedies* (Leiden/Boston: Martinus Nijhoff Publishers, 2008).

Wolfrum, Rüdiger, Peter-Tobias Stoll and Holger P. Hestermeyer (eds.), *WTO – Trade in Goods* (Leiden, Boston: Martinus Nijhoff Publishers, 2011).World

Bank and WTO, 'The Role of Trade in Developing Countries' Road to Recovery', Joint Policy Note, 2022.

World Bank, 'State and Trends of Carbon Pricing 2022', 2022.

'What Is Carbon Pricing?', https://carbonpricingdashboard.worldbank.org/what-carbon-pricing.

World Commission on Environment and Development, 'Our Common Future', Report, UN, 1987.

WTO, 'Chair Cites "Chronic" Low Compliance with Subsidy Notification Requirements', 27 October 2020, www.wto.org/english/news_e/news20_e/scm_27oct20_e.htm.

'Climate Change and International Trade', World Trade Report 2022, 2022.

Committee on Government Procurement – Report (2022) of the Committee on Government Procurement, GPA/AR/5, 8 December 2022.

Committee on SCM – Notification Provisions under the Agreement on Subsidies and Countervailing Measures – Background Note by the Secretariat – Revision, G/SCM/W/546/Rev.13, 31 March 2022.

Committee on SPS Measures – Existing Definitions of Private Standards in Other International Organizations – Note by the Secretariat – Revision, G/SPS/GEN/1334/Rev.1, 5 August 2014.

Committee on SPS Measures – Private Industry Standards – Communication from Saint Vincent and the Grenadines, G/SPS/GEN/766, 28 February 2007.

Committee on SPS Measures – Report of the Co-Stewards of the Private Standards E-Working Group to the March 2015 Meeting of the SPS Committee on Action 1 (G/SPS/55) – Submission by the Co-Stewards of the E-Working Group, G/SPS/W/283, 17 March 2015.

Committee on SPS Measures – Review of the Operation and Implementation of the SPS Agreement – Report adopted by the Committee on 14 July 2017, G/SPS/62, 25 July 2017.

Committee on SPS Measures – Summary of the Meeting Held on 29–30 June 2005 – Note by the Secretariat – Revision, G/SPS/R/37/Rev.1, 18 August 2005.

Committee on TBT – Actions to Increase Participation of Developing Country Members in the Work of Relevant International Standard Setting Organizations – Information from International Organizations – Report of the Director-General, G/TBT/W/172, 27 February 2002.

Committee on TBT – Agreement Reached by a Member with Another Country or Countries on Issues Related to Technical Regulations, Standards or Conformity Assessment Procedures – Notification – The Separate Customs Territory of Taiwan, Penghu, Kinmen and Matsu, G/TBT/10.7/N/146, 8 February 2018.

Committee on TBT – Agreement Reached by a Member with Another Country or Countries on Issues Related to Technical Regulations, Standards or Conformity Assessment Procedures – Notification – Japan and the Republic of Singapore, G/TBT/10.7/N/45, 17 July 2003.

Committee on TBT – Agreement Reached by a Member with Another Country or Countries on Issues Related to Technical Regulations, Standards or Conformity Assessment Procedures – The European Communities and Switzerland – Notification, G/TBT/10.7/N/44, 29 January 2003.

Committee on TBT – Agreement Reached by a Member with Another Country or Countries on Issues Related to Technical Regulations, Standards or Conformity Assessment Procedures – Notification – Japan and European Community – Telecommunications [. . .] Products and Medicinal Products, G/TBT/10.7/N/37, 31 May 2002.

Committee on TBT – Agreement Reached by a Member with Another Country or Countries on Issues Related to Technical Regulations, Standards or Conformity Assessment Procedures – Notification – Ukraine, G/TBT/10.7/N/147, 23 February 2018.

Committee on TBT – Agreement Reached by a Member with Another Country or Countries on Issues Related to Technical Regulations, Standards or Conformity Assessment Procedures – Notification – Ukraine, G/TBT/10.7/N/144, 30 March 2017.

Committee on TBT – Colombia – Proposed Modifications to Resolutions 910/2008 and 2604/2009 on Pollutant Emissions from Heavy Vehicles with Diesel Engines – (G/TBT/N/COL/185 and G/TBT/N/COL/186) – Statement by Mexico to the Committee on Technical Barriers to Trade – 6–7 March 2013, G/TBT/W/362, 21 March 2013.

Committee on TBT – Decisions and Recommendations Adopted by the WTO Committee on Technical Barriers to Trade since 1 January 1995 – Note by the Secretariat – Revision, G/TBT/1/Rev.14, 24 September 2019.

Committee on TBT – European Union – Amendments to the Directive 2009/28/EC, Renewable Energy Directive – Statement by the European Union to the Committee on Technical Barriers to Trade – 21 and 22 March 2018, G/TBT/W/474, 17 April 2018.

Committee on TBT – European Union – Draft Commission Regulation Laying Down Eco-Design Requirements for Electronic Displays Pursuant to Directive 2009/125/EC of the European Parliament and of the Council, Amending Commission Regulation (EC) No. 1275/2008 [. . .] – 6 and 7 March 2019, G/TBT/W/606, 22 March 2019.

Committee on TBT – European Union – Draft Commission Regulation Laying Down Eco-Design Requirements for Electronic Displays Pursuant to Directive 2009/125/EC of the European Parliament and of the Council, Amending Commission Regulation (EC) No. 1275/2008 [. . .] – 20 and 21 June 2019, G/TBT/W/672, 23 July 2019.

Committee on TBT – Fifth Triennial Review of the Operation and Implementation of the Agreement on Technical Barriers to Trade under Article 15.4, G/TBT/26, 13 November 2009.

Committee on TBT – Fourth Triennial Review of the Operation and Implementation of the Agreement on Technical Barriers to Trade under Article 15.4, G/TBT/19, 14 November 2006.

Committee on TBT – Minutes of the Meeting of 1 July 2004 – Chairperson: Mr. Sudhakar Dalela (India) – Note by the Secretariat, G/TBT/M/33, 31 August 2004.

Committee on TBT – Minutes of the Meeting of 10–11 November 2011 – Note by the Secretariat, G/TBT/M/55, 9 February 2012.

Committee on TBT – Minutes of the Meeting of 12–15 November 2019 – Note by the Secretariat, G/TBT/M/79, 30 January 2020.

Committee on TBT – Minutes of the Meeting of 13–14 May 2020 – Written Procedure on Specific Trade Concerns – Note by the Secretariat, G/TBT/M/81, 26 June 2020.

Committee on TBT – Minutes of the Meeting of 13–15 June 2012 – Note by the Secretariat, G/TBT/M/57, 18 September 2012.

Committee on TBT – Minutes of the Meeting of 15–16 June 2011 – Note by the Secretariat, G/TBT/M/54, 20 September 2011.

Committee on TBT – Minutes of the Meeting of 15–16 June 2016 – Note by the Secretariat, G/TBT/M/69, 22 September 2016.

Committee on TBT – Minutes of the Meeting of 16–17 June 2005 – Note by the Secretariat, G/TBT/M/36, 4 August 2005.

Committee on TBT – Minutes of the Meeting of 17, 19 and 20 June 2013 – Note by the Secretariat, G/TBT/M/60, 23 September 2013.

Committee on TBT – Minutes of the Meeting of 18–19 March 2009 – Note by the Secretariat, G/TBT/M/47, 5 June 2009.

Committee on TBT – Minutes of the Meeting of 18–19 March 2015 – Note by the Secretariat, G/TBT/M/65, 28 May 2015.

Committee on TBT – Minutes of the Meeting of 2 November 2005 – Note by the Secretariat, G/TBT/M/37, 22 December 2005.

Committee on TBT – Minutes of the Meeting of 20–21 June 2019 – Note by the Secretariat, G/TBT/M/78, 23 September 2019.

Committee on TBT – Minutes of the Meeting of 21–22 March 2018 – Note by the Secretariat, G/TBT/M/74, 22 May 2018.

Committee on TBT – Minutes of the Meeting of 23–24 June 2010 – Note by the Secretariat, G/TBT/M/51, 1 October 2010.

Committee on TBT – Minutes of the Meeting of 24–25 March 2010 – Note by the Secretariat, G/TBT/M/50, 28 May 2010.

Committee on TBT – Minutes of the Meeting of 24–25 March 2011 – Note by the Secretariat, G/TBT/M/53, 26 May 2011.

Committee on TBT – Minutes of the Meeting of 24–26 February 2021 – Note by the Secretariat, G/TBT/M/83, 21 April 2021.

Committee on TBT – Minutes of the Meeting of 25–26 June 2009 – Note by the Secretariat, G/TBT/M/48, 29 September 2009.

Committee on TBT – Minutes of the Meeting of 29–30 March 2017 – Note by the Secretariat, G/TBT/M/71, 2 June 2017.

Committee on TBT – Minutes of the Meeting of 30–31 October 2013 – Chairperson: Mr. Jingo Kikukawa – Note by the Secretariat, G/TBT/M/61, 5 February 2014.

Committee on TBT – Minutes of the Meeting of 4–6 November 2015 – Note by the Secretariat, G/TBT/M/67, 3 February 2016.

Committee on TBT – Minutes of the Meeting of 5–6 November 2014 – Note by the Secretariat – Revision, G/TBT/M/64/Rev.1, 6 March 2015.

Committee on TBT – Minutes of the Meeting of 5 July 2007 – Note by the Secretariat, G/TBT/M/42, 6 August 2007.

Committee on TBT – Minutes of the Meeting of 6–7 March 2013 – Note by the Secretariat, G/TBT/M/59, 8 May 2013.

Committee on TBT – Minutes of the Meeting of 6–7 March 2019 – Note by the Secretariat, G/TBT/M/77, 15 May 2019.

Committee on TBT – Minutes of the Meeting of 8–9 November 2017 – Note by the Secretariat, G/TBT/M/73, 6 March 2018.

Committee on TBT – Minutes of the Meeting of 9–10 March 2016 – Note by the Secretariat, G/TBT/M/68, 12 May 2016.

Committee on TBT – Minutes of the Meeting of 9 November 2006 – Note by the Secretariat, G/TBT/M/40, 26 January 2007.

Committee on TBT – Ninth Triennial Review of the Operation and Implementation of the Agreement on Technical Barriers to Trade under Article 15.4, G/TBT/46, 17 November 2021.

Committee on TBT – Notification – Switzerland – Diesel Passenger Cars, G/TBT/N/CHE/39, 5 March 2004.

Committee on TBT – Notification – Switzerland – Diesel Passenger Cars, G/TBT/N/CHE/67, 11 August 2006.

Committee on TBT – Second Triennial Review of the Operation and Implementation of the Agreement on Technical Barriers to Trade, G/TBT/9, 13 November 2000.

Committee on TBT – Sixth Triennial Review of the Operation and Implementation of the Agreement on Technical Barriers to Trade under article 15.4, G/TBT/32, 29 November 2012.

Committee on TBT – Twenty-Fifth Annual Review of the Implementation and Operation of the TBT Agreement – Note by the Secretariat, G/TBT/44, 19 February 2020.

Committee on Trade and Development – Special and Differential Treatment Provisions in WTO Agreements and Decisions – Note by the Secretariat, WT/COMTD/W/271, 16 March 2023.

Committee on Trade and Environment – Committee on TBT – Negotiating History of the Coverage of the Agreement on Technical Barriers to Trade with Regard to Labelling Requirements, Voluntary Standards, and Processes and Production Methods Unrelated to Product Characteristics – Note by the Secretariat, WT/CTE/W/10, G/TBT/W/11, 29 August 1995.

Committee on Trade and Environment – Communication on Trade and Environmental Sustainability – Communication from Australia; Canada; Chad; Chile; Costa Rica; EU; The Gambia; Fiji; Iceland; Japan; Korea; [. . .]; and the UK, WT/CTE/W/249, 17 November 2020.

Committee on Trade and Environment – Environment and Services, WT/CTE/W/9, 8 June 1995.

Committee on Trade and Environment – Environmental (Sustainability) Assessments of Trade Liberalization Agreements at the National Level – Item 2 of the Work Programme – Note by the Secretariat, WT/CTE/W/171, 20 October 2000.

Committee on Trade and Environment – Internationally Agreed Definitions of Environmental Labelling within the International Organization for Standardization (ISO) and Related Work – Communication from the ISO, WT/CTE/W/114, 31 May 1999.

Committee on Trade and Environment – Report of the Meeting Held on 24–25 November 1997 – Note by the Secretariat, WT/CTE/M/16, 19 December 1997.

Committee on Trade and Environment – Report of the Meeting Held on 30 June 2014 – Note by the Secretariat, WT/CTE/M/57, 30 September 2014.

Committee on Trade and Environment – Report of the Meeting Held on 29 September 2010 – Note by the Secretariat, WT/CTE/M/50, 2 November 2010.

Committee on Trade and Environment – Report of the Meeting Held on 14 November 2011 – Note by the Secretariat, WT/CTE/M/53, 27 January 2012.

Committee on Trade and Environment – Report of the Meeting Held on 5 June 2013 – Note by the Secretariat, WT/CTE/M/55, 16 August 2013.

Committee on Trade and Environment – Report of the Meeting Held on 20 June 2017 – Note by the Secretariat, WT/CTE/M/63, 27 September 2017.

Committee on Trade and Environment – Special Session – Report by the Chairman, Ambassador Manuel A. J. Teehankee, to the Trade Negotiations Committee, TN/TE/20, 21 April 2011.

Committee on Trade and Environment – Special Session – Report by the Chairman, Ambassador Manuel A. J. Teehankee, to the Trade Negotiations Committee for the Purpose of the TNC Stocktaking Exercise, TN/TE/19, 22 March 2010.

Committee on Trade and Environment – Special Session – Statement by the Chairperson of the Special Session of the Committee on Trade and Environment to the Trade Negotiations Committee, TN/TE/2, 4 July 2002.

Committee on Trade and Environment – Special Session – WTO Negotiations on Environmental Goods and Services – Addressing the Development

Dimension for a 'Triple-Win' Outcome – Communication from China and India, TN/TE/W/79, 15 April 2011.

Committee on Trade and Environment – Taxes and Charges for Environmental Purposes – Border Tax Adjustment – Note by the Secretariat, WT/CTE/W/47, 2 May 1997.

Council for Trade in Goods – Minutes of the Meeting of the Council for Trade in Goods – 7 and 8 July 2022, G/C/M/143, 6 October 2022.

Council for Trade in Services – Background Note on Environmental Services – Note by the Secretariat, S/C/W/320, 20 August 2010.

Council for Trade in Services – Energy Services – Background Note by the Secretariat, S/C/W/52, 9 September 1998.

Council for Trade in Services – Energy Services – Background Note by the Secretariat, S/C/W/311, 12 January 2010.

Council for Trade in Services – Special Session – Communication from Chile, Mexico, New Zealand and Panama – Exploratory Discussions on Market Access, JOB/SERV/282, 13 June 2018.

Council for Trade in Services – Special Session – Communication from Australia, Canada, the EU, the Republic of Korea, Mexico, New Zealand, Norway, Switzerland and the UK – Exploratory Discussions on Market Access: Environmental Services – Revision, JOB/SERV/299/Rev.4, 21 July 2022.

Council for TRIPS – Annual Report on Notifications and Other Information Flows – Note by the Secretariat – Revision, IP/C/W/687/Rev.1, 7 March 2022.

Council for TRIPS – Implementation of Article 66.2 of the TRIPS Agreement – Decision of the Council for TRIPS of 19 February 2003, IP/C/28, 20 February 2003.

Council for TRIPS – Report on the Implementation of Article 66.2 of the TRIPS Agreement – EU – Addendum, IP/C/W/656/Add.5, 6 February 2020.

Council for TRIPS – Report on the Implementation of Article 66.2 of the TRIPS Agreement – New Zealand – Addendum, IP/C/W/656/Add.7, 4 February 2020.

Council for TRIPS – Report on the Implementation of Article 66.2 of the TRIPS Agreement – Australia – Addendum, IP/C/W/656/Add.3, 10 October 2019.

Council for TRIPS – Report on the Implementation of Article 66.2 of the TRIPS Agreement – Canada – Addendum, IP/C/W/656/Add.4, 10 October 2019.

Council for TRIPS – Report on the Implementation of Article 66.2 of the TRIPS Agreement – Norway – Addendum, IP/C/W/656/Add.6, 10 October 2019.

Council for TRIPS – Report on the Implementation of Article 66.2 of the TRIPS Agreement – Switzerland, IP/C/W/656, 27 September 2019.

'Dispute Settlement', www.wto.org/english/tratop_e/dispu_e/dispu_e.htm.

'Eliminating Trade Barriers on Environmental Goods and Services', www.wto.org/English/tratop_e/envir_e/envir_neg_serv_e.htm.

'Environmental Database', https://edb.wto.org.

'Environmental Goods Agreement (EGA)', www.wto.org/english/tratop_e/envir_e/ega_e.htm.

'Environmental Services', www.wto.org/english/tratop_e/serv_e/environment_e/environment_e.htm.

European Union – Certain Measures Concerning Palm Oil and Oil Palm Crop-Based Biofuels – Request for the Establishment of a Panel by Indonesia, WT/DS593/9, 24 March 2020.

European Union and Certain Member States – Certain Measures on the Importation and Marketing of Biodiesel and Measures Supporting the Biodiesel Industry – Request for Consultations by Argentina, WT/DS459/1, G/L/1027, G/SCM/D97/1, G/TRIMS/D/36, G/TBT/D/44, 23 May 2013.

European Union and Certain Member States – Certain Measures Concerning Palm Oil and Oil Palm Crop-Based Biofuels – Request for Consultations by Malaysia, WT/DS600/1, G/L/1384, G/TBT/D/54, G/SCM/D131/1, 19 January 2021.

'Exploring the Links between Subsidies, Trade and the WTO', World Trade Report 2006, 2006.

'The Future of Services Trade', World Trade Report 2019, 2019.

General Council – 28 February and 1 March 2019 – The Continued Relevance of Special and Differential Treatment in Favour of Developing Members to Promote Development and Ensure Inclusiveness – Communication from China, India, South Africa and the Bolivarian Republic of Venezuela, [...] and Pakistan – Revision, WT/GC/W/765/Rev.2, 4 March 2019.

General Council – 7 May 2019 – Pursuing the Development Dimension in WTO Rule-Making Efforts – Communication from Norway; Canada; Hong Kong, China; Iceland; Mexico; New Zealand; Singapore and Switzerland – Revision, WT/GC/W/770/Rev.3, 8 May 2019.

General Council – 9–11 December 2019 – Draft General Council Decision – Procedures to Strengthen the Negotiating Function of the WTO – Decision of X Date – Revision, WT/GC/W/764/Rev.1, 25 November 2019.

General Council – Advancing Sustainability Goals through Trade Rules to Level the Playing Field – Draft Ministerial Decision, WT/GC/W/814, 17 December 2020.

General Council – An Undifferentiated WTO: Self-Declared Development Status Risks Institutional Irrelevance – Communication from the United States, WT/GC/W/757, 16 January 2019.

General Council – China's Proposal on WTO Reform – Communication from China, WT/GC/W/773, 13 May 2019.

General Council – Committee on SCM – Committee on Trade and Development – A Case for Rebalancing the Agreement on Subsidies and Countervailing Measures (ASCM) – Policy Space to Promote Industrialisation in Developing Countries – Communication from the African Group (Angola; Benin; [...]; Uganda; Zambia and Zimbabwe), WT/GC/W/880, G/SCM/W/589, WT/COMTD/W/274, 26 May 2023.

General Council – Council for Trade in Goods – Procedures to Enhance Transparency and Strengthen Notification Requirements under WTO Agreements – Communication from Argentina, Costa Rica, the EU, Japan, and the United States, JOB/GC/204, JOB/CTG/14, 1 November 2018.

General Council – Council for Trade in Goods – Procedures to Enhance Transparency and Improve Compliance with Notification Requirements under WTO Agreements – Communication from Albania; Argentina; Australia; Brazil; Canada; Chile; Colombia; Costa Rica; the EU; [. . .]; and Uruguay – Revision, JOB/GC/204/Rev.12, JOB/CTG/14/Rev.12, 2 November 2022.

General Council – Improving the Operation of WTO Bodies to Revitalise the WTO's Monitoring and Deliberative Function – Communication from Australia; Brunei Darussalam; Canada; Chile; Costa Rica; Guatemala; Iceland; Israel; Japan; Republic of Korea; New Zealand; [. . .]; and the UK, WT/GC/W/877, 4 May 2023.

General Council – Ministerial Statement on Fossil Fuel Subsidies – Revision, WT/MIN(21)/9/Rev.2, 10 June 2022.

General Council – Minutes of the Meeting – Held in the Centre William Rappard and in Virtual Format on 25–26 July 2022, WT/GC/M/200, 21 October 2022.

General Council – Reinforcing the Deliberative Function of the WTO to Respond to Global Trade Policy Challenges – Communication from the EU, WT/GC/W/864, 22 February 2023.

General Council – Strengthening and Modernizing the WTO: Discussion Paper – Communication from Canada, JOB/GC/201, 24 September 2018.

General Council – Waivers – 1995–2020 – Note by the Secretariat – Revision, WT/GC/W/718/Rev.1, 25 January 2021.

General Council – Waivers – 2021 – Note by the Secretariat, WT/GC/W/840, 17 December 2021.

General Council – WTO Reform: Incremental Changes to Improve the Functioning of the Various WTO Bodies – Communication from India, WT/GC/W/874, 1 May 2023.

Guide to GATT Law and Practice (Geneva: WTO, 1995), Analytical Index, Vol. 1.

'Investment Facilitation for Development in the WTO', January 2023, www.wto.org/english/tratop_e/invfac_public_e/factsheet_ifd.pdf.

'Lamy Calls for Dialogue on Trade and Energy in the WTO', 29 April 2013, www.wto.org/english/news_e/sppl_e/sppl279_e.htm.

Ministerial Conference – [Twelfth Session – Geneva, 30 November – 3 December 2021] – TESSD – Ministerial Statement on Trade and Environmental Sustainability – Revision, WT/MIN(21)/6/Rev.2, 14 December 2021.

Ministerial Conference – [Twelfth Session – Geneva, 30 November – 3 December 2021] – Informal Dialogue on Plastic Pollution and

Environmentally Sustainable Plastics Trade (IDP) – MC12 Ministerial Statement on Plastic Pollution and Environmentally Sustainable Plastics Trade – Revision, WT/MIN(21)/8/Rev.2, 10 December 2021.

Ministerial Conference – Tenth Session – Nairobi, 15–18 December 2015 – Ministerial Declaration on the Expansion of Trade in Information Technology Products – Nairobi, 16 December 2015, WT/MIN(15)/25, 16 December 2015.

Ministerial Conference – Twelfth Session – Geneva, 12–15 June 2022 – Ministerial Decision on the TRIPS Agreement – Adopted on 17 June 2022, WT/MIN(22)/30, WT/L/1141, 22 June 2022.

Ministerial Conference, Singapore – Ministerial Declaration on Trade in Information Technology Products – Singapore, 13 December 1996, WT/MIN(96)/16, 13 December 1996.

Negotiating Group on Rules – Report by the Chairman, H. E. Mr Wayne McCook to the Trade Negotiations Committee, TN/RL/28, 29 November 2017.

'Negotiations on Trade and the Environment', www.wto.org/English/tratop_e/envir_e/envir_negotiations_e.htm.

Report (1996) of the Committee on Trade and Environment, WT/CTE/1, 12 November 1996.

Report (2008) of the Working Group on Trade and Transfer of Technology to the General Council, WT/WGTTT/10, 11 December 2008.

'SPS & TBT Platform', https://eping.wto.org.

Structured Discussions on Investment Facilitation – Communication from Brazil, INF/IFD/W/1, 26 March 2019.

'Subsidies Committee Members Again Cite Concerns on Lack of Transparency', 30 April 2019, www.wto.org/english/news_e/news19_e/scm_30apr19_e.htm.

'Trade and Environmental Sustainability Structured Discussion: An Overview in Three Pages', www.wto.org/english/tratop_e/tessd_e/tessd_overview_in_three_pages.pdf.

'Trade in Natural Resources', World Trade Report 2010, 2010.

'Trade in Services: The Most Dynamic Segment of International Trade', 2015, www.wto.org/english/thewto_e/20y_e/services_brochure2015_e.pdf.

TPRB – Trade Policy Review – Report by the Secretariat – Australia – Revision, WT/TPR/S/396/Rev.1, 29 July 2020.

TPRB – Trade Policy Review – Report by the Secretariat – Bangladesh – Revision, WT/TPR/S/385/Rev.1, 21 May 2019.

TPRB – Trade Policy Review – Report by the Secretariat – China – Revision, WT/TPR/S/375/Rev.1, 14 September 2018.

TPRB – Trade Policy Review – Report by the Secretariat – Georgia – Revision, WT/TPR/S/328/Rev.1, 18 March 2016.

TPRB – Trade Policy Review – Report by the Secretariat – Indonesia – Revision, WT/TPR/S/401/Rev.1, 5 February 2021.

TPRB – Trade Policy Review – Report by the Secretariat – The State of Kuwait – Revision, WT/TPR/S/258/Rev.1, 28 February 2012.

Trade and Environmental Sustainability Structured Discussions – Meeting Held on 19 and 20 July 2022 – Informal Summary by the Coordinators, INF/TE/SSD/R/12, 20 September 2022.

Trade and Environmental Sustainability Structured Discussions (TESSD) – Experiences in the Promotion and Facilitation of Environmental Goods and Services – Note by the Secretariat, INF/TE/SSD/W/18, 23 March 2022.

Trade in Services – Lao PDR – Schedule of Specific Commitments, GATS/SC/150, 22 April 2013.

Working Group on the Relationship between Trade and Investment – Communication from UNCTAD – The Draft United Nations Code of Conduct on Transnational Corporations and the OECD Guidelines for Multinational Enterprises, WT/WGTI/W/52, 21 August 1998.

Working Group on Trade and Transfer of Technology – A Taxonomy on Country Experiences on International Technology Transfers – Note by the Secretariat, WT/WGTTT/W/3, 11 November 2002.

Working Group on Trade and Transfer of Technology – Provisions Relating to Transfer of Technology in WTO Agreements – Communication from Cuba, Egypt, Honduras, India, Indonesia, Jamaica, Kenya, Mauritius, Pakistan and Zimbabwe – Revision, WT/WGTTT/3/Rev.1, 21 October 2002.

Working Group on Trade and Transfer of Technology – Report 2021 of the Working Group on Trade and Transfer of Technology to the General Council, WT/WGTTT/23, 5 November 2021.

Working Party on Domestic Regulation – Communication from Switzerland – Proposal for Disciplines on Technical Standards in Services, S/WPDR/W/32/Rev.1, 28 October 2005.

Working Party on Domestic Regulation – Disciplines on Domestic Regulation Pursuant to GATS Article VI:4 – Chairman's Progress Report, S/WPDR/W/45, 14 April 2011.

Working Party on Domestic Regulation – Technical Standards in Services – Note by the Secretariat, S/WPDR/W/49, 13 September 2012.

Working Party on Professional Services – The Relevance of the Disciplines of the Agreement on Technical Barriers to Trade (TBT) and on Import Licensing Procedures to Article VI.4 of the General Agreement on Trade in Services – Note by the Secretariat, S/WPPS/W/9, 11 September 1996.

'WTO Members Engage in Exploratory Talks on Market Access for Environmental Services', 30 September 2019, www.wto.org/english/news_e/news19_e/serv_30sep19_e.htm.

Yada, Jurei et al., 'Harmonization of Product Energy Efficiency Standards and Free Trade Agreements: The Role of International Cooperation', European Council for an Energy Efficient Economy, Summer Study

Proceedings, 2017, www.eceee.org/library/conference_proceedings/eceee_Summer_Studies/2017/2-policy-governance-design-implementation-and-evaluation-challenges/harmonization-of-product-energy-efficiency-standards-and-free-trade-agreements-the-role-of-international-cooperation/.

Yamaguchi, Shunta, 'Greening Regional Trade Agreements on Investment', OECD Trade and Environment Working Paper No. 2020/03, 2020.

Yu, Dayong, 'The Harmonized System – Amendments and Their Impact on WTO Members' Schedules', WTO Staff Working Paper No. ERSD-2008-02, 2008.

Zachmann, Georg and Ben McWilliams, 'A European Carbon Border Tax: Much Pain, Little Gain', Policy Contribution No. 5, Bruegel, 2020.

Zee, Eva van der, 'Disciplining Private Standards under the SPS and TBT Agreement: A Plea for Market-State Procedural Guidelines', 52 *Journal of World Trade* 393 (2018).

Zhu, Ying, 'Corporate Social Responsibility and International Investment Law: Tension and Reconciliation', 2017 *Nordic Journal of Commercial Law* 90 (2017).

Zhuang, Wei, *Intellectual Property Rights and Climate Change: Interpreting the TRIPS Agreement for Environmentally Sound Technologies* (Cambridge: Cambridge University Press, 2017).

INDEX

Printed in the United Kingdom by TJ Clays Ltd.